MW01625740

Dutch Utopia

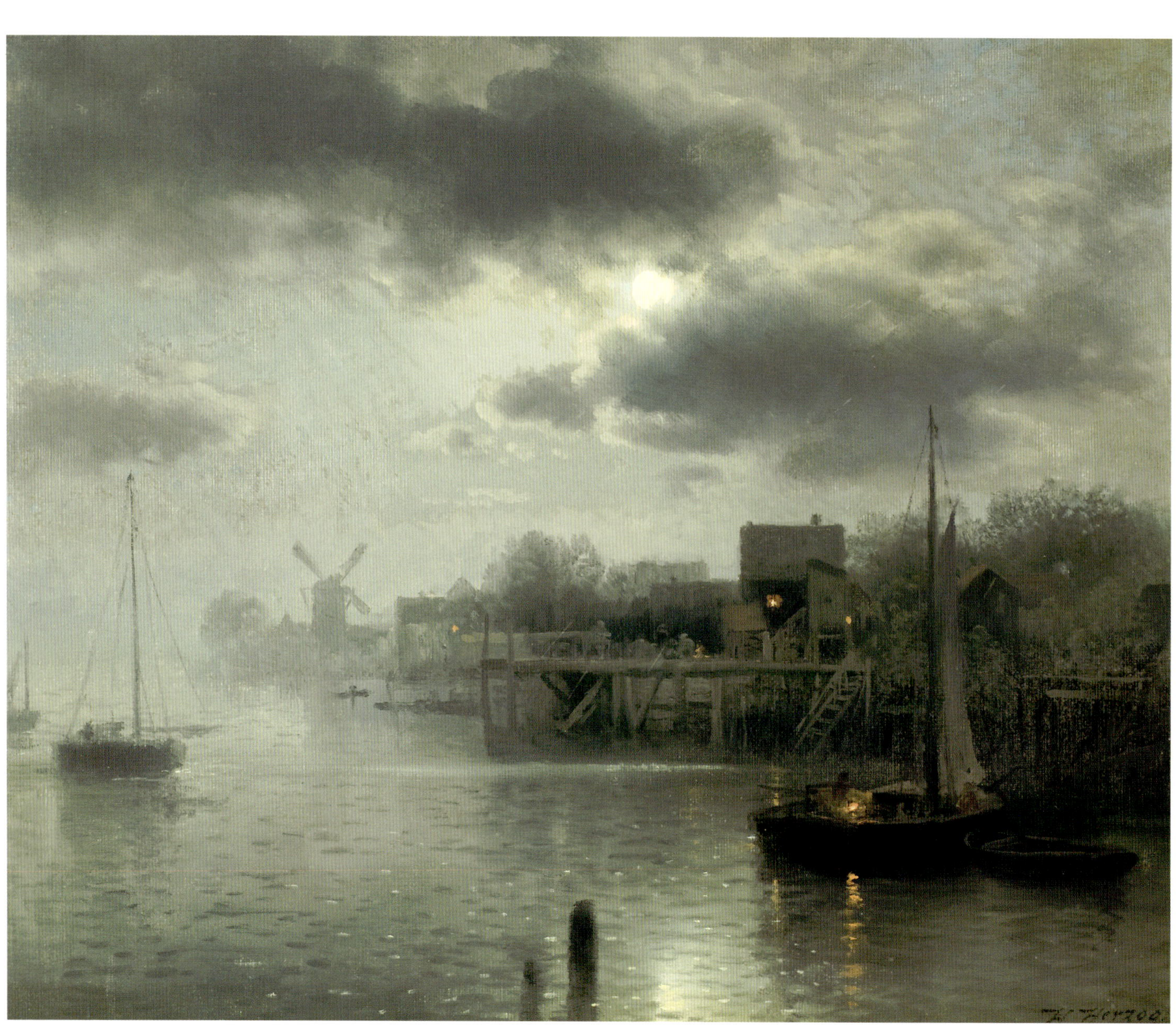

Dutch Utopia

American Artists in Holland, 1880–1914

EDITED and with an introduction by
Annette Stott

ORGANIZING CURATOR
Holly Koons McCullough

ESSAYS by
Nina Lübbren
Holly Koons McCullough
Emke Raassen-Kruimel
Kim Sajet
Annette Stott

Organized by the Telfair Museum of Art, Savannah, Georgia
in association with
the Singer Laren Museum, the Netherlands

Telfair Books
Savannah, Georgia

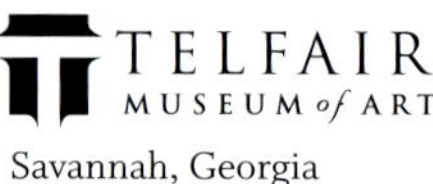

Savannah, Georgia
www.telfair.org

Library of Congress Catalogue
Control Number: 2008909950
ISBN: 978-0-933075-11-5

Distributed by the University of Georgia Press
www.ugapress.org

Frontispiece: Herman Herzog, *Moonlight in Holland*, n.d.; see cat. 21

Endsheets: John Henry Twachtman, *Windmills*, c. 1885, detail, see cat. 69; and Walter MacEwen, *Returning from Work*, c. 1885, detail, see cat. 33

Edited by Michelle Bolton King
Translated by Jennifer Kilian and Katy Kist (Dutch to English, Emke Raassen-Kruimel's essay, "American Artists in a Dutch Context," and catalog entries 2, 3, 46, 47, 48, 54, 60, 61, and 62)
Proofread by Ted Gilley
Indexed by Candace Hyatt
Designed by Jeff Wincapaw
Color management by iocolor, Seattle
Produced by Marquand Books, Inc.
www.marquand.com
Printed and bound in China by
C&C Offset Printing Co., Ltd.

EXHIBITION ITINERARY

Telfair Museum of Art, Savannah, Georgia
October 1, 2009–January 10, 2010

Taft Museum of Art, Cincinnati, Ohio
February 5–May 2, 2010

Grand Rapids Art Museum, Michigan
May 21–August 15, 2010

Singer Laren Museum, the Netherlands
De Hollandse Droom, Amerikaanse Kunstenaars in Nederland 1880–1914
September 16, 2010–January 16, 2011

Dutch Utopia: American Artists in Holland, 1880–1914 is organized by the Telfair Museum of Art, Savannah, Georgia, in association with the Singer Laren Museum, the Netherlands. This exhibition is made possible by the generous support of the Terra Foundation for American Art and the Henry Luce Foundation.

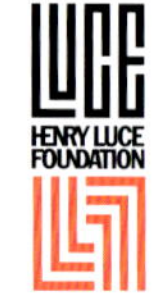

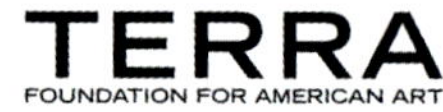

A special thank you to the Telfair Academy Guild, Mrs. Joanne Stanley Holbrook Patton, Mrs. Robert O. Levitt, and the Consulate General of the Kingdom of the Netherlands, who have generously provided additional support for this exhibition.

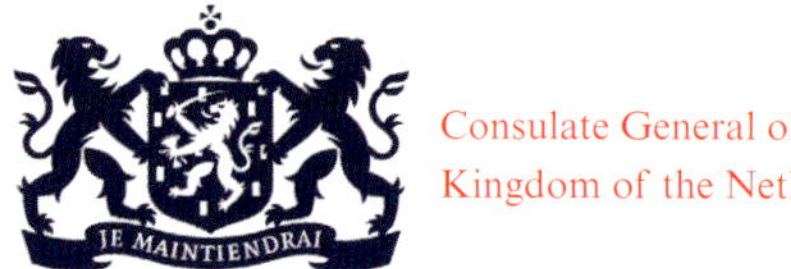

General operating support for the Telfair Museum of Art is provided in part by the Georgia Council for the Arts through the appropriations of the Georgia General Assembly. GCA also receives support from its partner—The National Endowment for the Arts.

Contents

Foreword

Telfair Museum of Art

THE TELFAIR MUSEUM OF ART has a long and engaging history. The oldest art museum in the American South, the Telfair was founded in Savannah, Georgia, in 1883 and opened to the public in 1886. Defining what this new museum would become was the task of its early leaders. Carl Brandt, the Telfair's first director, was called upon to assemble a collection for the Telfair Academy of Arts and Sciences. He commissioned an architect to adapt the Telfair mansion into a modern museum and, as an artist of some renown, he painted many murals for the Telfair, several of which still decorate the museum's galleries. He also traveled throughout Europe to purchase paintings and to commission plaster copies of antique statuary to bring back to Savannah. Following Brandt's death in 1905, the museum's trustees recruited the artist Gari Melchers to act as an artistic advisor. Forty-five years old at the time of his appointment, Melchers had firmly established a national and international reputation for his work. Over the course of his career, Melchers would embrace diverse styles of painting, from realism to impressionism, as well as a variety of subjects. However, it was his early paintings of daily life in the remote Dutch village of Egmond, where he settled in 1884, that cemented his early reputation. Although Melchers maintained active studios in New York and Paris, Egmond remained his primary residence from 1884 until he returned to America in 1915. During his tenure as the Telfair's fine arts advisor from 1906 to 1916, Melchers traveled back and forth between his studios and Savannah as he actively acquired more than seventy paintings for the museum's collection.

Melchers's acquisitions for the Telfair included works by many of his colleagues, some of whom had painted alongside him in Holland. So it is not surprising that several paintings by American artists focusing on Dutch subject matter are included in the Telfair's collection. George Hitchcock's *Early Spring in Holland* (c. 1890–1905; cat. 22) was one of the first works Melchers acquired, and James Jebusa Shannon's portrait of George Hitchcock (c. 1895; cat. 58) was purchased shortly after. The Telfair's later acquisition of Melchers's *Unpretentious Garden* (c. 1903–15; cat. 44) and the Walter MacEwen work known as *The Lacemakers* (c. 1885–1900; cat. 36) reinforced this interest in American painters working in Holland.

While researching works in the permanent collection, the Telfair's chief curator of fine arts and exhibitions, Holly Koons McCullough, became intrigued by this little-documented fascination with Dutch subject matter at the turn of the twentieth century. Working with Annette Stott, author of the groundbreaking publication *Holland Mania: The Unknown Dutch Period in American Art and Culture*, Holly began to explore the possibility of an exhibition on this period. Independently, Kim Sajet, then deputy director of the Pennsylvania Academy of the Fine Arts and now president and CEO of the Historical Society of Pennsylvania, was exploring this theme from a different perspective, also drawing upon Stott's research, and working closely with Ineke Middag of the Singer Laren Museum in Holland. They soon decided to work together to pursue the development of *Dutch Utopia: American Artists in Holland, 1880–1914*, and it is due to this collaboration of scholars that we now celebrate, in this book and exhibition, a fascinating period in American art history.

The Singer Laren Museum is an important partner in this exhibition, and we appreciate the energy and commitment of both Ineke Middag and her successor, Jan Rudolph de Lorm, as well as Reinier Sinaasappel, general director of the Singer. We are pleased that this project has resulted in such a strong international partnership between our two museums. Many museums in the United States and Europe have lent their art to this exhibition. They are listed separately elsewhere in this book, but I want to emphasize how grateful we are for their generosity in parting with these works for such a substantive period of time. Projects of this scale are becoming increasingly difficult to organize, and *Dutch Utopia* would have been impossible without the support of our lenders. We also want to acknowledge our two U.S. venues on the show's tour, the Taft Museum of Art, Cincinnati, Ohio, and the Grand Rapids Art Museum in Michigan, for their enthusiastic interest in the exhibition concept. Finally, I am pleased to recognize our generous sponsors for this exhibition and publication. At the Terra Foundation for American Art, Elizabeth Glassman, president and CEO, was an early supporter of this project. The Terra's significant grant reinforced our belief in *Dutch Utopia* and encouraged us to continue. Ellen Holtzman, program director for American art at the Henry Luce Foundation, was also an important advocate. Thanks to her vision, the Telfair was awarded a substantive two-year Luce grant to help fund the exhibition. Both the Terra and Luce foundations' support of new studies in American art is absolutely critical today as the costs of organizing, exhibiting, and traveling these exhibitions continue to escalate. Finally, I want to thank the Telfair Academy Guild, the museum's largest membership group, for its enthusiastic support of this exhibition from its very beginnings. *Dutch Utopia*, bearing close association to the founding of the Telfair's own collection, struck a chord with Guild members, and they have wholeheartedly embraced the project throughout its development.

Steven High
Director, Telfair Museum of Art

Foreword

Singer Laren Museum

IT IS HARD TO IMAGINE a more appropriate venue for an exhibition on American artists inspired by Dutch art colonies between 1880 and 1914 than the Singer Laren Museum. The illustrious past of the small Dutch village of Laren as an international artists' colony is actually the bedrock of the museum's very existence. When he came to Laren, the American landscape painter William Henry Singer Jr. knew exactly what artistic features he was seeking there, namely its unspoiled nature and the simple life of local farmers and weavers, which had been so poignantly captured by the Hague School painter Anton Mauve, among others. Mauve's works found great success among American collectors of the Gilded Age, including in Singer's native Pittsburgh, where he surely must have seen them. Like other American artists, Singer sought out that source. He first traveled to Laren in 1902, sojourning there for a while, and subsequently he and his wife Anna Spencer Brugh lived in the picturesque hamlet for longer periods of time. The couple began collecting art and in 1911 built De Wilde Zwanen (The Wild Swans), their handsome residence, which now forms the core of an active theatre and the museum devoted to their collection.

At the writing of this foreword in spring 2009, the opening of the exhibition *Dutch Utopia: American Artists in Holland, 1880–1914* in Savannah is still more than six months away, and its opening in Singer Laren a year and a half away. We embarked on this project four years ago, and in the meantime the career of Kim Sajet, one of the original initiators, has taken a radically different course, though she has remained involved in this project as a catalog essayist. The same can be said of Ineke Middag, museum director of Singer Laren, who was succeeded this spring by Jan Rudolph De Lorm. Moreover, in the course of 2009, curator and catalog essayist Emke Raassen-Kruimel, chief curator of Singer Laren Museum, is retiring. On the one hand, these changes symbolize the dynamics of the museological and scholarly enterprise of which *Dutch Utopia* is part and parcel; on the other, they make clear that the continuity of the practice and application of art history is not dependent on staff mutations. Singer Laren and the Telfair Museum of Art, with the assistance of Annette Stott and others, worked on this catalogue and exhibition in a spirit of harmony and cooperation.

We would like to thank everyone involved in this project. We are particularly proud of the exemplary collaboration with the Telfair Museum of Art, which has proven that neither time, nor distance, nor crisis form impediments to success. Our love of and dedication to art brought us together and will continue to do so.

Dolf van den Brink
Chairman of the Board of Trustees

Reinier Sinaasappel
General Director

Jan Rudolf de Lorm
Director of Museum Affairs

Singer Laren, April 2009

Acknowledgments

GARI MELCHERS (1860–1932) remains a formidable presence at the Telfair Museum of Art, where he served as fine arts advisor from 1906 to 1916. Melchers acquired cosmopolitan works of art from some of the most important living artists of his time for the Telfair, which still largely define the museum's collection a century later. It is perhaps a surprise to realize he did so while residing in a small village in the Netherlands. While working on the Telfair's catalog of the collection in 2004, I was struck by the relative paucity of information pertaining to artists who were, like Melchers, living or working abroad in Holland during the late nineteenth and early twentieth centuries. This realization led me to explore the concept of developing an exhibition on Melchers and his broader circle in Holland, some of whom, such as George Hitchcock and Walter MacEwen, were represented in the Telfair's permanent collection.

My interest in this subject was further excited after I met George Starke, a descendant by marriage of the artist Walter MacEwen, a friend and colleague of Melchers who had established his reputation on Dutch genre scenes. Mr. Starke shared a portfolio of MacEwen's work and a scrapbook documenting the artist's career—materials that he generously agreed to place on loan for further research. Moving ahead, I contacted Dr. Annette Stott, author of *Holland Mania: The Unknown Dutch Period in American Art and Culture* and one of the few scholars to publish research on American artists in Holland and the colonies they formed. Annette agreed to assist the Telfair in the development of the exhibition that would become *Dutch Utopia*. She has served as the chief curatorial advisor for this exhibition and the content editor of this catalog. Her scholarship and judgment have informed this project on nearly every level. I am grateful for her expertise, her professionalism, and her good-natured dedication to this venture.

I am also grateful to the other original members of the *Dutch Utopia* exhibition team. As Steven High mentioned in his foreword, the Telfair joined forces, albeit temporarily, with Kim Sajet and the Pennsylvania Academy of the Fine Arts. Although Kim has since departed to lead the Historical Society of Pennsylvania, she contributed significantly to the early thematic development of the project, and, happily, has remained involved as an essayist for this catalog. It was Kim who forged the initial connection with Ineke Middag and the Singer Laren Museum in the Netherlands, who remain vital partners in this exhibition. With great energy and enthusiasm, Ineke secured funding for a research trip to Holland for the exhibition team, and has provided critical advice and assistance throughout the duration of this project. Finally, Emke Raassen-Kruimel, curator at the Singer Laren at the time of this writing, has contributed her scholarly expertise and has provided valuable assistance with lenders in Europe.

As the exhibition developed, research queries were forwarded to a number of professionals in the field who responded with grace and generosity. On behalf of the exhibition team, I gratefully acknowledge the expertise and assistance of the following: Linda S. Ferber, executive vice president and director of the museum division of the New-York

Historical Society; H. Barbara Weinberg, the Alice Pratt Brown curator of American paintings and sculpture at the Metropolitan Museum of Art; Joanna Catron, curator of the Gari Melchers Home and Studio at Belmont; Stephen Phillips, director of the art program at the Federal Reserve Board, and his predecessor, Mary Anne Goley; Lisa N. Peters, director of research and publications at Spanierman Gallery; Bruce Weber, formerly of Berry-Hill Galleries, now at the National Academy of Design Museum; Gretchen Burch of Sotheby's; Sara Kyman of Bonhams and Butterfields; Cees List, Panorama Mesdag, The Hague, the Netherlands; and Ron van Vleuten, Bergen, the Netherlands.

I am also very grateful to our museum partners: Lynne Ambrosini, curator at the Taft Museum in Cincinnati, who advocated for the Taft as a venue for *Dutch Utopia;* and Celeste Adams, director of the Grand Rapids Art Museum in Michigan, who likewise secured the exhibition for her museum. Given the scholarship and effort invested in this project, it was important that it travel beyond Savannah, and we are delighted that audiences in Cincinnati and Grand Rapids, as well as visitors to the Singer Laren Museum in the Netherlands, will have the opportunity to experience *Dutch Utopia*, or, as it is called at the Singer Laren Museum, *De Hollandse Droom.* Finally, I am enormously grateful to all the lenders to this exhibition, who have quite literally made it possible.

A number of volunteers provided valuable support for this project. Karen Cassard, a Telfair docent, has tirelessly and meticulously translated numerous letters, emails, and documents in French pertaining to loans for this exhibition. Interns Josephine Warshauer and Melissa Shugart performed valuable research related to *Dutch Utopia.* Chuck Weiner and Ervin Houston assisted in the search for works on our checklist. Leigh Carter, former trustee of the Telfair, generously helped us to secure a loan that was critical to the exhibition. Olivia Nagel, Alexandra Gaba-van Dongen, André Groeneveld and Jannig Kwakman encouraged the support of important lenders to the project. Linda McWhorter, a longtime Telfair volunteer, advocated for *Dutch Utopia* within the Telfair Academy Guild, an important museum member group.

Thanks are also due to the editor of this publication, Michelle Bolton King, who handled a great deal of material in a very limited span of time, and whose thoroughness, patience, and efficiency were much appreciated. We are also grateful to the staff of Marquand Books in Seattle—particularly Sara Billups, Jeremy Linden, Adrian Lucia, Keryn Means, Marie Weiler, and designer Jeff Wincapaw—for this beautiful publication. Special thanks are due to Jeff, who patiently and diligently responded to design concerns, and is responsible for the final, very attractive results. Finally, we are proud to disseminate this publication through our distribution partner, the University of Georgia Press.

Dutch Utopia required sustained and diligent effort on the part of the Telfair's curatorial team. Two former employees of the Telfair's curatorial department, Diane Rixon and Johnna Gluth, conducted significant research pertaining to works and artists included in the exhibition. Beth Moore, assistant curator, worked tirelessly on rights and reproductions, photography, comparative images, and a multitude of other details. I am particularly indebted to Jessica Mumford, registrar, and Courtney McGowan, assistant curator, whose tireless efforts have enabled this exhibition to reach fruition. Jessica has good-naturedly handled the complex loan, shipping, insurance, and conservation arrangements with great confidence and skill. Courtney has provided critical support on nearly every level. From managing the checklist and overseeing extensive paperwork to contributing articulate entries for this catalog, Courtney's superior organizational skills and lively intelligence are everywhere evident.

I am grateful to the Telfair's former director, Diane Lesko, who encouraged me to pursue this project, and to Steven High, current director of the museum, who began his tenure in early 2007 after planning for *Dutch Utopia* was well underway. He recognized the scholarly value of the exhibition to the Telfair's history and mission and supported it, despite the considerable price tag. I would like to acknowledge Steven's leap of faith as well as that of the Telfair's Board of Trustees, who have been equally committed. I echo Steven's praise of the Terra Foundation and the Henry Luce Foundation, whose support has enabled us to present this exhibition and accompanying catalog, and I am deeply grateful to Mrs. Joanne Stanley Holbrook Patton and Mrs. Robert O. Levitt, who have provided generous private support for *Dutch Utopia*. Sincere thanks are also due to Lucita Moenir Alam, Consul General of the Kingdom of the Netherlands, for procuring cultural funds from the Netherlands Consulate General in support of this exhibition. I am especially gratified by the enthusiasm Ms. Alam and Esther van Geloven, senior commercial officer at the Consulate, have expressed for *Dutch Utopia* within the context of Dutch-American relations. Finally, I thank the members of the Telfair Academy Guild, who have not only offered extensive financial support, but have also provided a great deal of encouragement and enthusiasm for this exhibition that, in many ways, returns the Telfair to its roots.

Holly Koons McCullough
Chief Curator, Fine Arts and Exhibitions,
Telfair Museum of Art

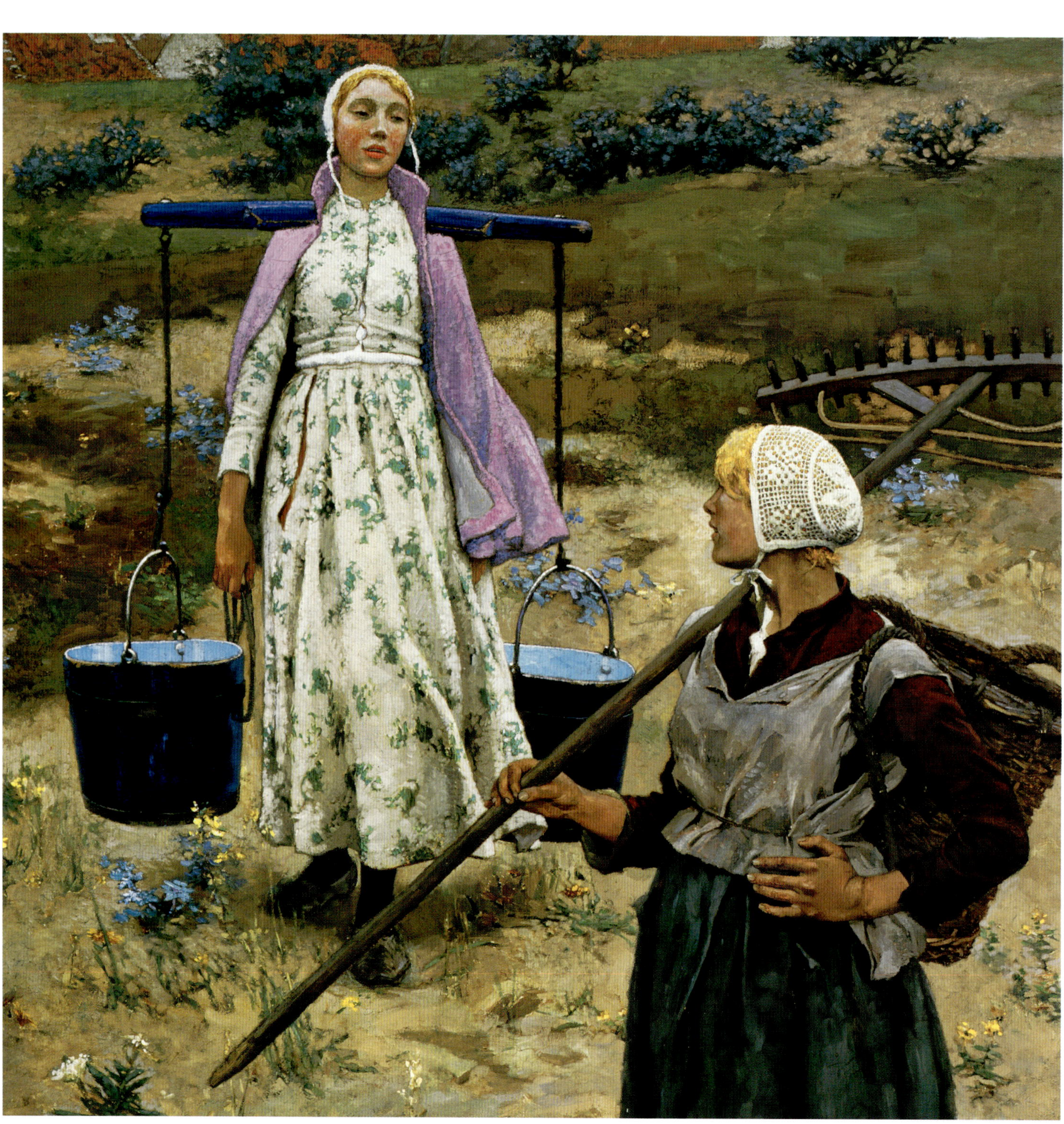

Introduction

Annette Stott

ONE DAY IN SEPTEMBER 2005, I received an email from Holly Koons McCullough, curator of the Telfair Museum of Art, asking whether any American museum had mounted an exhibition based on my book *Holland Mania: The Unknown Dutch Period in American Art and Culture* (1998). At that time, only one such exhibition had taken place and it was in the Netherlands. In 2001, the Zuiderzee Museum in Enkhuizen opened *Amerikaanse Hollandgekte*, a historical exhibition with paintings, books, and artifacts from the period when Americans became enamored of the Dutch, 1880–1914. The Telfair Museum was interested in exploring the Dutch period of three American artists to which it had ties: Gari Melchers, George Hitchcock, and Walter MacEwen. One week after we agreed to work together, I received a similar request from Kim Sajet, then deputy director of the Pennsylvania Academy of the Fine Arts and now president and CEO of the Historical Society of Pennsylvania. She was interested in a broader exhibition of the American painters working in the Netherlands at the turn of the twentieth century, the subject of my PhD dissertation, "American Painters Who Worked in the Netherlands, 1880–1914." William H. Gerdts had recently put her in touch with Ineke Middag at the Singer Laren Museum, and I suggested she work with the Telfair as well. Within weeks the three museums had embarked on the exhibition that—after many twists and turns—would become *Dutch Utopia: American Artists in Holland, 1880–1914*.

It is a delight to return to the subject that launched my professional life. Since my initial dissertation research twenty-five years ago, many things have changed. Many of the artists discussed in my dissertation were virtually unheard of in 1986, but have since become the subjects of exhibitions, articles, dissertations, and books. Joseph Raphael and Wilhelmina Douglas Hawley are good examples. Other American painters with Dutch oeuvres have emerged more recently, such as Mathias J. Alten. Scholarship on French and American impressionism, European realism and naturalism, peasant painting, and rural colonies has become more theoretical and nuanced. Nina Lübbren's *Rural Artists' Colonies in Europe, 1870–1910* (2001) considered the art colony movement as a new type of international art practice entrenched in a mythology of place. While American scholars of expatriate art have focused on artists and colonies in Italy, Scandinavia, France, and Germany, European scholars have taken a broader international approach and within that framework Dutch scholars have looked closely at the Netherlands. The Singer Laren Museum's *Schildersdorpen in Nederland* (Artists' Villages in the Netherlands) (2004) took up the subject of rural Dutch art colonies, generally. Dutch scholars and resident historians in Volendam, Laren, Hattem, Veere, Heeze, and Katwijk have examined the history of these places as artist and tourist attractions.[1] These scholars have established new contexts within which to examine the paintings created by American artists in Holland.

Detail of cat. 38

In the past twenty years, Dutch scholars have illuminated the extent to which their land became a haven for foreign artists in the nineteenth century, capturing this reality through the metaphor of dreams. Hans Kraan and John Sillevis may have been the first to apply this metaphor in an unrealized exhibition of American and European paintings of the Netherlands under development in 1987 with the working title *Holland, A Painter's Dream*. In 2002, Kraan published his book, *Dromen van Holland* (Dreaming of Holland), which examined the work of non-Dutch artists in the Netherlands during the nineteenth century, including some Americans. The same use of metaphor may be found in Alexandra Gaba-van Dongen's book, *Dromen van Rijsoord: Wilhelmina Douglas Hawley, 1860–1958*, about her grandmother, a permanent expatriate to the Netherlands whose work is included in *Dutch Utopia*. Still another exhibition, *Dromen van Dordrecht* (2005), examines foreign artists who painted the ancient city of Dordrecht in the period 1850–1920. The notion of Holland as the stuff of artists' dreams correlates well with the idea of Holland as a utopia. Both suggest a place of the imagination and that is certainly what the paintings in this exhibition reveal. Sometimes the imaginary was achieved through misunderstanding, when foreign artists misinterpreted what they saw, but more often it was the result of a willful viewing of the Dutch countryside, history, and people through a particular lens. The art of Americans, and of many other foreign painters in Holland, paints a picture of a place of the imagination more than a place in the world.

As the field of American art history matures, each generation of scholars asks new questions. A recent shift toward transatlantic perspectives and borderland studies makes the exploration of Dutch-American cultural relations in this exhibition especially timely. It is the first major art exhibition focused on Dutch-subject paintings by nineteenth-century American artists to be mounted in the United States, and it is a cross-cultural effort.[2] The five essays are written by historians and art historians from the Netherlands, England, and the United States. These scholars bring a breadth of perspectives to the subject that reflects some of the cultural perspectives of the original artists, their models, and their audiences. When the painters James Jebusa Shannon and Florence Kate Upton left their native land to study in England, and from there made trips to paint in Holland, they brought to bear on Dutch subjects the Anglo-American perspectives that their experiences had engendered. When Walter MacEwen and Gari Melchers painted views of contemporaneous Dutch villagers, they were thinking about the international audiences that would view their pictures in the major exhibitions throughout Europe and America to which they sent them. When artists of the Hague School, including Jozef Israëls and Hendrik Willem Mesdag, welcomed American painters into their Dutch studios, they offered a friendship based on shared interests in modern art and a common love of Holland. As Dutch villagers and American artists came to know each other through the long summers, there were disagreements and misunderstandings as well as neutral distances with reserved judgments, but close friendships also emerged. By bringing this exhibition to Dutch, American, and Dutch-American audiences, we offer a new generation the opportunity to discover the Holland of the American imagination that was recorded on canvases a century ago.

The curators and scholars collaborating on this work share a central understanding of the paintings that they have articulated through references to six themes, discussed below. They also bring a diversity of interpretations to individual pictures that reflects cultural biases and differing knowledge bases. So, for example, the British scholar Nina Lübbren reads Marcia Oakes Woodbury's painting of a mother and daughter spinning thread (cat. 73) as an exposition on the difficulty of women's lives in the absence of a male head of household. She suggests that the original audience would have made up narratives about these women's single state to account for the husband's demise and that they might have imagined a future family for the daughter. Dutch curator Emke Raassen-Kruimel, on the other hand, describes the same painting as a view of the daily work of women whose husbands were occupied in the local weaving factory. The drudgery of men's and women's separate work days and the poverty of their existence are the message for this curator who works in the same town that Woodbury depicted and bases her interpretation on her knowledge of the town's history. American scholar Kim Sajet takes a third perspective, seeing in the depiction of Dutch women's labors a model for nineteenth-century American reformers' attempts to introduce traditional crafts to urban immigrants through institutions such as Chicago's Hull House, and a symbolic reference to colonial America. These progressive and reformist ideas were widespread at the time the artist painted the picture. All three views are equally valid. They probably mirror a diversity of interpretations among the original audiences—Dutch models and their neighbors; Dutch artists and art lovers who saw these paintings in exhibitions in Amsterdam, The Hague, and abroad; international artists and tourists at some of the same exhibitions; and American collectors and art lovers who viewed them in exhibitions and sales in the United States. Dutch viewers often brought deeper knowledge of the circumstances depicted, while American and other foreign viewers did not necessarily even recognize where the pictures originated, but saw them in more universal terms of human behavior. American viewers sometimes shared a nationalistic perspective with the paintings' creators that other audiences missed. Thus, the same image of women spinning can be seen as a positive view of domestic industry, a negative view of unending drudgery, or anything in between. Titles sometimes clarified the artists' intentions, but more often revealed a desire to refrain from directing the viewers' experience. The title that Woodbury had carved into the frame of her triptych to ensure that it remained part of the painting is quite ambiguous: *Moeder en Dochter: Het Geheele Leven,* which can be translated as "mother and daughter: the whole of life" or "the whole life" or "the wholesome life."

In discussions among the curators working on the present exhibition, the Americans tended to accept images as closer to the reality of nineteenth-century American experiences in Holland, while Dutch curators were more skeptical. They did not readily accept the ideas, for example, that Dutch women weeded streets on their knees or wore purple flowered capes as the foreign painters George Henry Boughton and Gari Melchers depicted them. We know reality blended with imagination in American paintings of Holland, but the boundaries are not often clear. Interpretations depend on viewers' perspectives. To help contemporary audiences navigate some of the nineteenth-century perspectives, the pictures in this exhibition were assembled with six themes in mind. Many pictures embody several of the themes, and each essay in this book touches on at least two. I want to briefly describe them here in isolation and invite visitors to the exhibition to search for them in the pictures.

THE INFLUENCE OF SEVENTEENTH-CENTURY DUTCH PAINTING

The last quarter of the nineteenth century found American industrialists collecting in the international art market on an unprecedented scale. The most sought-after pictures were those by the old Dutch masters. As the newspapers reported record sales and exhibitions brought many Americans into contact with the real thing (although often misattributed), a heightened awareness of Golden Age Dutch art developed in the United States. When American painters traveled to the Netherlands, it was always, in part, to see more of these paintings. They brought with them expectations of the contemporary Dutch scene that were based on a combination of old master paintings, John Lothrop Motley's histories of the rise and fall of the Dutch republic, and literature that romanticized Holland and was often illustrated with old Dutch paintings. As a result, the paintings they created of contemporaneous Holland bore the imprint of the seventeenth century in multiple ways.

Conditioned to see Holland through the eyes of the old masters, Joseph Raphael painted a portrait of a Dutch town crier surrounded by his children (1905; cat. 52) in much the same pose as Frans Hals chose centuries earlier. *Dutch Soldier* (1907; cat. 19) and *Dutch Girl Laughing* (1907; cat. 18) by Robert Henri also owe a clear debt to Hals. Charles Yardley Turner re-created the palette of a seventeenth-century canal scene in *The Grand Canal, Dordrecht, Holland* (1881; cat. 67). Gari Melchers modernized Johannes Vermeer, painting cosmopolitan ladies in sunlit interiors. Even as they strove to perfect what they considered the most up-to-date, innovative style of painting, these artists remained steeped in the art of the seventeenth century. They were cognizant of their own American roots in Europe, and especially of New York's roots in Amsterdam during the seventeenth century when the Netherlands was a world power planting colonies on four continents.

THE INFLUENCE OF THE HAGUE SCHOOL

In the last two decades of the nineteenth century, a different class of American and British collectors discovered the contemporary Dutch painters centered in The Hague. They began collecting the art of the Hague School, often in the form of watercolors or small oil paintings that were far more affordable than the old Dutch masters. Because the painters of the Hague School also admired the old Dutch masters of the seventeenth century, the influence of the Hague School on American painters reinforced the influence of the older Dutch art tradition. Some American patrons specialized in collecting both contemporary Dutch and American images of the Netherlands. American artists saw the Hague School work in the United States, in exhibitions in Paris, and in the Netherlands. They struck up friendships with Dutch artists and invited them to the United States, often serving to connect painters with collectors and dealers.

The married Boston painters Marcia Oakes Woodbury and Charles Herbert Woodbury kept up a correspondence for many years with the Amsterdam painter Wally Moes, whom they saw in Laren when all three spent summers there. They, like several other American artists, communicated as easily in Dutch as in English. In letters from 1894 and 1897, Moes told them how discouraged she was over the response of Dutch art dealers who considered her work good but not saleable.[3] She thanked Charles Woodbury for letting her ship her paintings to him and for successfully selling them to his friends and dealers in the United States. In return, he sent her at least one student, and Moes kept the Woodburys informed about the paintings she was working on and all the Laren news until they recrossed the ocean to Holland. This is just one of many such personal and professional relationships among Dutch and American artists, who also exhibited together, socialized in the same artist clubs, crossed the ocean both directions to visit one another, and sometimes shared dealers and patrons.

Given such interactions and the presence of significant populations of American painters for up to half the year in rural Dutch art colonies, it would be surprising if the influences were not mutual. In fact, the critic R. W. P. de Vries, in discussing the work of a younger generation of Dutch artists in 1916, not only noted their debt to the Hague School and Vincent van Gogh, but also wrote: "These younger men of the new movement simply carry forward the discovery made by that open-eyed American painter Gari Melchers, who long since saw that Holland was not always enveloped in a drab and forbidding gray mist."[4] It is outside of the scope of the present exhibition to consider the ways in which the art of internationally successful

American artists such as Melchers, Hitchcock, MacEwen, and Elizabeth Nourse—with their foreign visions of Holland—influenced the younger Dutch artists. What *Dutch Utopia* suggests is that at the beginning of the period examined here, the influence between contemporary Dutch and American painters generally flowed from the older generation of Dutchmen to the young Americans in their midst. Over the course of the years this interaction became more of an exchange, with the younger group of both Dutch and American painters leaving the path of the Hague School to explore a brighter and broader palette. By the end of this period, there is evidence that some of the American artists' visual expressions of a different, brighter, flower-filled Holland were influencing a still younger generation of Dutch painters. This is something for scholars to look at more closely in the future.

ANTIMODERNISM AND THE AMERICAN PROGRESSIVE MOVEMENT

Antimodernism and progressivism are two sides of the same coin. When artists sought out remote Dutch villages where people wore traditional localized costume, and windmills or watermills still functioned to grind grain and saw lumber, they often did so out of nostalgia for the preindustrial, agrarian life, with its slower pace and greater community focus. This looking backward was a typical antimodern impulse.[5] At the same time, the reform fever that was so much a part of the Progressive Movement attempted to counteract many of the drawbacks associated with progress, from urban alienation and slum conditions to cheap factory-made goods and child laborers, by providing antidotes based on the lessons of the past. Progressives believed that new technologies, urbanization, industrialization, mass production, and man-made materials were essential components of a modern world; all they needed was to mitigate the darker side of this progress. Paintings of premodern corners of Europe provided models of those particular values that would do the mitigating. So Gari Melchers's painting of Dutch farm women with handmade wooden rake and pails (1887; cat. 38) seems to embrace the premodern method of farming with antimodern enthusiasm, while simultaneously upholding a progressive ideal of fresh air and companionship that reformers were trying to instill in American cities.

Another progressive notion embedded in paintings of premodern Holland was the idea that modernity must be founded on and rooted in older traditions. George Elmer Browne's *City of Leiden* (c. 1901–10; cat. 7) resembles seventeenth-century panoramic views of premodern Dutch cities, yet its central building was the site of an important discovery of modern physics. Cass Gilbert drew many pictures of old European tower structures, such as *Tower of the Cathedral of Utrecht, Holland* (1898; cat. 13), as he worked out the best designs for modern skyscrapers. By the same token, the art that Americans produced in the Netherlands ranged in style from extremely conservative academic pictures such as Julian Alden Weir's *Milkmaid of Popindrecht* (1881; cat. 71), to ultramodern scenes of old-fashioned industries and events, such as Paul Bernard King's *Hauling in the Anchor Line* (1905; cat. 30) and Charles Herbert Woodbury's *Dutch Kermis (Dutch Fair)* (1895; cat. 72). Old and new, antimodern and progressive were inextricably linked in the art of Americans in Holland.

BINDING TIES: POINTS OF CONVERGENCE IN NATIONAL IDENTITIES

Although certain aspects of Dutch character, as understood by American observers, were considered alien, many others seemed American. On the negative side, observers noted that the Dutch worked their women too hard, allowed small children to smoke and drink, and had a more phlegmatic approach to life than Americans. But like Americans, they were also industrious, inventive, self-reliant, freedom-loving, tolerant, and materialistic. These points of convergence in national identities were often traced to the Dutch colony in North America that eventually became New York, and to the colonists' descendants who spread out across eastern New York, New Jersey, Delaware, and Connecticut in the seventeenth and eighteenth centuries. Several artists painted not only scenes of contemporary Holland, but also imaginative history paintings of New Netherland, such as George Henry Boughton's *The Edict of William the Testy* (1877; cat. 4). Others painted those character traits they most admired. Charles Frederick Ulrich's *The Village Printing Shop, Haarlem, Holland* (1884; cat. 70) not only depicts the immaculate and efficiently organized interior of a small industry, but alludes to the seventeenth-century invention of moveable type and the basic ideal of freedom of the press. Gari Melchers's *The Family* (c. 1895; cat. 42) captures the social unit that provided the basic building block of Dutch and American society: a father, mother, and two children. His *Easter Sunday* (1910–11; cat. 45) is one of many pictures celebrating the Protestant faith of Dutch villagers that reminded many Americans of their own beliefs and church experiences.

Nineteenth-century Dutch immigrants to the United States helped reinforce the idea that Dutch and Americans shared histories and values. Unlike the larger numbers of Eastern European and Asian immigrants who might alter the basic fabric of American life, as feared by many conservative white Protestant Americans, blue-eyed blond immigrants from Holland with their Protestant work ethic and history of self-governance and personal freedoms seemed to fit into the establishment. One such immigrant, Edward Bok, rose to become a powerful spokesperson for the new American history of his era which held that Holland was the motherland of the United States.[6] Many arguments were advanced to support this historical interpretation, from the similarities between American founding documents (for example, the Declaration of Independence) and earlier Dutch documents, to Dutch support for the American Revolutionary War, Dutch precedents for American institutions, and the Dutch ancestry or training of many founding fathers, including the Pilgrims and Huguenots who took refuge in Holland before sailing to North America. The Dutch may have found such an interpretation increasingly palatable as the United States gained status in the world. At least some shared the belief that the geographies of American wilderness and Dutch placement below sea level shaped these two peoples similarly. On the surface, many paintings of the Netherlands look like paintings of any other rural European locale, but because of these binding ties, when viewers knew they were looking at a Dutch subject, overtones of national identity and history crept in.

ARTIST COLONIES IN HOLLAND

Most of the paintings in this exhibition were produced in rural art colonies in Holland. Summer art colonies became a staple of artists' lives abroad, and Dutch summer colonies offered many comforts of home: both Catholic and Protestant churches; an innkeeper with sufficient English to communicate, for those Americans who spoke no Dutch; modest, clean homes; and fresh fish or farm produce. The presence of friends and the ability to meet other artists at similar or more advanced stages of their careers in a casual setting also proved advantageous.

Colonies came about in several ways. Some, such as Katwijk, had long attracted Dutch artists and had roots in seventeenth-century Dutch art. Americans including Mathias J. Alten, Walter Castle Keith, Paul Bernard King, Carl Eugene Mulertt, William Edward Norton, William Ritschel, and Stephen Salisbury Tuckerman chose

Katwijk because of its proven paintability for marine artists and readily available accommodations.

Other colonies had been discovered more recently by Dutch painters whose pictures attracted additional artists. For example, Laren's Hague School artists and their widely exhibited paintings of sheep on the dunes, peasant farmers with their cows, and women in poor interiors lured Martin Borgord, Emma Lampert Cooper, Amy Cross, William Henry Howe, Joseph Raphael, William Henry Singer Jr., and Marcia Oakes Woodbury, among many others.

One of the smaller colonies that catered primarily to young art students, Rijsoord probably began attracting Americans because it was the birthplace of John Vanderpoel, a Dutch-American art teacher at the Art Institute of Chicago who escorted his students there. German teachers also brought students to Rijsoord, but not with the same numbers or persistence as the Americans. In this exhibition, only Anna Stanley and Wilhelmina Douglas Hawley represent the Rijsoord colony, but Hawley was its longest American artist resident. She went there first as a student, then as a teacher of watercolor painting, married a local man named Bastiaan de Koning, and settled permanently. Similarly, Hattem is represented only by Walter MacEwen, possibly one of its earliest foreign artists.

Still another colony was begun by two Americans, George Hitchcock and Gari Melchers, whose Salon paintings garnered admiration and followers such as James Jebusa Shannon. Among many others, Alice Blair Ring and Letta Crapo Smith came to Egmond as students to study with George Hitchcock.

Volendam became the quintessential rural Dutch colony, marketed to tourists as the picture-perfect image of the old Netherlands. Dutch scholars attribute its discovery to French travel writer Henry Havard, whose book about the dead villages of the Zuider Zee brought the British and American artists George Clausen and Dewey Bates to investigate in 1876.[7] In the summer of 1880, George Henry Boughton and Edwin Austin Abbey, funded by an American publisher, made their own journey and published a highly successful series of illustrated articles that had a greater impact on other American artists than had Clausen and Bates. Anna Richards Brewster, Robert Henri, Elizabeth Nourse, John Rettig, and Charles Herbert Woodbury are just a few of the diverse American artists to work in this idiosyncratic Dutch fishing village and international art colony. Many others, such as Walter MacEwen, painted in studios elsewhere but used parts of the Volendam costume in their pictures. The Volendam image became the most easily recognized by the American public as Dutch.

The presence of enough artists to form a colony invariably altered the towns that hosted them. One of the most obvious ways was in the impact on local economies, directly through the spur to pensions, hotels, and restaurants; the new jobs for models, servants, and interpreters; antique buying; and indirectly through the sale of pictures that brought tourists in their train. The image of the art colony tourist was captured by John Singer Sargent and James Jebusa Shannon.

HOLLAND IMAGINED: CONSTRUCTING DUTCHNESS

Artists constructed an image of Holland as a utopian country through selective vision, creative alteration, and vivid imagination. The image conveyed by individual paintings varies quite a lot, but the composite image formed by bringing together more than seventy paintings in this exhibition suggests that American artists invented a Holland that suited their preconceptions and their ideals. For these visual interpreters, Holland provided source material for pictures of honest labor, unadulterated nature, beautifully crafted objects, healthy lifestyles, spiritual faith, domesticity, community harmony, individuality, self-reliance, parental affection, tradition, and

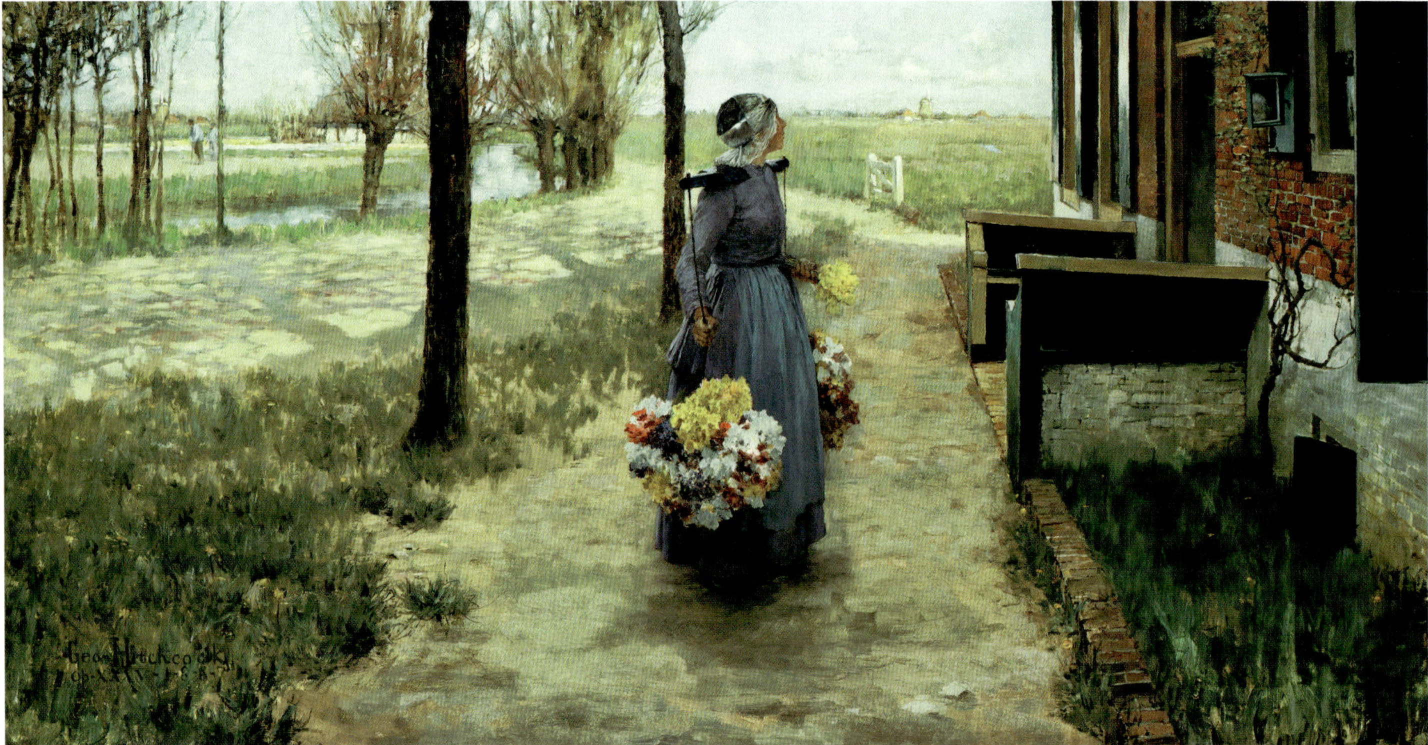

Fig. 1. George Hitchcock, *Flower Girl in Holland,* 1887, oil on canvas, 31⅛ × 58", Art Institute of Chicago, Illinois, Potter Palmer Collection, 1888.169.

continuity. John Henry Twachtman's *Windmills* (c. 1885; cat. 69) conveys a mood of tranquility through its horizontal lines and harmonious tonal palette, while subtly suggesting the industriousness underlying these picturesque icons of the Dutch people's fight against the sea, centuries of technological prowess, and ability to gain the greatest productivity from the smallest patch of land. It is an image with which most middle-class Europeans and Americans could identify. It had its counterparts in windmill-studded landscapes in France, England, Spain, and Long Island. Yet viewers of the time recognized it as a peculiarly American take on a characteristically Dutch scene.

One of the most common manipulations that cosmopolitan artists indulged in was the collection of costumes and artifacts from many different parts of the Netherlands to use as props in their paintings. The congregation in a chapel in Egmond would have worn the local costume with slight personal variations and might have included a visitor from another region, but Melchers frequently painted that place and those people wearing the headdresses that were normally only seen in the province of Brabant on the other side of the country. Other artists combined costumes from many different towns and regions. Architectural settings suffered from the same manipulations. When George Hitchcock created his famous view of a Dutch flower seller in front of a home in Egmond (fig. 1), he deleted all the other houses beyond it, causing it to appear as if it were out in the countryside to a greater extent than it really was.[8] These are the normal tools of artists, who felt no obligation to faithfully re-create what they saw, but rather a higher calling to create something more beautiful or more evocative than what nature and humankind presented to them. *Dutch Utopia* presents these diverse utopian images of Holland, painted by Americans in an era when people expected art to have an elevating influence on society.

The five essays that follow discuss American painters in Holland from multiple perspectives, starting with the macro view and moving toward the micro. The first essay, by Emke Raassen-Kruimel, places the artists in their Dutch contexts, from the Golden Age paintings they came to study, to the contemporary Hague School artists with whom they exchanged ideas, to the Dutch subjects they painted. The second essay, by Kim Sajet, places the art within an American context of mixed antimodern and progressive trends that helped push the artists toward the Netherlands in their search for answers to America's modernizing challenges. The third essay, by Nina Lübbren, examines the narrative qualities of some of the figure and landscape paintings, within the context of international art developments. The fourth essay, my own contribution, takes a closer look at a single art colony, Egmond. The final essay, by Holly Koons McCullough, looks closely at an individual artist, Walter MacEwen. Together, the paintings, essays, and catalog entries provide a new look at an important cross-cultural phenomenon in late-nineteenth-century American painting.

NOTES

1. See for example, Dick Brinkkemper, Peter Kersloot, and Kees Sier, *Volendam Schildersdorp, 1880–1940* (Zwolle: Waanders, 2006); *"Zij waren in Laren . . .": Buitenlandse kunstenaars in Laren en 't Gooi* (Laren: Singer Laren Museum, 1989); D. Koel, G. Kouwenhoven, and H. Schulte Nordholt, *Schilders van Hattem* (Hattem: Stichting Streekmuseum Hatten Voermanhuis, 1991); Kees Leeman, *Heel de Wereld trekt naar Veere: Kunst en Cultuur in een klein Zeeuws Stadje, 1870–1970* (Goes: 2003); Jean Coenen, *Heeze: Geschiedenis van een schilderachtig dorp* (Weert: 1998); *Katwijk in de Schilderkunst* (Katwijk: Katwijks Museum, 1995); and Carole Denninger-Schreuder, *De Onvergankelijke Kijk op Kortenhoef: Een Schildersdorp in Beeld* (Bussum: Thoth, 1998).

2. Mary Anne Goley curated an early exhibition of work by nineteenth-century Dutch and American painters, *The Hague School and Its American Legacy* (Washington, D.C.: Federal Reserve, 1982).

3. Wally Moes, Amsterdam, letter to Mr. Charles Woodbury, Boston, December 6, 1894, and February 20, 1897, Smithsonian Institution, Archives of American Art, Woodbury Papers, microfilm 1255.

4. R. W. P. de Vries, in J. Nilsen Laurvik, *The Netherlands (Holland) Art Exhibition* (San Francisco: Independent Pressroom, 1916), 6.

5. I first introduced this concept of an antimodern approach to Dutch subject matter in the article, "Dutch Utopia: Paintings by Antimodern American Artists of the Nineteenth Century," *Smithsonian Studies in American Art* 3, no. 2 (Spring 1989): 47–61.

6. This fairly short-lived historical interpretation is more fully explored in chapter three of Stott, *Holland Mania: The Unknown Dutch Period in American Art and Culture* (Woodstock, N.Y.: Overlook Press, 1998), 78–100.

7. Brinkkemper, Kersloot, and Sier, *Volendam Schildersdorp*, 62.

8. Ron van Vleuten identified the setting of Hitchcock's *Flower Girl in Holland* (1887, Art Institute of Chicago) in "Amerikaanse schilders in Egmond (2)," *Geestgronden: Egmonds historisch tijdschrift* 2 (July 1995): 27–42.

Dutch Utopia

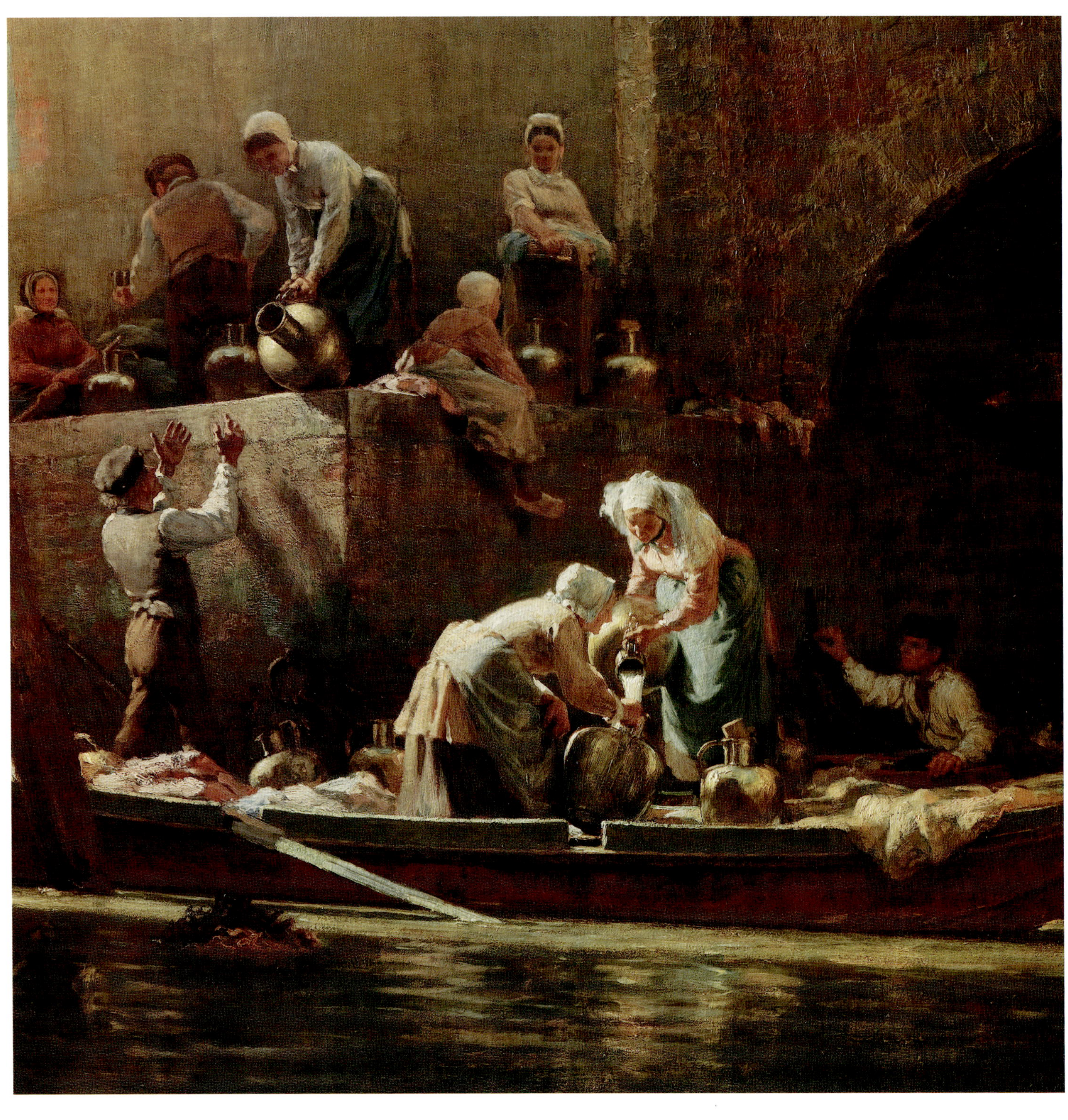

American Artists in a Dutch Context

Emke Raassen-Kruimel

THE KEEN INTEREST AMERICAN ARTISTS began evincing in the Netherlands in the 1880s was an extension of their attraction to Dutch seventeenth-century and Hague School painting. Both had an impact on the work of the Americans. Because they were active outside of The Hague as well, Hague School painters also exerted great influence on their nineteenth-century Dutch contemporaries. They played a particularly crucial role in the development of the artists' colony at Laren, which was sought out by large numbers of American artists in the wake of their Dutch confreres.

THE HAGUE SCHOOL

The village of Oosterbeek played a key role in the Hague School's early history. Around 1840 several Dutch artists came to work there and in nearby Wolfheze, drawn by the splendid surroundings with woods and pastures on the edge of the Veluwe region in the heart of the Netherlands. In the 1850s and 1860s Gerard Bilders, Anton Mauve, Paul Gabriël, and Willem Maris—all young at the time—began to work out of doors directly from nature. With their freer approach they succeeded in breaking away from the academic tradition and the artificiality of romanticism, thereby laying the foundations for what would later come to be called the Hague School.

Deriving inspiration directly from the rural surroundings was also a distinctive feature of the Barbizon School in France. Oosterbeek has been referred to as the "Dutch Barbizon." Gerard Bilders died at a young age in 1865, but the other three soon created a furor as painters of the Hague School, the collective name of a group of influential landscape and genre painters working in The Hague.[1]

This city emerged as the center of Dutch painting in the 1870s. Part of its appeal lay in the fact that its immediate surroundings were still rural compared to those of Amsterdam and Rotterdam. Polders, waterways, pastures, as well as the beach with ships and fishermen were close at hand, all eminently suitable subjects for painters bent on working out of doors. His genre scenes of the fisherman's life had already earned the somewhat older Jozef Israëls a great reputation. Anton Mauve was building a career as a landscape painter and later, in the 1880s, moved to Laren, where he played a prominent role. Hendrik Willem Mesdag became a leading figure in The Hague; in addition to being a celebrated seascape painter, he assembled and gave to the nation a large collection of work by Dutch and French contemporaries. Mesdag also extended his hospitality to many artists, including Americans. Jacob Maris painted landscapes and cityscapes in The Hague. Willem Maris, mentioned above in relation to Oosterbeek, specialized in pastures with cattle. In addition to Gabriël, other landscapists, such as Willem Roelofs and Jan Hendrik Weissenbruch, should not go unnoticed here. Albert Neuhuys painted interior scenes and would become one of the founders of the artists' colony in Laren. Bernardus Johannes Blommers,

Detail of cat. 67

too, was a practitioner of this genre and also painted beach scenes with children.[2] All these artists shared a desire to render freely and directly what they observed, whether a landscape or a genre scene. In 1875, the art critic J. van Santen Kolff was the first to speak of a "Hague School," noting a new "realism."[3] Characteristic was the use of a tonal color scheme leaning to gray, brown, and green tints rather than more vibrant colors.

Gerard Bilders expressed his quest for tonality as early as 1860: "I am looking for a tone, which we call colored gray; that is, the merging of all colors, no matter how strong, into an entity, such that they make the impression of a fragrant, warm gray."[4] This quote touches upon the essence of the Hague School. The paint was often loosely brushed onto the canvas, giving an impression of the landscape. Even though it was totally different in color from French impressionism, in fact the Hague School is a Dutch variant of it. Also influential was the free execution and tempered palette of the Barbizon School. Moreover, seventeenth-century landscapes and interiors were an important source of inspiration for the painters of the Hague School. Many artists kept in touch and regularly gathered at Pulchri Studio, the meeting point of the Hague School artists. Along with oil paint, watercolor was favored as an artistic medium: well-executed watercolors make up a substantial share of the oeuvres of Israëls, Jacob Maris, Mauve, and Neuhuys. This medium, furthermore, became popular among the many painters who followed in the footsteps of the Hague School.

The Hague School experienced its heyday between around 1870 and 1885. The work of these painters gradually gained in popularity and was exported on a wide scale, in particular to Anglo-Saxon patrons in England, Scotland, Canada, and the United States.

In the meantime, many of them no longer worked solely in The Hague but also headed out to the countryside, where artists' colonies emerged during the 1870s in villages such as Katwijk and Laren. Urbanization, which also affected The Hague, eroded the natural character of the immediate surroundings of the city, prompting Anton Mauve, for example, to move to Laren for good. Hence, the painting style of the Hague School was continued in different places throughout the Netherlands.

In a number of instances, American artists who visited the Netherlands had direct contact with the Dutch painters. As noted above, Mesdag was very hospitable, but Israëls, Mauve, and many others also received colleagues. John Henry Twachtman, who traveled with Julian Alden Weir to the Netherlands, met Anton Mauve in 1881.[5] At Mesdag's invitation in 1903, William Merritt Chase took the pupils in his summer class, which he held in Haarlem, to The Hague to see Mesdag's collection. Chase's acquaintanceship with Mesdag dated to the 1880s. Israëls received the group on the same day.[6] A few Americans, such as Amy Cross, studied at the Royal Academy of Art in The Hague; she took lessons from Jacob Maris and Neuhuys. Charles Paul Gruppe, too, trained at the academy and had classes with Israëls and Blommers. During his lengthy sojourn in the Netherlands, he became acquainted with many artists. Cross and Gruppe were also members of Pulchri Studio, where they met Dutch colleagues and participated in Dutch exhibitions.[7]

THE INFLUENCE OF THE SEVENTEENTH CENTURY

For many American artists, the paintings of the Dutch Golden Age were an important reason to travel to the Netherlands. They generally went to the Frans Hals Museum in Haarlem and the Rijksmuseum in Amsterdam to copy masterpieces hanging there, though sometimes they visited other collections as well.[8] The seventeenth-century portraits, interiors, landscapes, sea- and riverscapes, and cattle pieces left their mark on the work of the Americans. Rembrandt and Hals, as well as others such as De Hooch, Vermeer, and Van Ruisdael, were emulated. Various examples of this are cited in the discussion of artists who worked in Laren, but several other sea- and riverscape painters are worth noting here.

For his *Dutch Coast* (1885; cat. 15), William Stanley Haseltine may well have been inspired by Willem van de Velde II or Jacob van Ruisdael: the dramatic cloud-filled sky, the low horizon, and the cresting waves point in that direction. However, the somewhat theatrical lighting also recalls the romantic realism of the German painter Andreas Achenbach, whose work Haseltine knew from a sojourn in Düsseldorf.[9] More naturalistic is *Marine View* (1885; cat. 66) by Stephen Salisbury Tuckerman. Tuckerman lived for a long time in The Hague and also painted in Katwijk.[10] The subject of a fishing boat cleaving through the waves has its origin in the seventeenth century, but the placement of a single boat in the middle of the composition, the loose execution and the fairly tonal palette reveal his kinship with the work of Mesdag. Dwight William Tryon betrays his response to art of the seventeenth century in his precise observation in *The River Maas at Dordrecht* (1881; cat. 65). In the nineteenth century, Dordrecht's seventeenth-century character appealed tremendously to foreign artists. Charles Yardley Turner perceived Dordrecht in an entirely different way. His *The Grand Canal, Dordrecht, Holland* (1881; cat. 67) affords a somewhat nostalgic view of the quayside hustle and bustle in the seventeenth-century town center. Turner, who also painted genre scenes, here combined genre and architectural elements, both facets of seventeenth-century painting. The powerful *clair-obscure*, for instance, in the highlighting of the figures and embankment wall, is reminiscent of Rembrandt. The theatrical atmosphere, however, is hardly Dutch and sooner related to seventeenth-century Italian art. Herman Herzog in his *Moonlight in Holland* (n.d.; cat. 21) followed the tradition of nocturnal landscapes like those, for example, that established the reputation of Aert van der Neer in the seventeenth century.

LAREN DISCOVERED BY PAINTERS

Laren is one of the places where many Americans stayed for longer or shorter periods of time. Located approximately twenty miles (thirty kilometers) east of Amsterdam, the village is nestled amid a gently rolling landscape of sandy ground with heaths in the Gooi region. In the nineteenth century it was still a modest rural hamlet of farmers and weavers, with sheep grazing on the moors.

The first painters to visit Laren in the 1870s encountered a rather poor community, whose inhabitants lived in old farms or laborer's cottages (fig. 2). The painter Wally Moes, who went to Laren in 1884, wrote:

> When Laren was still the old Laren, it lay still and peaceful surrounded by sweeping fields, and the houses along the gritty sand roads stood stoic and silent, . . . the farms spread apart, tucked behind hedges, the small dwellings in groups or in rows. . . . The grayish-brown thatched roofs almost reached the ground.[11]

Initially the village was somewhat isolated, but that changed with the arrival of the Gooi Steam Trolley in 1882, when a direct connection to Amsterdam was introduced. An ever-growing number of artists and tourists discovered Laren: "The old village emanated a serene charm. The inn with its weathered signboard 'De Vergulde Postwagen' (the Gilded Mail Coach) was located on a very handsome large church green. It was entirely planted . . . with long rows of slender elms."[12]

The town center was and still is graced by a village square known as De Brink, in the middle of which is De Koesweerd Pond. This was the spot from which shepherds and their sheep would head out to the moors in the early morning and return in the evening. The above-mentioned guesthouse was the village hotel run by the widow

Fig. 2. Laren models in front of their house, about 1900, Singer Laren Museum, the Netherlands.

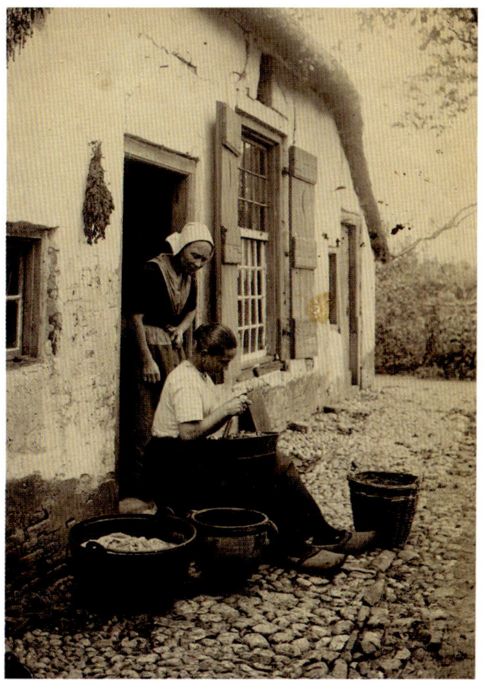

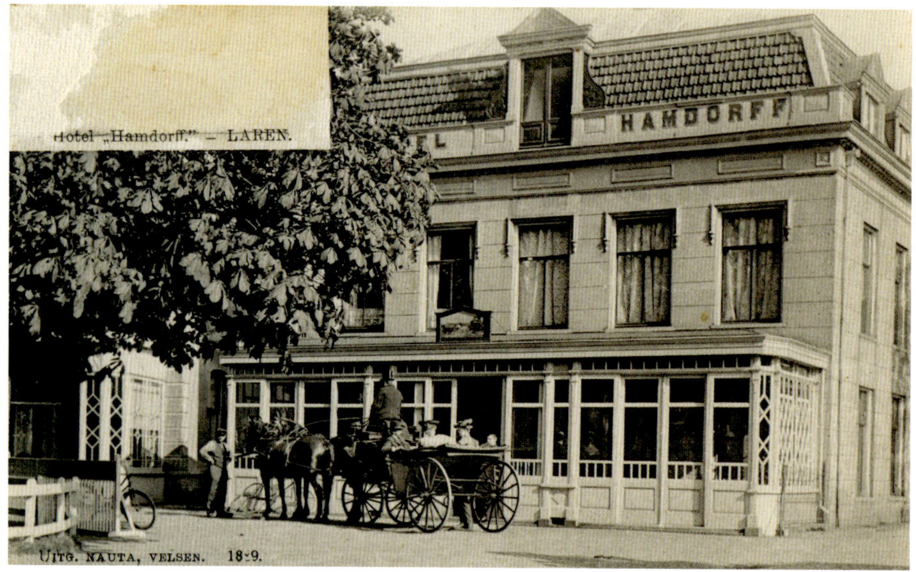

Fig. 3. Postcard of the Hotel Hamdorff, Laren, about 1900, Singer Laren Museum, the Netherlands.

Hamdorff and her son Jan. Jan Hamdorff soon became Laren's most famous hotelier. In 1905 he radically expanded the inn, which in the meantime had been rechristened Hotel Hamdorff (fig. 3). It gained a certain renown in the Netherlands and abroad. The hotel's café, Het Kroegje or the Little Tavern, became a watering hole for artists and intellectuals. Jan Hamdorff not only provided lodging, he also facilitated artists looking for studios and models and brokered sales of works of art with dealers. To top it off, he also played a prominent role in local politics.

Hotel Hamdorff was not the only accommodation. One could also stay at De Gouden Leeuw hotel (The Golden Lion) or with Mrs. Kam-Redcliffe, who settled in Laren in 1895 and set up a boarding house in Villa Van Dijk on the St. Janstraat. She was English by birth, which appealed to her English-speaking guests. Around 1905 her guesthouse was relocated to 't Witte Huis (The White House) on the Neuhuysweg.[13] Artists staying for protracted periods of time also rented rooms from private individuals or even built a house with a studio, many of which can still be found in Laren and in the neighboring village of Blaricum.[14] As far as painting is concerned, Blaricum really was an extension of Laren. Many artists lived and worked in both villages, though the cultural center was in Laren.

Laren's appeal was not limited to visual artists. Around 1900, it also counted many intellectuals, writers, composers, philosophers, and idealists.[15] At the beginning of the twentieth century they were joined by affluent individuals from Amsterdam eager to live in the splendid Gooi region. The village's rapid expansion with large mansions eroded its bucolic character, bringing changes which did not exactly meet with everyone's approval.

The discovery of Laren as an artists' haven is credited to Jozef Israëls, who visited it certainly as early as 1874.[16] Israëls drew the village to the attention of his younger colleague, Albert Neuhuys, who moved from Amsterdam to The Hague in that same year and became part of the Hague School. He specialized in interior scenes. Laren provided ample inspiration in this respect because, "In the houses everything was still as it had been for hundreds of years. The fire burned under the large chimney directly on the plate or in the brazier, above which the kettle hung, the floors were mostly still red-tiled and the walls white-washed."[17] The inhabitants of these old interiors wore traditional Laren costumes. That this appealed to Israëls is understandable given his interests, despite the fact that there is not much work by him that can be directly connected to Laren (fig. 4). Neuhuys, however, became *the* painter of Laren interior scenes, and in this he was most certainly influenced by the older Israëls, who in turn responded to seventeenth-century interior scenes. Neuhuys himself also drew direct inspiration from the Golden Age. In 1883 he moved

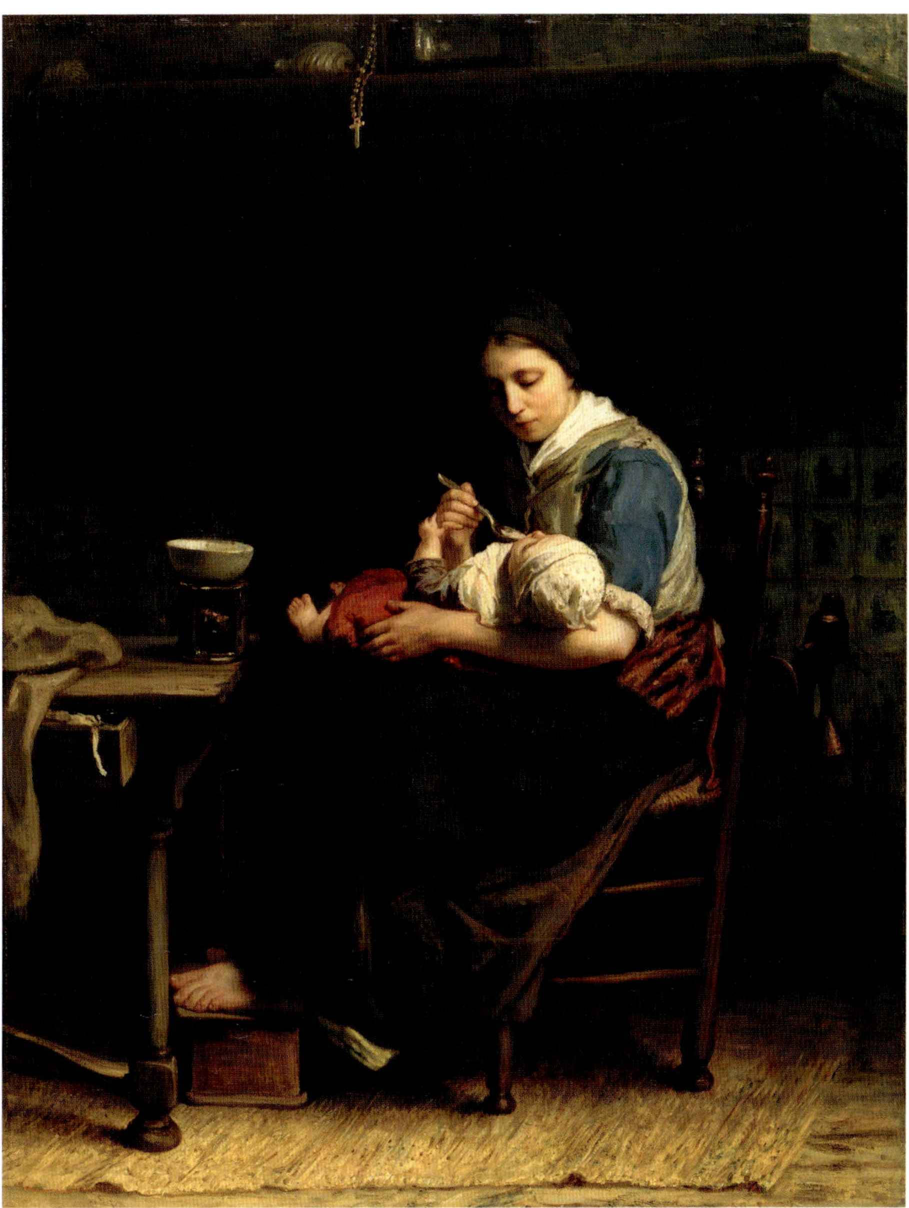

Fig. 4. Jozef Israëls, *The Cottage Madonna,* c. 1867, oil on canvas, 71½ × 54", The Detroit Institute of Arts, Michigan, Bequest of Nell Ford Torrey.

Fig. 5. Albert Neuhuys, *Laren Woman at the Cradle,* before 1904, oil on canvas, 24 × 21¼", Singer Laren Museum, the Netherlands.

to Laren and spent several years there, also returning later on many occasions.[18] Domestic scenes of mothers and children became his trademark, the woman usually busy sewing or doing some other household chore. Neuhuys was captivated by the picturesqueness of the subject. His paintings and watercolors present a friendly and serene image of daily life, in which nothing alludes to the dire poverty suffered by Laren's inhabitants. His "realistic" painting style is actually rather romantic and contributed to his enormous success; his work sold at a brisk rate as far away as America.[19] Neuhuys's genre scenes stimulated other painters to create comparable work, if not actually emulate them, and he is considered one of the founders of painting in Laren, referred to by some as the Laren School, but which was in fact an extension of the Hague School (fig. 5).[20]

Other successful painters of interior scenes were Jacobus Simon Hendrik ("Hein") Kever and Evert Pieters, who shared Neuhuys's rosy vision of Laren life. Kever had been working in Laren and vicinity since the 1870s and spent every summer there as of 1887.[21] He converted one of the rooms in his house into a Laren peasant abode in which his models posed. This allowed him to work in peace, unencumbered by the inconvenience of the filthy farms—apparently, that aspect of realism went a bit too far for him. This working method was not uncommon, for Neuhuys and Pieters also had such niches in their houses, as did Jozef Israëls, who built a replica of a cottage interior in his studio in The Hague.[22]

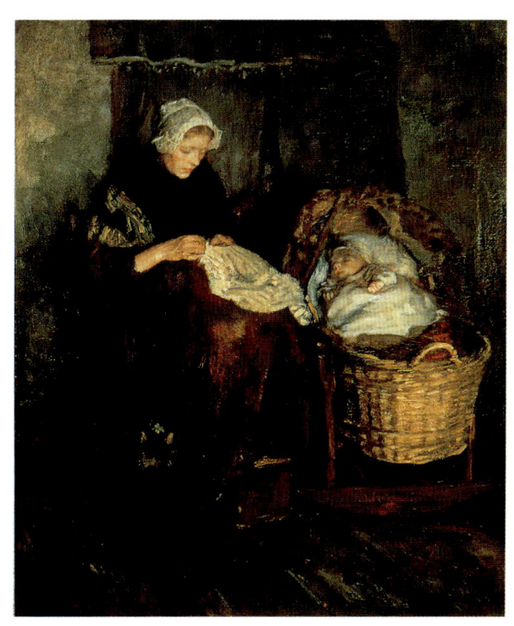

The most celebrated Dutch painter at this time whose name is indelibly linked to Laren was Anton Mauve, one of the most successful members of the Hague School. He visited Laren for the first time in 1882, and wrote his wife that it was easy to reach from Amsterdam with the steam trolley. In the same letter he noted: "It is a beautiful region, with wonderful heaths, and sheep as well, magnificent straw roofs and very friendly spots . . . in short, large and small nuggets of gold for artistic hands."[23] At that moment, his close friend, Neuhuys, was residing with his family in Laren. The steadily growing urbanization of the area around The Hague prompted Mauve's decision to move to Laren for good in 1885; he bought a house, adding a studio, on the edge of the village, on the Naarderstraat, which he named Villa Ariëtte after his wife.[24] Prior to settling in Laren, he painted beach scenes, polder landscapes with ditches, dune views with flocks of sheep, and foresters at work. In Laren, sheep roaming on the heaths became his favorite subject; other treasured subjects in those years included a farmwoman in her vegetable garden or with a goat in an orchard, farm workers harvesting potatoes, and unpopulated landscapes with a cottage here and there (fig. 6).

Mauve shared the "gold" he panned in Laren with others. For example, he encouraged the painter Arina Hugenholtz, whom he knew from The Hague, to come to Laren and in particular to work out of doors. She took up residence in De Vergulde Postwagen in 1885 and became the pivot of the artists' community. Hugenholtz befriended countless artists.[25] Mauve's circle of friends also included Wally Moes, who in 1886 rented the house next door, where Albert Neuhuys had once lived.[26] Moes, too, played a key role in Laren and like Arina Hugenholtz is mentioned below in relationship to the Americans.[27]

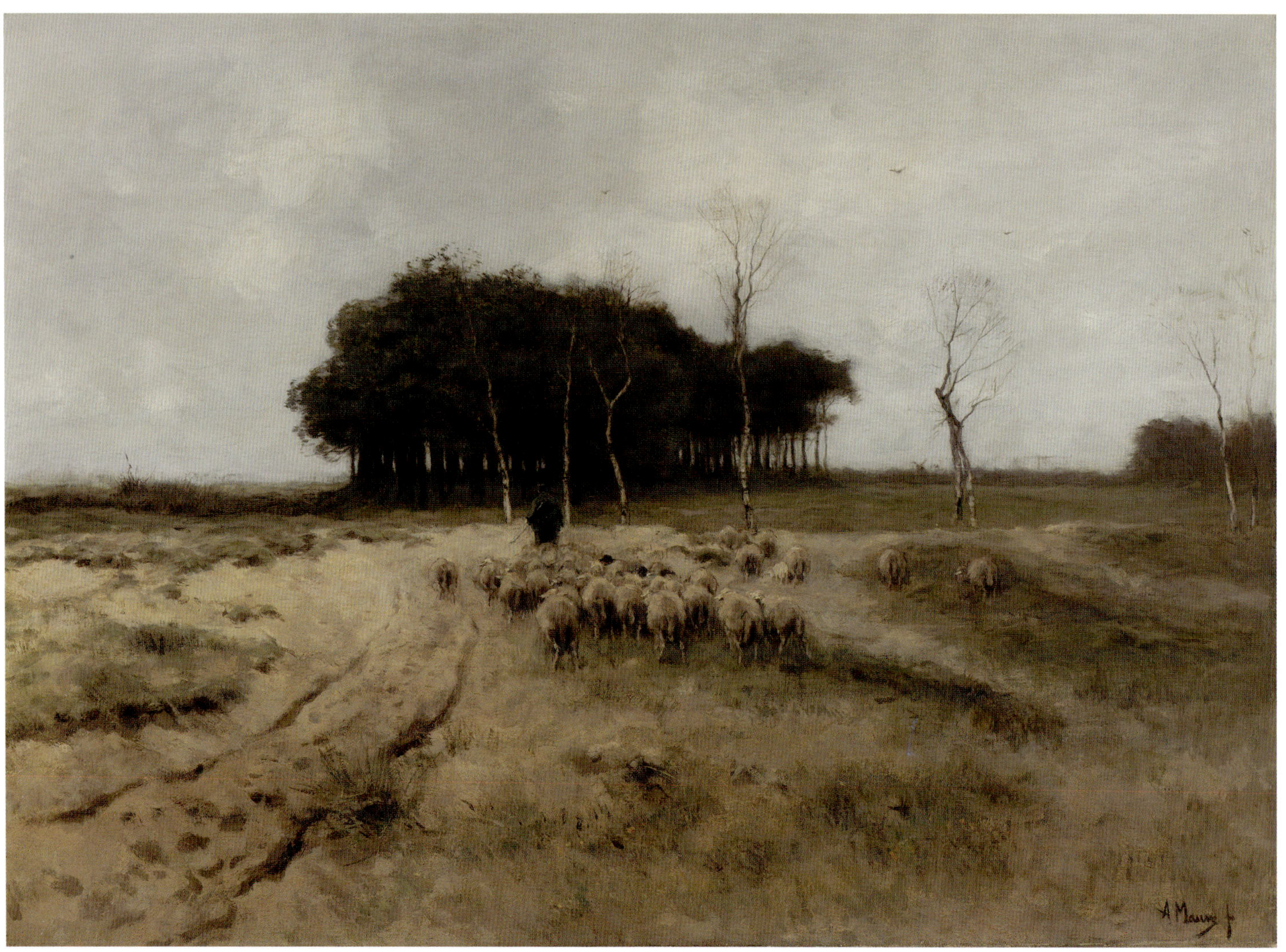

Fig. 6. Anton Mauve, *Heathland at Laren,* 1887, oil on canvas, 30¼ × 41", Rijksmuseum, Amsterdam, the Netherlands.

Mauve died unexpectedly in 1888, at a relatively young age, but Laren continued to profit from his reputation for a long time to come. In the following decades Mauve's success prompted many Dutch and American painters to adopt his subject matter, albeit with varying levels of quality, but in any case under his influence. Many of these artists visited Laren or sojourned there for some time. When Nico van Harpen opened his Larensche Kunsthandel, or Laren Art Gallery, in 1905, he shrewdly christened his premises Villa Mauve and called the bulletin he published as of 1906 *Het Land van Mauve*. The commercially oriented Van Harpen exported works by Laren painters to the United States on a large scale. To satisfy the great demand, quickly executed oil paintings and watercolors of popular subjects (but of mediocre quality) were often produced. Made solely for money, these "potboilers" gave Laren a bad name and were soundly criticized in the Netherlands at the time.[28]

THE FIRST AMERICAN ARTISTS IN LAREN: THE LANDSCAPE

Soon after Laren emerged as a painters' village, during the 1880s the first Americans began arriving there. Colleagues from The Hague drew their attention to Laren's picturesque possibilities, and these often still-young artists were eager to explore the "beautiful land" of Mauve. Several of them are well documented as actually having worked in Laren. Others can only be associated with Laren on the basis of the subjects of their works.[29]

One of the first of them was Henry Ward Ranger, who traveled throughout Europe in the 1880s and spent a fair amount of time in the Netherlands. In America he had become fascinated by the Barbizon School, many works of which had by then been imported to the New World. He discerned the successors of Barbizon in the Hague School:

> I went to Holland. My first sight of the works of Israel[s], Maris, Bosboom, and Mauve gave me the same thrill which I had received from my first acquaintance with the Barbizon painters; and I wanted to know them also. I felt them to be the lineal successors of the Barbizon School.[30]

Ranger most likely met some of the Hague School painters in The Hague in the mid-1880s. Mauve had moved to Laren for good in 1885, and Ranger remembered speaking with him there. He found the Dutch to be sympathetic and open, always ready to help and offer advice. Mauve was "a very delightful man" and told him that he made sketches out of doors, which he worked out further on canvas back in his workshop, like the old masters had done. This working method appealed to Ranger. In any case, Ranger was in Laren in 1888, a few weeks before Mauve died unexpectedly.[31] He also had discussions there with other painters, such as Israëls, in "a little inn," probably the Kroegje of De Vergulde Postwagen (later Hotel Hamdorff), where he lodged.[32] His circle of friends furthermore included Albert Neuhuys and Jacob ("Jack") Maris. Later, in 1899, with Laren in mind, Ranger encouraged American painter friends to work in Old Lyme, Connecticut, where an artists' colony arose.

In the Netherlands, Ranger painted landscapes and harbor and river views, such as *Dutch Harbor* (c. 1890; cat. 51). The powerful expression of the atmosphere of a gloomy day and the highly tonal character with the many shades of gray in the sky and water are entirely in keeping with the Hague School. The gray skies by Jacob Maris and Anton Mauve instantly come to mind.

At the end of the 1880s William Henry Howe was in Laren, where he also met Ranger.[33] Howe specialized in cattle painting and made several cattle pieces there. The work of seventeenth-century Dutch painters such as Aelbert Cuyp and Paulus Potter was popular in America, and Howe particularly admired Potter's *The Young Bull* (fig. 7). Howe's *Evening at Laren* (1890; cat. 28) recalls the sensibility of Potter's

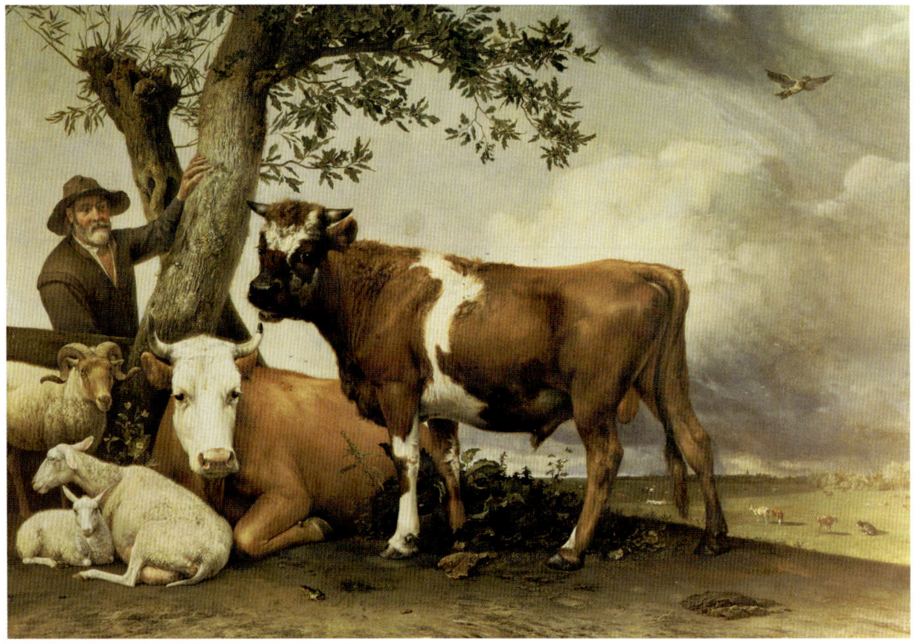

Fig. 7. Paulus Potter, *The Young Bull*, 1647, oil on canvas, 92¾ × 133½", Royal Cabinet of Paintings Mauritshuis, The Hague, the Netherlands.

icon: almost perfect cows in a perfect landscape. A more realistic image is afforded by *Reclining Cow in the Stall* (1890; cat. 27), which he gave as a present to Jan Hamdorff in 1890. With its loose brushwork, this work fits in well with the Hague School. Howe was certainly familiar with the cows and stable interiors that Mauve had been painting since the beginning of his career, as well as those by Willem Maris and the slightly older Willem Roelofs, both known for their meadow landscapes with cattle. Like Ranger, Howe later worked in Old Lyme where he—and many other artists—painted door panels in Florence Griswold's boarding house for artists, including one of a cow lying in a stable.

Some Americans, such as Charles Paul Gruppe (sometimes also written as Gruppé), actually lived in the Netherlands for many years. Gruppe ranked among the better painters and he reaped success with his work. He was part of the Hague School artists' milieu for so long that he almost came to be seen as a Dutch artist. An extensive article on him in *Elsevier's Geïllustreerd Maandschrift* in 1904 even noted that: "art-historically he belongs to Holland."[34] Originally from Canada, Gruppe was an almost entirely self-taught artist. He lived in the Netherlands between around 1890 and 1910 and in addition to The Hague, he also stayed in Laren and Katwijk. The themes and painting manner of the Hague School are reflected in his oil paintings and watercolors. Landscapes with a ditch and a farm or with sheep or woodcutters are subjects drawn from the surroundings of The Hague or Laren and have their roots in the work of Anton Mauve. Gruppe's titles sometimes refer to the place of origin; various Laren titles are listed in a catalog of the Frans Buffa art gallery from around 1906.[35] Admiration for Mauve, who had died several years earlier, undoubtedly brought Gruppe to Mauve's village. Gruppe subsequently built a house in Katwijk in 1906, where he lived for three years. He had previously worked in Katwijk, painting coastal scenes of fishing boats on the beach or in the sea as well as children playing along the shore. The latter theme was equally popular with the Hague School painter Bernard Blommers, whose work was highly sought after in America. The two artists were neighbors in Katwijk.[36] Gruppe's interest in seascapes may have been stimulated by Mesdag, with whom he studied.

Gruppe's *October Skies, Holland, Near Voorburg* (1890s; cat. 14), a view of a mill along the water and boats in the vicinity of The Hague, bespeaks yet another influence. The typical cloudy Dutch sky, the low horizon, and the water in the foreground call to mind related canvases by Jacob Maris (fig. 8). In turn, Maris was in part inspired by seventeenth-century landscapes by Jacob van Ruisdael, whose grand panoramas are distinguished by vast cloudy skies and low horizons. Gruppe certainly would have seen Van Ruisdael's famous *View of Haarlem* (fig. 9) in the Mauritshuis in The Hague, or his *The Windmill at Wijk bij Duurstede* in the Rijksmuseum in Amsterdam. The subject matter of *October Skies* is akin to that of the latter painting.

Walter Castle Keith from Detroit lived in various places in the Netherlands from 1901 to 1921. In his first years he spent some time in Katwijk, where his *Beach Scene* originated (1905; cat. 29). Its subject and the loose execution of the tide line and sky are related to the Hague School. Striking, however, is the pronounced accent on the left part of the composition with a *bomschuit* (fishing boat) and a standing fisherwoman, both partly laid out in simple planes of color without detail. The cropping was undoubtedly influenced by photography. More in keeping with the Hague School are Keith's landscapes with sheep in the manner of Mauve, and meadows with cows. All of his work, however, is distinguished by a fresh use of color. He probably also painted similar subjects as well as interior scenes in Laren, where he stayed a few times and eventually lived from 1914 to 1917.[37] In 1917 he moved

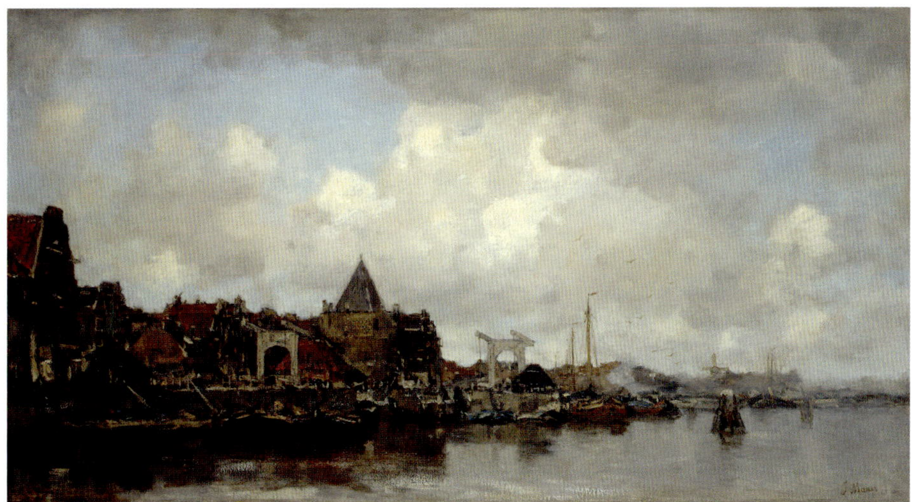

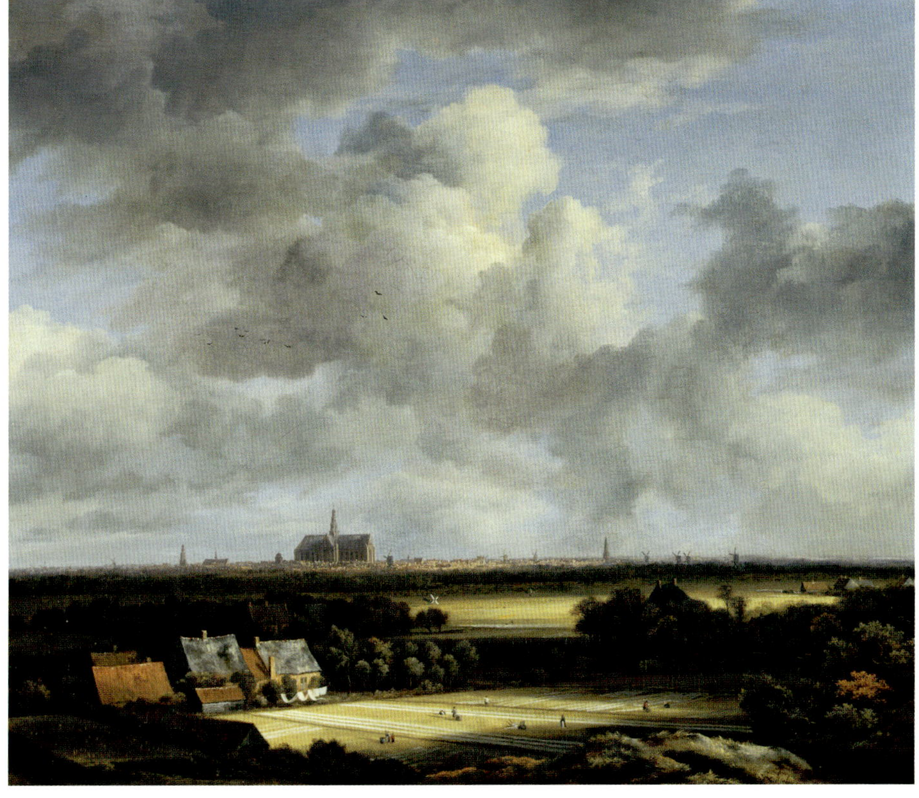

Fig. 8. Jacob Maris, *The Schreierstoren, Amsterdam*, c. 1890, oil on canvas, 31½ × 58¼", Gemeentemuseum Den Haag, The Hague, the Netherlands.

Fig. 9. Jacob van Ruisdael, *View of Haarlem with Bleaching Grounds*, c. 1670–75, oil on canvas, 21⅞ × 24⅜", Royal Cabinet of Paintings Mauritshuis, The Hague, the Netherlands.

to the Heeze artists' colony in Brabant and continued to treat similar themes. It is difficult to identify where he made his paintings because their titles often fail to mention any specific location, as is apparent in the catalog of the commemorative exhibition organized by Frans Buffa and Sons in 1929.[38] Apart from the individual artists we know by name, many groups also came to Laren, chiefly in the 1890s. Newspapers sometimes took notice of this phenomenon: ". . . Laren distinguished itself by the peculiarity of affording lodging to several American ladies: almost all of them painters, or wanting to be. . . . They seemed to believe that if one paints where Mauve painted, art would simply flow from their brushes."[39] Although the quote is unflattering, it probably gives a reasonably accurate idea of the situation. Moes, too, expressed herself in this vein in her *Nagelaten Vertellingen*.[40]

GENRE PAINTING IN LAREN

A surprising number of female American artists worked in Laren. They specialized in genre scenes and often worked in watercolor, a medium used by Hague School artists as well. Amy Cross, chaperoned by her mother, stayed in De Vergulde Postwagen around 1890 and was in Laren again in 1892.[41] She studied at the Royal Academy of Art in The Hague in the late 1880s and early 1890s under Jacob Maris and Albert Neuhuys, among others.[42] For one of her gouaches, Cross chose an unusual subject: not an interior with a mother and child, but a vegetable vendor with his client out of doors in front of an attractive farm (*The Holland Vegetable Vendor*, c. 1890s; cat. 12). Like the familiar interior scenes, here, too, an overly rosy image of life in Laren is presented. A Dutch painter would not have chosen the subject so readily, but its rural informality evidently appealed to this American artist. In Laren, Cross had contact with Tony Offermans,[43] Arina Hugenholtz, and Wally Moes, whom she met at Hamdorff's. She also worked in Katwijk and Nunspeet, where she painted interior scenes.[44]

Charles Herbert Woodbury and his wife, Marcia Oakes Woodbury, first visited Laren at about the same time as Amy Cross. They spent their honeymoon in Europe in 1890 and visited the Netherlands, among other countries. Subsequently they would return regularly to the Low Countries until 1908. Marcia was fascinated by Dutch and Flemish painting, about which she wrote extensively, and fairly soon in Dutch. She conveyed her understanding of Dutch culture and the past in paintings of genre scenes and especially subjects with children wearing the traditional costumes of Laren, Volendam, Katwijk, and Veere.[45] In the Woodburys' third year in Laren, Marcia painted a triptych in watercolor entitled *Moeder en Dochter: Het Geheele Leven (Mother and Daughter: The Whole of Life)* (1894; cat. 73). In this exceptional work the painter expressed her concern for the women of Laren, who were condemned to a life of spinning. While the subject may now seem nostalgic, in 1894 it was a reality. The men worked in the textile factories of Laren; the women spun wool at home or in the collective spinning mill, the Laren Vlasschuur, which is also known from an 1887 painting in the Berlin National Gallery by the German painter Max Liebermann, *The Spinners of Laren, Holland (Flachsscheuer in Laren)*. Perhaps the painter Wally Moes, with whom the couple became acquainted, opened Marcia's eyes to life in Laren. Moes wrote: "Given that the wages were very low, poverty was great. . . . Spinning with highly primitive wheels, done standing and turning a spoke with one's right hand . . . was extremely unhealthy work."[46] Other artists also addressed the subject of spinning, but not in this symbolic sense. With their restrained and nearly devotional character, the two female faces could almost be contemporary variants of portraits by Flemish primitives, such as Hans Memling or Rogier van der Weyden. The choice of the triptych format, which originally had a religious function, also points in this direction.

Throughout his life Charles Woodbury was primarily a painter of sea and shore, but in the Netherlands he turned his hand to other themes as well. In Laren he concentrated on the landscape and the village.[47] The annual fair in Volendam, the fishing village where he worked on numerous occasions, provided him with the subject of his *Dutch Kermis* (1895; cat. 72). Just like many Dutch and foreign artists, he portrayed the event in a bright color scheme. Woodbury delineated the crowd on the dyke near the harbor in fluid brushstrokes, a loose execution also characteristic of his later work.

Somewhat before Marcia Woodbury's triptych, the theme of spinning had already inspired a friendly genre scene by Emma Lampert: *The Breadwinner* (1891; cat. 11). The mood of this watercolor of a woman spinning is entirely in keeping with the model of Jozef Israëls's interior genre scenes. The subject is timeless: a woman working quietly, surrounded by the tools of her trade, a broom in the corner, and a cat in the window. Although the watercolor is in the first place related to the Hague School, the attention to detail recalls seventeenth-century interior scenes by Jan Steen or Gabriël Metsu, for example. Equally striking are the light accents on the skeins of wool and the floor. This highlighting was also a feature of the Laren painter Hein Kever, whose interiors enjoyed great success and who had taught Lampert.[48] She married Colin Campbell Cooper in 1897, who had also painted in Laren but focused more on the landscape and farmers. Cooper also specialized in city views and was interested in architecture. That he looked at seventeenth-century art can be demonstrated by his painting *Dordrecht Harbor* (c. 1898; cat. 10). Many foreign artists, including famous American ones such as James Abbott McNeill Whistler and John Twachtman, visited Dordrecht in the nineteenth century. With its old houses and harbor, it had retained much of its seventeenth-century character and was where the illustrious Aelbert Cuyp had worked. Cooper rendered the Grote Kerk (the Dordrecht Minster) and the houses along the harbor in great detail and very true to life, rather than in the loose manner of the Hague School. In this, the painting is related to seventeenth-century city views, but it shares its nostalgic conception with romantic pictures from the mid-nineteenth century.

Not long ago a sketch of a Laren subject by Elizabeth Nourse, a very well-known artist in America, was discovered. It is part of a sketchbook containing drawings of mostly Volendam figures. Nourse worked in Volendam in 1892, at which time she also visited Laren. A fairly precise study of a woman in traditional Laren costume is annotated "Laaren Sept 1892." She reaped success with her highly realistic figure pieces of Volendam women and children on the dyke, at home, or in church.[49] Some works contain reminders of seventeenth-century influence, either with regard to their subject matter or the calm reserve exuded by the figures in the tradition of Johannes Vermeer.

Laren's fame also drew American artists after the turn of the century. Joseph Raphael lived in Laren on and off between 1904 and 1912.[50] He sometimes lodged at Mrs. Kam-Redcliffe's boarding house, where his compatriot Wilder Darling resided for years, and where the English painting couple Harold and Laura Knight stayed as well.[51] Raphael painted figures in his early years in Laren. Differing entirely from the prevailing interiors is his large group portrait *The Town Crier and His Family* (1905; cat. 52), which is inspired by the seventeenth century in a number of ways. Raphael's town crier with his rattle takes center stage in the composition, like Captain Banninck Cocq in *The Nightwatch* (fig. 10) by Rembrandt. The pose of the girl at the left is reminiscent of that of the brightly lit girl in Rembrandt's monumental canvas, and like the seventeenth-century master, Raphael also used a dark, neutral architectural background. The town crier's gesture—arm akimbo with his palm facing forward—is well known from, for example, civic guard pieces by Frans Hals; and, there are more elements deriving from seventeenth-century

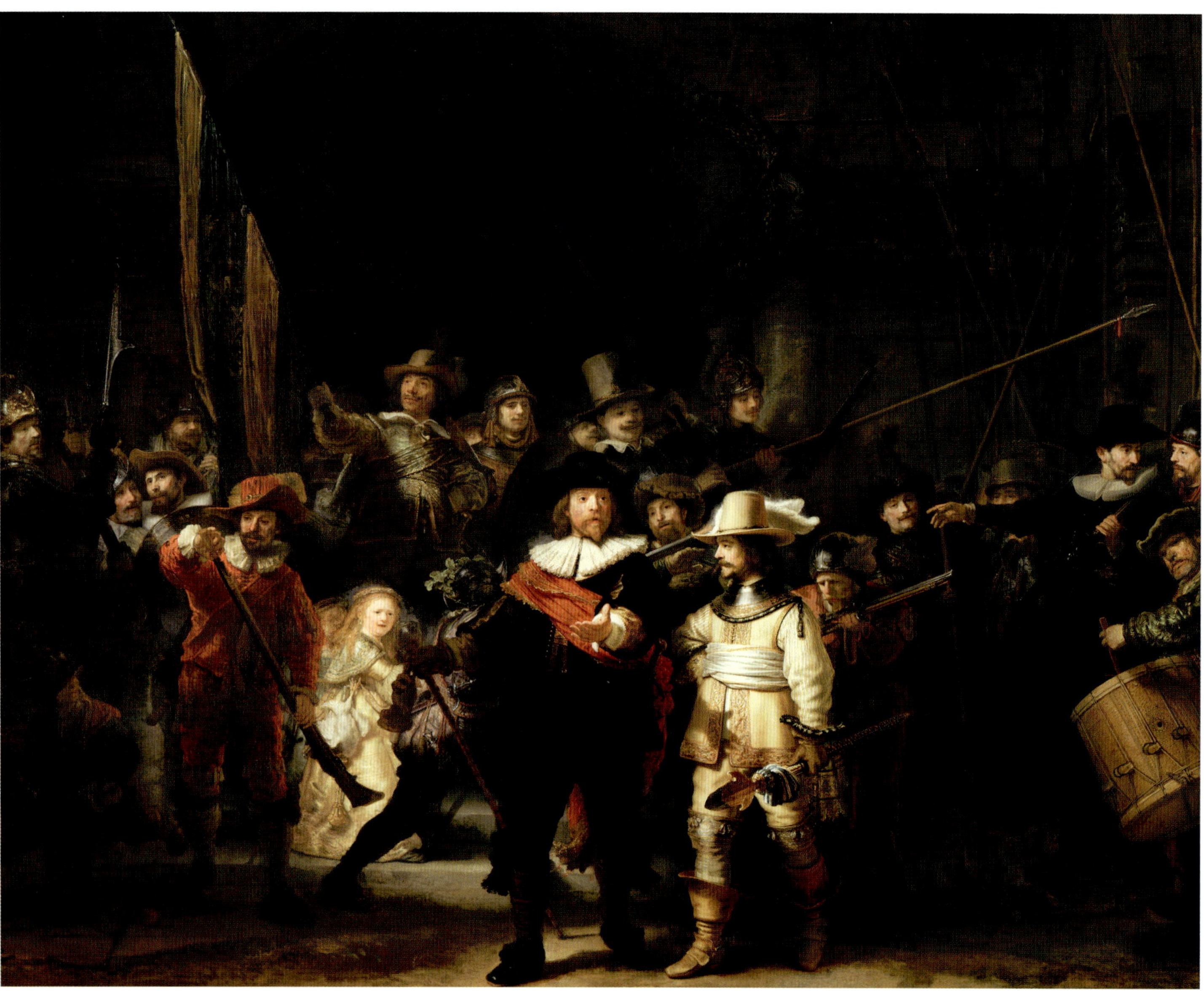

Fig. 10. Rembrandt, *The Nightwatch*, c. 1642, oil on canvas, 142⅞ × 172", Rijksmuseum, Amsterdam, the Netherlands.

artists. Here, Raphael devised an interesting painting whose subject matter, moreover, was original at the time. His dark palette and accurate rendering, however, soon gave way to the riot of color of French divisionism, as is evident in his *Holland Tulip Fields* (1913; cat. 53). Raphael, who had meanwhile married a Dutch woman, lived in Ukkel, Belgium, from 1912 on, yet undoubtedly regularly visited the Netherlands.

WILLIAM SINGER AND HIS CIRCLE

William Henry Singer Jr., his wife, Anna Spencer Brugh, and their friend, the Norwegian American painter and sculptor Martin Borgord, arrived in Laren in May 1902.[52] Singer had taken lessons in the late 1890s from Borgord, who had been the head of the Allegheny School of Art, founded in 1898 in a suburb of Pittsburgh.[53] Following a brief period of study in Paris, the threesome set off for Laren. Singer's interest in the work of Anton Mauve most likely informed his choice of destination. In his fatherland Singer had already made landscape studies and before leaving for Paris he had spent some time painting on Monhegan, an island off the coast of Maine that was popular among American artists. *Landscape with Sheep, Monhegan Island* (1901, Singer Laren Museum) explicitly betrays the influence of Anton Mauve. Singer could have known works by Mauve owned by friends of his parents.[54] The Singers and Borgord initially took up residence in the Hotel Hamdorff. Singer later rented a house and studio on the Oude Naarderweg from 1903 to 1905.[55] In this period he painted various subjects in the spirit of Mauve.

Singer made several renderings of the moors with sheep, for instance the large *Heathland near the Tafelberg, Blaricum* (1902; cat. 60).[56] He used fairly coarse loose brushwork and a tonal palette, in line with the painters of the Hague School. Many of his Laren paintings were on view in Pittsburgh in 1903 in a solo exhibition at the J. J. Gillespie gallery. They received due attention and appreciation in the newspapers: "All the scenes show the landscape in the luxuriant verdure of midsummer, varied with spectral cloud effects, the glare of a harvest sun and the softening tints of fading twilight."[57] In the summer of 1903 the Singers traveled with Martin Borgord to his native Norway. Singer was immediately taken with the beautiful, unspoiled mountain landscape. Even though he returned to Laren and also traveled a great deal in the following years, Norway was the country where he would work the most. His palette gradually lightened and became more colorful. He responded to American impressionism, which he came into contact with in 1907 during a stay in Old Lyme, Connecticut. Singer became friends with Willard Metcalf and Walter Griffin, who, like many American contemporaries, had developed their own variations of the colorful French impressionism during their stay in France.[58] In 1911 the Singers moved into De Wilde Zwanen, the house they had built in Laren. Located in the garden was a large double studio, half of which was used by Martin Borgord. In these Dutch years, the villa and the garden were Singer's subject matter of choice, often rendered in a vivid and sunny manner, as in *In My Garden, Spring* (1912; cat. 61). However, the Norwegian landscape continued to exert its pull: as of 1913 the Singers were spending a great deal of time in Norway, and Singer painted the lion's share of his oeuvre there.

In Laren, Singer met many Dutch artists, some of whom became friends for life, such as Evert Pieters and Arina Hugenholtz. Their circle of friends also included Hein Kever, who lived across the street, as well as Albert Neuhuys, Tony Offermans, Willy Sluiter, and Hendrik Jan Wolter, to mention just a few. Their names are inscribed in the guestbook of De Wilde Zwanen, which Anna instituted in 1912. The Singers acquired works of art by these artists for their collection, a part of which constituted the basis of the Singer Laren Museum in 1956.[59] Moreover, the Singers received visits in Laren from American artist friends. In addition to Martin Borgord, who lived with them for years, their guests included Walter Griffin, Richard E. Miller, and the sculptors Gutzon Borglum and Paul Bartlett.[60]

While it is true that Martin Borgord was Singer's first teacher, he was not a landscape painter. Borgord was born in Norway and emigrated to the United States at a young age.[61] In the period 1902–5, when he was staying with the Singers in Laren, he concentrated on interior scenes and portraits. Dating from these years are some Laren interiors, which are illustrated in *The Pittsburg Index* of 1903, including *Motherhood* and *A Lonely Meal*. Their subject matter and painting style dovetail with canvases by painters such as Neuhuys and Kever, both of whom Borgord knew well.[62]

Borgord manifested a greater sense of realism in a number of portraits of Laren sitters. In 1904 he made studies on paper, a few of which present the somewhat worried face of a woman wearing the Laren so-called "square" cap.[63] The Singer Laren Museum owns likenesses in oil paint, such as the *Portrait of Japie Wiegers* (1903; cat. 2) and *Lammert Wortel, a Laren Farmer* (1905; cat. 3). The sitters give the impression of leading an arduous life. One wonders how Borgord arrived at this incisive realism. Like many contemporaries, he studied seventeenth-century portraits by Frans Hals and Rembrandt. Sometimes Hals's portrayal of his sitters is earnest and serious, for instance in his *Regentesses of the Old Men's Home* (fig. 11), while at other times it is exuberant, as in *The Merry Drinker*. Hals's vivacious and high-spirited renderings inspired Americans such as Robert Henri, but Borgord was

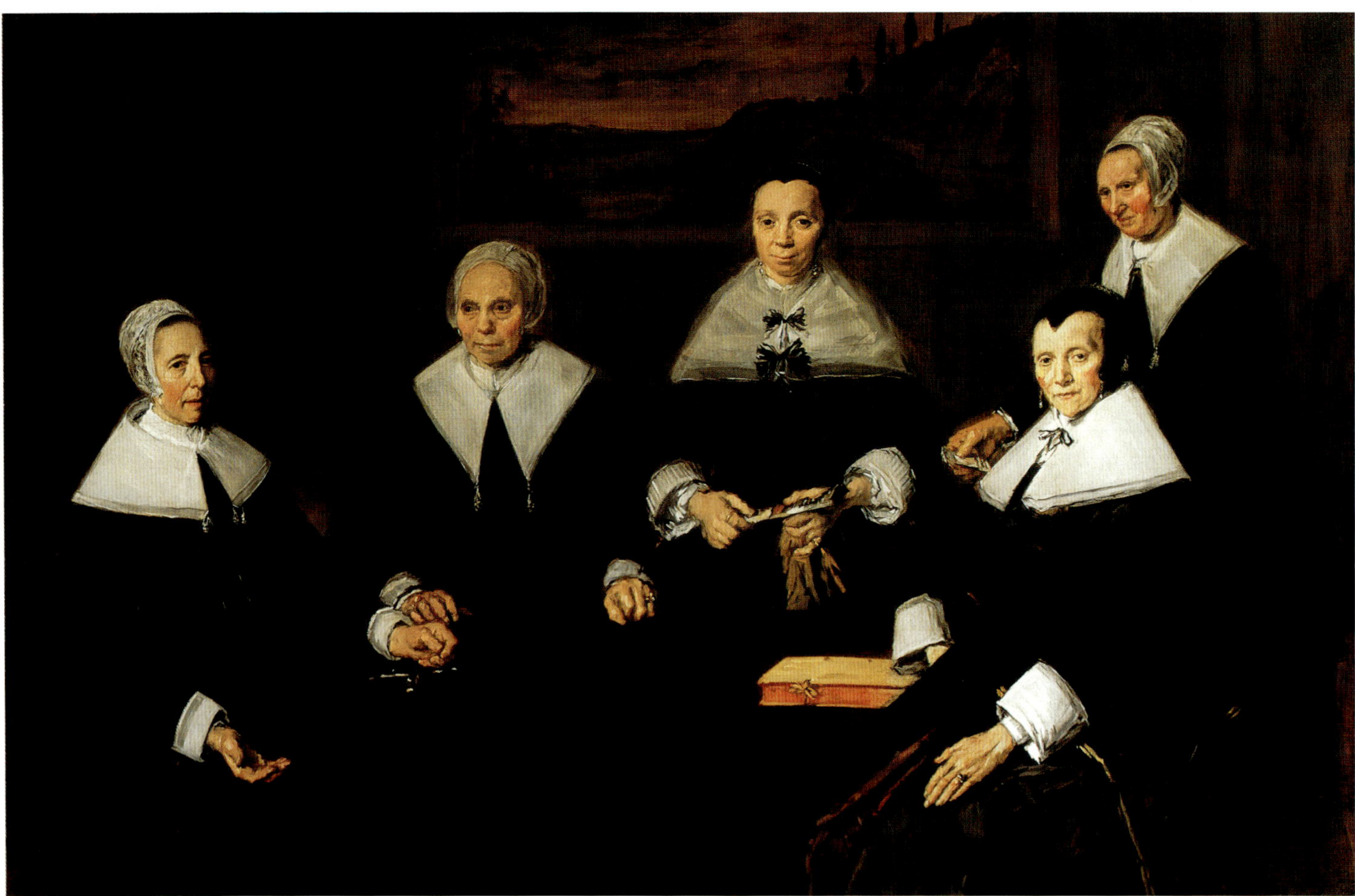

Fig. 11. Frans Hals, *The Regentesses of the Old Men's Home, Haarlem,* 1664, oil on canvas, 67⅞ × 100¾", Frans Hals Museum, Haarlem, the Netherlands.

one of the relatively few painters in Holland to respond and give expression to the more sober aspect.

Even though Borgord did travel now and then, in the period 1911–19 he lived mostly in the Singers' villa, De Wilde Zwanen.[64] During this time, his subject matter and style changed under the influence of American impressionism. He also made sculptures redolent of Rodin's sensibility.

Among the Singers' guests in their new house in 1912 was Richard E. Miller.[65] Miller studied at the Académie Julian in Paris in 1899–1900 and sojourned in the French capital regularly thereafter. Probably under the influence of Dutch painting, he depicted women in interiors that were sometimes somewhat dark, somber, and realistic, such as in *Woman at the Table* (before 1908; cat. 46), which was sold in 1908 to the Royal Museum of Fine Arts in Antwerp. Miller most likely traveled within the Netherlands; a few other subjects point in this direction, such as a girl in traditional Zeeland costume and the *Vieille Hollandaise* in the Musée d'Orsay in Paris.[66] Usually, though, he portrayed rather more frivolous ladies partaking in Paris's nightlife or elegantly dressed women in the intimacy of their interiors.[67]

The Singers probably became acquainted with Miller in Paris when they were there in the summer of 1905. Both artists were members of the Paris American Art Association, and Singer rented an apartment with an atelier on the boulevard Montparnasse, while Miller lived around the corner on the rue Boissonade.[68] Little is known about their subsequent contact other than that Miller visited them in Laren in 1912. In the meantime he had developed into a true American impressionist, painting charming subjects such as women sitting in the garden or inside before an open window, done in light, summery colors. Miller was one of the Americans who painted such themes in Giverny, like the better-known Frederick Carl Frieseke. The light tone of a *Double Portrait of Anna and William Singer with a Palette* (West Norway

Museum of Decorative Art, Bergen, Norway, on loan to the Singer Laren Museum) fits into this atmosphere, even though we are not sure when or where it was painted. In any event, it can be seen in a photograph of De Wilde Zwanen of 1912/1913 (private collection, on loan to the Singer Laren Museum). Miller's *Portrait of Martin Borgord* (before 1912; cat. 47) also cannot be precisely dated, but it, too, can be seen in this photograph and must have originated in the same time period. In so far as is known, Miller did not paint any other Laren subjects.

One of Singer's very good friends was the landscape painter Walter Griffin, whom he knew from Old Lyme. Griffin visited the Singers in Laren several times between 1910 and 1913. His oeuvre also includes some Norwegian landscapes, which he painted when he was there with Singer.[69] No Laren work by him, other than the *Garden of De Wilde Zwanen* (fig. 12) of 1912, is known. Formerly attributed to Singer, this painting is now attributed to Griffin on account of its coarse, thick buildup of paint.[70]

Singer and Borgord are among the last American painters to have worked in Laren. Singer returned there several times after World War I and painted Dutch subjects again in the 1930s. For most of the other Americans, however, 1914 marked the end of their Dutch time. The heyday of the traditional Laren interior and landscape was over. Younger and more modern artists such as Piet Mondrian and Bart Antony van der Leck came to Laren and manifested themselves in a more individual fashion.

Fig. 12. Walter Griffin, *Garden of De Wilde Zwanen*, 1912, oil on canvas, 18¼ × 21⅞", Singer Laren Museum, the Netherlands.

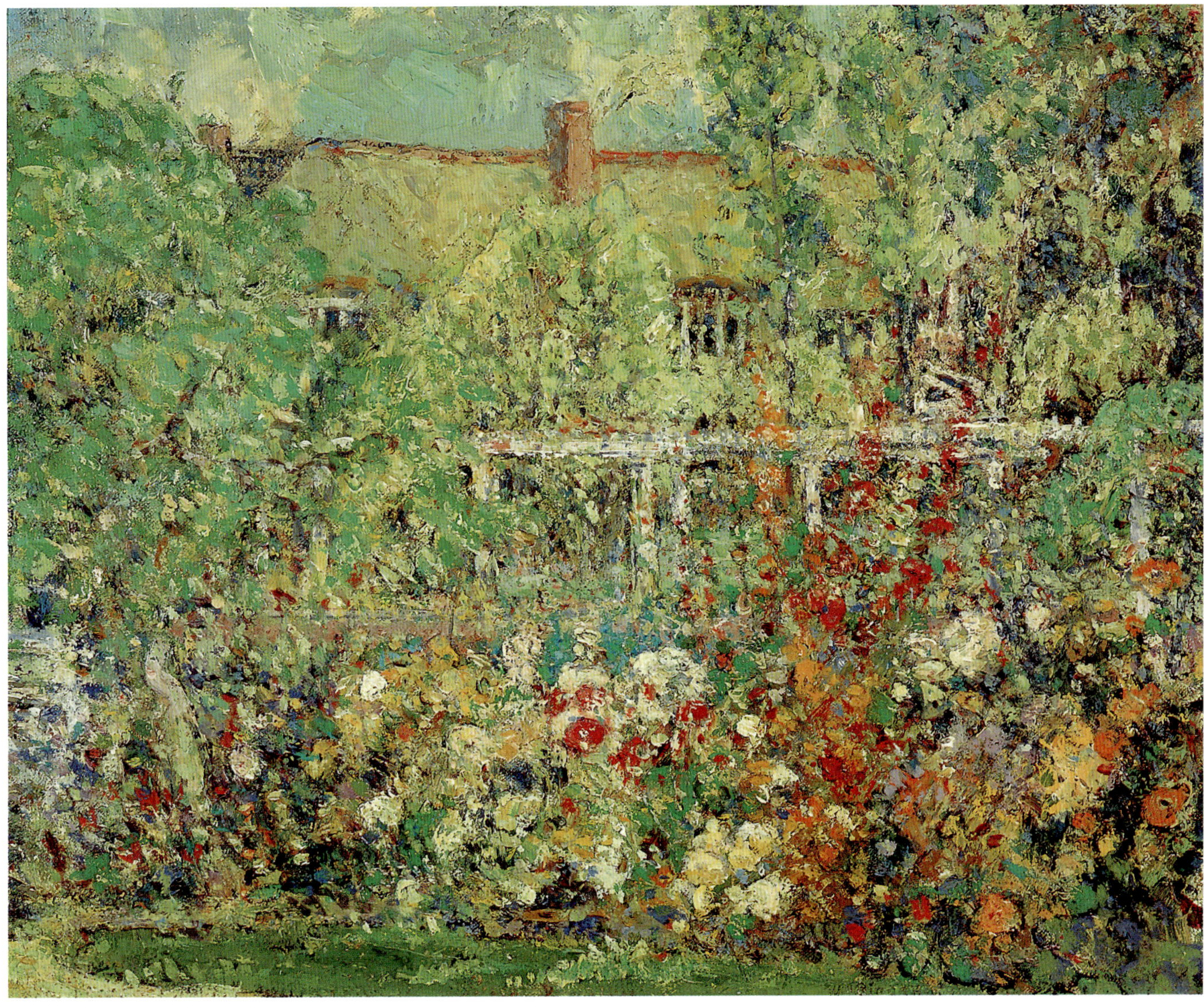

NOTES

1. On Oosterbeek, see Saskia de Bodt, "Oosterbeek en Wolfheze: Een Magische Streek," in *Schildersdorpen in Nederland* (Warnsveld: Terra and Laren: Singer Laren Museum, 2004), 12–20.

2. This information is derived in part from Ronald de Leeuw, "Introduction," in *The Hague School: Dutch Masters of the Nineteenth Century*, ed. Ronald de Leeuw, John Sillevis, and Charles Dumas (The Hague: Gemeentemuseum, London: Royal Academy of Arts, and Paris: Grand Palais, 1983), 14.

3. Jacob J. van Santen Kolff, "Een Blik in de Hollandsche Schilderschool Onzer Dagen, dl.IV," *De Banier, tijdschrift van "Het Jonge Holland"* I (1875): 158–59, quoted in John Sillevis, "The Heyday of the Hague School (1870–1985)," in *The Hague School*, 81–82.

4. Gerard Bilders, letter to Johannes Kneppelhout, July 10, 1860, published in Wim Zaal, *Gerard Bilders: Vrolijk versterven. Een keuze uit zijn dagboek en brieven* (Amsterdam: Meulenhoff, 1974), 67.

5. Richard J. Boyle, *John Twachtman* (New York: Watson-Guptill, 1979), 28. Twachtman was on his honeymoon. He painted and etched in Holland, together with J. Alden Weir and his brother John. His wife, Martha Scudder, was also an artist.

6. Ronald G. Pisano, *A Leading Spirit in American Art: William Merritt Chase 1849–1916* (Seattle: University of Washington, Henry Art Gallery, 1983), 135–36.

7. Annette Stott, "American Painters Who Worked in the Netherlands, 1880–1914" (PhD diss., Boston University, 1986). On Cross, see 190 and 192; on Gruppe, 188 and 204.

8. For documentation from Dutch archives on the activities of American artists in the Netherlands, see Stott, *Holland Mania: The Unknown Dutch Period in American Art and Culture* (Woodstock, N.Y.: Overlook Press, 1998), 265–77.

9. Marc Simpson, Andrea Henderson, and Sally Mills, *Expressions of Place: The Art of William Stanley Haseltine* (San Francisco: Fine Arts Museums of San Francisco, 1992), 156.

10. Stott, "Amerikaanse kunstenaars," in *Katwijk in de schilderkunst* (Katwijk: Katwijks Museum, 1995), 110–11.

11. Wally Moes, *Dorpsvertellingen* (The Hague: Nijgh and Van Ditmar, 1957), 136. Wally Moes visited Laren from Amsterdam a number of times and finally moved there permanently. When she could no longer paint due to illness, she wrote three collections of village tales, the first of which appeared in 1913. The 1957 edition cited here is an anthology of all three.

12. Wally Moes, *Heilig ongeduld: Herinneringen uit mijn Leven* (Amsterdam: Wereldbibliotheek, 1961), 184. Moes penned her memoirs during World War I. They were published posthumously.

13. Bep de Boer, "Het Boarding House ofwel het Engelse pension," *Kwartaalbericht Historische Kring Laren* (December 1997): 14–15. The Laren inhabitants referred to it as the English boarding house. Mrs. Kam-Redcliffe lived in Laren until 1915 (Laren County Register 1895–1925, Hilversum Regional Archive).

14. On the artists' houses, see Margriet van Seumeren, *"Een mooi land": Wandelen door het kunstenaarsverleden van Laren en Blaricum* (Laren: Singer Laren Museum, 2000).

15. Lien Heyting, *De wereld in een dorp: Schilders, Schrijvers en wereldverbeteraars in Laren en Blaricum 1880–1920* (Amsterdam: Meulenhoff, 1994).

16. Jozef Israëls, notes in his archive, the Netherlands Institute for Art History (RKD), The Hague, also mentioned in Heyting, *De wereld in een dorp*, 13, n. 1. The painter Gerrit Alexander Godart Filip Mollinger has also been called the discoverer of Laren.

17. Moes, *Heilig ongeduld*, 185.

18. See also Margriet van Seumeren-Haerkens, *Albert Neuhuys (1844–1914): Schilderijen, aquarellen en tekeningen* (Laren: Singer Laren Museum and Eindhoven: Museum Kempenland, 1987).

19. Seumeren-Haerkens, *Albert Neuhuys*, 11–12. He was warmly received in many places while traveling in the United States in 1904.

20. See also Emke Raassen-Kruimel, "Bestaat er eigenlijk wel een Larense School?," *Tussen Vecht en Eem: Tijdschrift voor Regionale Geschiedenis* 24: 3 (September 2006): 179–84.

21. Cornelis Willem Verster, "J. S. H. Kever," *Elsevier's Geïllustreerd Maandschrift* 22: 43 (1912): 116.

22. Israëls's studio is described in Wally Moes, *Heilig ongeduld*, 155. General information on Laren and its painters is found in Carole Denninger-Schreuder, *Schilders van Laren* (Bussum: Thoth, 2003).

23. Anton Mauve, letter to his wife, Jet Carbentus, Laren, June 3, 1882, RKD, The Hague. Mauve wrote that he is staying at the "vergulde leeuw" [he meant De Gouden Leeuw] guest house, because the first boarding house he tried was full of families with children. This was most likely De Vergulde Postwagen.

24. The house still exists and is located diagonally across from Singer Laren.

25. Nico van Harpen, "Het Land van Mauve. Laren en zijn schilders: Arina Hugenholtz," *Boon's Geïllustreerd Magazijn* 7 (1905): 258–63. Hugenholtz painted views of Laren, shepherds with flocks of sheep, and other Mauvesque subjects.

26. Anton Mauve, letter to Arina Hugenholtz, Laren, February 24, 1886, RKD, The Hague. The house no longer exists. Moes rented it together with her friend, the painter Etha Fles. See also Moes, *Heilig ongeduld*, 198.

27. Moes was acquainted with many artists and writers and was socially active. She did not paint *en plein air*, but produced genre scenes in the manner of Neuhuys, as well as independent figures.

28. See Raassen-Kruimel, "Bestaat er eigenlijk wel een Larense School?," 180, and Heyting, *De wereld in een dorp*, 103–115.

29. Stott, "American Painters," chapter 5 "Laren," 178–220, mentions many artists who were in Laren but about whom little is known or whose works cannot be traced.

30. Ralcy Husted Bell, *Art-Talks with Ranger* (New York: G. P. Putnam's Sons, 1914), 42. Ranger's views on painting and his memories are recorded in this book. See also Jack Becker, *Henry Ward Ranger and the Humanized Landscape* (Old Lyme, Conn.: Florence Griswold Museum, 1999).

31. Bell, *Art-Talks with Ranger*, 44 and 139.

32. Ibid., 93. Ranger is mentioned in De Vergulde Postwagen's hotel account book for the period 1888–90. Present whereabouts of account book unknown.

33. Stott, *Holland Mania*, 77, and on Howe, 53–55.

34. Pieter Andreas Martin Boele van Hensbroek, "Ch. P. Gruppe," *Elsevier's Geïllustreerd Maandschrift* 14, no. 28 (November 1904): 291. It was exceptional for this periodical to devote an article to a foreign painter. See also Antoine de Cluny, *Holland as Painted by Charles P. Gruppé* (Leiden: A. W. Sijthoff's Uitgevers-Maatschappij, n.d.).

35. *Tentoonstelling van schilderijen en aquarellen: Charles P. Gruppe* (The Hague: Frans Buffa and Sons, n.d.).

36. Stott, "Amerikaanse kunstenaars," 112. In the same book (184) Gruppe is listed with his own house "Nellie," 1906–1908 (information probably from the Community Archives).

37. Laren County Register 1890–1925, Hilversum Regional Archive. See also Raassen-Kruimel, "De Amerikanen," in "*Zij waren in Laren . . .": Buitenlandse kunstenaars in Laren en 't Gooi* (Laren: Singer Laren Museum, 1989), 30–31.

38. *Memorial Exhibition Castle Keith* (Amsterdam and New York: Frans Buffa and Sons, 1929). The locations were often given for American and French subjects, but not for the "Dutch Period." In any case, the exhibition took place in Amsterdam as appears from a review in the *Nieuwe Rotterdamse Courant* and perhaps also in New York, given that the text is in English.

39. Quote from *Gooi en Eemlander,* January 2, 1892, *Gooi and Eemlander* Archive, Naarden Municipal Archive. In this article the newspaper looked back to the previous year. The ladies in question were in Laren in May 1891.

40. Wally Moes, *Nagelaten vertellingen* (Amsterdam: Scheltema and Holkema's Boekhandel, n.d. [1920]), 132. The Laren artist Toon de Jong later also noted that groups of up to twenty-five Americans were at work on the moors (*Bussumsche Courant,* August 9, 1941, repeated in Heyting, *De wereld in een dorp,* 101–2).

41. De Vergulde Postwagen account book 1888–90; on December 10, 1892, the *Gooi en Eemlander* reported that the first telegram in Laren had been received for the Cross ladies who were staying in the Hotel Hamdorff, as De Vergulde Postwagen was then already called (Naarden Municipal Archive, *Gooi and Eemlander* Archive).

42. For biographical information on Cross, see Sandra C. Davidson and Ann H. Murray, *Eleanor Norcross. Amy Cross. Edith Loring Getchell* (Fitchburg, Mass.: Fitchburg Art Museum and Norton, Mass.: Watson Gallery, Wheaton College, 1980), 10–13.

43. Offermans did not paint interiors with mothers and children, but craftsmen at work in their workshops. He also painted a portrait of Mrs. Cross (private collection).

44. Stott, *Holland Mania,* 57–58.

45. David O. Woodbury, "Marcia Oaks Woodbury (1865–1914)," in *Charles H. Woodbury N.A. (1864–1940). Marcia Oakes Woodbury (1865–1914)* (Boston: Vose Galleries of Boston, 1980), 14–20.

46. Moes, *Heilig ongeduld,* 186.

47. Stott, "American Painters," 194. On his subjects, see also *Charles H. Woodbury N.A.*

48. Stott, *Holland Mania,* 56.

49. See Stott, *Holland Mania,* 219–21. Dick Brinkkemper, Peter Kersloot, and Kees Sier, *Volendam schildersdorp, 1880–1940* (Zwolle: Waanders, 2006), 76–77.

50. See also Raassen-Kruimel, *Joseph Raphael 1869–1950* (Laren: Singer Laren Museum, 1981) and *Joseph Raphael (1869–1950): An Artistic Journey* (New York: Spanierman Gallery, 2003).

51. Laura Knight, *Oil Paint and Grease Paint* (London: Ivor Nicholson and Watson, 1936), 141, 156–57. In this autobiographical book Knight describes her memories of Laren, which she visited three times between 1903 and 1907.

52. Recent research on William Singer has brought to light a great deal of new information. See Helen Schretlen, *American Impressionist William H. Singer Jr. 1868–1943* (Laren: Singer Laren Museum, 2008; Dutch and English edition). With thanks to the author for bringing various documents to my attention.

53. *The Pittsburg Bulletin* (March 16, 1901). See also Schretlen, *American Impressionist,* 20: Singer lived in Allegheny City.

54. See Schretlen, *American Impressionist,* 21.

55. Schretlen, *Loving Art: The William & Anna Singer Collection* (Laren: Singer Laren Museum and Zwolle: Waanders, 2006), 54. The house was at 11 Oude Naarderweg.

56. For Laren subjects, see also Schretlen, *American Impressionist,* 29–31.

57. "Won Honor with Brush at Paris: William H. Singer, of Allegheny, Returns from Two Years in Europe," unannotated clipping, 1903, in a scrapbook kept by Anna Singer, collection West Norway Museum of Decorative Art, Bergen. See also Schretlen, *American Impressionist,* 31–33.

58. Schretlen, *American Impressionist,* 38.

59. Anna founded the Singer Memorial Foundation in Laren in 1954. The foundation manages a museum, of which the art collection of the Singers serves as the basis; a theater; and the De Wilde Zwanen house. The Singer complex was opened in 1956. The collective name is Singer Laren.

60. Guestbook of De Wilde Zwanen, Singer Laren Museum.

61. Harald Kleiven, "Martin Borgard—verdskjend Malar og skulptor fra Gausdal," article, source unknown, gives the genealogy of his family and mentions that Martin was born in 1866. Other sources give 1869; also the Laren County Register 1890–1925, Hilversum Regional Archive, gives 1869 as his date of birth. The family name was originally Borgard, and later changed to Borgord.

62. "Dutch Paintings by Martin Borgard," *The Pittsburg Index,* January 31, 1903. According to notes by Anna Singer in this article in her scrapbook (West Norway Museum of Decorative Art, Bergen), most of the illustrated works were sold, and *A Lonely Meal* went to W. H. Singer, who must be William's father. The title was changed to *The Pipe of Consolation.* Perhaps the art dealer thought this was more commercial.

63. A white lace cap with a rectangular starched flap folded upward on each side. This cap was primarily depicted in Laren and Blaricum painting but was worn in much of the Gooi region. Anna glued the sketches in her scrapbook (West Norway Museum of Decorative Art, Bergen).

64. Laren County Register 1890–1925, Hilversum Regional Archive. Schretlen, *Loving Art,* 85.

65. Guestbook, De Wilde Zwanen.

66. *Woman Knitting in an Interior,* 1903, oil on canvas, 28¾ × 21¼", auctioned in New York, April 21, 1982 (William Doyle Galleries), present whereabouts unknown. Depicted is a girl in the traditional clothing of Walcheren in the province of Zeeland. *La tasse de thé* or *Vieille Hollandaise,* before 1912, oil on canvas, 28¾ × 22¾", acquired by the Musée du Luxembourg, Paris, now in the Musée d'Orsay, Paris.

67. On Miller, see also Marie Louise Kane, *A Bright Oasis: The Paintings of Richard E. Miller* (New York: Jordan-Volpe Gallery, 1997).

68. Schretlen, *Loving Art,* 60–61. On Miller, see also William H. Gerdts, *American Impressionism* (New York: Abbeville Press, 1984), 266–70.

69. In 1910 Griffin visited the Frans Hals Museum with Singer and Borgord (Stott, *Holland Mania,* 270) and signed the guestbook of De Wilde Zwanen in 1912 and 1913. See also Raassen-Kruimel, "Buitenlandse kunstenaars in de collectie: Het werk van William Singer en zijn Amerikaanse en Franse collega's," in *Collectie Singer: Schilderijen* (Laren: Singer Laren Museum and Zwolle: Waanders, 2002), 47–48. Schretlen, *Loving Art,* 66–67 passim. The Singers owned quite a few works by Griffin.

70. Schretlen, *American Impressionist,* 49, 50, attributes the work to Griffin.

The author wishes to acknowledge the following individuals who provided valuable assistance with this essay:

Bep de Boer, Laren Historical Society, the Netherlands

Kristin Bonk, Denver University, Colorado, U.S.A.

Amy Dawson, Cleveland Public Library, Ohio, U.S.A.

Ursula de Goede, Netherlands Institute for Art History, The Hague, the Netherlands

André Groeneveld, Katwijk Museum, the Netherlands

Hilversum Regional Archive, the Netherlands

Annemarie Kingmans-Claas, Katwijk Museum, the Netherlands

Anton Kos, Hilversum Museum, the Netherlands

Jannig Kwakman, Hotel Spaander, Volendam, the Netherlands

Naarden Municipal Archive, the Netherlands

Netherlands Institute for Art History, The Hague, the Netherlands

Moniek Peters, Dordrecht Museum, the Netherlands

Helen Schretlen, Bussum, the Netherlands

Marianne de Voogd, Netherlands Institute for Art History, the Netherlands

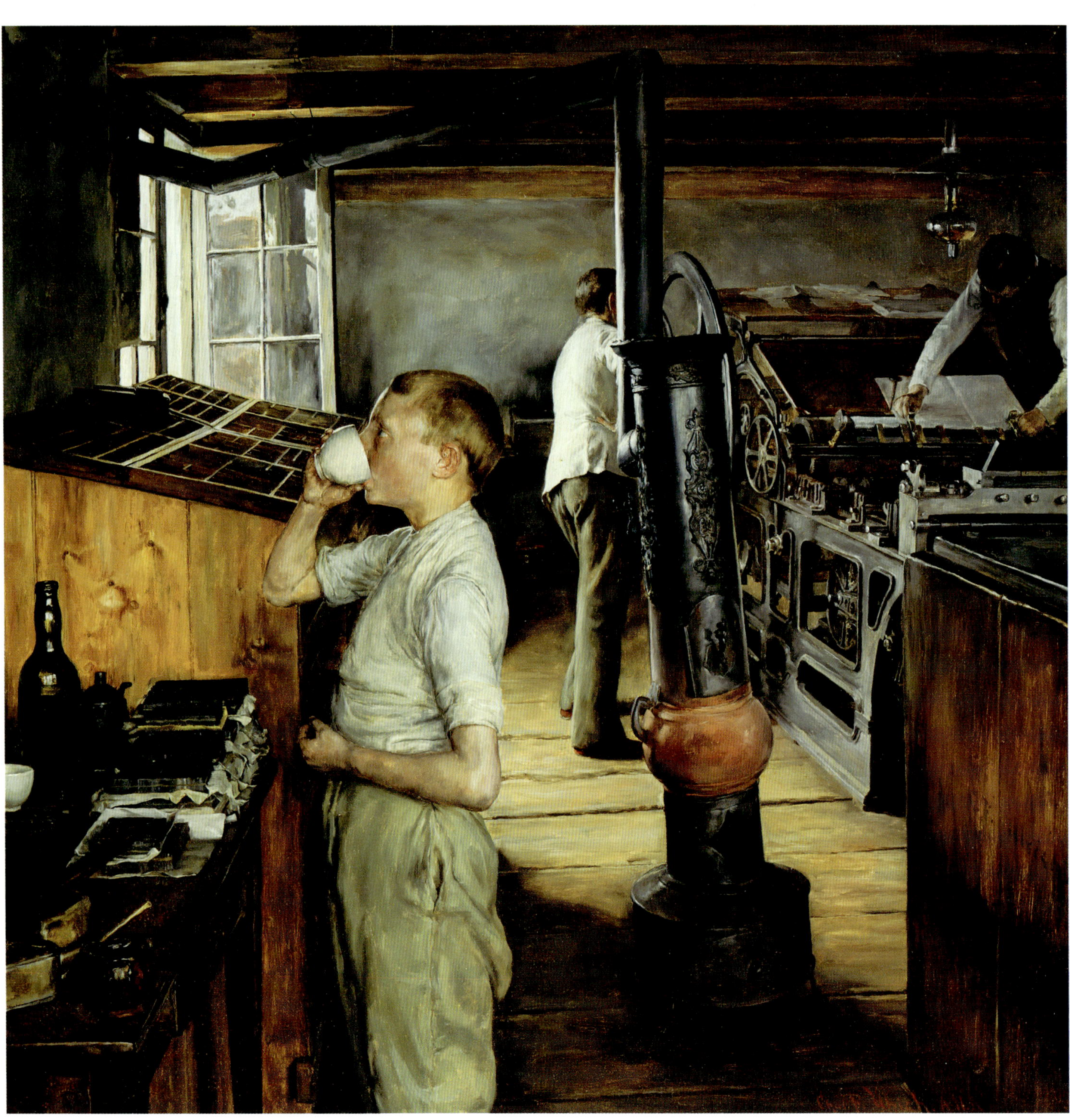

Providing Solace in the Age of Discontent

Kim Sajet

> *Early twentieth century Dutchness was in America essentially a work of rhetoric and visual fiction: the Dutch were reinvented as idealized counterparts of the Americans and they often wore more American traits than European marks.*[1]

IF WE LOOK CAREFULLY AT THE IMAGERY of the *Dutch Utopia* artists—the nobility of the farmer and virtuousness of the peasants, the idolization of women as mothers and homemakers, the centrality of the family and the importance of community over individuality, the guidance of the church, and even the uniformity of the people depicted, both in terms of class hierarchies and ethnicity—it becomes apparent that there is more at play than a reaction against modernism and a return to traditional values. Placed in the context of late-nineteenth-century America, there is a direct parallel between the philosophical messages transmitted through the art, and the moral values held by vast sections of the American middle class during the rise and fall of the Progressive Movement that occurred between 1870 and 1920.

Described as a time of "fierce discontent," the Progressive Era had risen out of the crises of civil war, the pain of reconstruction, and the humility of economic depression, and manifested itself in a growing sense of panic caused by rapid industrialization. Having no clearly defined agenda, crossing societal boundaries, and employing various methods of protest, reformers of the period were not a coherent group. The most unifying goal they shared was also the most audacious—nothing less than the complete social transformation of America. The ascension of Theodore Roosevelt to the presidency, the youngest man ever to reach the White House, was as symbolic of the "reformatory impulse" as the rise in middle-class activism.

The Progressive Era champions were numerous and effective, ranging from Eugene V. Debs, the founder of the Social Democratic Party, to Elizabeth Cady Stanton the suffragette, Samuel Gompers the union organizer, Carrie Nation the temperance activist, and Booker T. Washington the educator. Their various agendas were advanced through published research such as the 1890 census reports, specialized studies such as Robert Hunter's *Poverty*, popular magazines such as *The Century*, the investigative reporting of the so-called muckraking press, the photo-realism of Jacob Riis, and the imagery of artists. In the words of historian Michael McGerr, progressivism was an "explosion, a burst of energy that fired in many directions across America."[2]

Migration and movement can be said to have precipitated the Progressive Era experience. Whereas at the turn of the nineteenth century only ten percent of the population lived in cities, by 1901 as a result of industrialization, forty percent of the population were urbanized and held manufacturing or service-sector jobs. While

Detail of cat. 70

in 1801 just over five million people had lived mostly along the Atlantic seaboard, a century later a staggering seventy-seven million people of all racial, religious, and social backgrounds were spread across forty-five states.

By 1890 it became obvious that America had moved away from its mercantile roots and had embraced capitalism. A key discontent was that over fifty percent of the nation's resources was controlled by one percent of the industrial elite. This unbalance had become painfully obvious when Congress was forced to borrow more than sixty million dollars from Wall Street financier J. P. Morgan in order to stabilize the economy after the Depression of 1893. Squeezed by the self-involved upper class, and the overworked working class, reformers came largely from the middle class, and their approach was to elect politicians willing to tax the rich and legislate adult behavior in order to create new codes of conduct. "I take it for granted that wiping out the idle rich is to be one of the first steps in a programme of national advancement," stated Frederick Townsend Martin, a New York socialite.[3]

In the area of tax reform the progressives found allies in the four presidents that spanned the period of 1897 to 1921: William McKinley, Theodore Roosevelt, William Howard Taft, and Woodrow Wilson. While the first three Republican leaders were reluctant to interfere in economic matters, they all nevertheless courted the middle class and enacted a slew of legislation against the wealthiest top ten percent of the population. McKinley, for example, imposed excise taxes on corporations, restricted the anti-union practices of employers, and executed safety legislation on behalf of transportation workers. Roosevelt established the Department of Commerce and Labor to regulate both domestic and international commerce and oversee mining, manufacturing, shipping, and transportation. William Howard Taft shepherded in the Sixteenth Amendment, which allowed Congress to collect federal income taxes and paved the way for a modest but pathbreaking one-percent tax on annual incomes up to twenty thousand dollars, with an additional surtax for higher incomes. And Woodrow Wilson, the first Democrat elected in twenty years, launched the New Freedom program, designed to remove the privileges of special interests and literally create a "new social age, a new era of human relationships and a new stage-setting for the drama of life."[4]

It was particularly in the area of social reform that the influence of the progressives manifested itself in the work of the artists included in this exhibition, the Dutch Utopians. While largely middle class, these artists had little quarrel with more equitably distributing the nation's wealth. More profoundly, they shared a growing belief that living standards for the poor could be improved by changing the environment in which people lived. Not simply antimodern, the reformers and the Dutch Utopians saw that the American system of democracy was failing its citizens by becoming disconnected from the core values that had served America during settlement, revolution, independence, and economic prosperity. Reformers and artists alike fought "to preserve the society that had given their lives meaning."[5]

On the surface, the Dutch Utopian paintings seem far removed from the frantic reforming activities taking place in America. Conjuring romantic images of a bygone era reminiscent of seventeenth-century Holland, and re-creating everything from costumed peasants, tulip fields, slow-turning windmills, and even Amsterdam in the 1600s, these American artists may have seemed to be living in a fantasy world far removed from their own. The opposite was in fact true. While certainly taking pains to exclude Holland's own modernization, the Dutch Utopians tapped into an enormous reservoir of Progressive Era nostalgia that was underpinning the very foundations of social change. Evidence of their appeal was the voracious art-buying market for their work, which was so strong that dealers in the United States sometimes financed artists' trips to Holland to replenish their stock.[6]

Henry James had once speculated that the challenge for artists at the turn of the twentieth century was the "thinness" of American life on which to draw.[7] It was not that American life was not real, but rather that it was almost hyper-real in the sense of a fast-moving train. Because America was so much in flux, it failed to conjure up the types of value associations that came so easily by using established European stereotypes. For example, George Hitchcock, recalling the picturesque qualities of Holland, wrote of the "soulful" work of the Dutch farmer whose spirit was not linked to that of a machine. "It is this which makes the ordinary American interior so absolutely unpaintable, and excuses the expatriation of those who seek, from a picturesque standpoint, the sympathetic evidences of man in his objects of daily use and toil."[8]

When George Henry Boughton and Edwin Austin Abbey traveled through Holland in the hope of capturing a world they considered frozen in time, to their dismay they found that the "demon of improvement" was all over the country.[9] And despite confrontation with a clock made in Connecticut, steam engines imported from the United States, and one rather unpleasant experience where Boughton fancied himself in "some back street of Chicago," they and the other Dutch Utopians engaged in selective "reality research" that brought back to urban American audiences a romantic version of authentic Dutch life.[10] The appeal rested upon a contemporary desire to return to a time when "honest labor was no disgrace and time not too short with which to do things well and beautifully."[11] It rested also on romanticizing the Dutch countryside as a source of spiritual renewal in contrast to the large American cities, which had grown rapidly as a result of large-scale manufacturing and appeared almost uncontrollable in terms of crowding, poverty, crime, and corruption.

Pervasive throughout the Progressive Era was the fear that the city was not simply replacing a former way of life, but rewriting the laws of nature, neglecting God, and alienating citizens from their national purpose. In the simplest terms, many believed that cities would destroy American civilization: "This life of great cities is not the natural life of man," complained Henry George in 1883. "He must under such conditions deteriorate physically, mentally, and morally."[12]

Never planned and poorly governed, American cities between 1860 and 1910 grew voraciously out of rural villages that expanded as a result of industrializing mills, factories, railroads, and clusters of manufacturers.[13] Fed by a steady stream of European immigrants and native-born rural workers, by 1900 the ten largest cities in America accounted for thirty-five percent of industrial goods produced within the country.[14] Overcrowded, vulnerable to disease, with a confusing stew of ethnic cultures creating a volatile atmosphere, urban reformers saw their efforts in city planning quite simply as anti-chaos. Characterized as "reasoned activists," reformers relied on specialized studies and statistical reports that contextualized urban disorganization as something wholly preventable. Robert Hunter's 1904 book *Poverty*, for example, declared the lack of food, lodging, and clothing a result of "low wages, employment, ill health and accidents."[15]

Jacob Riis's pioneering study of New York tenement life, *How the Other Half Lives* (1890), featuring documentary-style photographs of sweatshops, flop houses, and boarding rooms in the slums of New York City, was one of many published calls-to-action for the American middle class who recognized the seeds of a social uprising (fig. 13). By 1910 as many as one-third to one-half of all urban Americans were living and working in shared quarters with no indoor running water and waste collection haphazard at best. In response, reformers organized the groundbreaking 1899 Tenement-House Exhibit that mapped areas of the highest poverty and disease and called for a wide range of improvements such the provision of bathhouses

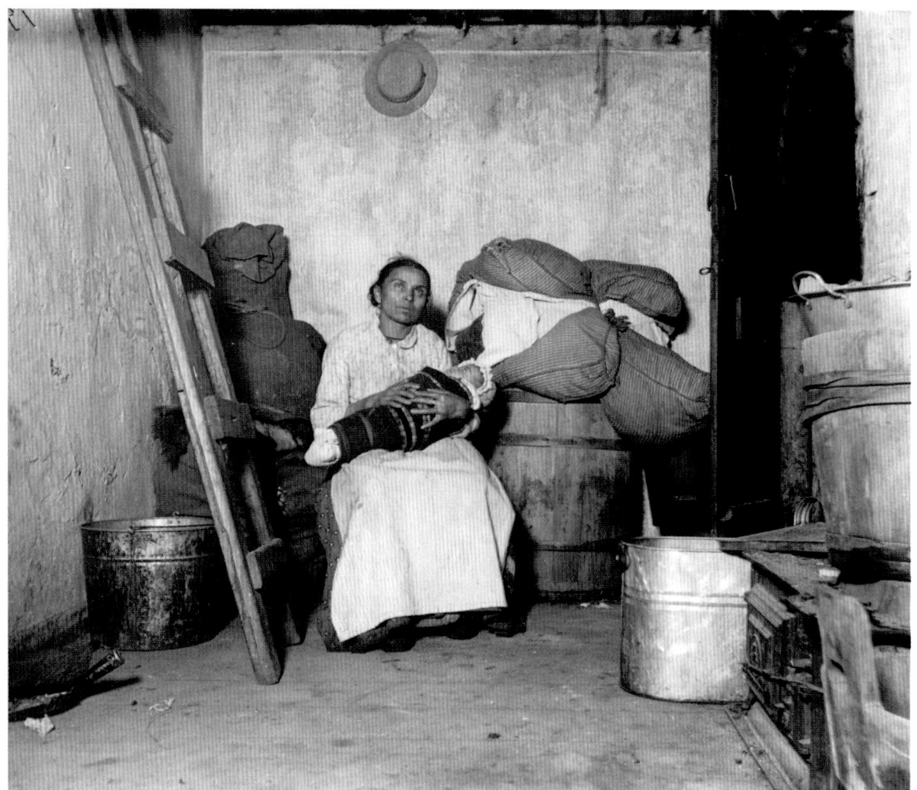

Fig. 13. Jacob Riis, *In the Home of an Italian Rag-picker, Jersey Street,* c. 1890, Museum of the City of New York, Jacob A. Riis Collection, 90.13.1.160.

and parks. The exhibit was followed by a two-volume report to the New York State Tenement House Commission, and led directly to Theodore Roosevelt passing the 1901 Tenement House Act that set standards on the size of living quarters, required fire escapes, prioritized fresh air and light, and mandated the disposal of garbage, bilge water, and waste.

Walter MacEwen's painting known as *The Lacemakers* (c. 1885–1900; cat. 36) and William Henry Singer Jr.'s *My Studio* (1913; cat. 62) provide two examples of spacious, window-lit interiors that would have pleased the housing reformers. In fact, both these paintings also complemented a fashion for Dutch-inspired architecture that swept America in the late nineteenth century.[16] Based on rural farmhouses, the "Modern Dutch Colonial" became an identifiable style of architecture that featured a gambrel roof, large windows, a covered porch, and occasionally a "Dutch door" that permitted additional air and light into the home. The Dutch Colonial was also one of the "model homes" Edward Bok, editor of the *Ladies Home Journal* and one of the most famous and outspoken Dutch immigrants in America, featured in his popular magazine. Chosen because of its cottagelike appeal, the Dutch Colonial incorporated modern sanitary features such as indoor bathrooms, cross-ventilation, central heating, and easy-to-clean surfaces.

Close on the heels of housing reform came workplace reforms that were fought within the volatile atmosphere of labor unions and business owners clashing over the inequalities of the wage labor system. For middle-class progressives, the issue was one of encouraging interclass harmony with special attention paid to the physical, psychological, and social conditions of industrial-era production. Utopian ideals sprang up around the concept that farmers, workers, and business owners in a properly governed society could share the fruits of economic prosperity. Although the task was not easy, as reformers quite literally found themselves caught in the middle of two warring factions, they were nevertheless remarkably successful in the years before World War I in passing regulatory authority over workplace practices—particularly in relation to women and children.

By 1908 large sections of American businesses restricted women's work to under ten hours a day and limited their involvement in certain dangerous occupations, such as mining and grinding metals. Similarly, child labor laws began to take effect that limited industrial work for minors under the age of fourteen. In general, the courts were willing to approve such legislation because women and children were physically weaker and considered dependent on the protection of men. In this respect, reformers had allies in the organized labor movements who felt that working women and children forced down wages and impinged on male job security. For all their sympathy toward the working class, however, what the reformers most wanted was a "moral revolution" whereby both employees and their employers would join together with a sense of shared social purpose. "We have been sighing for labor and capital to get together; we have been telling them they are brothers, that the interest of one is the other," wrote the journalist Ray Stannard Baker.[17]

The Dutch Utopians very clearly echoed the sympathies and values of the reformers in terms of meaningful collective work, undertaken in pleasant surroundings and in harmony with the larger goals of their society. A wonderful example can be found in Charles Frederick Ulrich's *The Village Printing Shop, Haarlem, Holland* (1884; cat. 70), which shows a boy, presumably a printer's apprentice, having a drink during his work break while two men in the background work on a handpress. While one contemporary reviewer saw the picture as "extremely American" because of the mode of dress, others saw an affirmation that the Dutch shared with Americans a number of democratic institutions, such as freedom of the press.[18] However, also demonstrated are the ideals of workplace reform that show a clean, centrally heated workplace, lit by natural light, and ventilated by fresh air, where machinery is used in harmony with human labor. The young man is precisely that—not a child—and conceivably apprenticed to the printers as he learns his new profession.

What this picture also shows is the approach that urban progressives took to transplant village intimacy and rural values into the city—either directly by creating homes, parks, and workplaces that brought back a sense of human scale to the metropolis, or indirectly by attempting to cultivate a sense of brotherhood and compassion among workers and their employers. The sense that people living in cities were becoming part of an "overcivilized" society cut off from experiencing "real life" was a very strong sentiment amongst the Dutch Utopians who themselves modeled a collective ideal within the artists' colony. Viewed as small experimental communities based on the tenets of freedom, friendship, and work, the colonies suspended some of the usual strictures of social etiquette—particularly for women—and allowed artists to graft reformist values onto themselves.

While cities were considered inherently dangerous and necessitated rigorous reorganization, the American middle class almost unnaturally, and certainly unrealistically, mythologized the concept of farm life as intensely heroic. Anna Stanley's

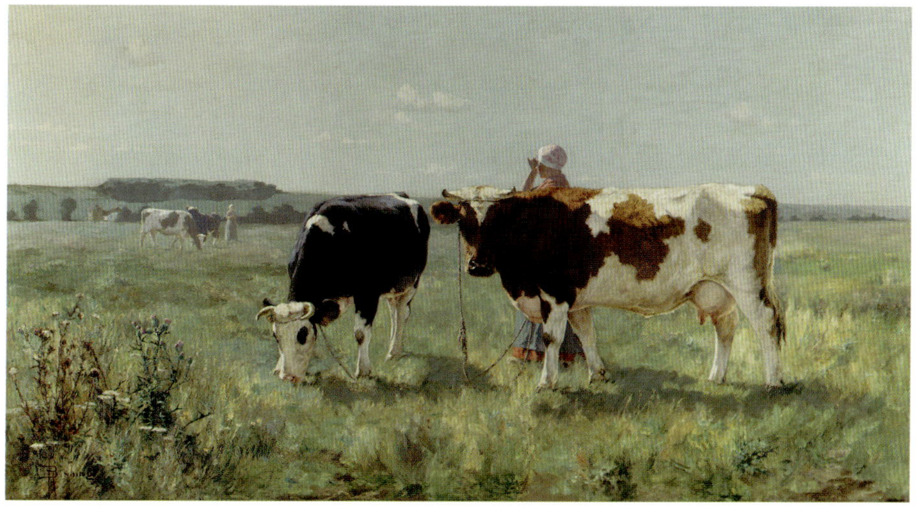

Fig. 14. Henry Singlewood Bisbing, *In the Meadow*, 1888, oil on canvas, 79 × 138", Pennsylvania Academy of the Fine Arts, Philadelphia, Gift of Colonel Thomas Fitzgerald.

Girl Carrying Sheaves (c. 1895; cat. 64), Walter MacEwen's *Returning From Work* (c. 1885; cat. 33), and Henry Bisbing's *In the Meadow* (fig. 14), all offer pictorial examples of how the American middle class romanticized rural life and farming as almost a sacred vocation: "It seems most natural that people living in the country should be more pious than those in the city, is it not?" commented the artist Elizabeth Nourse to her sister as they witnessed peasant women praying at a wayside shrine.[19]

The reality for farmers during the Progressive Era, however, did not match the stereotype. While on the one hand they were admired for their hard work and moral respectability, on the other, their political, economic, and social status was on the decline. Previously, Thomas Jefferson had romanticized farmers as "yeomen" whose strength of purpose and self-sustainability demonstrated a vision of hardworking American industry. After the Civil War, however, while the heroic nature of farm life was still being assiduously promoted, the impact of the growing capitalistic economy was making it more expensive to work the land and less profitable for rural sons to follow in their fathers' footsteps.

Between 1870 and 1900 millions of acres of virgin land came under new cultivation, and crop production grew correspondingly. But agricultural prices did not keep pace. The economic depression in 1873, compounded by towering interest rates, higher-priced manufactured goods, and the greater cost of employing seasonal labor, made it harder for rural families to remain self-sustaining. In contrast to the artist Daniel Ridgeway Knight's observation that rural workers were "as happy and contented as any similar class in the world . . . they all save money and are small capitalists and investors," by 1900 over a third of all American farms were operated by tenants, and not their original farming families.[20]

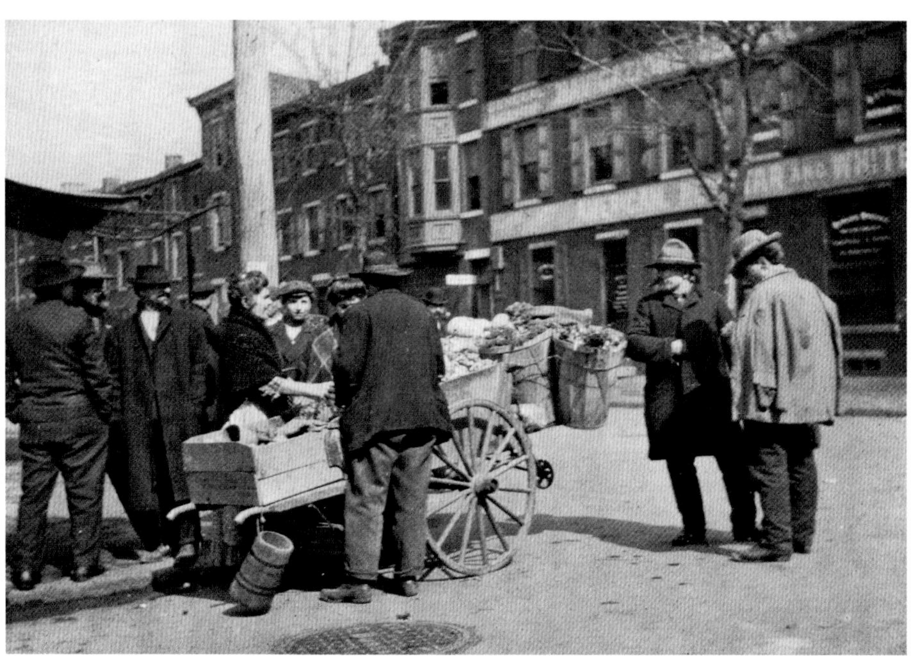

Fig. 15. Street near Casa Ravello Milk Station, Philadelphia, 1911. From the Starr Center Association annual report. Collection of The Historical Society of Pennsylvania, Philadelphia.

In the minds of the Dutch Utopians and the Progressive Era middle class, however, much of this rural angst was either unknown or ignored, and the myth of the yeoman farmer became a part of the country's nationalistic ideology. "There is neighborliness in the country," remarked Kenyon Butterfield, a sociologist and president of the Massachusetts State College of Agriculture, "there is intense democracy; there is a high sense of individual responsibility; there is initiative . . . which in turn reacts powerfully upon the general life of the family."[21]

Idealization of country life provided a way to "recover a reusable past" after national conflict and in the face of a slowly encroaching urban-centered future.[22] Even more compelling was the transformation of the yeoman farmer into the ideal of the suburban homeowner: the salary-earning man, providing for his family by purchasing a single house with a yard and garden. A comparison of Amy Cross's *The Holland Vegetable Vendor* (c. 1890s; cat. 12) to vendors operating in the streets of American cities (fig. 15), for example, reveals an unflattering contrast between the crowded streets of city living and rural homes where children were still able to play safely in their front yards. Certainly Gari Melchers's *The Unpretentious Garden* (c. 1903–15; cat. 44) provided the American middle class with a visual example of the American dream.

By 1920 the size of the American family had dramatically shrunk to include two or three children as opposed to an average of seven a century earlier. Particularly in the cities, child labor laws and the subsequent push for compulsory education helped this decline, as children could not be put to work as quickly. Improved medical care also promised parents that their offspring were more likely to survive into adulthood, with the result that the concept of "childhood" emerged as a distinct life stage where young minds were nurtured at home before entering society.

Joseph Raphael's *The Town Crier and His Family* (1905; cat. 52), focused on a father proudly surrounded by his children, and Gari Melchers's *The Family* (c. 1895; cat. 42), showing a nursing mother with a toddler at her feet and a doting husband by her side, are examples of the value connection between a well-managed, peaceful, and well-appointed rural home and family life. The home was expected to be a place for children to grow and adults to provide guidance. As Riis put it: "Brethren, upon our home rests our moral character; our civic and political liberties are grounded there; virtue, manhood, citizenship grow there. For American citizenship in the long run will be, must be, what the American home is."[23]

In the spirit of home ownership, and influenced by the principles underlying the Arts and Crafts movement that stated "wherever you can rest, there decorate," the Dutch Utopian artists and their patrons particularly admired the coziness and handmade furnishings of traditional Dutch interiors that provided a sense of familial permanence and reliability in a rapidly changing world.[24] For example, the array of family china and a silver tea set in Richard E. Miller's *Woman at the Table* (before 1908; cat. 46) and the glowing hand-painted Delft tiles in Gari Melchers's *Arranging the Tulips* (late 1880s; cat. 40), privilege craftsmanship above mass production, and uncover a desire for the "honest labor," dependability, and cooperative work that reformers asked employers to develop in the workplace and families to nurture in their children. "How many had been born in this room, lived with it all their lives and left it as they happily found it?" gushed George Henry Boughton after finding a picturesque Dutch room to copy. "May they rest happily in their tombs for that one virtue alone."[25]

The wish to replicate on a large scale the traditional activities of preindustrial family life and essentially equip poorer citizens with the skills to improve their lives was at the heart of the settlement housing movement which numbered more than four hundred houses across America by the mid-twentieth century. The best known of its kind, Hull House, was established in 1886 by Jane Addams and Ellen Gates Starr in Chicago and described as "an experimental effort to aid in the solution of the social conditions of life in a big city."[26] While some settlements provided housing, their main purpose was to provide a mixture of educational, social, and welfare services such as night schools, kindergartens, children's clubs, and art and craft classes that would guide the development of poor and immigrant families. At the heart of the effort was a desire both to advance American culture by interpreting democracy in social terms and to engineer a system of social work that reflected a preindustrial and largely rural past.

Walter MacEwen's *The Lacemakers* (c. 1885–1900; cat. 36) and *The Ghost Story* (1887; cat. 34) offer two idealized examples of communal activity that is both pleasurable and productive in the spirit of the settlement movement. But also, these pictures make a distinction about the proper place of women who work together in a sunlit room, largely without the presence of men. Part of the impetus underlying the settlement house concept by Jane Addams was to provide a safe environment for women and children. Reformers laid much of the blame for urban violence on men who, with increased wages and leisure time, resorted in ever-increasing numbers to drunkenness, solicitation of prostitutes, and gambling.

Controlling the use of alcohol became a particularly important focus throughout the 1880s and until Prohibition was legislated in 1919. From strong drink it was felt that illicit sex and other vices followed, and in the insistence of controlling adult behavior to force social change, reformers called for its removal. Curious in this respect is Gari Melchers's *The Pilots* (1887–88; cat. 39), showing a gathering of men resting after work, with no alcohol present. Surely this scene seems highly contrived, particularly in Holland—a country famous for the quality of its beer and gin?

While reformers in the Progressive Era tried to remove the causes of poverty and crime, they also encouraged reverent obedience to Christian values, particularly in regard to the "Americanization of the immigrant." Numerous multicultural unions, clubs, and societies formed to promote the American-Christian value system and influence social behavior. The first stated purpose of the Junior Order of the Ladies Pennsylvania Slovak Catholic Union, for example, was to assist its members to become "strong spiritually, alert mentally and to adapt themselves so as to become useful American Citizens."[27] Religious identity gave comfort at a time of enormous social change. However, the role of the church as the foundation of moral teaching was being undermined by the secularizing forces of modern life, and more liberal theological views emerged that blended contemporary concerns with spiritual values. The Dutch Utopian artists particularly fell into this category.

Elizabeth Nourse's *In The Church at Volendam* (1892, private collection), and Gari Melchers's *The Sermon* (1886; cat. 37), provide two excellent examples of approved Christian behavior interpreted through art. In Nourse's picture, two young girls sitting in the front pew are holding a prayer book or Bible, as behind them older women listen to the sermon. To the right sits a little boy, possibly the focus of their later affections and representative of the sons they will bear. In Melchers's picture, a young girl has fallen asleep, to the deep approbation of the elderly woman sitting next to her. Placed in the context of the church, the first picture points with Christian approval to the education and community involvement of the young. In contrast, the act of falling asleep is not only sinful, but shown in the company of generations of women, uncovers a growing concern about the future of womanhood. Notable again is the clear separation of men and women.

In the late nineteenth century the idea of the "New Woman" surfaced as a means to modernize and reposition the role of females. Where previously women had worked alongside their husbands and children in the fields or family business, now they attended college in ever-increasing numbers and entered the workforce. Symbolic of women's growing freedoms, the restrictive clothing of the hourglass corset was abandoned, makeup widely used, and contraception quite common. While women had not yet achieved the vote, it was generally acknowledged that it was only a matter of time. The attributes ascribed to the New Woman, widely perpetuated in popular imagery and women's magazines, included intelligence, beauty, physical fitness and health, self-confidence, self-sacrifice, and financial savvy (fig. 16). However, all women's attributes were a prelude to their ultimate "profession"—motherhood and "domestic statesmanship." Into their realm fell squarely the responsibility of the efficient running of the home, the education and supervision of the children, and the maintenance of the family's religious and moral values. "The home has ever

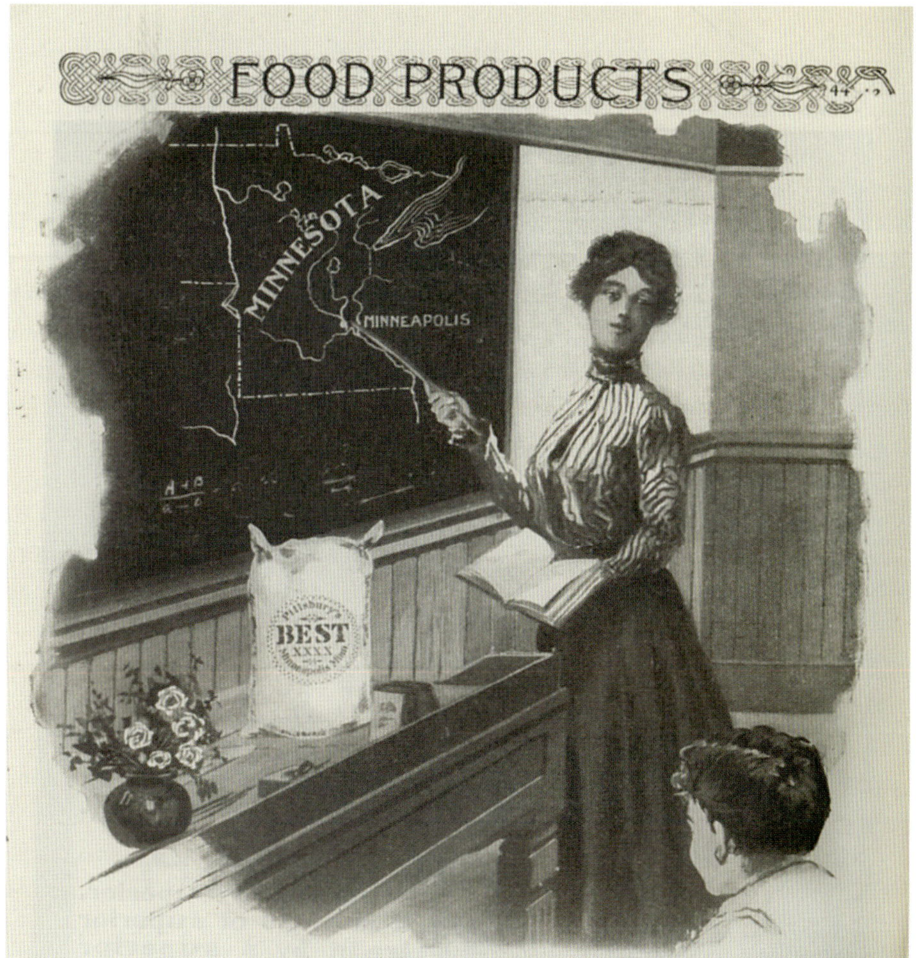

Fig. 16. Advertisement for Pillsbury-Washburn Flour Mills Co., Ltd., in *The Century Illustrated Monthly Magazine* 61, no. 1 (November 1900): 164, Collection of The Historical Society of Pennsylvania, Philadelphia.

been the woman's truest sphere and it will ever remain so . . . there lies her greatest power," claimed *The Ladies Home Journal.*[28]

The Dutch Utopian artists tapped into the idealization of women as pillars of virtue who operated in the private rather than the public sphere—despite the fact that women in large numbers were involved in social activism and in many respects were the backbone of the reform movement. An excellent example can be found in Joseph Raphael's *The Town Crier and His Family* (1905; cat. 52), where the father fills the center of the family and his wife is almost totally hidden behind him in the shadows. Picking up the metaphors associated with farming that exhorted women to "in-graft," "sow," and "root" steadfast principals of virtue in their children, the Dutch Utopians' idealization of the female peasant reinforced women's role as the cultivators of the future generation.

The honest labor of women in the home or in the field was a recurring theme for the Dutch Utopian artists that in some respects calmed anxieties that educating women would cause them to abandon their traditional roles as wives and mothers. By 1910 forty percent of college students were female—more than double the number after the end of the Civil War—and this rise in advanced education was credited by some contemporary social observers for the soaring divorce rates and the steep decline in childbirth.

Theodore Roosevelt characterized these changes as "a bane to any nation, a curse to society, a menace to the home." In his 1905 speech to the National Congress of Mothers, he went on to summarize:

> The woman's task is not easy—no task worth doing is easy—but in doing it, and when she has done it, there shall come to her the highest and holiest joy

> known to mankind; and having done it, she shall have the reward prophesied in Scripture; for her husband and her children, yes, and all people who realize that her work lies at the foundation of all national happiness and greatness, shall rise up and call her blessed.[29]

Romanticizing homemaking and motherhood in spiritual terms, such as in George Hitchcock's *Maternité (Maternity)* (1889; cat. 24), which frames the head of the young mother with a halo in the form of a wicker basket; or Walter MacEwen's *L'Absente (The Absent One on All Souls' Day)* (1889; cat. 35), which casts a Christian blessing on a daughter reading her Bible by an approving maternal ghost, performed a type of secular imagery that was nevertheless clearly founded on biblical teaching.

One of the most interesting aspects of the Dutch Utopian artists, however, was that many of them were women. Anna Mary Richards, Amy Cross, Wilhelmina Douglas Hawley, Elizabeth Nourse, Alice Blair Ring, Letta Crapo Smith, Anna Stanley, and Marcia Oakes Woodbury—all represented in this exhibition—were able to become professional painters as a direct result of the inroads made by the women's movement. Some, like Elizabeth Nourse, never married. Woodbury married an artist whose profession enabled her own continued practice after marriage. Some went to college, and all postponed childbearing. Most benefited from the tremendous growth in female art associations and the admission of women to art schools such as the Pennsylvania Academy of the Fine Arts in Philadelphia, and the Académie Julian in Paris.

Holland was particularly suited to this new brand of female, who typically came to Paris to study art, lived at the American Girls' Club on the rue de Chevreuse, and enjoyed a form of emancipation that even within art circles of Europe was seen as particularly American.[30] During the summer, or after formal studies were completed, Holland offered women easy and safe access via the clean and efficient railway service, a familiar Protestant social order, and a widespread facility with the English language. Like the south of France or Spain, Holland offered ample examples of preindustrial life but without the worries over personal safety or a lapse in social proprieties.

What is particularly intriguing to note are some of the subtle differences in subject matter between the male and female Dutch Utopians. For instance, while earlier in this essay Walter MacEwen's *The Ghost Story* and *The Lacemakers* were

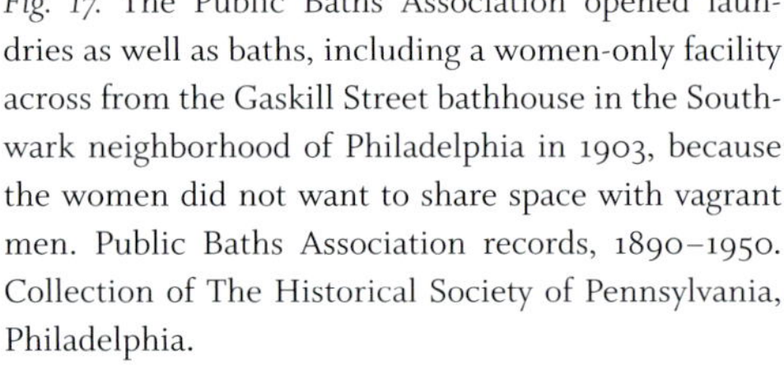

Fig. 17. The Public Baths Association opened laundries as well as baths, including a women-only facility across from the Gaskill Street bathhouse in the Southwark neighborhood of Philadelphia in 1903, because the women did not want to share space with vagrant men. Public Baths Association records, 1890–1950. Collection of The Historical Society of Pennsylvania, Philadelphia.

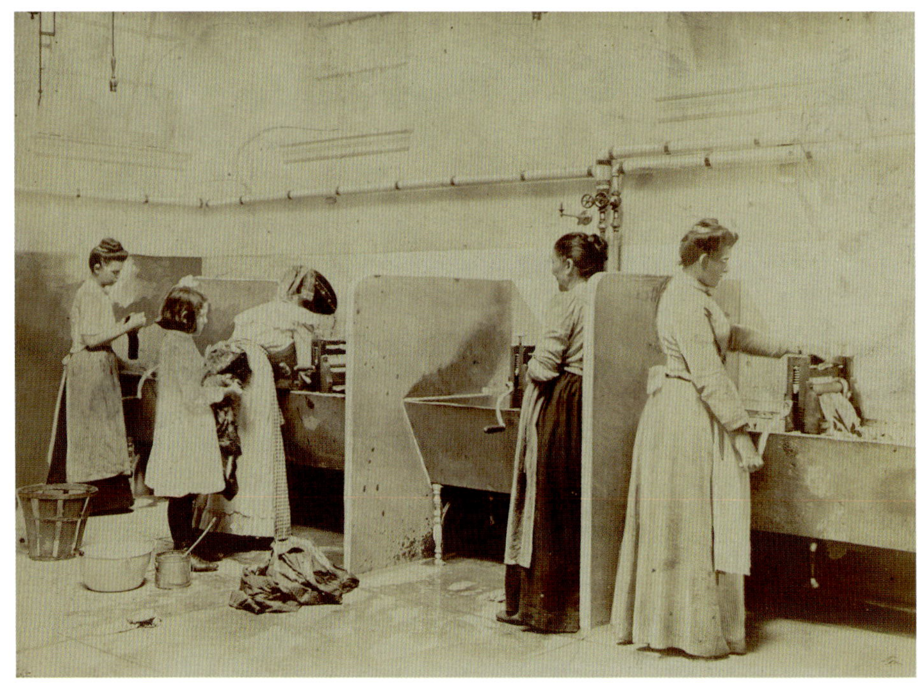

given as examples of the idealization of female work, these light-filled interiors contrast sharply with Marcia Oakes Woodbury's *Moeder en Dochter: Het Geheele Leven (Mother and Daughter: The Whole of Life)* (1894; cat. 73), and Emma Lampert Cooper's *The Breadwinner* (1891; cat. 11), showing women confined in rather small and singly lit rooms spinning wool. The images in these situations seem more of an approbation of women's labor than a celebration of it.

It is not within the scope of this essay to question whether there is a gendered difference in the Dutch Utopian artists' depiction of Dutch life. But certainly Wilhelmina Douglas Hawley's *Two Women near the River Waal* (1894; cat. 16), Elizabeth Nourse's *On the Dyke at Volendam* (1892; cat. 50), and Alice Blair Ring's *Morning Sunshine* (1906; cat. 55) all show strong confident women as stalwarts within their communities, which could be taken as evidence of the artists' desires for female equality. Perhaps more reliably, however, these images tie into the notion of "domestic science" that was promoted as a concept for unpaid female work and seen to hold the same qualities as a man's profession: education, time management, delegating tasks to others, and a sense of mission.

Julian Alden Weir's *Milkmaid of Popindrecht* (1881; cat. 71) and Gari Melchers's *In Holland* (1887; cat. 38) share a similar vision of women's strength of purpose and admiration for Dutch working women as expressed by George Henry Boughton: "I am not particularly fond of the idea of women doing the hard field work, but the women do in Holland a number of masculine tasks and very temptingly most of them 'compose' for the sketcher's benefit," he wrote. "As solid well-set-up specimens of healthy humanity the women have often the advantage of the men. It is a great treat to see a powerful young Dutch woman handle a rope on a pull boat."[31] Admiration for the strength and independence of women no doubt did reflect Progressive Era standards about housework and cleanliness that were particularly linked with stereotypes of Dutch fastidiousness, cleanliness, and efficiency. For example, Boughton's *Weeding the Pavement* (1882; cat. 5) compares favorably with an image of a public bathhouse in 1903 (fig. 17) and advertisements for Old Dutch Cleanser (fig. 18) with its trademark Dutch woman chasing dirt with a stick.[32] The Dutch example of paved roads, uncluttered interiors, and tiled surfaces that could be quickly wiped clean provided American cities with a standard for civic pride.

Many reform programs during the Progressive Era, such as the Public Baths Association of Philadelphia, were dedicated to improving the sanitary conditions of urban centers and the health of the poor. But also at work in some corners of society was a prejudicial fear that the large numbers of immigrants who settled in the damp, dilapidated tenement districts were truly the "great unwashed." Anti-immigration, otherwise known as nativism, and the promulgation of "whiteness" emerged as a result of the breakdown in the relative homogeneity of the American population. Supported by a type of social Darwinism that claimed some races to be better than others, Northern Europeans—such as the Dutch—were privileged above those who feared the "browning of America."

Nativism in the mid-nineteenth century first manifested itself as anti–Roman Catholic, particularly along the Eastern seaboard where a greater concentration of Irish and other Catholic immigrants settled. In 1844, for example, mobs attacked Irish neighborhoods and several Catholic churches in Philadelphia, burning St. Augustine's to the ground.[33] In 1882 Congress enacted the Chinese Exclusion Act, and in 1907 America and the Japanese entered into the so-called Gentleman's Agreement, whereby Japan agreed not to issue passports for Japanese citizens wishing to work in the United States.

The Dutch, however, fell into the favorable racial category, presenting to Americans a homogeneous white, Protestant, and republican identity to which they felt a direct kinship. Recalling famous Dutch Americans such as William Penn,

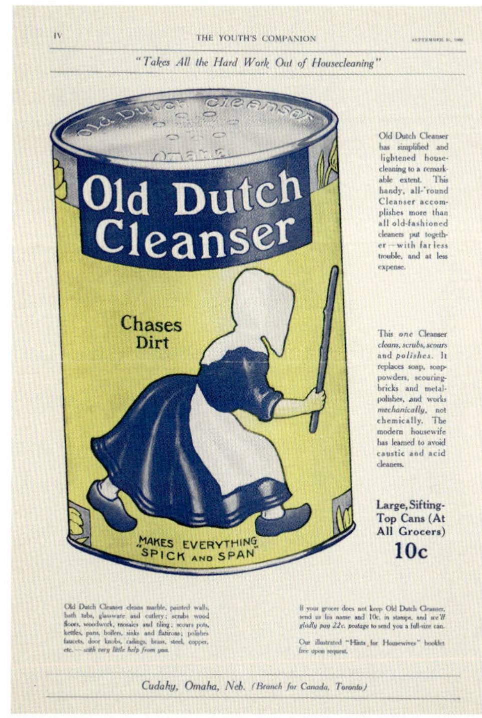

Fig. 18. Advertisement for Old Dutch Cleanser, in *The Youth's Companion* 83, no. 37 (September 16, 1909), Courtesy of the Library of Congress, Washington, D.C.

Herman Melville, Walt Whitman, Edward Bok, and most notably, the Roosevelt family, white Americans identified personally with the Dutch, and at a less admirable level, envied their apparent racial cohesiveness. "They have not changed much in appearance these sailor and fisher folk during the last two hundred years," wrote George Henry Boughton.[34] The same could not be said of American workers, particularly in rural areas that increasingly depended on seasonal migrants to bring in the harvest.

Small wonder then, that images of healthy blonde children such as Robert Henri's *Dutch Girl Laughing* (1907; cat. 18), Gari Melchers's *The Sisters* (c. 1895; cat. 43), and Letta Crapo Smith's *The First Birthday* (1902; cat. 63) appealed to a host of middle-class Americans who worried that the future of their national values was increasingly under attack by outside forces. The Dutch Utopians soothed a whole series of societal fears that blended into the great white American heartland.[35]

Because Holland industrialized relatively late, the Dutch government was better able to anticipate the unfolding development of modern culture and counteract some of its most socially disruptive effects. By freely allowing different factions to be given a seat at the governing table, some of the earliest political reforms and labor organizing were carried out within Christian communities with the blessing of the ruling parties. To the Americans, whose politics were characterized by fierce partisan fighting, most notably demonstrated by Theodore Roosevelt's splitting of the Republican Party in 1912, the Dutch ability to modernize without losing its moral compass was worthy of emulation.[36]

This admiration however, was to stop with the onset of World War I in Europe, when it became clear that even the enlightened Dutch were unable to protect themselves from enemy attack. Suddenly the idealization of a rural premodern way of life was horribly upset by the realities of modern weaponry. While the Progressive Era did not end—some would argue it was strengthened by war—the close association with the Dutch and social reform did. Artists began to look toward America itself for inspiration, believing that their country was now alone in creating a new and enlightened world order, and reformists began a second phase of work that embraced scientific and industrial improvements as the way of the future.

Where hitherto a rural template and traditional way of life, best represented by European examples, had overlaid urban planning and social values, after World War I it became apparent that "the time had come when it was no longer necessary for a first rate artist to go to Europe."[37] Certainly, artists and reformers could no longer claim the superiority of the Dutch way of life, in a world where progress was measured by how technically advanced a nation was, compared to other nations. Reflecting back on the Dutch-inspired paintings, one reviewer reminisced: "They told us how much better it would be to live quietly and peacefully than to rack brain and body with a mile-a-minute pace. Though we might entertain no such serious intention of taking to a cottage and courting rural bliss, it was no harm to contemplate the advantages of such a course."[38]

NOTES

1. Willem Frijhoff, "Dutchness in Fact and Fiction," in *Going Dutch: The Dutch Presence in America 1609–2009*, ed. Joyce D. Goodfriend, Benjamin Schmidt, and Annette Stott (Leiden: Brill, 2008), 352.

2. Michael McGerr, *A Fierce Discontent: The Rise and Fall of the Progressive Movement in America, 1870–1920* (New York: Oxford University Press, 2003), xv.

3. Frederick Townsend Martin, *The Passing of the Idle Rich* (London: Doubleday, 1911), 109–11.

4. Woodrow Wilson, *The New Freedom: A Call for the Emancipation of the Generous Engines of a People* (New York: Doubleday Page, 1918), 7.

5. Robert H. Weibe, *The Search for Order* (New York: Hill and Wang, 1967), 44.

6. Annette Stott, *Holland Mania: The Unknown Dutch Period in American Art and Culture* (Woodstock, N.Y.: Overlook Press, 1998), 38.

7. Henry James, *The American Scene* (London: Chapman and Hall, 1907), 322.

8. George Hitchcock, "The Picturesque Quality of Holland: Interiors and Bric-a-Brac," *Scribner's Magazine* 5, no. 2 (February 1889): 166.

9. George H. Boughton, *Sketching Rambles in Holland* (New York: Harper and Brothers, 1885), 227.

10. For a discussion of "reality research," see Nina Lübbren, *Rural Artists' Colonies in Europe, 1870–1910* (New Brunswick, N.J.: Rutgers University Press, 2001), 42–43.

11. Annette Stott, "Dutch Utopia: Paintings by Anti-modern American Artists of the Nineteenth Century," *Smithsonian Studies in American Art* 3, no. 2 (Spring 1989): 47–61, quote by George Hitchcock, 54.

12. Henry George, *Social Problems* (Garden City, N.Y.: Doubleday Page, 1883), 235.

13. Richard Hofstadter, *The Age of Reform* (New York: Vintage Books, 1955), 174.

14. Walter Licht, *Industrializing America: The Nineteenth Century* (Baltimore: Johns Hopkins University Press, 1995), 125.

15. Thomas J. Schlereth, *Victorian America: Transformations in Everyday Life, 1876–1915* (New York: Harper Perennial, 1991), 258.

16. Stott, *Holland Mania*, chapter 6, "An American Renaissance of Dutch Architecture," 152–83.

17. Ray Stannard Baker, quoted in McGerr, *A Fierce Discontent*, 135.

18. Stott, *Holland Mania*, 110–13.

19. Mary Alice Heekin Burke, *Elizabeth Nourse, 1859–1938: A Salon Career* (Washington, D.C.: Smithsonian Institution Press, 1983), 35.

20. Daniel Ridgeway Knight, quoted from 1885 in Burke, *Elizabeth Nourse*, 135.

21. Kenyon L. Butterfield, "Rural Life and the Family," in *American Sociological Society Papers and Proceedings*, Third Annual Meeting, 106–10. Reprinted in McGerr, *A Fierce Discontent*, 105.

22. Mary Weakes-Baxter, *Reclaiming the American Farmer: The Reinvention of a Regional Mythology in Twentieth-Century Southern Writing* (Baton Rouge: Louisiana State University Press, 2006), 200.

23. Jacob Riis, *The Peril and Preservation of the Home* (Philadelphia: George W. Jacobs, 1903), 24.

24. John Ruskin, "The Lamp of Beauty," in *The Seven Lamps of Architecture* (London, 1849; repr. E. P. Dutton, 1910); reprinted in *The Theory of Decorative Art, 1750–1940: An Anthology of European and American Writings*, ed. Isabelle Frank (New Haven: Yale University Press, 2000), 43. Although neither Ruskin nor William Morris ever visited the United States, their followers such as Walter Crane, Charles Robert Ashbee, and Morris's daughter May Morris made extensive lecture tours around the country. John Ruskin's *The Two Paths* was reprinted nineteen times in America between 1859 and 1892.

25. Boughton, *Sketching Rambles in Holland*, 117.

26. Schlereth, *Victorian America*, 257–60.

27. "Constitution and By-Laws of the Junior Order of the Ladies Pennsylvania Slovak Catholic Union, revised and adopted at the XXV convention held at Scranton, PA, September 7–11, 1952," collection of the Historical Society of Pennsylvania, Philadelphia.

28. Helen Damon-Moore, *Magazines for the Millions: Gender and Commerce in the Ladies Home Journal and the Saturday Evening Post, 1880–1910* (Albany: State University of New York, 1994), 92.

29. Theodore Roosevelt, report of the National Congress of Mothers, March 13, 1905, Washington, D.C. Accessed online April 10, 2009, http://books.google.com/books?id=JLUDAAAAMAAJ&pg=PA168&dq=Theodore+Roosevelt+National+Congress+of+Mothers+1905&client=safari#PPA3,M1.

30. Mariea Caudill Dennison, "The American Girls' Club in Paris: The Propriety and Imprudence of Art Students, 1890–1914," *Woman's Art Journal* 26:1 (Spring–Summer 2005): 32–37.

31. Boughton, *Sketching Rambles in Holland*, 21.

32. Stott, *Holland Mania*, 209.

33. For more information about Philadelphia's nativist riots, see Bruce Dorsey, "Bibles, Public Schools, and Philadelphia's Bloody Riots of 1844," *Pennsylvania Legacies Magazine* (May 2008): 12–17.

34. Boughton, *Sketching Rambles in Holland*, 39.

35. The appeal for Dutch-derived pictures and the influence of "Dutchness" was fairly strong, for example, in Cincinnati, Ohio, as Stott points out in *Holland Mania*, chapter 8, "Cincinnati, a Case Study," 212–37.

36. In 1898, for example, the Dutch prime minister, Abraham Kuyper, was given an honorary doctorate by Princeton University and delivered the Stone lectures, titled "Christianity and the Class Struggle," which essentially laid out the belief that government, religion, and business could work together to create a democratic, Christian, and modern nation. For further information refer to James W. Skillen and Stanley W. Carlson-Thies, "Religion and Political Development in Nineteenth-Century Holland," *Publis*, 12, no. 3 (Summer 1982): 43–64.

37. Henry McBride, "American Expatriates in Paris," reprinted in *Dial* (April 1929); quoted in Wanda M. Corn, *The Great American Thing: Modern Art and National Identity, 1915–1935* (Berkeley: University of California Press, 1999), 219.

38. "Notes on the Art Exhibit of Holland," *Brush and Pencil* (February 1905): 133–34, quoted in Stott, "Dutch Utopia," 51.

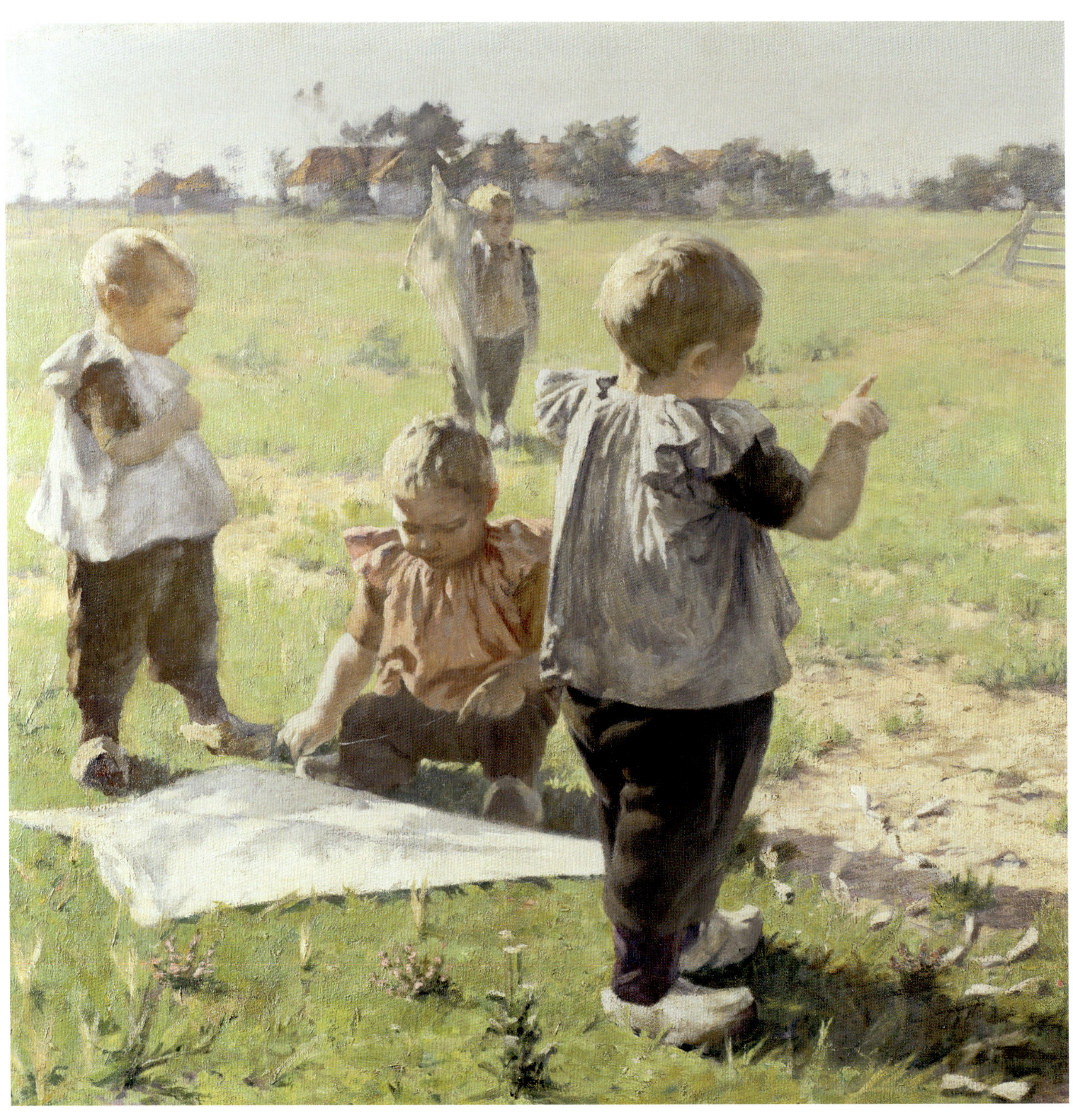

Narratives of Rural Life

Nina Lübbren

NINETEENTH-CENTURY ARTISTS IN EUROPEAN RURAL REGIONS painted the landscape and the people they encountered in the countryside. They represented rural areas as places of timeless nature where the same activities repeated themselves year after year, following the cycle of the seasons. Singular events played much less of a role in such representations of nature than they did in contemporary history painting or in urban genre painting. Rural images told their own stories in their own way, and representative examples from *Dutch Utopia* illustrate the distinctive modalities of narration developed to fit in with notions of nature and village life.

MINIMAL NARRATIVE

A close look at Walter MacEwen's *Returning from Work* (c. 1885; cat. 33) reveals a group of Dutch peasants on a sandy path in the countryside. The landscape is flat, with low-growing grasses and flowers, stretching to an equally flat horizon that is broken only by a few clumps of trees. The sky is overcast, with gray clouds massing at right. The light is diffuse; there are no strong cast shadows, nor dappled effects of sunlight.

MacEwen's painting depicts a type of landscape that was immensely popular among rural painters of the late nineteenth century. I call this type "minimal landscape." Minimal landscapes are characterized by the depiction of stark, flat terrains, with the horizon bisecting the canvas into two rectangular halves.[1] Gone are the mountain silhouettes, masses of foliage, and trees balanced against each other across the composition—all devices favored by an earlier generation of romantic landscape artists. Painters of minimal landscape eschewed Alpine or wooded regions, and instead chose wide open heath, moor, or coastal landscapes. Indeed, the countryside of the northern Netherlands was eminently suited to representing this kind of stark, flat landscape. In addition, minimal landscapes often went hand in hand with a preference for gray daylight over direct sunshine.[2] This mode of painting has sometimes been identified with the distinctive gray or silver illumination of the Hague School in the Netherlands.[3] It should be noted, however, that both the choice of flat terrain and overcast weather was representative of painters throughout Northern Europe during this period. Indeed, artists sought out northern locations in preference to Mediterranean sites precisely in order to paint diffuse light, unencumbered by the changing effects of dappled sunlight. MacEwen's canvas is typical of this landscape trend; compositions similar to *Returning from Work* may be found in the oeuvre of contemporaries such as Peder Severin Krøyer in Denmark or Otto Modersohn in Germany.[4]

While one could describe MacEwen's *Returning from Work* as simply some figures in a minimal landscape, doing nothing of any note, let us examine the painted

Detail of cat. 32

people's activities in more detail. The figures face away from us and are shown walking down a path, into the painting. A young woman and a young man are singled out for closer attention. The woman stands in the left foreground; she is dressed in the clothes, bonnet, and wooden clogs of a Dutch peasant. We watch her bending over toward us and hitching up her skirt, as if to adjust her stocking. At the same time, the woman twists around in order to look back over her shoulder; she gazes toward the receding group but in particular at one young man—or so we are invited to assume. This young man stands to the right of the vertical axis and lags a little way behind the rest of the group. The youth has paused in his progress, one foot in front of the other, as he looks back at the young woman in the foreground.

MacEwen's canvas is not a pure landscape painting. It is a figurative painting with a narrative twist. The narrative is not of the grand dramatic type associated with many contemporary history paintings, nor is it of the melodramatic or humorous kind associated with contemporary genre paintings. We see no tale of intrigue and murder, as we do in Jean-Léon Gérôme's history painting *Death of Caesar* (1867, Walters Art Gallery, Baltimore), but we also see no gently funny incident, as we do in Jean-Georges Vibert's *The Reprimand* (1874, Metropolitan Museum of Art, New York). Above all, we see nothing affecting or complex. If anything, MacEwen's *Returning from Work* hovers on the very edge of not being narrative at all.

I would argue, however, that the picture, despite its non-dramatic content, does invite viewers to reconstruct a narrative—a basic, minimal narrative, set in a minimal landscape. The definition of the minimum requirements for a story is controversial; however, most narrative theorists tend to agree that a basic or "minimal story" needs at least two events taking place in chronological succession, linked to each other by causal connections, and enacted or experienced by narrative agents, that is, by characters.[5] In MacEwen's painting, we have two figures looking at each other. They constitute the events. The woman's bending down could be termed one event while the man looking over his shoulder is a second event. These two events are connected by causal means: the young man looks at the woman *because* she has stopped on the road; the woman, in turn, looks at the man *because* he is waiting for her. The picture even invites us to conjecture about further causal relationships: the woman has possibly stopped to adjust her stocking and to show her ankle precisely *in order to* entice the young man to look at her.

The action of looking and bending over can perhaps hardly be graced by the term "event." It is true that these humble activities are not on a par with the more elaborate actions found in contemporary narrative paintings, such as the killing of a tyrant or the rejection of a suitor. Indeed, the modest actions of bending down and looking over one's shoulder can barely be said to constitute anything as dramatic as plot, action, or story. However, nineteenth-century viewers were primed to expect narrative content from figurative pictures. Spectators arrived at a gallery or at the reproductions of images in periodicals with the anticipation of being told stories in pictorial form. MacEwen's canvas plays to and rewards such narrative expectations. The painting invites viewers to spin out a tale from very minimal givens. The tale probably involves some romantic attraction between the two principal protagonists, the young woman and man on the sandy path.

The mutual connection of the two main figures in fore- and middle ground by means of their exchanged glances furnishes a sufficient narrative clue. It should be noted that the young heterosexual couple formed a staple of many narrative pictures, and in this sense, viewers could readily slot the depicted peasants into a familiar framework. For example, Gari Melchers's *Skaters* (c. 1892; cat. 41), or Jules Bastien-Lepage's *Rural Love* (fig. 19) both contain a rustic flirting couple as their center of attention. Viewers who were familiar with a range of such scenes of courtship could easily pick out the germ of a similar story in MacEwen's *Returning from Work*.

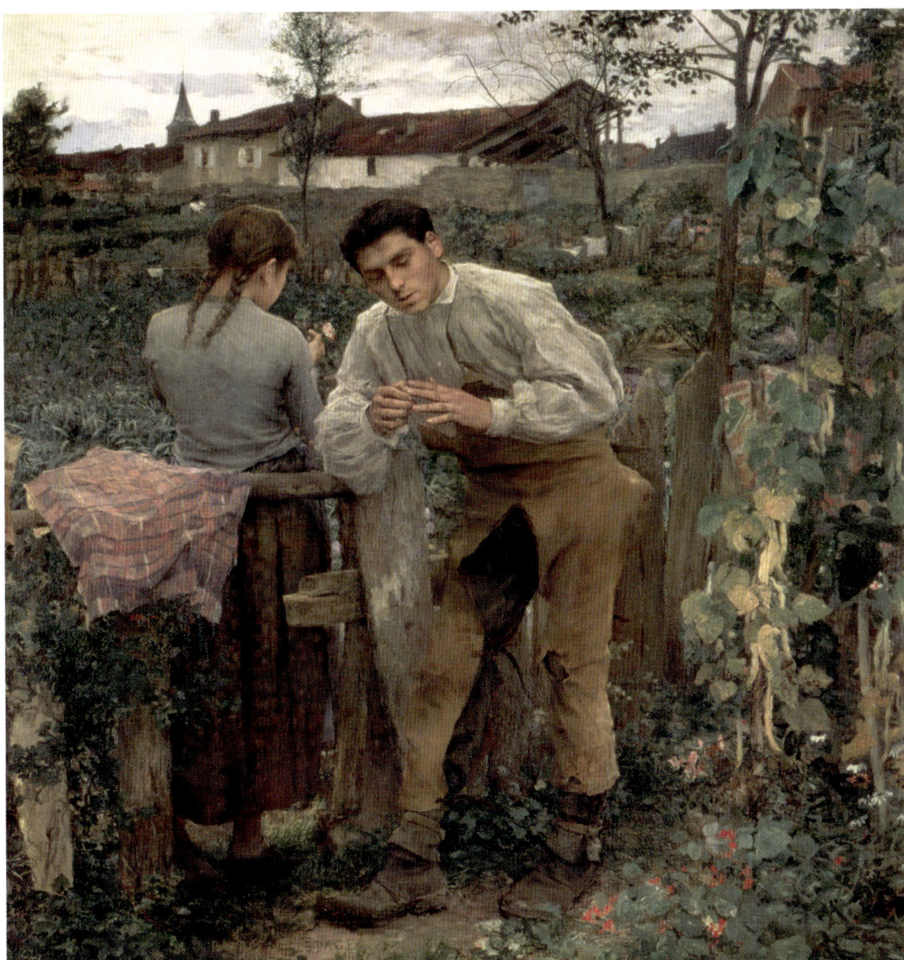

Fig. 19. Jules Bastien-Lepage, *Rural Love,* 1882, oil on canvas, Pushkin Museum, Moscow, Russia.

MacEwen's painting furnishes the additional twist of making the young woman the instigator of the flirtation.

NARRATIVE AND GENRE

Narrative painting is usually associated with history or genre painting. History painting involves the depictions of unique actions that were perpetrated by named and famous historical, literary, or mythical heroes, such as Hercules or Julius Caesar. Historical actions are unique because they happened only once, to particular individuals. Genre painting, by contrast, involves the delineation of everyday, non-unique occurrences that happen on a regular or cyclical basis. This is why genre scenes often appear to be "timeless," as they could take place during any time. Because generic actions are not unique, they are often not registered as particularly narrative in character. They seem to show general human conditions rather than causally linked plots. In addition, the events in genre paintings happen to non-named, anonymous persons who could be "anybody" or "everyman." Generic characters are not heroic and tend to be defined by such categories as age or working status. Common generic types are, for example, that of "child," "old woman," or "peasant."

MacEwen's *Returning from Work* would seem to fall comfortably within the category of genre painting. It is, however, a particular kind of late-nineteenth-century genre painting. It is a "historicized" and "narrativized" genre painting. In *Returning from Work,* the unique, unrepeatable moment of story time invades the timeless, cyclical condition of generic time. The group in the middle ground of the picture is generic: peasants (a generic class of interchangeable persons) returning from work (a generic activity that repeats every day). However, the mini-narrative of the foreground woman and the man introduces an element of the unique into this scenario. We are here no longer dealing with only a generic "return from work" (as suggested by the title) but also with a specific romantic story between two particular individuals.

It could, of course, be argued that the exchange of flirtatious glances is in itself a generic, repeatable action. It certainly seems rather repeatable when one looks through all of the scores, if not hundreds, of nineteenth-century pictures that feature coquettish interactions between young women and men.[6] However, one must consider to what extent each of these many couples is made distinctive and unique in some way. Nineteenth-century pictures of the act of courtship personalize and individualize this universal theme. This tendency becomes especially apparent when one draws a comparison with the Dutch seventeenth century. All Western nineteenth-century genre painters modeled themselves to a large degree on their Dutch seventeenth-century predecessors, but for those artists active in actual locations in the Netherlands, the painting of "everyday life" of the so-called Golden Age held a particular charge. Not only did Dutch Baroque genre painting come to epitomize genre painting per se, but the actualities of present-day Holland were experienced as a direct continuation of the supposed "realities" seen in seventeenth-century paintings.[7] In the words of the English painter Arthur George Bell, who visited the country in the 1890s:

> They still go on wearing costumes that were worn hundreds of years ago. You are continually coming across the same type of face and figure that Teniers painted, and there is a man who drives me about who reminds me of one of Van Eyke's saints. Even the horses do not seem to have changed since the days of Wouvermans. . . . and I often notice a hound that at once makes me think of Snyders.[8]

Given this notion of the continuity of traditions and types over a period of centuries in Holland, one would expect there to be more resemblance between seventeenth-century and nineteenth-century genre paintings than is actually the case. As we have seen, romantic couples were a staple of nineteenth-century genre, so it is striking to note how comparatively few pictures with this subject matter exist in Dutch Baroque art. To be sure, we do encounter seventeenth-century couples but they tend to be either respectably married, or involved in a brothel scene, with more or less allegorical import, as happens, for example, in Frans van Mieris's *Brothel Scene* (c. 1658–59, Royal Picture Gallery, Mauritshuis, The Hague) or Gerard Terborch's *Young Couple Drinking Wine* (c. 1662–63, Staatliche Museen zu Berlin [National Gallery]). Scenes may show bawdy dancing or the like, but invariably within a larger scene of merry-making. Very rarely, if ever, does the heterosexual couple emerge as the anchor point for an anecdote of the kind seen in MacEwen's composition.[9] In Dirck Hals's *Loose Company in an Interior* (fig. 20), we even see a woman looking right out at the viewers and lifting her glass, as if to demonstrate to the audience exactly which kind of moral laxness is being illustrated here. Hals's woman addresses the spectators and thereby breaks the illusion of the "fourth wall," making this picture profoundly non-narrative. MacEwen's couple shows no awareness of being watched by anybody outside the composition. They do not interact with the viewers; they interact only with each other, and this enhances the narrative power of their interaction. The couple does not so much illustrate the general, transtemporal nature of sexual attraction, but gives us a very particularized instance of it. In this regard, the hitching up of the skirt provides the fulcrum of uniqueness; the generic figure of "peasant woman" is thereby transformed into a unique, quasi-novelistic character.

Not only does the courtship anecdote in MacEwen's painting draw upon intertextual resonances of couples in paintings, novels, and plays, but it also crucially

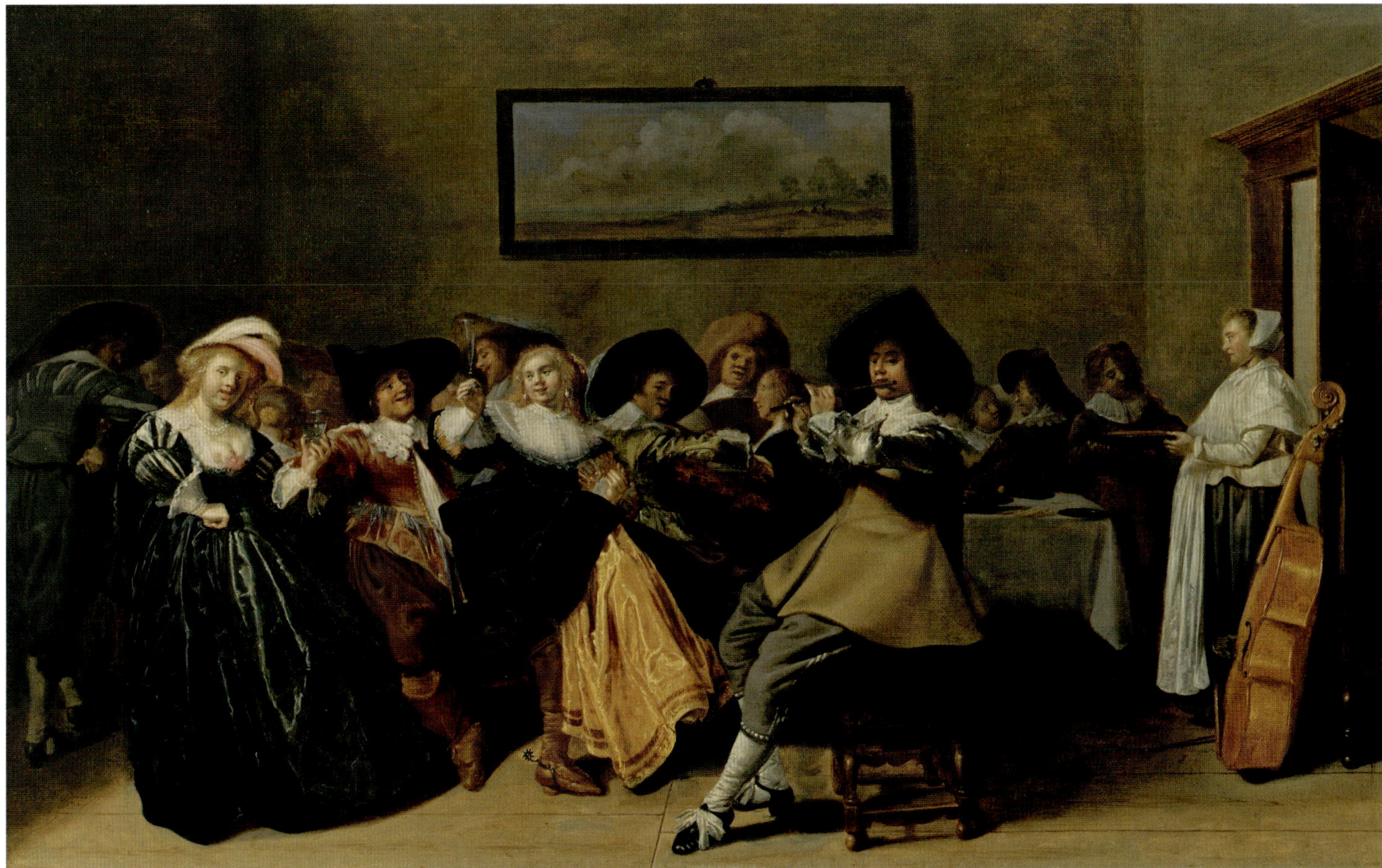

Fig. 20. Dirck Hals, *Loose Company in an Interior*, c. 1620s/30s, oil on panel, 17⅝ × 27¾", Niedersächsisches Landesmuseum, Hannover, Germany.

evokes a range of possible narrative outcomes and futures. Again, this is what differentiates MacEwen's scene from its seventeenth-century forebears and what places it firmly within the bounds of nineteenth-century narration. Viewers are invited to speculate about what will happen next in a way they were not when faced with seventeenth-century genre paintings.

Marcia Oakes Woodbury's triptych *Moeder en Dochter: Het Geheele Leven (Mother and Daughter: The Whole of Life)* (1894; cat. 73), set in the agricultural town of Laren, tells the story of two women without a man. The title might suggest that mother and daughter, left to their own devices without a breadwinner, have to work for their own living. The mother, old and shaped by a lifetime of labor, has left her man behind in her past; the daughter, young but already serious and sad, possibly has a man still in her future. We are encouraged to make assumptions about this family: Did the *pater familias* drown at sea? Will the young girl ever find a suitor? Woodbury's painting invites viewers to imagine the pasts and futures of the figures depicted, weaving small tales around these present moments.

LANDSCAPE, NATURE, AND TIME

During the nineteenth century, genre painting became increasingly infected with the narrative bug, and the genre paintings that were produced and set in the countryside present a special case. MacEwen's *Returning from Work* combines genre with landscape. It is a painting of a rural setting, and it is not coincidental that it represents no grand dramatic event. Rural paintings rarely did.

The idea of landscape developed along a particular trajectory in nineteenth-century art and culture. Whereas genre moved from the representation of timeless scenes to narrativized events, landscape moved from the tradition of historical landscapes with figures (exemplified by Nicolas Poussin or Claude Lorrain) to landscapes devoid of historical, or in many cases, even any figurative content.[10] This development was crucial to the way landscape and nature were viewed during the nineteenth century.

The evolution of landscape may be illustrated by the early career of the French painter Camille Corot. Corot's *Hagar in the Wilderness* (1835, Metropolitan Museum of Art, New York) is an early example of a historical landscape. The woods and rocks of the Forest of Fontainebleau near Barbizon have been harnessed to provide a backdrop for the biblical story. However, the painter combined topographical motifs taken from different sites: the rocks in the background are taken from studies Corot did at Civita Castellana near Rome; the boulders and vegetation in the foreground are based on Fontainebleau.[11] This mix-and-match procedure and the transformation of the natural environment into a setting for a mythical narrative found no favor with later generations who came to the countryside in order to be immersed in vegetative nature. If we compare *Hagar in the Wilderness* with *Rocks in the Forest of Fontainebleau* (1860/65, National Gallery of Art, Washington, D.C.), a later scene by the same artist and painted in the same region of the forest of Fontainebleau, we can see how Corot has eliminated the figurative content in favor of a scene of pure nature.[12]

Landscape which had, in the eighteenth century, been largely historical and hence narrative, became, in the nineteenth century, a vehicle for non-narrative depiction. Viewers of pictures such as the Dutch artist Anton Mauve's *The Marsh* (fig. 21), painted near the village of Laren, or the American William Henry Singer Jr.'s *Heathland near the Tafelberg, Blaricum* (1902; cat. 60), also painted near Laren, were asked to contemplate the scenery before them and to immerse themselves in the remembered sights, sounds, and other sensual impressions of being in the country-side. In his memories of sketching studies in the forest of Fontainebleau in the 1870s, the American painter Will Hicok Low summed up the experience of many nature painters:

Fig. 21. Anton Mauve, *The Marsh,* 1885, oil on canvas, 23⅝ × 35½", Rijksmuseum, Amsterdam, the Netherlands.

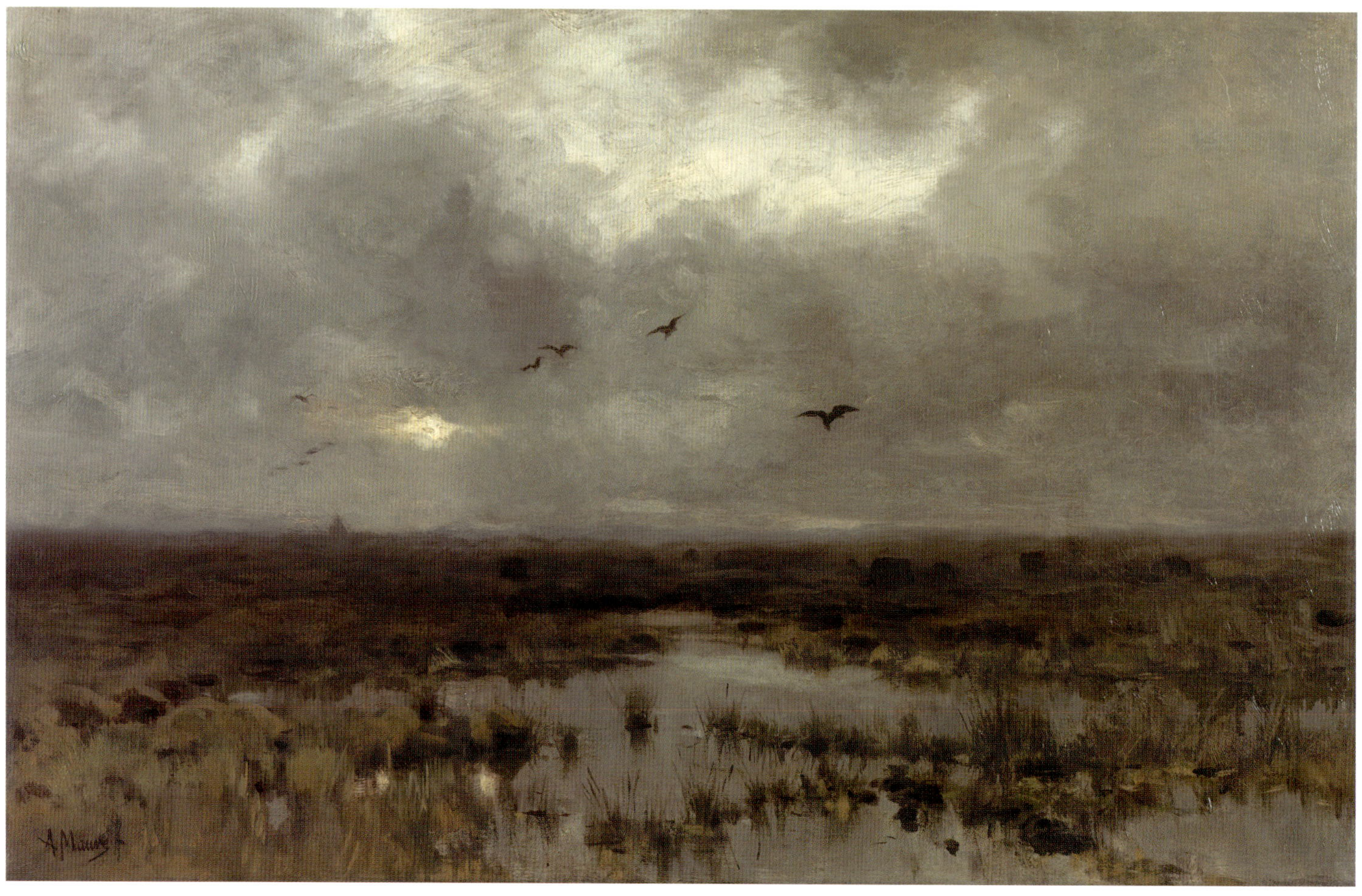

> In after years, . . . [the artist] shall perchance look upon his despised study and, through its darkened tones, the sunlight of the morning in the Bas Bréau or upon the plain, or the sharp storm when, crouching in the shelter of a wheatrick, he dashed a few rapid colour notes on his canvas, will live again for him . . .[13]

The Scottish writer Robert Louis Stevenson evoked a similar experience of being immersed in the sights, sounds, and tactile sensations within nature. Stevenson wrote of his time spent near Barbizon in the 1870s:

> I am here in my dear forest, all day in the open air. It is very be—no, not beautiful exactly, just now, but very bright and living. There are one or two song birds and a cuckoo: all the fruit-trees are in flower, and the beeches make sunshine in a shady place.[14]

I have written elsewhere on these landscapes of immersion.[15] For now, let us examine how these experiences of nature played themselves out in Singer's *Heathland near the Tafelberg, Blaricum*. The landscape in Singer's painting is not dissimilar to the one seen in MacEwen's *Returning from Work*. To be sure, Singer's heath near Laren is somewhat less flat than the plain chosen by MacEwen. However, there is the same forked sandy path, leading the eye and the imagination into the scene; we see a similar mix of sand and short, scruffy scrubland; there is the same overcast, cloudy sky and the shadowless gray illumination; and in both paintings, we have a bare landscape without dwellings, fences, or overt signs of human interference. However, there the similarities stop. Unlike *Returning from Work*, Singer's *Heathland* contains no narrative, not even a minimal one. In *Heathland*, nothing happens. There is no event, no before and after, no causal connection; there are no protagonists. The only animate creatures visible are a flock of sheep, and these could hardly be said to constitute "characters" in the narrative sense. We are not asked to imagine a story unfolding through time, but rather a timeless scene of nature.

The introduction of narrative into such a painting would amount to the introduction of history, and history was precisely what painters (and their audiences) sought to evict from nature. Within the discursive contexts of nineteenth-century urban cultures, nature was placed outside of time and the effects of industrialized modernization.[16] Nature was outside historical time, and it was even outside generic, cyclical time; it seemed to exist in a space outside of any time, or in a time that was unfathomable to humans. Of course, nature yielded to seasonal change, but the way painters represented natural scenes had little to do with, say, the ordered march of spring to winter, each season accompanied by its appropriate human activity, as seen in medieval illuminations (for example, the Duc de Berry's book of hours, painted by the Limbourg Brothers, 1412–16) or in Pieter Brueghel's sixteenth-century paintings of the four seasons.[17] Nineteenth-century landscapes do not show human control of, or even interaction with, nature's changes. Instead, nature exists in and for itself. In Singer's painting, there is no evidence of human presence, and this is in the province of North Holland, one of the most densely populated and highly regulated agrarian terrains of Europe.[18]

Other rural paintings, such as the American John Leslie Breck's *Autumn, Giverny (The New Moon)* (1889, Terra Foundation for American Art, Chicago) or Anna Stanley's *Girl Carrying Sheaves* (c. 1895; cat. 64) do contain human figures but in these rustic scenes, we have what amounts to a "landscapefication" of figurative painting. Figures are placed within nature, immersed in its textures and shapes, as if they were themselves sheep or windblown trees. Such images conjured a dream of rural nature, a modern idea of the supposed authenticity and affinity with nature of the European peasant. History, and therefore narrative, played no role in these images of a nature outside of time.

DESCRIPTION AND NARRATION

The introduction of narratives into representations of interiors and village life was, perhaps, easier to effect, as the settings of churches, inns, or cottages were not subsumed under the rubric of "natural nature" to the same degree as landscapes. Painters often inserted humorous or affecting anecdotal content into scenes of village life, as can be analyzed in Gari Melchers's painting *The Sermon* (1886; cat. 37), executed in the Dutch coastal settlement of Egmond.

A glance is sufficient to detect a narrative stimulus in *The Sermon*. We see a congregation of women and men in regional costume during a religious service in Egmond Binnen's Protestant church. The focus is on the young woman in the center foreground who is slumped forward in her chair, asleep. Our attention is drawn to her by the old woman seated two chairs beyond the sleeper, the only figure to turn her face in our direction. The others all look "off-screen," as it were, beyond the left edge of the canvas, presumably at the clergyman giving his sermon. The pictorial strategies employed include placing the main focus of attention outside of the painting, presenting a variety of listening attitudes and poses, including details that are not immediately relevant to the main theme (such as the numbers on the chair backs or the discarded cloak hung on the back of a chair) and, most prominently, centering the scene around a story that is subsidiary to the main theme of sermon but essential in that it adds light-hearted human interest. All of these devices serve to draw the viewers into the scene by encouraging them to use their imaginations to fill in the gaps in the story. Indeed, the empty chair in the right foreground seems to invite the viewer to join the congregation. The thematic strategy is similar to the Anglo-German painter Hubert von Herkomer's *The Last Muster* (1875, Lady Lever Art Gallery, Port Sunlight, England). Herkomer's picture shows a congregation of veterans, one of whom has slumped forward in his chair, dead, noticed only by his pew neighbor. Melchers's story is less portentous but makes use of equally effective narrative visual devices.

The Sermon is a genre scene, similar to other rural church pictures, such as the Swiss-German painter Benjamin Vautier's *Devout Congregation in the Village Church* (1858, Stiftung Kunsthaus Heylshof, Worms, Germany) or Elizabeth Nourse's *In the Church at Volendam* (1892, private collection).[19] However, *The Sermon* is a genre scene infused with a bead of narrative. Costume, headdresses, the woodwork of the chairs, the details of the church interior—all of these are displayed as a kind of ethnographic spectacle. These details are scrupulously described and add up to a cumulative effect of reality, to borrow a term from the literary critic Roland Barthes.[20] But there is, in addition, an overriding narrative impulse. As viewers, we cannot resist homing in on the story and speculating, in however minor a way, about the reasons for the girl's fatigue (boredom? exhaustion? a late night?), about the thoughts expressed by the matron's searching look, and about the consequences for the girl upon waking. Arguably, this narrative, minimal though it may be, draws attention away from all of the other elements in the picture—at least initially. This is not necessarily an exclusive reaction, of course. A twentieth-century Egmond audience of *The Sermon*, for one, zeroed in not on the anecdote but on the "realism" of the costume, commenting in 1980 that the women looked underdressed in their lace caps and that in church they should have been wearing bonnets.[21]

As soon as a plot is inserted into a descriptive scene, and be the plot ever so minimal, the scene becomes narrative. In a different context, the photographer John Hedgecoe wrote that even the tiniest figure in a landscape irresistibly draws the beholder's eye.[22] Narrative works in a similar way: even the most trivial of plots will compel our attention. We viewers are story seekers. A plot response is, arguably, the first and primary response elicited by figurative pictures: Who are these people? What are they doing, and why? What will happen next? Narrative will always tend to overwhelm pictorial description in any given image. Painters who wished to resist the narrative drive in their images needed to evict plot forcefully, as did Singer in his *Heathland*. Those who wished to retain narrative content could count on viewers' readiness to tell stories in front of pictures, and painters need furnish only minimal clues to infuse their paintings with plot interest, as did Melchers in *The Sermon*.

Paintings set in village locations could be complex and highly dramatic although they rarely attempted the sensationalism of some of their history and urban counterparts.[23] We do not find the murders, executions, assassinations, battles, sexual temptation, and political intrigue that play a prominent role in story-telling pictures set in the city, in the past, or in mythical fiction.[24] Death does feature in images of the countryside but it generally features as a natural occurrence, not as a man-made murder; instead, we have death by old age or death by drowning. For example, Elizabeth Nourse's painting of female figures, anxiously awaiting the return of their menfolk from the sea, in *On the Dyke at Volendam* (1892; cat. 50) obliquely addresses the popular theme of fisherwomen threatened by their husbands' deaths.[25] We may assume that the women in Woodbury's previously discussed triptych *Moeder en Dochter* were bereaved; although the work was painted in landlocked Laren, non-Dutch viewers could easily assume that the husband and father may have drowned at sea. Other viewers might speculate that he was taken by illness. Overall, the stories set in agrarian or fishing locations tended to be more muted, more minimal, more gently humorous and anecdotal.[26] Village life was seen as being closer to nature than city life or historical events, and it is as if the pull of the presumed timelessness of nature exerted itself on rural genre pictures, also.

GENRE IN THE NINETEENTH AND SEVENTEENTH CENTURIES

Even a seemingly non-narrative picture such as Walter MacEwen's interior with women sewing, the work known as *The Lacemakers* (c. 1885–1900; cat. 36), contains a kernel of plot. We see three women in Dutch regional costume seated on wooden chairs in a plain room. Two of the women, wearing white bonnets, are busy working on a large sheet. The third young woman sits with her head in her hand, in the manner of traditional representations of melancholy, her other hand idle upon the sheet in her lap. This woman is also marked out as slightly different from the other two by the cap she wears and by her location on her own at left. In the middle ground, standing next to one of the windows, is a man whose head twists round to look at the young thoughtful woman. The turn of head is similar to that of the young man in MacEwen's *Returning from Work*, and it creates a mental connection between him and the woman at left. This is a very minimal allusion to what could possibly develop into a romantic plot, but it is enough.

MacEwen's scene is patterned on Dutch seventeenth-century genre precedents, such as interiors by Pieter de Hooch. However, if we take a look at a specific seventeenth-century painting with a similar topic, we may be able to refine our understanding of the particularities of MacEwen's nineteenth-century version of the theme. The seventeenth-century artist Nicolaes Maes's *The Lacemaker* (fig. 22) shows one woman absorbed in her task. This lace maker interacts neither with us, the viewers, nor with anybody else within the picture. She is self-contained. The scene is entirely descriptive; no narrative element intrudes. The print on the wall, showing a male portrait, may possibly represent the woman's husband, but no causal connection is explicitly set up between his likeness and her lace-making. The stillness of Maes's woman and the descriptive attention paid to the objects displayed in the interior evoke the universal or static quality of generic time.

In her study of Dutch art, art historian Svetlana Alpers famously contrasts narrative with descriptive painting, and distinguishes the seventeenth-century Dutch

Fig. 22. Nicolaes Maes, *The Lacemaker,* 1655, oil on oak, 22½ × 17¼", National Gallery of Canada, Ottawa, Ontario.

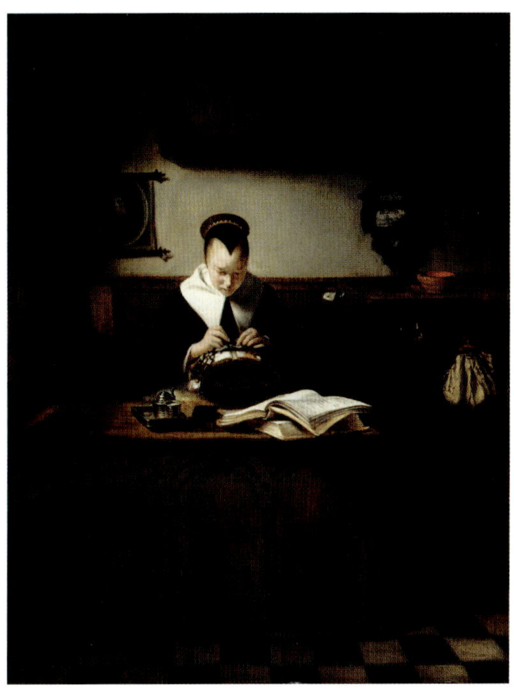

"descriptive" mode of picture-making from that of pictorial narration indebted to the Italian Renaissance. The author also makes a connection between realism and description in her discussion: "'Descriptive' is . . . one way of characterizing many of those works that we are accustomed to refer to casually as *realistic.*"[27] Alpers's point about description being aligned with realism can be linked to Roland Barthes's argument about the reality effect. Barthes develops his points with respect to nineteenth-century literature, not painting, but his case can, arguably, be used to understand nineteenth-century painting as well. Barthes argues that a surfeit of seemingly insignificant and narratively "useless" items works to produce a "reality effect."[28] Because the described things appear to have no bearing on the plot, we, the readers, interpret them to signify "reality." Maes's picture, and Dutch seventeenth-century genre paintings in general, contain such a surfeit of seemingly irrelevant detail. In recent decades, the "realism" of Dutch genre paintings of the Golden Age has been controversially debated, but for the nineteenth century, their verisimilitude was unquestioned. It is notable to what extent MacEwen has evacuated descriptive detail from both *The Lacemakers* and *Returning from Work.* The minimal quality of the interior in the former and the landscape in the latter help to focus viewers' attention on the narrative element. The bare floorboards and unadorned walls of *The Lacemakers* signify, on the one hand, a plain and non-luxurious lifestyle, one associated by Americans in particular with the austere virtues of Protestantism,[29] and on the other hand, this plain interior does not detract the eye from the exchange of glances among the human protagonists. In Maes's seventeenth-century painting, by contrast, we are constantly enticed to stray from the central figure and let our eyes roam across the surfaces of pot, bowl, cloth, or pouch.

Barthes contrasts descriptive detail with narrative flow; for him, narrative is essentially temporal and predictive whereas description's structure is "purely additive."[30] Nothing *happens* in time in description. In this sense, Maes's picture is more akin to Singer's *Heathland* than to MacEwen's *Lacemakers.* In both the paintings by Maes and Singer, we are presented with a situation but there is little sense of "before" or "after," of causality, or of "what will happen next?" MacEwen's *Lacemakers,* by contrast, provides a strong stimulus for questions such as "what will the man say?" or "what is the woman going to do?" or even "what is everybody thinking?" We are invited to speculate about these figures' actions, their motivations and their inner lives. In other words, we are invited to turn the depicted figures into *characters,* in a process that does not apply to the woman in Maes's *Lacemaker,* let alone the sheep in Singer's *Heathland.*

NARRATIVES OF INNER LIFE

Toward the end of the nineteenth century, pictorial narrative turned increasingly inward. Dramatic plots were replaced with quiet scenes verging on the non-narrative. Carl Eugene Mulertt's *Fishergirl by the Old Church, Katwijk* (1910; cat. 48) focuses almost entirely on the inner life of the girl depicted in the foreground. She stands in profile, cropped at mid-chest, and gazes out beyond the picture's edge at left. In the middle- and background, we see two bonneted women before a looming church tower and some cottages. A sandy path, of the kind familiar from pictures by MacEwen and Singer, connects the foreground girl visually with the distant women.

Nothing happens here. There is no romantic subplot and no overt exchange of glances. We do not see the girl's body, so we cannot discover what her posture or gestures may be. All we see is her rather intent gaze into the unseen distance. Viewers on the lookout for plot (and particularly viewers used to nineteenth-century narrative pictures) may well pose some sort of connection between the women and the girl in front. The narratologist Shlomith Rimmon-Kenan suggests that causality could often, if not always, be projected onto temporality.[31] In pictorial terms, temporality can be translated into spatial juxtaposition. The women and the girl in Mulertt's painting are connected spatially, and this leads us to assume a causal connection, however tenuous, between the two figurative elements. All three figures are linked to the church by similar devices of juxtaposition. To today's viewers, it may seem easy, if far-fetched, to posit a whole series of speculative narrative connections: Did the girl transgress religious convention in some way, as did the sleeping girl in Melchers's *The Sermon*? Is the girl on the brink of womanhood, soon to be welcomed into the folds of adulthood and the church? It should be pointed out that such narrative speculations did not seem far-fetched to contemporary audiences. By 1910, however, when Mulertt's picture was painted, the overriding narrative impulse of the late nineteenth century had been muted by both the developments within art toward antinarrative abstraction, and by audiences' defection from painting toward other forms of narrative entertainment, notably comic strips and the movies. Mulertt's painting represented a late phase of story-telling painting, a phase when stories turned subjective.

Faced with Mulertt's *Fishergirl by the Old Church, Katwijk*, we speculate not so much about what will happen next as about the thoughts going through the characters' minds. To be sure, narrative speculation about mental operations had been present in earlier plot pictures as well, but in Mulertt's picture this comes to the fore. His painting is akin to subjective narrations such as John William Godward's

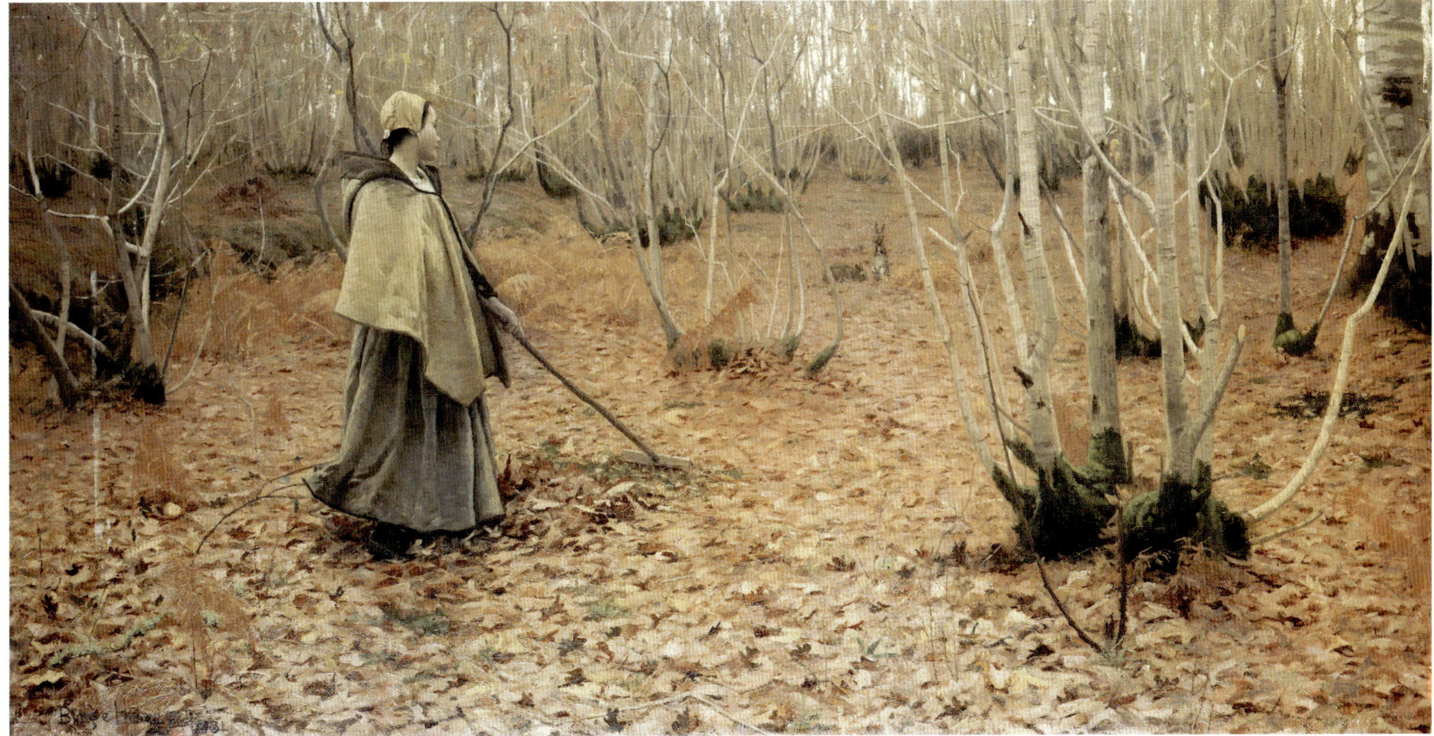

Fig. 23. Birge Harrison, *November*, 1881, oil on canvas, 52 × 97⅝", Musée des Beaux-Arts, Rennes, France.

Memories (1892, Art Gallery, Auckland, New Zealand), Birge Harrison's *November* (fig. 23), or Alexander Harrison's *Castles in Spain* (c. 1882, Metropolitan Museum of Art, New York). These pictures show one figure in a natural setting, gazing into space and lost in reverie. External narrative clues are extremely minimal: a rabbit to look at; a stalk of grass to chew on. The narratologist Mieke Bal's discussion of "focalization" may help us in deciphering what can possibly be going on here at the level of story or plot.[32]

In stories, we must differentiate between the narrator and the focalizor.[33] The narrator tells the story; the focalizor is the character through whose eyes we see the story. The narrator is not necessarily part of the story itself; the focalizor always is. In visual images, such as Mulertt's or Melchers's, we are invited to think our way into the thoughts of a main protagonist. In Melchers's *The Sermon,* the old woman looking at the sleeping girl functions as a kind of focalizor; we are encouraged to see the events through the old woman's eyes.[34] Mulertt's *Fishergirl* functions in a similar way; we are, it could be argued, invited to see the scene through her eyes. We could even conjecture that the landscape is slightly out of focus not because of the "realism" of any actual mist but because of the dreamy nature of the girl's thoughts. It is, perhaps, in *her* mind that the church looms large and that the women take on a strangely important role with their billowing dresses and undefined faces. Mulertt's style is itself not the precise, descriptively neutral style of earlier painters but partakes a little of concurrent experiments with facture and distortion. These distortions are not represented, however, as technical experimentation but as narrative expressions of the protagonist's inner thought processes.

Mulertt's *Fishergirl* is focalized narration. It has its forebears in such pictures as Nourse's *On the Dyke at Volendam,* Stanley's *Girl Carrying Sheaves,* and Walter Castle Keith's *Beach Scene* (1905; cat. 29). All of these paintings contain female figures, not doing much in particular. The idleness of the women and girls in Nourse's and Keith's paintings is accounted for by the fact that they are waiting for their menfolk who have gone to sea, fishing. In this sense, the pictures are highly dramatic, as they deal with the threat of death and drowning, although not much action is shown explicitly. Wind and waves are outward expressions of the women's internal worries as much as they are causal indications for a narrative of possible drowning. The anxiety about a possibly grim fate is located within the women's heads. Stanley's peasant girl is presented as working in the fields, and arguably this is not a state of reverie. However, she is shown as a "creature of nature," and her labor is represented as an activity that is at one with her natural environment.

In this sense, it may be seen how pictures of reverie could grow out of the depiction of peasants and fisherfolk in nature, which, in turn, grew out of notions of agrarian workers leading a more "natural" life than their modern urban counterparts.

CONCLUSION

Rural imagery does not appear to lend itself to grand narrative. However, as we have seen, minimal narratives and plots that work with little exterior activity but with great dramatic impact were inserted into what otherwise seem to be scenes of unchanging and premodern rural life and nature. Nineteenth-century painters and their middle-class urban audiences were anxious to shore up the encroachment of modernity and preserve agrarian locations as places of untouched, "timeless" nature. However, the historicism of nineteenth-century modernity inevitably crept into pictures of generic agrarian timelessness, in the guise of minimal narratives. In the painting of rural narratives, the pressures to narrate entertaining tales to a story-seeking mass audience collided with the paradigms available to view and experience uncorrupted nature, and this collision resulted in a productive tension that informs nineteenth-century paintings of rural life.

NOTES

1. Nina Lübbren, *Rural Artists' Colonies in Europe, 1870–1910* (New Brunswick, N.J.: Rutgers University Press, 2001). I thank Annette Stott for her astute and thoughtful comments on the penultimate draft of this essay.

2. Nina Lübbren, "North to South: Paradigm Shifts in European Art and Tourism, 1880–1920," in *Visual Culture and Tourism*, ed. David Crouch and Nina Lübbren (Oxford: Berg, 2003).

3. See *The Hague School: Dutch Masters of the Nineteenth Century*, ed. Ronald de Leeuw, John Sillevis, and Charles Dumas (The Hague: Gemeentemuseum, London: Royal Academy of Arts, and Paris: Grand Palais, 1983).

4. See examples in Lübbren, *Rural Artists' Colonies*.

5. Gérard Genette, *Narrative Discourse: An Essay in Method* (Ithaca, N.Y.: Cornell University Press, 1980); Gerald Prince, "Revisiting Narrativity," in *Grenzüberschreitungen: Narratologie im Kontex/Transcending Boundaries: Narratology in Context*, ed. Walter Grünzweig and Andreas Solbach (Tübingen: Gunter Narr Verlag, 1999); Shlomith Rimmon-Kenan, *Narrative Fiction: Contemporary Poetics* (New York: Methuen, 1983). See also David Lodge, *The Art of Fiction* (Harmondsworth, Middlesex: Penguin, 1992).

6. A short selection: Franz von Defregger, *Courtship (Brautwerbung)* (c. 1889, Essen, Villa Hügel), reproduced in Doris Edler, *Vergessene Bilder: Die deutsche Genremalerei in den letzten Jahrzehnten des 19. Jahrhunderts und ihre Rezeption durch Kunstkritik und Publikum* (Münster and Hamburg: Lit Verlag, 1992), fig. 85; Marcus Stone, *Love at First Sight*, reproduced in Philip Hook and Mark Poltimore, *Popular 19th Century Painting: A Dictionary of European Genre Painters* (Woodbridge, Suffolk: Antique Collectors' Club, 1986), 320; Johann Hamza, *The Curious Hunter (Der neugierige Jäger)* (private collection, Vienna), reproduced in Heinrich Fuchs, *Die österreichischen Maler des 19. Jahrhunderts* (Vienna: Dr. Heinrich Fuchs, self-published, 1972), 133; Max Volkhart, *The Eavesdropper*, reproduced in Hook and Poltimore, *Popular 19th Century Painting*, 169; Ilya Repin, *Preparations for the Exam (The Blown Kiss)* (1864, The Russian Museum, St. Petersburg); Edmund Blair Leighton, *My Next-Door Neighbour* (1894), reproduced in Hook and Poltimore, *Popular 19th Century Painting*, 322.

7. Annette Stott, *Holland Mania: The Unknown Dutch Period in American Art and Culture* (Woodstock, N.Y.: Overlook Press, 1989), 51–52, 101–2, 133–35. On Dutch genre painting as the epitome of all genre painting, see *Genremalerei*, ed. Barbara Gaehtgens (Berlin: Reimer, 2002).

8. Arthur G. Bell, "Letters from Artists.—Sketching Grounds, No. 2.—Holland," *The Studio* 1, no. 3 (1893): 117.

9. One rare example is Adriaen van Ostade's print *Village Romance* (c. 1667, Harris Schrank Fine Prints). This image, however, does not so much tell a ministory as show a representative illustration of "love" (or "lust," depending on one's interpretation). Arguably, Ostade's print (and similar seventeenth-century representations of couples) demonstrates an emotion or illustrates commonly held adages about the nature of sexual affection. These pictures do not tell a story in the manner of nineteenth-century anecdotes of courtship.

10. I owe some of my thinking on this topic to Patricia Mainardi's stimulating paper, "Historical Landscape: The 'Other' History Painting," given at the College Art Association's annual conference in Atlanta, Georgia, 2005.

11. Michael Clarke, *Corot and the Art of Landscape* (London: British Museum Press, 1991), 56–7; Peter Galassi, *Corot on Italy: Open-Air Painting and the Classical Landscape Tradition* (New Haven, Conn.: Yale University Press, 1991), 81. Further discussion in my PhD diss., "Rural Artists' Colonies in Nineteenth-Century Europe," University of Leeds, "Excursus: Corot and Barbizon."

12. To be sure, vestiges of historical landscapes persisted into the late nineteenth century, for example, Fritz von Uhde's *The Hard Path (The Road to Bethlehem)* (1890, Neue Pinakothek, Munich) which transposes Joseph and Mary looking for an inn to the contemporary rural setting of the Bavarian village of Dachau, or George Hitchcock's *Maternité (Maternity)* (1889; cat. 24) with its thinly disguised halo-as-winnowing basket hovering around the head of a mother holding a baby and making her way through the dunes near Egmond.

13. Will Hicok Low, *A Chronicle of Friendships, 1873–1900* (London: Hodder and Stoughton, 1908), 125.

14. Robert Louis Stevenson, Barbizon, letter to Frances Sitwell, April 1875, in *The Letters of Robert Louis Stevenson*, ed. Bradford A. Booth and Ernest Mehew, vol. 2, April 1874–July 1879 (New Haven, Conn.: Yale University Press, 1994), 127, letter no. 376.

15. Lübbren, *Rural Artists' Colonies*, chapter 5, "Landscapes of Immersion."

16. See Robert L. Herbert, "City vs. Country: The Rural Image in French Painting from Millet to Gauguin," *Artforum* 8 (1970): 44–55; Nicholas Green, *The Spectacle of Nature: Landscape and Bourgeois Culture in Nineteenth-Century France* (Manchester: Manchester University Press, 1990); John Urry, *Sociology Beyond Societies: Mobilities for the Twenty-first Century* (New York: Routledge, 2000), chapter 6, "Dwellings."

17. Brueghel's paintings of the seasons: *The Gloomy Day (February), The Return of the Herd, Hunters in the Snow* (all 1565, Kunsthistorisches Museum, Vienna); *Haymaking* (1565, National Gallery, Prague); *The Harvesters* (1565, Metropolitan Museum of Art, New York).

18. On Laren as a tourist resort, see Lübbren, *Rural Artists' Colonies*.

19. For a sociological/theological perspective on Vautier's picture, see Stefan König, "Calvinistischer Heilsaspekt und ideale Gemeinschaft: Benjamin Vautiers 'Andächtige in der Dorfkirche'," *Kunst + Architektur* 45, no. 4 (1994): 354–60.

20. Reprinted as Roland Barthes, "On the Reality Effect in Descriptions," in *Realism*, ed. Lilian R. Furst (Harlow: Longman, 1992), 135–41; originally published as "L'effet de réel," *Communications* 11 (1968): 84–89.

21. Ronald van Vleuten, "Egmond Remembers Gari Melchers," in *Gari Melchers: A Retrospective Exhibition*, ed. Diane Lesko and Esther Persson (St. Petersburg, Fla.: Museum of Fine Arts, 1990), 162–63.

22. "The human figure is the most potent of all introduced objects and therefore an element that needs to be handled with great care. The figure draws the eye, and can easily dominate the view, so that even a tiny figure on the horizon is a counterpoint for a towering landscape." John Hedgecoe, *Practical Landscape Photography: A Complete Guide to Creative Techniques* (New York: Simon and Schuster, 1988), 86–87.

23. For example, Frank Bramley's *A Hopeless Dawn* (1889, Tate Britain, London), or Adolf Echtler, *A Family's Ruin* (c. 1883, Staatliche Kunstsammlungen Dresden, Gemäldegalerie Neue Meister, Dresden); reproduced in Aleksa Celebonovic, *The Heyday of Salon Painting: Masterpieces of Bourgeois Realism* (London: Thames and Hudson, 1974), 149, show scenes of bereavement, gambling, and emotional turmoil. These rural scenes, however, are tame in comparison with examples such as Jean-Léon Gérôme's grisly *Christian Martyrs' Last Prayer* (1863–83, Walters Art Gallery, Baltimore) or Jakub Schikaneder's disturbing *Murder in the House* (1890, National Gallery, Prague).

24. Some examples: Karl Theodor von Piloty, *Seni with the Corpse of Wallenstein* (1855, Neue Pinakothek, Munich); Jean-Léon Gérôme, *The Death of Caesar* (1867, Walters Art Gallery, Baltimore); Henri Regnault, *Execution without Trial among the Caliphs of Granada* (1870, Musée d'Orsay, Paris).

25. On the theme of fisherfolk, see Nina Lübbren, "'Toilers of the Sea': Fisherfolk and the Geographies of Tourism in England, 1880–1900," in *The Geographies of English Art: Landscape and the National Past in English Art 1880–1940*, ed. David Peters Corbett, Ysanne Holt, and Fiona Russell (New Haven, Conn.: Yale University Press, 2000).

26. Exceptions prove the rule. Rural crime is a theme, for example, in Ludwig Knaus's *Funeral Procession in the Forest* (1856, Arnot Art Museum, Elmira, New York) and in Benjamin Vautier's *An Arrest* (c. 1882, whereabouts unknown), reproduced in *Die Kunst für Alle*, 4 (1888–89): 214.

27. Svetlana Alpers, *The Art of Describing: Dutch Art in the Seventeenth Century* (Chicago: University of Chicago Press, 1983), xxi. See also Alpers, "Describe or Narrate? A Problem in Realistic Representation," *New Literary History* 8, no. 1 (1976): 15–41.

28. Barthes, "On the Reality Effect in Descriptions," 140.

29. See Annette Stott, "American Painters Who Worked in the Netherlands, 1880–1914" (PhD diss., Boston University, 1986), 29–30.

30. Barthes, "On the Reality Effect in Descriptions," 136.

31. Rimmon-Kenan, *Narrative Fiction*, 18.

32. Mieke Bal, *Narratology: Introduction to the Theory of Narrative*, 2nd ed. (Toronto: University of Toronto Press, 1997), part 2, chapter 7, "Focalization."

33. See Bal, *Narratology*; Genette, *Narrative Discourse*.

34. It may be argued that we remain at the same time outside of the woman's take on events. Viewers do not necessarily share the woman's slight disapproval and are perhaps more inclined to feel sympathy toward the sleeping girl. These ambiguities, though, simply highlight the subtle and complex multilayeredness of nineteenth-century pictorial narration.

Thanks are due to Holly Koons McCullough and Annette Stott for their helpful suggestions, and to Michelle Bolton King for her thorough reading and editing of this text.

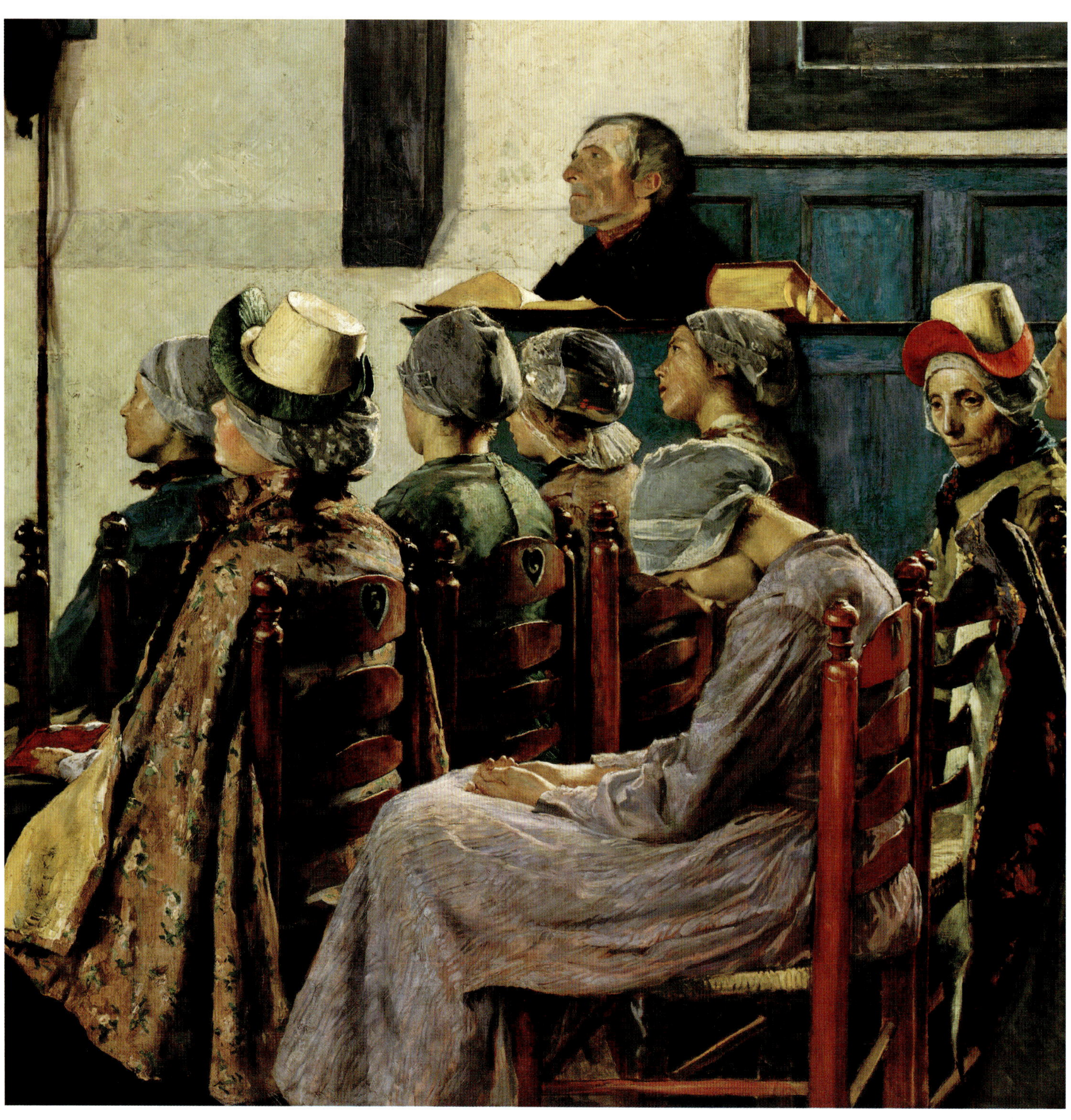

The Egmond School of American Impressionism

Annette Stott

IN THE 1880S, A SMALL GROUP OF AMERICAN PAINTERS with summer studios in Egmond, North Holland, attracted notice at exhibitions in Paris, London, New York, and Berlin. Led by George Hitchcock and Gari Melchers, this remote artists' colony became an international phenomenon.[1] The art of Egmond was very much in tune with the trends of the time: the rise of *plein air* painting, impressionist concern with color and light, the emergence of professional women artists, the supremacy of oil painting challenged by watercolor and etching revivals, the pull of Arts and Crafts values, the use of large canvases to gain notice at Paris Salons, the appeal of narrative within academic realism, and the tug-of-war between the cosmopolitan sophistication to which artists aspired and the rural peasantry that they studied. From Egmond arose a Dutch-subject art that embodied both conservative and progressive American values and impacted modernist color theories in the United States. With historical hindsight we might call this the Egmond School of American Impressionism, a title that is not unproblematic.

Egmond presents the first conundrum—a single word to describe three villages, each of which played a different role in the history of the artists' colony. In the period 1881–84 when the American painter George Hitchcock first saw it, Egmond aan Zee was a remote Dutch fishing village on the Atlantic shore with a small, mixed Catholic and Protestant population and one hotel, the Zeezicht. Hitchcock always took credit for discovering and popularizing Egmond among artists. He had a stone building erected on a dune overlooking the sea, into which he and his wife moved and which he shared as a studio with fellow American Gari Melchers. All three became official residents of Egmond aan Zee on December 17, 1884, according to the Registry of Residents.[2] Within two years, Melchers was painting pictures in the Protestant church at Egmond Binnen, a few miles southeast of Egmond aan Zee. Hitchcock had also traveled inland to paint his first pictures in a flower field. Their large exhibition canvases prompted other artists to seek out Egmond aan Zee, which was becoming a popular spot for German and British vacationers, with more pensions and hotels appearing each year. As the character of Egmond aan Zee changed, Hitchcock and Melchers moved inland to Egmond aan den Hoef about 1891. More agricultural than seafaring, the Hoef inspired figurative compositions and floral landscapes. All three Egmonds provided lodging and models for painters as the colony grew, but Egmond aan den Hoef became its heart and the place where both Hitchcock and Melchers would eventually own homes. Egmond Binnen figured in the pictures of the Egmond colony more than in colony life.

School has two distinct meanings in art: an educational establishment and a group of artists with a recognizable style. Egmond became an art school in both senses of the word. Students came here from the American art schools in Cleveland, Chicago, New York, and Boston—most often via schools in Paris—to study formally

Detail of cat. 37

with George Hitchcock and less officially with Gari Melchers during the summer. In time, Hitchcock's students came from many other countries, as well. When Hitchcock left the colony in 1904 or 1905, others stepped in to teach, as reported by a local newspaper, which noted that a Belgian painter was offering lessons in a house in Egmond aan Zee and had already secured six students at the end of August, 1905.[3] Melchers generally refused to take pupils before Hitchcock defected, but granted spontaneous critiques to some of the artists working around town and inspired many to call him their teacher. In all, perhaps a hundred painters and photographers studied in Egmond.

The other notion of a school of art indicates a unity of subject, content, and style. In Egmond, this can be seen not only in the way that Hitchcock and Melchers influenced one another and their pupils, but in the general stylistic development from academic gray-brown seascapes and figure paintings of poor fisherfolk to brighter, more impressionistic paintings of colorful flower fields and richly costumed women, to cosmopolitan interiors lacking any sense of Dutchness beyond an obvious formal debt to Vermeer. Although they changed over time, the style and subjects of Egmond were relatively unified at each point in its history.

American is a problematic term by definition, since it refers equally to a country and two continents, but in the context of the Egmond School it is even more complicated. Before 1900 at least three Dutch painters were living or working in the Egmond area and the colony eventually attracted the Scottish painter Fanny G. Plimsoll, Irish landscapist Edward L. Lawrenson, Canadians Henry E. Dey and Montague Castle, Londoners James Jebusa Shannon and Florence Kate Upton, Germans Heinrich Heimes and Hans Hermann, the French painter Ernest Noir, Russian Varvara de Wesselitsky, and others.[4] Simply by surveying the titles of paintings exhibited in the Paris Salons between 1890 and 1905, one finds evidence of this international contingent. Even the colony's founders, although firmly rooted in the country of their birth, became cosmopolitan expatriates. Gari Melchers moved among studios in Paris, Berlin, Egmond, New York, and Chicago; exhibited annually throughout Europe and the United States; and won much acclaim abroad. When the young Virginian Corinne Mackall sailed to Europe in 1902, she recorded her fellow passengers by name and city of origin, listing Melchers as a resident of "the world."[5] Clearly, the Egmond colony contained an international element on several levels.

Yet despite this seeming internationalism, the Egmond School was thoroughly American in spirit and character. Not only were Melchers and Hitchcock born, raised, and initially trained in the United States, but they thought of themselves as representatives of that country everywhere they went. Both took charge of organizing American artists abroad for international exhibitions. The paintings they created were sometimes criticized in their native land as too foreign, but more often found acceptance as representative of the best modern "American" art. Most of the international contingent in Egmond also had strong ties to the United States. The Montreal-born Henry Dey actually made his reputation as an illustrator for *Life Magazine* in New York City, where he became a naturalized American citizen and visualized American life for others. Upton was born and raised in the state of New York with only brief trips to England to visit relatives before she turned eighteen. She continued thereafter to make trips to the United States, where her genre paintings generally found their homes. Shannon was also born and spent his early childhood in the United States before moving to Canada and then to England to study art. American critics such as Christian Brinton continued to claim Shannon as an American during the period he worked in Egmond. Cecil Jay, a young British miniature painter who came to Egmond to study with Hitchcock in 1903, was perhaps the least American of all, and even she ended up marrying George Hitchcock and exhibiting regularly in the United States. The founders of the colony and the vast majority of students were American by birth, training, and attitude, and they participated in the internationalism of their age.

Impressionism is a category of art so distinctive that the general public has little difficulty recognizing it, yet recent art historical scholarship has revealed how problematic this label is. American impressionism has been claimed as a subcategory differing from French impressionism in its greater emphasis on the figure and lesser concern with the scientific examination of light or the modernity of urban life.[6] The Egmond School commenced, thoroughly steeped in the academic realist and naturalist movements of the Parisian and Düsseldorf art worlds with a strong dash of the Hague School thrown in. From this and ongoing avant-garde French influences, combined with Hitchcock's and Melchers's tendency to experiment with intuitive color combinations, it grew into its own particular brand of impressionism and post-impressionism. It was more closely allied with American than French versions of impressionism as we now understand them, but very clearly indebted to the latter. As Melchers once said: "We should thank Monet for the good he did in teaching us to view things with clear eyes."[7] In addition to concerns with sunlight and color, several Egmond artists paid close attention to broad flat color applications that owe less to typical impressionist brushwork and more to a strong tradition of illustration and decorative art. To call all of this impressionism stretches the definition, but captures the Egmond artists' central concern with light and color. With this understanding in place, we can embark upon an exploration of the Egmond School of American Impressionism.

ORIGINS AND EARLY YEARS IN THE EGMOND COLONY

George Hitchcock traveled in the Netherlands in 1880, signing the visitor's book at the Frans Hals Museum, Haarlem, in September that year; again in May 1881; and in May 1884. It is not clear exactly when he first came to Egmond, but he was there by the summer of 1884. During these years, the Hague School had a pronounced influence on Hitchcock. He frequently painted marine subjects in watercolors, exhibiting with both the New York Water Color Club and the American Watercolor Society. Some of the beach scenes he painted in Scheveningen and Katwijk feature women and children waiting on the shore or gathering and selling shellfish. Once in Egmond, he continued to focus on marine subjects, emulating the famous Hague School painter Hendrik Willem Mesdag despite the Dutchman's apparent rejection of Hitchcock as a pupil. After Hitchcock became a well-established artist, he enjoyed recounting variations on the story: "Mesdag told me very crudely . . . that though I might some day draw well, I should never be able to paint. At his advice I turned my back on Holland and tried Paris."[8] An article in a regional Dutch newspaper that could only have originated with Hitchcock noted that the artist received instruction from Mesdag, who was of the opinion that Hitchcock would never become a landscape painter and advised him to try portrait painting.[9] Most other sources record Hitchcock as Mesdag's pupil, but after 1888 Hitchcock himself only named the French artists Gustave Boulanger and Jules Lefebvre at the Académie Julian as his teachers.[10] On the other hand, Hitchcock and Mesdag exhibited some "Dutch Motives" together in London—along with Melchers, Bernardus Johannes Blommers, and a few other Dutch artists—at the Gladwell Gallery in the early 1880s.[11] Whatever the truth of their personal relationship, when Hitchcock first came to Egmond, he focused on pictures of fishing boats riding the Egmond surf, atmospheric beach scenes, and tonal seascapes that owe quite a lot to Mesdag's marine paintings.

Melchers also admired the modern Dutch painters, with whom he was on friendly terms. Having studied first with his German-born wood-carver father in Detroit and then from 1877 until the spring of 1881 at the Royal Academy of Fine

Arts in Düsseldorf, followed by a shorter period in the École des Beaux-Arts in Paris, Melchers's early work in Holland evinced strong connections with German art, tempered by influence from French and Dutch peasant painters.[12] Melchers's 1886 Salon picture *The Sermon* (1886; cat. 37) announced Egmond to the international art community. He set *The Sermon* in the Dutch Reformed church in Egmond Binnen and painted many more Protestant pictures through the years, such as *The Communion* (1887, Cornell University), *The Offertory* (private collection), and *Easter Sunday* (1910–11; cat. 45). Religion would become an important aspect of the Egmond School, visible in the symbolic use of peasants as Madonnas, contemporary church scenes, biblical subjects in which Egmonders served as models, and pictures of Jesus and various saints.

The Sermon also offered a bit of humorous narrative, something Melchers excelled at. Unlike the engrossed parishioners surrounding them, the two central figures appear to be paying no attention to the words of the unseen preacher. The young woman in the foreground bows her head and the older woman near her turns sharply to regard her, whether in concern or disapproval depends on whether the viewer interprets the young woman's posture as an expression of grief, devotion, or sleep. Melchers left the construction of the narrative to his viewer with characteristic ambivalence. The consensus among American, French, and Belgian viewers seems to have been very positive, regardless of the particular interpretation.[13] Melchers's palette of turquoise applied in broad swaths with accents of red and yellow also made a strong visual statement.

The attention gained for Egmond by *The Sermon* in Paris expanded the next year when Hitchcock experienced his first important Salon success with *La Culture des Tulipes* (*Tulip Culture*, 1887, private collection). This painting represented a turning point for Hitchcock away from the lower key atmospheric tones of the Hague School toward an exploration of harmonious color combinations in sunlight. It was one of a series of paintings exploring bulb horticulture, some of which Hitchcock labeled "opus" and numbered. An opus is a "work," or more commonly, a series of musical compositions, numbered in the order in which they are presented. Hitchcock's 1887 *The Tulip Garden*, inscribed "op. 33," is similar to *La Culture des Tulipes* in its subject of a woman standing in the middle of beds of yellow, pink, and white tulips. His

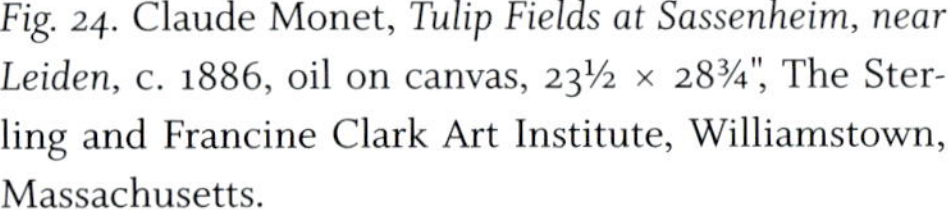

Fig. 24. Claude Monet, *Tulip Fields at Sassenheim, near Leiden*, c. 1886, oil on canvas, 23½ × 28¾", The Sterling and Francine Clark Art Institute, Williamstown, Massachusetts.

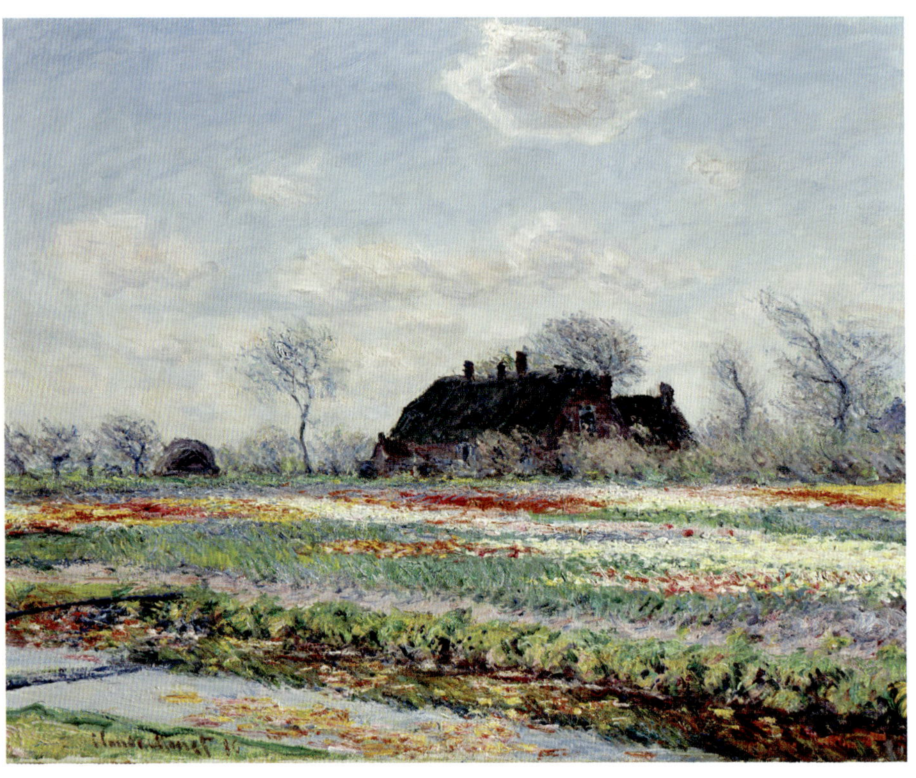

opus 35, *Flower Girl in Holland* (fig. 1, p. xx), depicts a woman standing in the road selling tulips from buckets suspended on her shoulder yoke to an unseen resident of the house named *Overslot* for its location across a small moat from the Egmond castle ruins.[14] *Overslot* became a favorite spot for artists to paint, and *Flower Girl in Holland* became Hitchcock's best known and loved painting in the United States through its reproduction in prints. The excitement generated by *La Culture des Tulipes* and expressed in rapturous reviews was so great that W. H. Tailer cabled his offer of $5,000 and bought the picture out of the exhibition, sight unseen.

Claude Monet had already visited Holland several times before Hitchcock and Melchers arrived there. He spent five months painting waterscapes and windmills at Zaandam in 1871, probably returning in 1872 and 1874. Then in 1886, Monet traveled to The Hague at the invitation of a friend of a friend, specifically to paint the tulip fields. He produced at least five brightly colored bulb field pictures, exhibiting them at the prominent Georges Petit Gallery in Paris in May 1886 (fig. 24). It is quite possible that Hitchcock saw Monet's bulb field paintings there and was inspired to try his hand at this unusual subject.[15] Monet used some of the strongest colors and most violent juxtapositions of his career in his attempts to capture the bright hues of what he described as "enormous fields in full flower . . . [that] drive the poor painter mad: they are unrenderable with our poor colours."[16] Hitchcock took a more conservative approach the next year when he painted *La Culture des Tulipes* with blended stokes and more subdued, yet still bright color to suggest the experience of viewing the flowers through a humid atmosphere. He struck the right note to avoid the criticisms that Monet's avant-garde approach evoked.

Then in 1888, Hitchcock turned in quite a different direction. He traveled to London, Paris, and Florence to study and make copies of Botticelli's Madonnas, which he published in an article about the Italian Renaissance painter at the end of the year. Hitchcock admired Botticelli's drawing, his color, and his naturalism, excusing the stylized flowers and gold leaf halos as requirements of his Catholic patrons or holdovers from Byzantine art. Convinced that Botticelli studied many of his figures in the open air, Hitchcock copied Botticelli's paintings in an attempt to improve his own work with the figure. Hitchcock claimed that Botticelli painted contemporary Italian models as they really looked, and admired these images of "the purest and most perfect type of womanly beauty," writing, "his creations of the Madonna are more perfect in piety, more Christian in sentiment, and more truthful in detailed perfection than any the world has ever seen."[17] In his own work, Hitchcock attempted increasingly to express these same ideas, but with greater naturalism. *Maternité (Maternity)* (1889; cat. 24) represents a Dutch woman walking through the dunes with a winnowing basket on her back that forms a natural halo. The child at her side and baby in her arms allude to Jesus and John. Comparison of Hitchcock's copy of Botticelli's Louvre *Madonna* (fig. 25) with his own *Magnificat (Annunciation)* (1894; cat. 25) shows the extent of Botticelli's influence. Both place the female figure in a shallow picture plane in front of a hedge. One major difference is Hitchcock's decision to turn his subject's eyes up to heaven in the song of praise referenced by the title. He may have adapted this rapt gaze from Jules Bastien-Lepage, whose *Joan of Arc* critics had greeted with enthusiasm nine years before. The same gaze appears in many of his later paintings, including *St. Genevieve*, a haloed Dutch shepherdess among her sheep on a flower-dotted hillside, and *The Last Moments of Sappho* (Indianapolis Museum of Art). One critic called this expression "refined, ethereal beauty, quite different from the placid, matter-of-fact type that appears in the peasant pictures."[18] But Hitchcock's contention that "No man, however great, can paint as Botticelli, without the living and ever-present belief in the truths of Christianity," seems to confirm his desire to express his own faith through paint.[19]

Fig. 25. George Hitchcock, copy after Sandro Botticelli, *Madonna*, 1888, The Louvre. Illustration from Hitchcock, "Sandro Botticelli," in *Scribner's Magazine* 4, no. 6 (December 1888): 716, fig. 25, Courtesy of the Library of Congress, Washington, D.C.

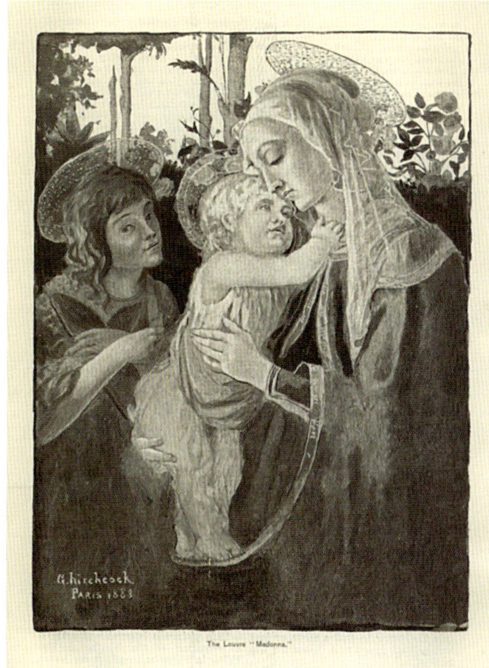

In addition to exhibiting *The Sermon* at the 1886 Salon, Melchers showed the enormous *In Holland* there in 1887 (1887; cat. 38) and *The Pilots* in 1888 (1887–88; cat. 39), and Hitchcock followed his 1887 success, *La Culture des Tulipes*, with *The Annunciation* in 1888 (cat. 25, comparative illustration). In just three years, then, the picturesqueness of the Egmond subjects and the potential of this environment to inspire international success was amply demonstrated to the art world. Hitchcock let it be known in Paris and London that he was available to take pupils and by the summer of 1888 he attracted at least two: Alice Buell and Agnes O'Halloran. He even published a series of enthusiastic articles in *Scribner's Magazine* in 1887, 1889, and 1891, detailing Holland's many paintable qualities as an inducement to other artists. It is probably not pure coincidence that the well-established American cattle painter William Henry Howe, who had painted all over France and Holland, exhibited a new work in the 1889 Salon called *Environs d'Egmond, Holland* (unlocated). For the next twenty years, paintings with Egmond subjects regularly appeared in the Salons, painted by artists from throughout the United States and Europe.

THE EGMOND SCHOOL MATURES

In 1891 the official Egmond Register of Residents recorded Hitchcock's move from Egmond aan Zee to Egmond aan den Hoef. He bought a house named Schuylenburg from the estate of the recently deceased mayor of Egmond and this became the social center of the artists' colony during the next twelve years. While Hitchcock built a new studio at Schuylenburg, Melchers began staying at Bult's inn in Egmond aan den Hoef, but continued to use the studio building in Egmond aan Zee for painting.[20] Bult's was a small tavern with rooms to rent upstairs and it often figured in Egmond paintings after 1890, such as Alice Blair Ring's *Morning Sunshine* (1906; cat. 55) and Melchers's *The Family* (c. 1895; cat. 42).

Another important member of the Egmond School, James Jebusa Shannon, began visiting in the early 1890s at the invitation of George Hitchcock.[21] A renowned portrait painter in London society, Shannon made figurative pictures modeled by family and friends in Egmond. *On the Dunes (Lady Shannon and Kitty)* (c. 1900–10; cat. 59) represents his wife and daughter as tourists relaxing near the beach. His portrait of Hitchcock, exhibited at the Salon of the Société Nationale des Beaux-Arts in 1894 as #1126, *M. George Hitchcock*, may be the painting now called *George Hitchcock* (c. 1895; cat. 58).[22] Like so many other Egmond paintings, it reveals a figure outside in sunlight in the midst of flowers, but in making that figure a painter holding a palette instead of a costumed Dutch woman, Shannon turned the picture into a symbol of the Egmond art colony. The focus on the figure, shallow picture plane, and combination of naturalism with impressionistic interest in the effects of color and light are all characteristic of the Egmond School.

The year after the Telfair acquired this painting, it loaned it as *Portrait of a Painter* to the Corcoran Gallery of Art in Washington, D.C., where the new title apparently stirred its subject to protest. Giving society portraits anonymous titles when they were on exhibition was a widely accepted practice that may not have suited Hitchcock's ego. A note added to correspondence between the Corcoran's director and the Telfair's chairman when the painting was returned says, "It was during the showing of Shannon's picture of Hitchcock at the Corcoran that began Hitchcock's explosion about his name."[23] Thereafter, Hitchcock's name appears once again in the painting's title and the Telfair made a point of correcting the director of the Albright Art Gallery a few years later when she called it *Portrait of a Man*.[24]

Although very close friends, Hitchcock and Melchers appear to have been opposites. Melchers was known for his modesty, geniality, generosity, and kindness. Hitchcock developed a reputation among the Egmonders as a rather wild, party-

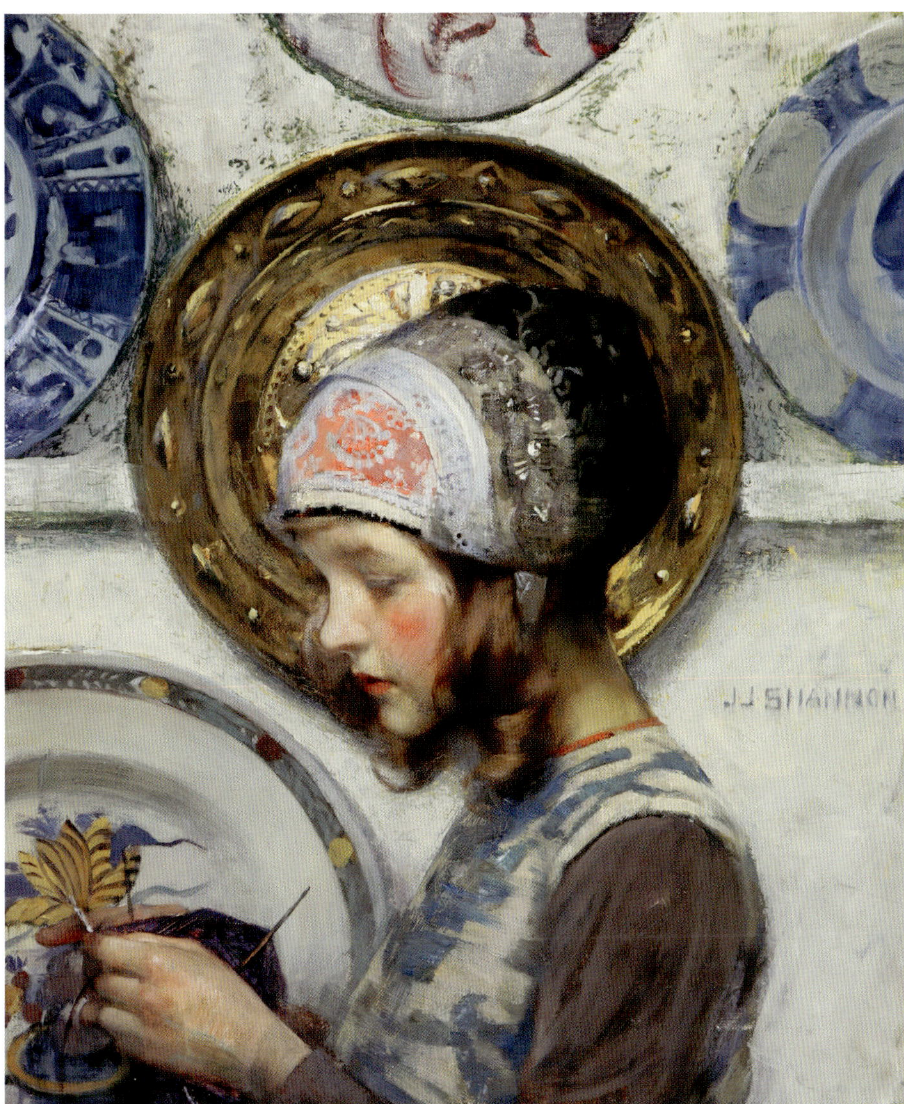

Fig. 26. James Jebusa Shannon, *The Purple Stocking*, c. 1894, oil on canvas, 22 × 18", South African National Gallery, Cape Town.

loving man who kept a racehorse.[25] A ladies' man, Hitchcock had already been accused of running off to Calais with his student Agnes O'Halloran, whom he supposedly got pregnant and abandoned in 1889.[26] Kitty Shannon described Melchers as someone who paid no attention to fashion, ignored his own physical comfort, and had little use for the social graces. Hitchcock dressed so beautifully that the Shannons nicknamed him "Gorgeous," and Kitty reported that "he walked with the most tremendous swagger. My father painted a portrait of him painting."[27] This is the Telfair Museum's *George Hitchcock*.

Many of the Egmond painters shared a love of antiques. Kitty Shannon's memoir describes traveling by horse and carriage with her parents and the Hitchcocks all over the Dutch countryside: "Whole days were spent in picture galleries, churches and bric-a-brac shops."[28] Many of the acquisitions from these journeys ended up as props in Egmond paintings. Shannon's colorful picture of Kitty in Dutch costume knitting, *The Purple Stocking* (fig. 26), shows her head and upper torso in profile against a wall of decorative plates, one of which forms a kind of halo. Melchers painted Henrietta Hitchcock handling a Delft horse from her collection and handing china from an antique cupboard to her Dutch maid. Hitchcock devoted one of his articles on picturesque Holland to bric-a-brac, admiring its "honesty" and "beauty" because it was handmade with great care for structural integrity, usefulness, and aesthetic quality, as opposed to American manufactured products that he considered artificial and ugly. These value judgements reflect an Arts and Crafts notion that an environment of beautiful objects could make one a better person. A local Egmond man, J. Kraakman, erected a building in Egmond aan den Hoef to house his dual businesses, a flourishing antiques trade on the first floor and rental of artist studios on the second. He said he catered exclusively to American and British artists and tourists.[29]

Throughout this period, Hitchcock built on his success with many more figure paintings in floral settings, as well as pure landscapes in meadows, bulb fields, and dunes. His landscapes became steadily more high key in palette and experimental in colors under the influence of French impressionism. *Early Spring in Holland* (c. 1890–1905; cat. 22) and *The Stork's Nest* (c. 1890–1906; cat. 23) are excellent examples of the mature impressionist style on which his fame rested.

STUDENTS

It appears from the names recorded in the local paper, the *Egmond Bad-Bode*, in 1903 that at the school's height Hitchcock may have taught twelve to fifteen students who arrived and departed at different times throughout the summer. Cecil Jay from England, Clara Fuch of Düsseldorf, Emmy Rose from Berlin, and the Americans Adeline Piper, Alice Worthington Ball, Eleanor Bristol Stone, Josephine Grainger Cochrane, Jessie Barrows Jones, Nannie Homans, Alice H. Barrie, Florence Kate Upton, Mr. M. Homelberg, Anna Woodward, Rudolph Loman, and Jane H. Valentine all worked in Egmond that summer and are likely to have made up the class of 1903, Hitchcock's last. The formal instruction in Hitchcock's school consisted of the master setting specific subjects and problems for his pupils, visiting them for critiques where they worked outdoors or in their studios, giving individual lessons on atmosphere and color, and inviting them to his home to talk about art. The students sometimes posed for one another or shared a model for a few hours.

Corinne Mackall's mother described the 1902 class in a letter home: "There are a half dozen students and they all work alone. He makes them do large canvases and [it] is said he is a very fine teacher! Fine on colour and atmosphere. He is a great swell."[30] She went on to describe how her daughter rode her rented bike from Egmond aan Zee, where they were staying, along the brick paved road to the studio she secured in Kraakman's building at the Hoef. Corinne Mackall also called Hitchcock a "swell" who loved to show off his pictures to the students on Sunday afternoons at his home and admired them as if they had been painted by someone

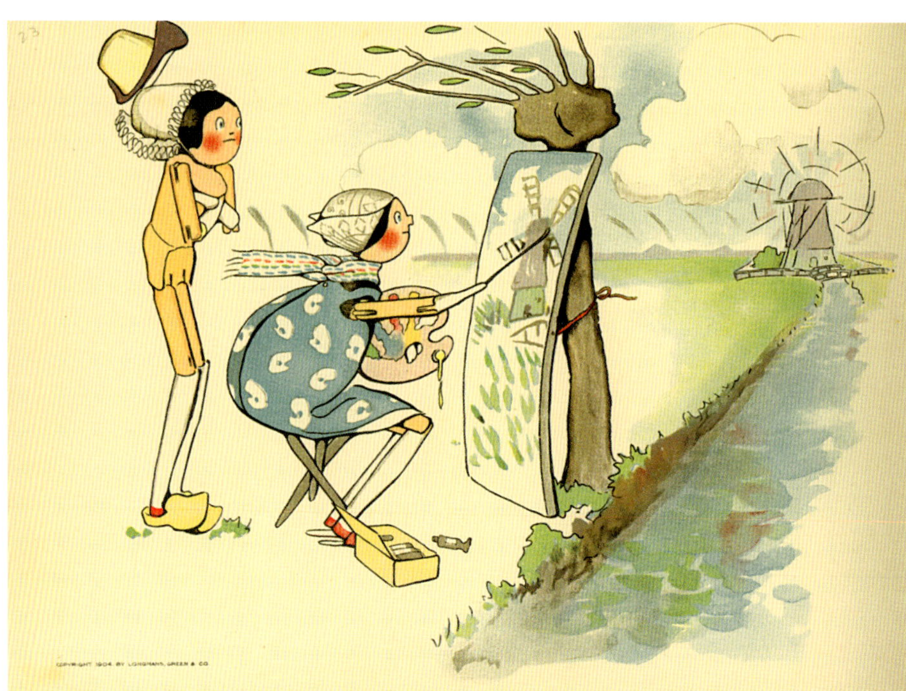

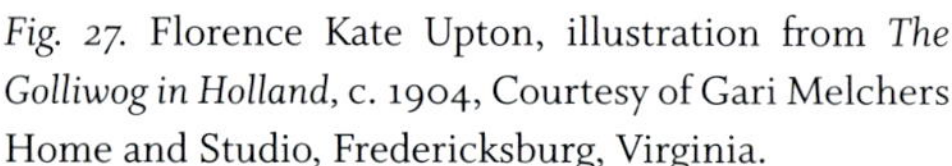

Fig. 27. Florence Kate Upton, illustration from *The Golliwog in Holland*, c. 1904, Courtesy of Gari Melchers Home and Studio, Fredericksburg, Virginia.

else. An inexperienced painter, she disparaged Hitchcock's overwhelming praise of her work, quoting him from a lesson a month after her arrival: "'Remarkable quite incredible talent' 'Wonderful progress!' Can he think I believe him?"[31] She prized Melchers's rare criticisms more highly, perhaps for personal reasons, as she married Melchers the next year. Although suspicious of Hitchcock's hyperbole, Mackall could not help but be flattered by it, and his encouragement and enthusiasm spurred some students on to success.

Hitchcock's insistence on large canvases painted *en plein air* is well documented. Letta Crapo Smith painted *The First Birthday* (1902; cat. 63) on a canvas so big that her neighbor in the Kraakman studio building, Corinne Mackall, had to help her carry it outside. Hitchcock's purpose was to push his pupils beyond their student perspectives and abilities by asking them to make pictures of a size, scale, and quality suitable for major exhibitions. Crapo Smith was forty years old when she painted this picture and already an accomplished artist with over a decade of American and European art training behind her. But most of her experience before entering Hitchcock's class the previous summer had been with smaller crayon studies, pastels, and watercolors, some of which she had exhibited at the Paris Salons and Philadelphia Art Club in the 1890s. It appears to have been Hitchcock's influence that propelled her out of her "drawing" mindset and into the oil painting section of the 1902 Salon with her previous summer's work, *A Daughter of Egmond* (1901, unlocated). Of course, a certain amount of credit reflected back onto the teacher when his purpose succeeded. Crapo Smith's *The First Birthday* was hung "on the line," meaning it was placed in the enviable position of being at eye level, in the Paris Société Nationale des Beaux-Arts Salon of 1903. The committee of the Art Institute of Chicago chose it out of the Salon for their *Sixteenth Annual Exhibition of Oil Painting and Sculpture by American Artists* and it received a bronze medal when Crapo Smith submitted it to the 1904 Louisiana Purchase Exposition in St. Louis. *A Daughter of Egmond* and *The First Birthday* marked Letta Crapo Smith's maturity as an artist and she continued to work in Egmond for years after Hitchcock left.[32]

Although he usually worked with his pupils individually, Hitchcock also arranged sketching days when they would all go together to work outdoors. Florence Kate Upton and Alice Worthington Ball found the emphasis on outdoor work both rewarding and challenging. Ball wrote:

> It is so windy there that the canvas must be anchored . . . and then my materials blow about and sometimes I am almost blown away myself. And the sunshine is so vagrant. On a beautiful day one starts hopefully to work and then the sun goes in, and one must drag the canvas back day after day, perhaps, for weeks before there will be another such sunshiny day again.[33]

Upton pictured the same experience in her children's book, *The Golliwog in Holland* (fig. 27).

Of course Hitchcock emphasized color in his lessons. The Egmond artist Charles Hovey Pepper said that Hitchcock used to tell his pupils, "If a landscape painter is an artist, he paints effects, not things."[34] Hitchcock showed them how to use color to attain those effects. Pepper's style was very different from Hitchcock's, consisting of broad areas of local color laid within drawn outlines in an illustrative manner, as seen in his watercolor illustration of the cheese market at Alkmaar, near Egmond (fig. 28). Pepper was deeply impressed with the simplicity, line, and color of Japanese prints, about which he wrote a book in 1905, *Japanese Prints.* Hitchcock encouraged such individuality with his indiscriminate praise.

Quite a number of Hitchcock's students came from the School of the Museum of Fine Arts, Boston. Ball was listed as part of the 1892–93 painting class along with Marion Eliza Crocker, Carl Gordon Cutler, William Homer Haskell, Martha Silsbee,

Fig. 28. Charles Hovey Pepper, *Alkmaar, Holland,* c. 1895, watercolor, Colby College Museum of Art, Waterville, Maine, Gift of Stephen Pepper.

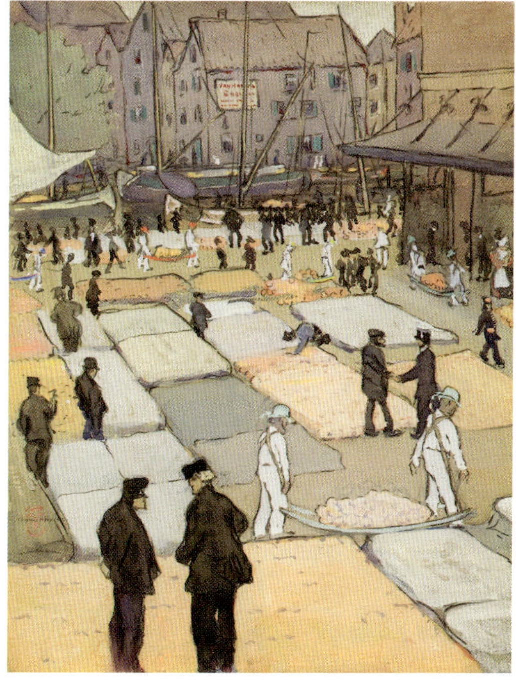

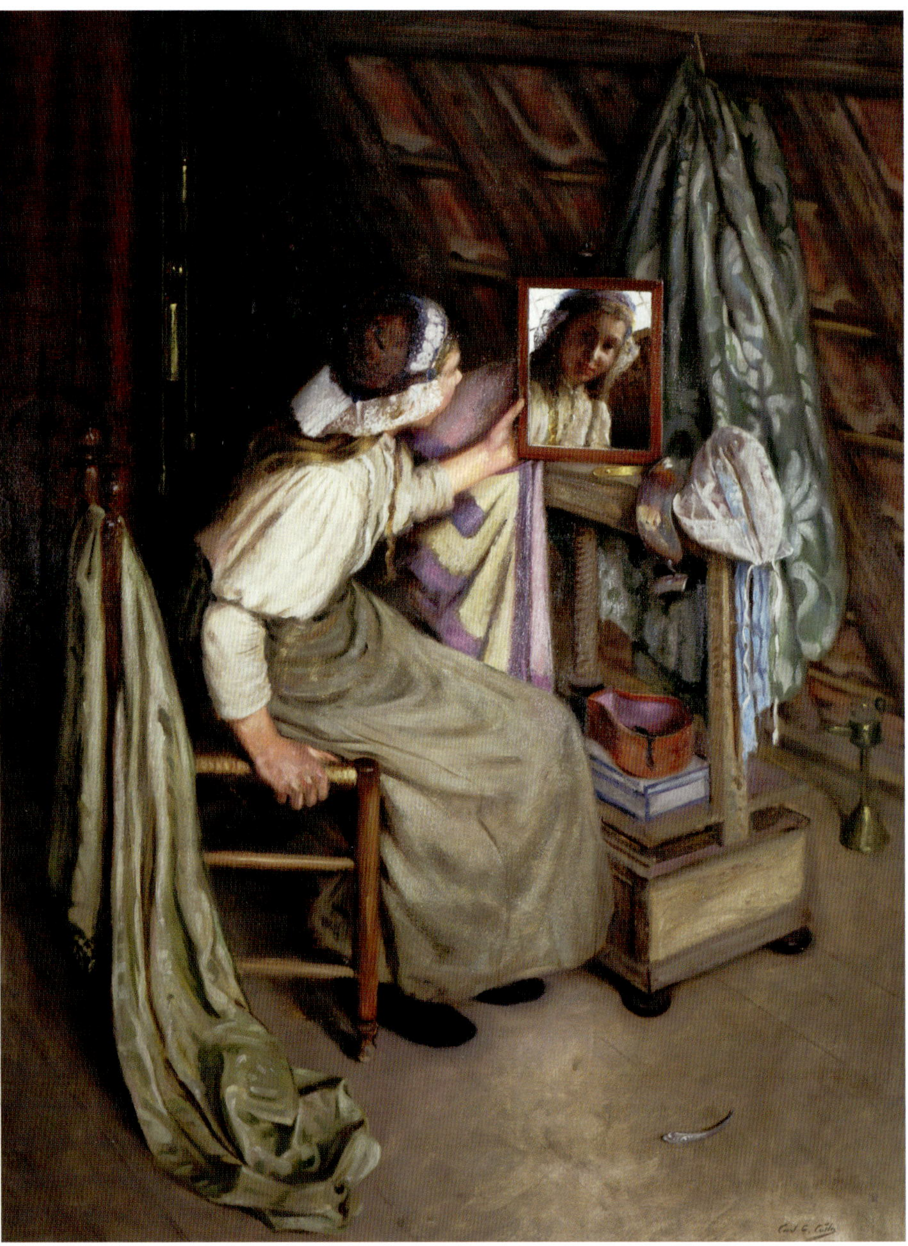

Fig. 29. Carl Gordon Cutler, *The Attic,* c. 1898, oil on canvas, 51 × 38", The Hainsworth Collection.

and Edwin Ambrose Webster, all of whom subsequently studied in Egmond.[35] Edmund Tarbell and Frank Benson were their life drawing and painting instructors, while Philip Hale taught drawing from the cast. These teachers may have instilled a love of Vermeer and impressionism that caused their students to seek out Egmond as an appropriate place to continue that trend. Shannon's *On the Dunes (Lady Shannon and Kitty)*, for example, fits very closely with the kinds of pictures painted by the Boston impressionists—women in light-colored dresses at their leisure sitting in full sunlight or partial shade.

For Cutler and Webster it was Hitchcock's reputation as a colorist that proved the greatest attraction. Finding that the teachers at the Académie Julian "paid no attention to color, teaching mostly drawing," they headed for Egmond in the summer of 1897.[36] Cutler's 1899 Salon picture, *The Attic* (fig. 29), is composed of harmonious tones with strong accents of his teacher's favorite violet and green, but he soon experimented with other effects. *The New Accordian* (n.d., collection of the artist's estate) depicts a mother and daughter in a rosy-hued interior lit by an open fire with the mother's white dress reflecting all the colors of the rainbow. As their styles developed, Cutler and Webster both modified Hitchcock's ideas with more modernist formulas of their own. Webster founded a school in Provincetown, Massachusetts, and published a small book, *Color.* Cutler also worked in Provincetown and collaborated with Pepper's son Stephen on a longer book called *Modern Color* (1923). It set forth a very controlled theory of applied color, related to Webster's but more complex, and contrasting with the intuitive process used by Hitchcock. *Modern Color* became a standard textbook in American art schools and influenced the thinking of a whole group of early American modernists. After 1900 Cutler, Webster, and Pepper exhibited together in Boston with increasingly shocking canvases in "ultra-modern terms, using pure color in a very high key, and with considerable originality."[37] It is this transformation of Hitchcock's once radical, but now dated color sense into a newer modernist color theory by his students that proved the longest-lasting legacy of the Egmond School (fig. 30).

THE LATE PERIOD

In 1903 George Hitchcock fell in love with his twenty-two-year-old British pupil, Cecil Jay.[38] At this time he left Henrietta and Egmond for good, marking the start of the colony's final phase. Hitchcock and Jay spent part of the next year on tour in the United States with their paintings, and when Hitchcock visited the Hals Museum with Melchers and E. M. McKay in June, he gave his address as Providence, Rhode Island, instead of Egmond for the first time since the early 1880s. On July 25, 1905, he divorced his wife of twenty-five years and as of August 7, officially departed from Egmond to live in France.[39] He sold Schuylenburg to Henrietta through the agency of their friend Shannon. Hitchcock married Jay in late 1905 and the two of them spent winters in their Paris studio and most summers painting in the Dutch province of

Fig. 30. E. Ambrose Webster, *Cliffs Azores*, 1913, oil on canvas, 29¼ × 39", Courtesy Babcock Galleries, New York, New York.

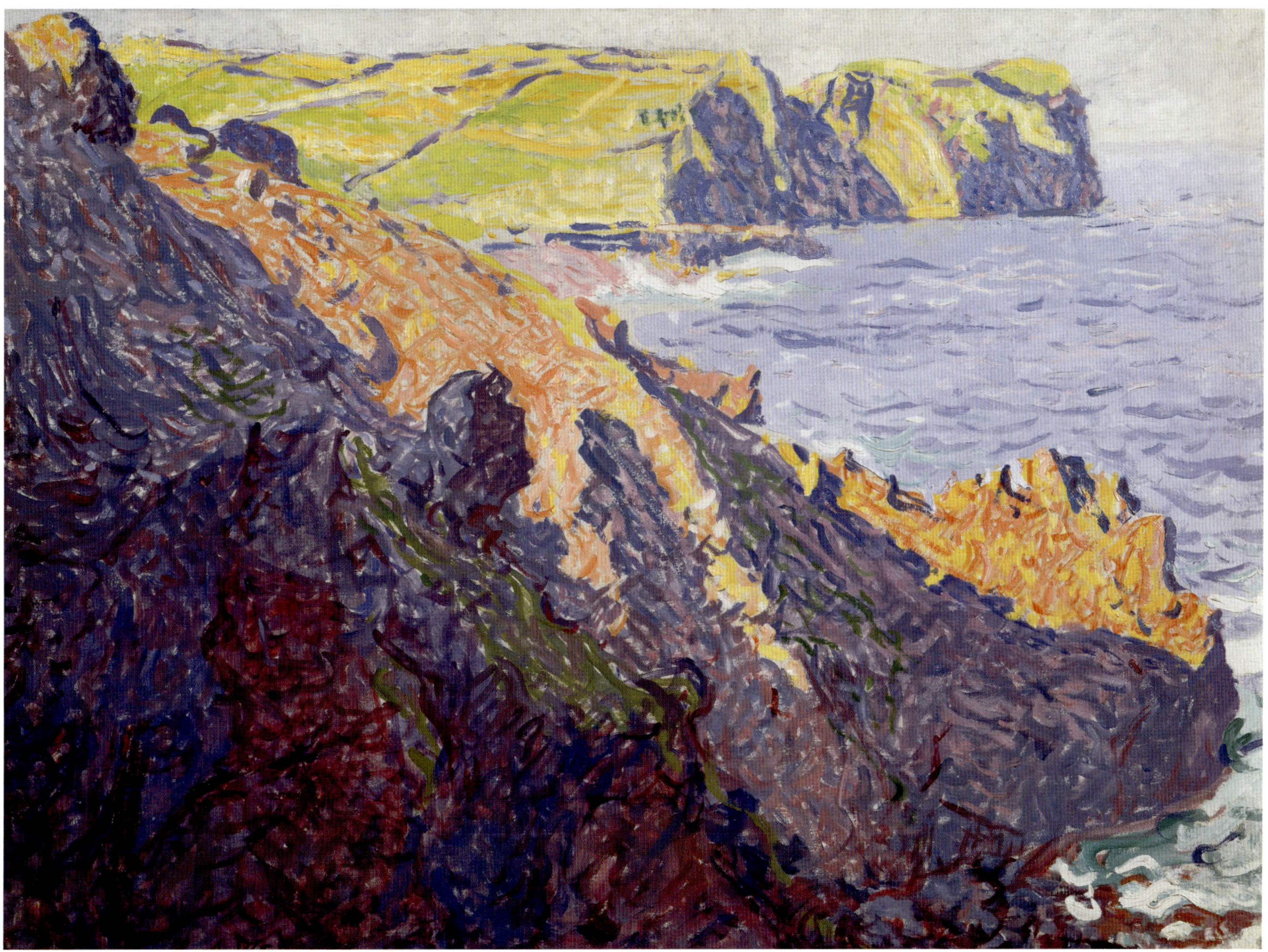

Zeeland. Jay's Zeeland miniatures reflect her one summer season in Egmond and ongoing association with Hitchcock (fig. 31). Until his death on the island of Marken in 1913, Hitchcock would continue to base his reputation on Dutch subject paintings in bright sunlight.

Back in Egmond, the school continued with Melchers as the dominant influence among a circle of now-mature former Hitchcock pupils who returned at regular intervals. If Botticelli inspired many of the religious peasant pictures of the 1890s, Vermeer became the primary old master influence for the post–1903 Egmond painters. Newly married, Melchers turned to domestic themes, painting intimate pictures of his wife in their home and garden (1903–09; cat. 44). He also worked in Hitchcock's abandoned studio and at the house at Schuylenburg, where Corinne,

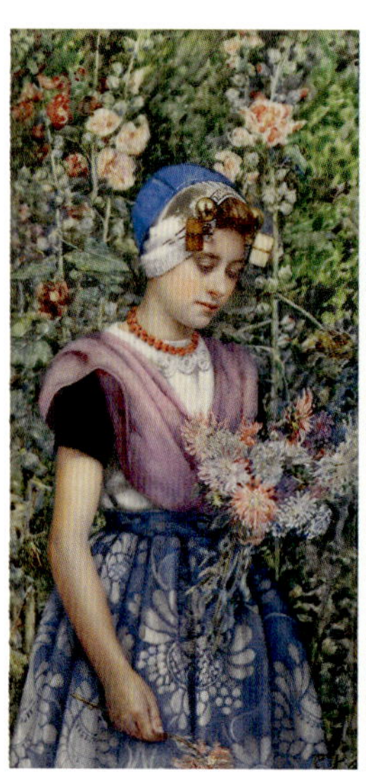
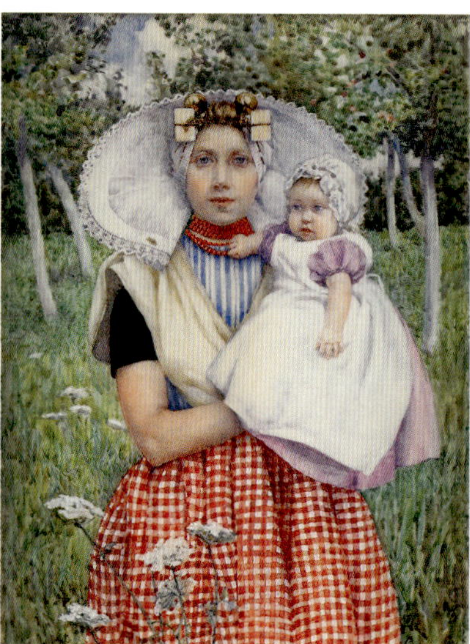
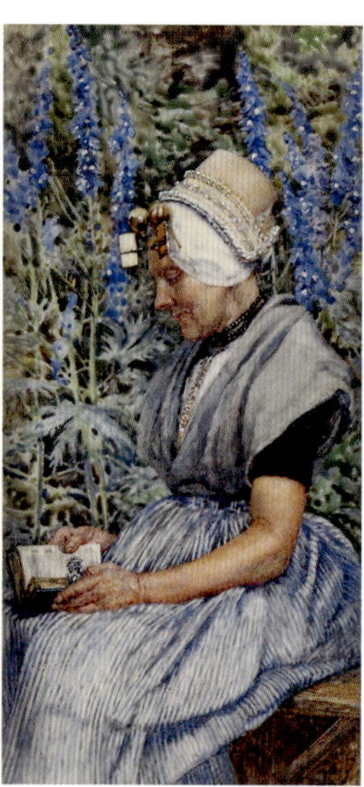

Fig. 31. Cecil Jay, *La Vie Paysanne,* c. 1908, watercolor on ivory, Walker Art Gallery, National Museums Liverpool, England.

Henrietta, and their Dutch maids posed for him. He produced cosmopolitan urban domestic scenes with little suggestion of anything Dutch about them, other than their obvious debt to Vermeer. Sunlight shines through an open window on women visiting in a parlor, a maid waits outside the doorway, a well-dressed lady works at her embroidery (fig. 32). The peasant pictures and biblical themes with which he had established his career became a thing of the past.

Many of Egmond's artists in this period were financially independent women, devoted to painting and teaching art. Alice Worthington Ball and Josephine G. Cochrane, who lived together in Baltimore when they weren't traveling, produced windmill-dotted landscapes and interior genre pictures filled with Dutch antiques. Both painted quiet parlor scenes peopled by women taking tea, admiring jewelry or china, and visiting. A critic noted, "Miss Ball forcibly indicates her predilections for that particular style of painting of which Gari Melchers is the strongest American exponent."[40] Crapo Smith's domestic genre scenes from this period also relate closely to work by Melchers.

Alice Blair Ring continued to paint Dutch subjects, including eighteen canvases exhibited in a 1910 solo show in Cleveland. The first was her picture from the 1906 Salon, *La veille du marché aux fromages, en Hollande* (*The Day before the Cheese Market, North Holland*) (c. 1906, Pilgrim Congregational Church, Pomona, Calif.), a large picture of two women preparing the brilliant orange balls of cheese in the yard under the trees on an autumn day. *Morning Sunshine* (1906; cat. 55) was the second picture listed in the catalog and others depicted fields of poppies and hyacinths, windmills, a characteristic Dutch drawbridge, and a shepherdess—a subject portrayed earlier by Hitchcock and Melchers as well as many of their pupils. In another solo exhibition by Ring, two Dutch pictures were called out for special attention: *Antiques,* depicting "two Dutch girls examining pieces of lovely Delft ware and pieces of glass," and

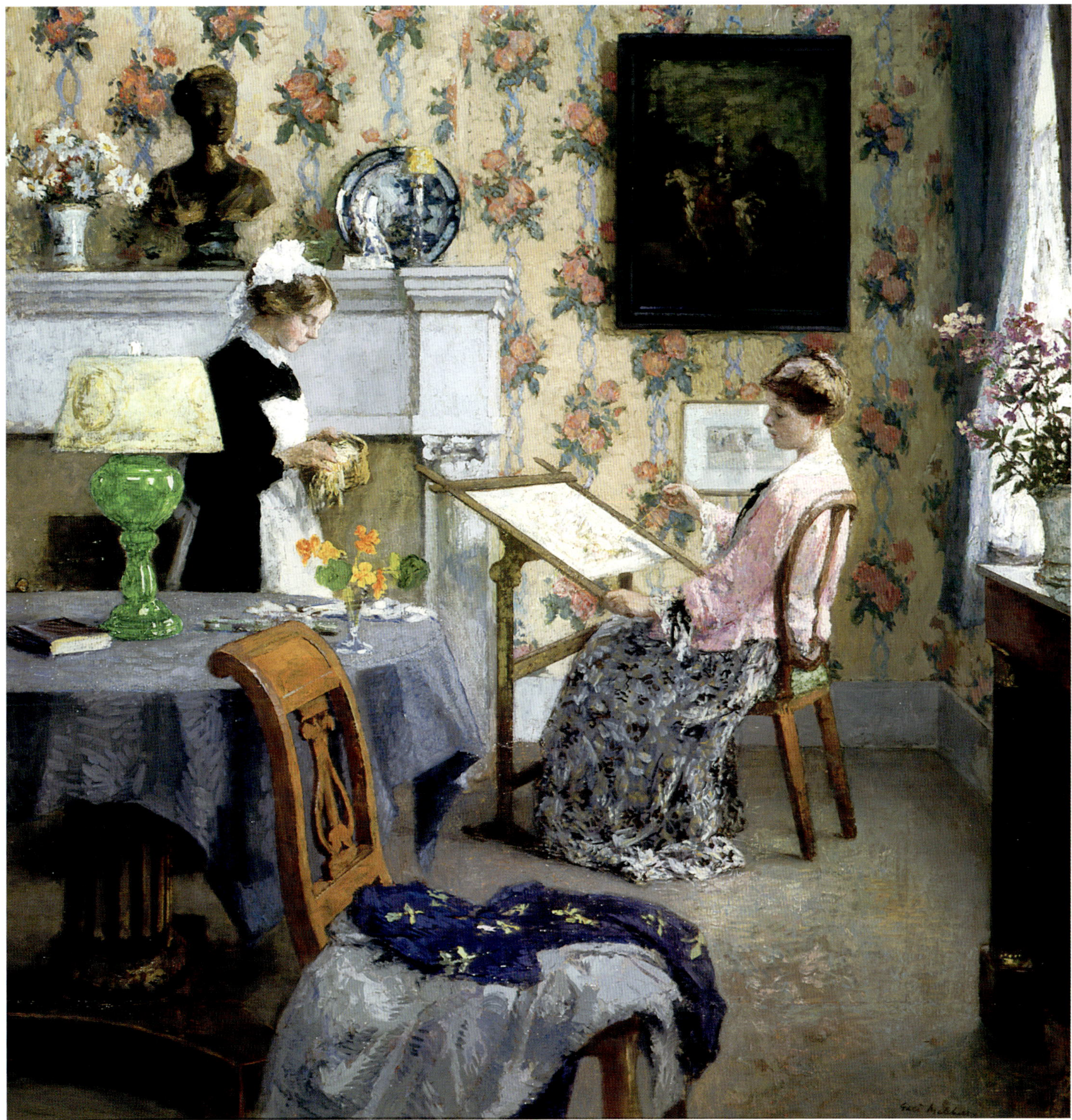

Fig. 32. Gari Melchers, *Penelope*, 1910, oil on canvas, 54½ × 50⅞", Corcoran Gallery of Art, Washington, D.C., Museum Purchase, Gallery Fund, 11.1.

Milking Time, showing a "Dutch girl carrying two huge brass milking cans" in the evening with "blue shadows falling from the sky on the upper part of the face of the girl, and the yellow reflections from below light the lower part of her face."[41]

In this way, the Egmond colony continued until World War I. After 1903, the religious element receded in favor of domestic genre, and the costumed Dutch peasant often gave way to cosmopolitan models, but Egmond's legacy of color moved forward in the hands of a few former pupils who founded their own art colonies and schools in the United States.

NOTES

1. Annette Stott, "American Painters Who Worked in the Netherlands, 1880–1914" (PhD diss., Boston University, 1986), chapter 4, "Egmond," 118–78.

2. Bevolkingsregister, City Archives, Egmond Binnen.

3. *In en Om Kennemerland*, August 31, 1905, Alkmaar, North Holland.

4. Plimsoll spent the summers of 1896 and 1897 in Egmond aan Zee, exhibiting *Marie, Laitière Hollandaise* in the 1897 Salon (Baschet catalog #1356) and *Les Dunes en Fleurs, Hollande* in the 1899 Salon (Baschet catalog #1899). Henry or Heinrich Heimes gave his address as Egmond aan Zee for the 1894 and 1898 Salons, in which he exhibited Egmond beach and dune views and a sunset over the North Sea. His presence was also noted in the local paper, *In en Om Kennemerland*. British painter Alfred Hitchins painted a picture of a woman and child on one of the door panels in the Hotel Zeezicht. Miss Varvara de Wesselitsky, who was born in Germany of Russian parents, described herself as a student of George Hitchcock. Mrs. Thamine Tadema-Groeneveld exhibited two oil paintings of Dutch fishing boats in the 1902 Salon and described herself in the catalog as a student of Hitchcock.

5. Corinne Lawton Mackall, diary entry for April 29, 1902, Gari Melchers Home and Studio, Fredericksburg, Virginia.

6. On American impressionism, see especially William H. Gerdts, *American Impressionism* (New York: Abbeville Press, 2001) and Susan G. Larkin, *American Impressionism: The Beauty of Work* (Greenwich, Conn.: Bruce Museum of Arts and Sciences, 2005).

7. Gari Melchers, quoted in Rilla Evelyn Jackman, *American Arts* (Chicago: Rand McNally, 1928), 216.

8. Charles Henry Meltzer, "A Painter of Sunlight," *Hearst's Magazine* 22, no. 7 (July 1912), 132.

9. "Beeldende Kunst te Egmond aan Zee," *In en Om Kennemerland*, January 1, 1905, Alkmaar, North Holland.

10. Hitchcock dropped Mesdag from his Salon entries in 1889 and the handwritten form he submitted to the Art League Publishing Company of Chicago for inclusion in the *Artists' Year Book, 1890*, makes no mention of Mesdag (Smithsonian Institution, Archives of American Art, microfilm roll D-10, frame 1285). He admitted to taking a few lessons at Heatherley's School of Fine Art in London and finishing his formal education with a winter term in Düsseldorf.

11. An invitation and cover of the catalog for this undated exhibition (Gari Melchers Home and Studio, Fredericksburg, Virginia) are illustrated in *Gari Melchers: A Retrospective Exhibition*, ed. Diane Lesko and Esther Persson (St. Petersburg, Fla.: Museum of Fine Arts, 1990), 62.

12. On Melchers's education see George Mesman, "The Student Years, Düsseldorf and Paris," in *Gari Melchers*, 49–54.

13. For extensive analysis of *The Sermon's* reception, see Jennifer A. Martin Bienenstock, "Gari Melchers and the Belgian Art World, 1882–1908," in *Gari Melchers*, 75–110. I have revised the opinion I expressed in the same catalog, that because modern Egmonders identified the central girl's cap as a mourning cap she might have been interpreted by Dutch viewers as deeply grieving rather than sleeping. The empty chair cannot symbolize a lost husband or father, since only women sat in that section. It could represent a lost female relative, but there is no reason to consider this over other interpretations.

14. Ron van Vleuten, "Amerikaanse schilders in Egmond (2)," *Geestgronden* 2 (July 1995): 27–42.

15. Previously, Jean-Léon Gérôme (*Tulip Folly*, 1882, Walters Art Gallery, Baltimore) and Vincent van Gogh (*Flower Beds in Holland*, 1883, National Gallery of Art, Washington, D.C.) were two of the very few painters who had ever painted the subject. Hitchcock would later follow Gérôme's lead and paint a historical picture of a soldier in the bulb fields, called *Vaincu* (*Vanquished*, c. 1898, Musée d'Orsay, Paris).

16. Claude Monet, quoted in *Monet in Holland* (Zwolle: Waanders, 1986), 167–68. See also 36–45.

17. George Hitchcock, "Sandro Botticelli," *Scribners Magazine* 4 (December 1888): 712, 718.

18. A. H. C., "Art Notes and Exhibitions: Holland Scenes at Memorial Gallery Glow with Sunlight and Color . . . ," review of exhibition of paintings by George Hitchcock and Paul Dougherty, unidentified newspaper clipping, January 1915, curatorial files, Memorial Art Gallery, Rochester, New York.

19. Hitchcock, "Sandro Botticelli," 712.

20. Ron van Vleuten noted the sale of Schuylenburg from his own family to Hitchcock (1893) and the construction of a studio in conversations with the author. Kitty Shannon, among others, noted that Melchers "had a studio on the sand dunes overlooking the North Sea, in the fishing village of Egmond Zee, a/d Houf, but he lived at an inn at a village two or three miles inland," Kitty Shannon, *For My Children* (London: Hutchinson, n.d.), 26.

21. Shannon's only daughter, Kitty, wrote that she was almost five years old the first time they went to Egmond. Shannon, *For My Children*, 18–19. They continued these trips at least until 1908 when they visited the museum in Haarlem with Mr. and Mrs. Lewis Hind (formerly Mrs. George Hitchcock), Stott, "Documentation of American Artists' Activities in Holland from Dutch Archives," in *Holland Mania*, 275. See also Barbara Dayer Gallati, "Portraits of Artistry and Artifice: The Career of Sir James Jebusa Shannon, 1862–1923," 2 vols. (PhD diss., City University of New York, 1992).

22. The Telfair's *George Hitchcock* was originally thought to be undated, but a 1979 conservation report says the date 1897 was revealed next to the signature upon cleaning, and Michael Quick published it as 1897 in *American Expatriate Painters of the Late Nineteenth Century* (Dayton, Ohio: Dayton Art Institute, 1976). If this is accurate, it cannot be the 1894 Salon painting, unless it was repainted in 1897. However, the conservation report of July 1985 mentions no date and none is present on the painting today. There is no record of what happened to the date on the portrait or why.

23. F. B. McGuire, Corcoran Gallery, letter to A. R. Lawton, Telfair Museum of Art, January 25, 1911, curatorial files, Telfair Museum of Art, Savannah, Georgia.

24. A. R. Lawton, Telfair Museum of Art, letter to Miss Cornelia B. Sage, November 13, 1914, curatorial files, Telfair Museum of Art, Savannah, Georgia.

25. Ron van Vleuten, conversation with the author at Schuylenburg in Egmond aan den Hoef, September 2, 1982; audio tapes made at the exhibition *Gari Melchers in Egmond* by the local historical society, Stichting Hart voor Egmond, c. 1980.

26. Annette Blaugrund discovered this article and kindly sent me a copy: "Hitchcock Elopes," *New York Herald Tribune*, June 25, 1889. The reporter claimed that

O'Halloran came from St. Paul, Minnesota, to Paris to study art, where Hitchcock met and persuaded her to become his student in Egmond for the summer of 1888. She produced several pictures there, as evidenced by her painting #2031 *La Fin des dunes* (*The Edge of the Dunes*) in the 1889 Salon. She also placed #230 *A Study* and #231 *Une Chaumière sur les dunes hollandaise (Cottage on the Dutch Downs)* in the American section of the 1889 Paris Universal Exposition, for which Hitchcock served as secretary of the American jury. Whatever the true story—the Hitchcocks remained married and O'Halloran dropped from view—the persistence with which such stories followed Hitchcock suggests he had conflicted relationships with female pupils.

27. Shannon, *For My Children*, 19.

28. Ibid., 25.

29. "De Oudheidkenner," *In en Om Kennemerland*, August 15, 1904, Alkmaar, North Holland.

30. Mrs. Mackall, Egmond aan Zee, letter to Leonard Mackall, Undercliff, New York, August 3, 1902, the Gari Melchers Home and Studio, Fredericksburg, Virginia.

31. Mackall, diary, September 6, 1902 entry.

32. A 1907 article ends by noting that Crapo Smith "is now in Holland working among the subjects she delights in," "New Pictures in the Galleries," *Bulletin of the Detroit Museum of Art* (July 1907): 3. The *Egmond Bad-Bode* recorded a Miss A. C. Smith staying in Egmond in August 1911, which may also refer to Letta Crapo Smith.

33. "Woman Artists of Baltimore—Miss Alice W. Ball," *Baltimore Morning Sun*, March 5, 1911.

34. Joseph Coburn Smith, *Charles Hovey Pepper* (Portland, Maine: Southworth-Anthoensen, 1945), 25.

35. *Seventeenth Annual Report of the School of Drawing and Painting* (Boston: Museum of Fine Arts, 1893).

36. Vivien Raynor, *E. Ambrose Webster, 1869–1935: A Retrospective of Paintings* (New York: Babcock Galleries, 1965), n.p. Their presence in Egmond was recorded in the *Egmond Bad-Bode* July 15 and September 1, 1897, Alkmaar Archives, North Holland.

37. *Boston Transcript*, August 20, 1914, clipping in E. Ambrose Webster Papers, Smithsonian Institution, Archives of American Art.

38. According to research by Dr. Peter J. H. van den Berg, who generously shared information from his forthcoming book, *De Uitdaging van het Licht: George Hitchcock 1850–1913* (Bahlmond, 2009), Cecil Jay was born in 1881 in Hertford, England.

39. Egmond bevolkingsregisters for 1905, Town Hall, Egmond Binnen. Henrietta married the London art critic and author Charles Lewis Hind in New York on November 18, 1907, and they became official residents of Egmond as recorded in the Bevolkingsregister June 16, 1908, although they traveled extensively.

40. W. E. B., "Baltimore, MD." *American Art News* 10, no. 4 (January 13, 1912): 7.

41. I am grateful to Connie Constant for sending me the newspaper article "Society to Show Colorful Paintings at Ebell," *Pomona Progress*, April 29, 1925.

I am particularly grateful to Ron van Vleuten and Joanna Catron for their research help and great generosity over the years that I have studied Egmond. The work of many other scholars, including some of my graduate students, has also been very valuable. I have tried to thank everyone in the appropriate footnotes, but have undoubtedly missed some. Please take this as my thanks to you all. Twenty-six years of intermittent research tends to accumulate more debt than can be adequately acknowledged. It has been a great pleasure to work with Holly Koons McCullough, Courtney McGowan, Ineke Middag, Michelle Bolton King, and the essayists on this project.

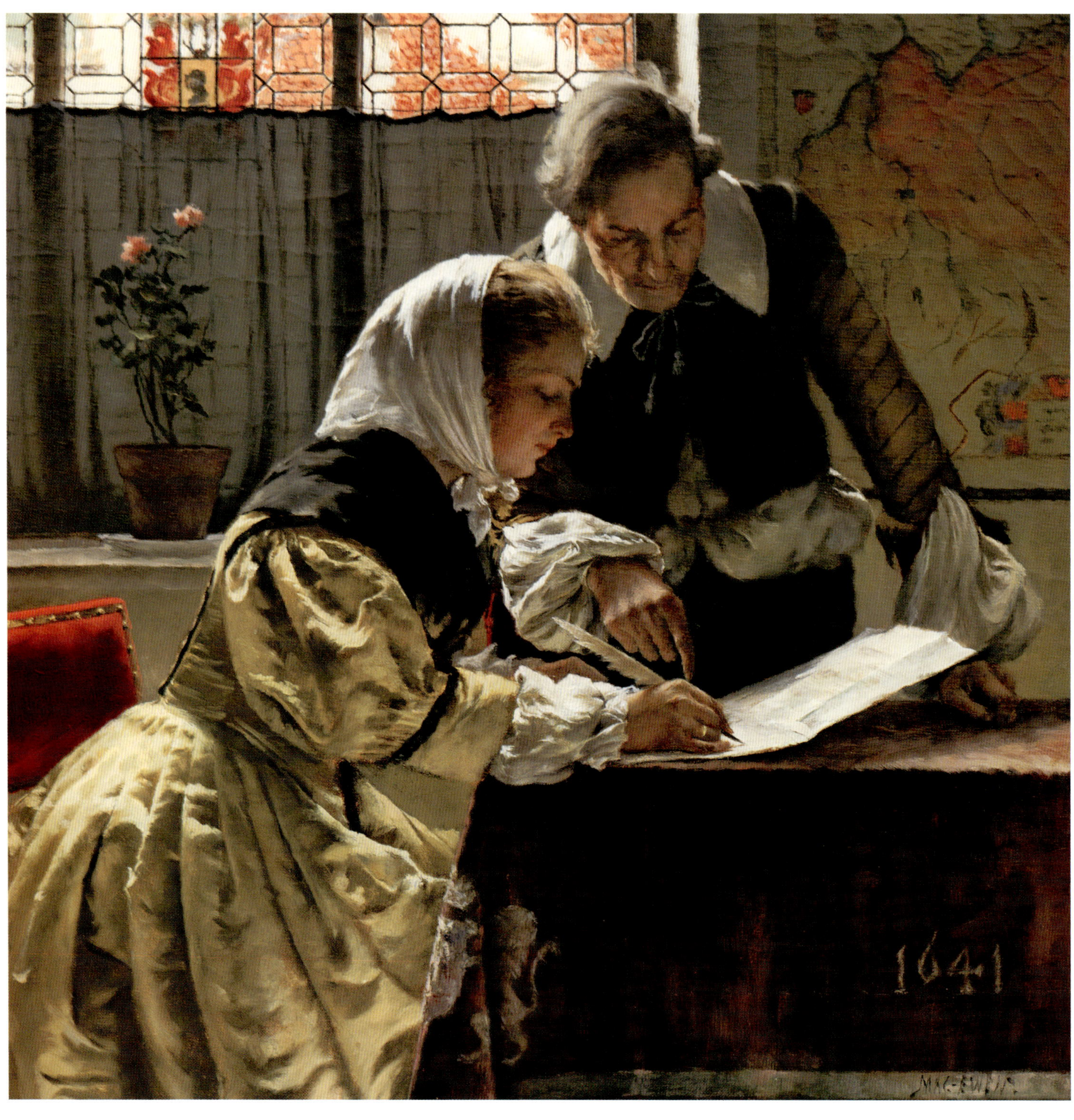
1641

Picturing Holland: The Case of Walter MacEwen

Holly Koons McCullough

A CHICAGOAN BY BIRTH, A PARISIAN BY RESIDENCE, and a Dutchman by artistic inclination, Walter MacEwen (fig. 33) was one of the most highly decorated American artists of the late nineteenth century. Versatile and business-savvy, he produced works in varying genres and styles ranging from intimate domestic scenes to society portraits to classical and Rococo-style mural decorations, but his reputation was firmly established on paintings of Dutch village life. MacEwen's prolific genre scenes of traditionally dressed Dutch women in spotless, radiant interiors tapped into the late-nineteenth-century nostalgia for preindustrial society, and helped to establish the popular notion of Holland as a pastoral haven. His paintings manifest both the allure of traditional life in Holland and the ongoing stylistic influence of the great painting tradition of the Dutch Golden Age. Yet, despite spending summers in rural Holland for many years, MacEwen was largely an urban dweller, a sophisticated expatriate American seeking success within the established European academic system. His painting style—a synthesis of seventeenth-century Dutch art, the Munich School, French academic principles, and the stylistic trends and innovations of his own time—reflected his cosmopolitan, peripatetic existence. In his work and in his life, Walter MacEwen was an important transitional figure who straddled the line between urban realities and pastoral ideals, between academic tradition and progressive modernism, and between American ambition and the European establishment.

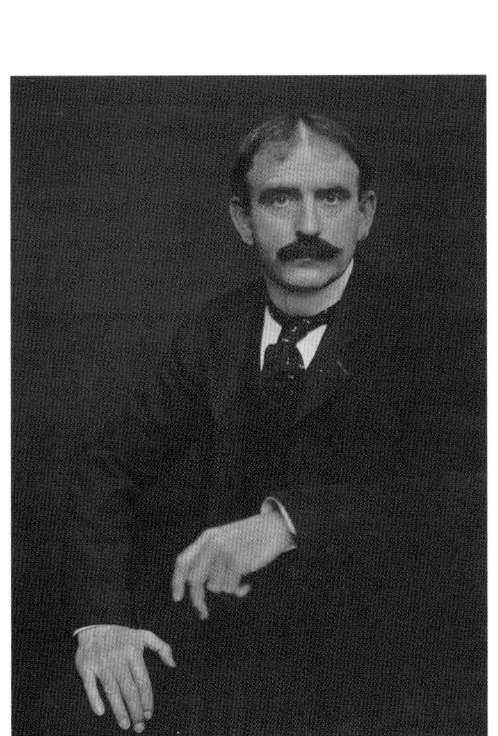

Fig. 33. Photograph of Walter MacEwen, 7⅞ × 5⅜", Starke Family Archives.

Walter MacEwen was born into a prosperous Chicago family on February 13, 1858, the eldest son of Elizabeth (Brennan) and John McEwen.[1] Walter, who later changed the spelling of his surname to "MacEwen," attended public schools as a child before enrolling in prep school at Lake Forest Academy.[2] Details of the artist's early life are limited. A journalist at the *Philadelphia Evening Post* reported:

> As a boy he did not display remarkable precocity in the field of effort in which he has since received several of the highest European honors open to Americans, and he never passed through the period of struggle and starvation so generally expected in early life of the young painter. . . . the most notable struggle of his artistic career was in overcoming parental objections to "fooling away time in making pictures."[3]

According to another source, MacEwen's parents recognized his youthful talent and procured private art lessons for him with Eliza Allen Starr, a local author and illustrator.[4] After a brief stint at Northwestern University, MacEwen enrolled at the Royal Academy of Fine Arts in Munich, Germany, in May 1877, commencing a residence of over six decades in Europe.[5] He remained at the Royal Academy for one year, but, eager to study painting and finding no room in the studio of his preferred instructor, Wilhelm von Diez, he began to teach himself with the informal

Detail of cat. 31

assistance of Frank Duveneck and other American artists in Munich. During this period, MacEwen absorbed the solid lessons of the academic Munich School: the use of a dark, earthy palette and bold, fluid brushwork; the naturalistic and unsentimental portrayal of ordinary subjects; and the cultivation of a deep respect for the Dutch and Spanish masters of the Baroque era. The artist showed early promise, earning a silver medal at the academy by the end of his first year, and exhibiting at the Munich International Exposition in 1883. Around the same time, MacEwen was exhibiting his work in Chicago, Boston, and New York, where his paintings found ready favor among American audiences and sold briskly.[6]

A well-attended exhibition of MacEwen's work at Stevens Gallery in Chicago in 1884 featured several Dutch scenes, currently unlocated, including *Returning from Milking*, *Dutch Genre*, and *Garden in Holland*.[7] MacEwen had visited Holland as early as 1878, where his exposure to the work of Frans Hals and other seventeenth-century Dutch masters, as well as to the artists of the contemporary Hague School, exerted a considerable impact upon his developing style. MacEwen adopted a lighter palette and began to produce genre scenes of Dutch villagers. By 1881, he had opened a studio in Hattem, a quiet medieval village in the province of Gelderland, where he began to spend his summers. Hattem was home to a few other American artists including Henry Bisbing, a Philadelphian who specialized in painting animals, and Amy Cross of Milwaukee, who devoted herself to genre scenes.[8] For MacEwen, agrarian village life in Hattem inspired dozens of Dutch genre paintings that would come to define his mature career. Although he is often associated with the Egmond colony and its famous American founders, Gari Melchers and George Hitchcock, to date there is no conclusive evidence that MacEwen ever had a studio in the Egmonds, and, unlike his colleagues, Holland was not his primary residence. However, it is certainly likely that MacEwen, as a close friend of Melchers, visited the Egmond colony.

Around 1886, MacEwen moved from Munich to Paris, where he studied at the private atelier of Fernand Cormon and at the Académie Julian under Tony Robert-Fleury.[9] Nevertheless, MacEwen cultivated the idea that he was largely self-taught, refusing to name a master in his first five appearances at the Paris Salon. A journalist in the *Chicago Times-Herald*, commenting on MacEwen's success in Paris, observed, "He carried his own eyes to Paris, and, although his brush gained there in dexterity, no teacher among those in whose ateliers he sought instruction affected to the slightest degree his individuality."[10] Of the twenty-one pictures that MacEwen exhibited in the Paris Salon prior to 1900, at least sixteen portrayed Dutch subjects, beginning with his first entry in 1885, a domestic interior entitled *The Letter* (believed destroyed). His submission of *The Judgment of Paris* (fig. 34) to the Salon the following year further solidified his growing reputation, earning him an honorable mention. In this painting, MacEwen presents the time-honored mythological theme of the shepherd boy Paris, whose hapless decision in a beauty contest between Aphrodite, Hera, and Athena ultimately led to the Trojan War. The three goddesses and Paris are dressed in the garb of contemporary Hattem villagers; Paris calmly holds the apple to be awarded to the fairest, and the maidens seem poised to argue their merits. The artist upended the conventional treatment of this subject by exchanging the traditionally nude goddesses with prim Dutch maids, and the usual classical trappings for a simple Gelderland interior, causing one critic to enthusiastically declare the painting the "least mythological work that I know."[11] *The Judgment of Paris* is an early example of a type of genre scene that MacEwen would render repeatedly over the course of his career.

MacEwen's other submission to the Salon of 1886, *Returning from Work* (c. 1885; cat. 33), reveals his stylistic assimilation of the contemporary Hague School, whose adherents produced matter-of-fact images of traditional agrarian or seafaring life in compositions that recalled seventeenth-century Dutch art.[12] Depicting villagers

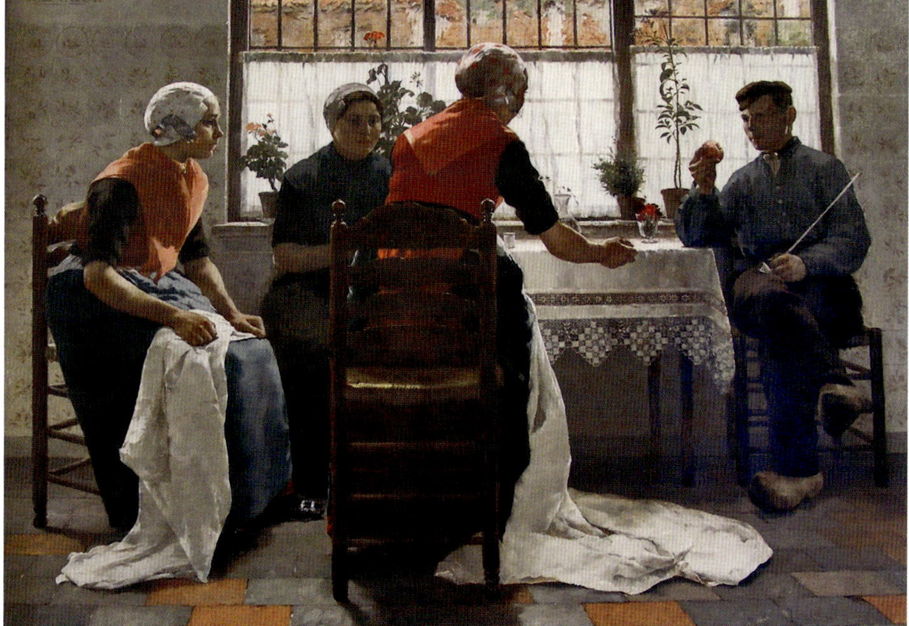

Fig. 34. Walter MacEwen, *The Judgment of Paris*, c. 1886, oil on canvas, 36¾ × 50¼", Tennessee Wesleyan College, Athens, Tennessee.

trudging home through a rugged meadow toward a village in the distance, *Returning from Work* captures an insignificant moment in time. A peasant woman stops to adjust her garter during the return from a typical workday; ahead, a young man pauses, looking back for her. In contrast to the artist's carefully delineated oeuvre, the paint application in *Returning from Work* is relatively fluid. The work's suggestive narrative, which is largely implied by the exchange between the bending woman and the man who awaits her, is also loosely structured. Critics responded positively to the naturalistic subject matter and execution of *Returning from Work*, which was judged a remarkable interpretation of local color. One French critic pronounced it a work of "exquisite grace" and observed: "I find in Mr. MacEwen's work . . . this inclination foreigners have to focus on modern customs and things that are truly alive. For you will not see their signature at the bottom of any antiquated academic painting, any pompous allegory, any over-idealized, conventional, stupid construction."[13]

Contemporary critics often compared MacEwen to the naturalist German artist Fritz von Udhe, who, along with Max Liebermann, had mined rural Holland as a source of imagery in the late 1870s, providing an example for the American artists who would follow. In so doing, they linked MacEwen to the naturalist movement that swept European art in the late nineteenth century. Naturalism advocated the unsentimental, sometimes unsparing depiction of rural peasant life at a time when traditional lifestyles were being threatened by encroaching industrialism and urbanization.[14] The Hague School, one manifestation of the naturalist movement, certainly exercised a significant influence on MacEwen's work. The composition, palette, and subject of *Returning from Work*, for instance, bear comparison to the work of Hague School artist Anton Mauve, particularly if one replaces MacEwen's workers with a herd of sheep. However, MacEwen generally avoided the harsh realism that characterized much naturalist work; his pictures, in fact, were often described as optimistic and uplifting, and his peasants were considered more than usually attractive. As one critic mused:

> Mr. McEwen finds beauty even in Dutch peasant girls, which would seem the superlative of the impossible if one were to judge the race merely through the hundreds of pictures in which our artists have portrayed them. He gives us these people in countless picturesque vocations, clothes them in color-harmonizing, and surrounds them in sunny light.[15]

MacEwen never allowed reality to disfigure his canvases. His paintings rarely depict overt poverty, and, with a few notable exceptions, the majority feature attractive, relatively youthful women. One critic flatly stated that MacEwen's interiors, in particular, did not represent the humbler side of life, but depicted people of a higher class.[16]

MacEwen specialized in two kinds of Dutch scenes: domestic interiors and images of children playing outdoors. The former is well represented by the work in the Telfair's collection known as *The Lacemakers* (c. 1885–1900; cat. 36) featuring three Dutch women sewing in a spare but spacious room, with a male figure behind them, his foot propped on a chair, smoking a pipe. The room is suffused with a subtle glow emanating from the paned windows in the background, a characteristic feature of MacEwen's work. The artist was, in fact, quite well known for "backlighting" his subjects in this manner, and for his technical prowess in handling light in general. This painting is representative of dozens of domestic scenes the artist produced over the course of his career, many of which reflect the influence of seventeenth-century Dutch painters, particularly Johannes Vermeer and the little Dutch masters such as Pieter de Hooch and Gerard Terborch. MacEwen's domestic interiors are often distinguished by repetitive elements that clearly establish their Dutch provenance: heavily paned window casements; painted Delft tiles; Vermeeresque maps on the walls; and potted plants on the windowsills. These pictures helped to construct a stereotype of traditional Dutch life that clearly appealed to audiences on both sides of the Atlantic.

Eh! Eh! les autres, allons jouer! en Hollande (also known as *Dutch Urchins Calling;* fig. 35), which MacEwen exhibited in the Salon of 1889, exemplifies his other specialty: children arranged in homely interiors or, more frequently, playing in the sunlight.[17] One critic observed of this work, "Mr. McEwen is most exceptional in his work with children. He has keen insight into their emotions and a sympathy with their joys and sorrows which vivify every child's face he portrays."[18] In fact, facial expressions are rarely important in MacEwen's genre works, with the exception of those that feature children, who are often highly animated and full of character. During the late 1880s, MacEwen completed a related series of works of small boys, clad in colorful smocks and wooden shoes, flying kites (cat. 32). The treatment of outdoor light and the broad application of paint in these pictures reveal MacEwen's assimilation of impressionism. These subjects also reflect the widespread taste for charming images of children that existed during the latter half of the nineteenth century.

MacEwen's submission to the Salon of 1888, *The Ghost Story* (1887; cat. 34), firmly sealed his reputation, becoming the artist's most popular and most frequently reproduced work. The painting presents a group of women in a typical Dutch interior, pausing at their domestic duties to listen, rapt, to one of their party telling a ghost story. It received enthusiastic reviews from the all-important French critics, including Paul Leroi, respected editor of *L'Art:*

> Mr. MacEwen . . . has reached the highest rank of genre painters with *The Ghost Story.* Old women and girls are studied, analyzed and drawn to perfection, painted as skillfully as one could wish, spaciously, generously, in an interior marvelously bathed in air. It is Holland caught alive by a very accomplished painter and an artist with the keenest of intellects.[19]

In addition to Leroi's glowing review, the painting garnered a number of significant awards. At the Paris Universal Exposition in 1889, *The Ghost Story* won a silver medal and placed MacEwen *hors concours,* beyond awards, in Paris. It later won medals at Antwerp and Vienna, and was eventually acquired by the Cleveland Museum of Art.

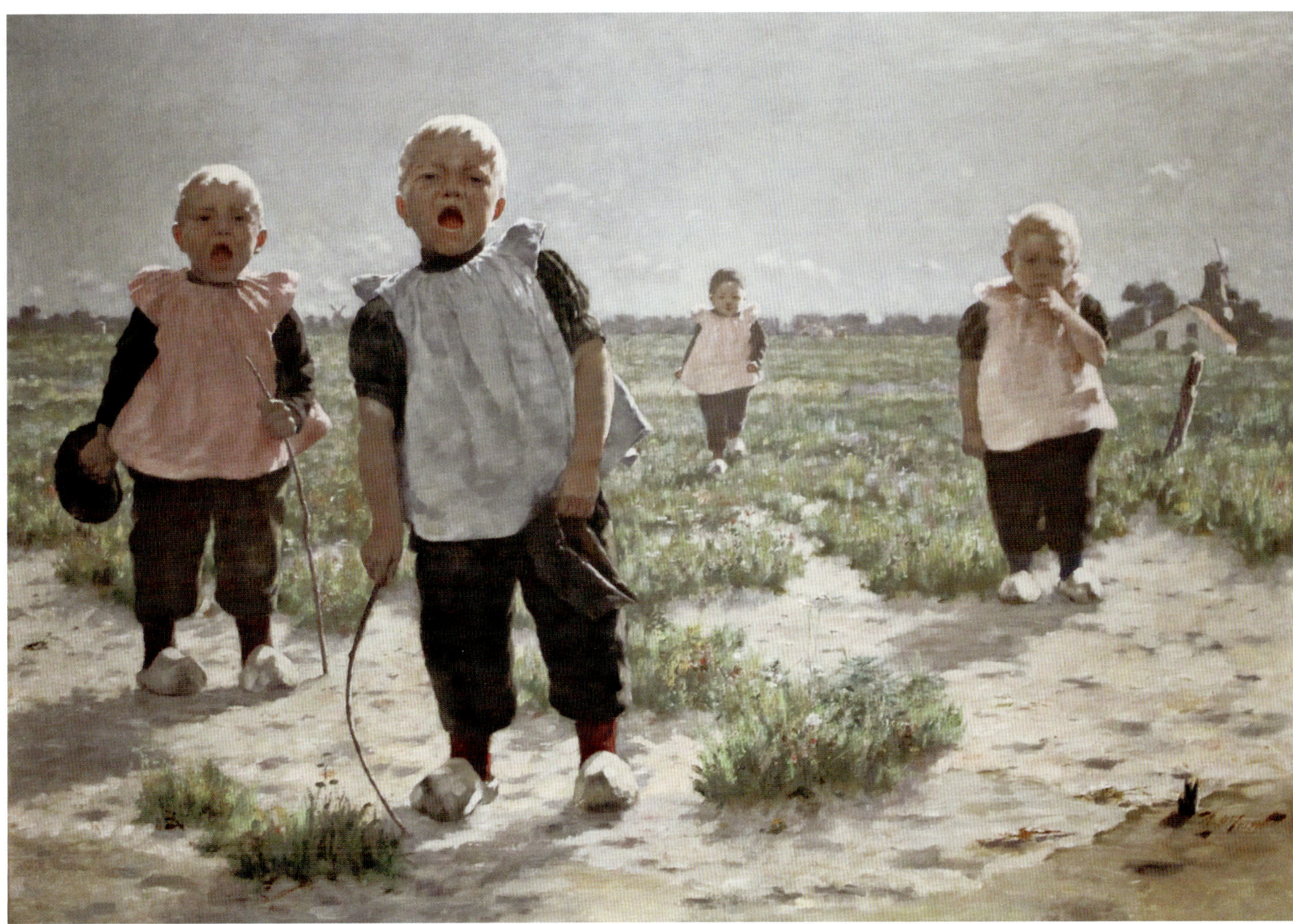

Fig. 35. Walter MacEwen, *Eh! Eh! les autres, allons jouer! en Hollande,* 1889, oil on canvas, 36 × 52", Roughton Galleries, Dallas, Texas.

Although the work was painted in the Hattem studio, MacEwen outfitted the women in the distinctive costume of Volendam, a picturesque fishing village that attracted scores of foreign artists. This disparity suggests that the artist utilized provincial costumes primarily for aesthetic effect rather than regional veracity, a practice not uncommon among American artists in Holland.[20]

The Ghost Story reveals a strong inclination toward narrative that characterizes much of MacEwen's work. The critics of the day detected this with varying degrees of approval. One enthusiastically observed, "This artist has a . . . keen feeling for the picturesque aspects of life's comedy and pathos. He loves a good story a little too much, perhaps; but he tells it extremely well, with admirable insight into human character."[21] Another more ominously declared, "A weakness for the anecdotal quality, for motives merely illustrative, is the defect of some of these pictures—a defect which tells against the permanence of their influence."[22] Indeed, in contrast to that of the other American purveyors of Dutch scenes, MacEwen's work was considered more narrative and sentimental.[23] Perhaps as a direct result, his paintings were also frequently described by contemporaries as uplifting: "It is refreshing to find an artist who is persistently an optimist in these pessimistic days, one who delights in the joyous aspects of life. . . . Mr. McEwen leaves to the reformers the misery of life; he feels that the artist must pursue beauty."[24] This reference to reformers suggests that MacEwen's calm, cozy domestic scenes were perhaps the visual equivalent of comfort food when measured against the various social ills of the late nineteenth century—child labor, prostitution, poverty—that were the target of various progressive reform movements in America.

While *The Ghost Story* earned MacEwen both medals and adulation, it also drew some dissenters:

> Walter MacEwen is too clever a painter, it seems to us, to go on for ever repeating himself. Here is the same girl, only more of her, and the same red dress in more positions, and, to be sure, the same clever painting showing well-studied relations between red dresses and white caps seen against the same well-understood reflected light; but this is the third or fourth Salon in which this artist has favored us with this scheme, and though *The Ghost Story* . . . is an advance in many ways, we should really like a change.[25]

Having found a successful formula for treating Dutch domestic interiors, MacEwen pursued numerous variations on the theme, and continued to do so long after strong popular interest in the subject matter had subsided. The artist also preferred to work in series, so that when he began painting images of women in empire gowns around 1900, for instance, he essentially repeated the same composition with minor surface variations. This tendency unquestionably contributed to his declining reputation in later years.

During the waning years of the nineteenth century, however, MacEwen enjoyed a considerable reputation, establishing himself as a central figure within the community of American artists in Paris. His contemporaries included James Abbott McNeill Whistler, John Singer Sargent, and a host of other American expatriates for whom he expressed admiration, including Richard E. Miller, Alfred Maurer, Julius Stewart, and Frederick Carl Frieseke.[26] In an 1895 interview, MacEwen was asked to voice his thoughts on the contemporary art scene in Paris. The artist opined, "Don't think I belittle impressionists if I say no fad can last. There is good in all fads, and we learn it and it remains; the rest passes away. Certain canons of art are everlasting. It is by them that we judge Velasquez, Terburg [Terborch], or Whistler and Manet." MacEwen goes on to decry the lack of interest in traditional training among younger artists ("They don't want to study even, lest it imperil their precious originality"), and then to ridicule Adolphe William Bouguereau, the standard-bearer of traditional academic art: "He is the only living artist, I believe, entirely uninfluenced by the modern movements."[27] This exchange is of interest in establishing MacEwen's perception of himself as occupying a middle ground between trendy impressionism and stolid, uninspired academic art. The artist considered himself a progressive, modern painter possessed of appropriate stylistic decorum and proper esteem for past masters. His respect for tradition was probably the reason that MacEwen elected to continue showing at the time-honored Salon sponsored by the Société des Artistes Français, rather than the progressive new Salon established in 1890 on the Champ de Mars. One contemporary observer noted MacEwen's middle-of-the-road posture: "McEwen is a strange admixture. He paints pictures for the Champs-Élysées, procures the single decoration allowed to a new world painter, and then caters to the Champ de Mars . . . After all this shows versatility."[28]

MacEwen continued to devote himself largely to Dutch peasant subjects during the 1890s. His painting *L'absente (The Absent One on All Souls' Day)* (1889; cat. 35) was one of the most celebrated American works of the Salon of 1890. A somberly dressed daughter and her father are seated in an interior. The daughter reads Scripture while her father inadvertently dozes; an apparition of the absent family member, the deceased mother, occupies the third chair. Critics on both sides of the Atlantic lauded *The Absent One*, in particular MacEwen's skillful rendering of the ghostly figure of the mother, which is tangible yet ethereal. Although the work reflects a general taste for spiritual themes common to late-nineteenth-century painting, it inspired a variety of religious interpretations. One journalist, discussing a study for *The Absent One* that MacEwen included in his 1890 exhibition at the Art Institute of Chicago, reported:

> Walter McEwen's imaginative little study, *All Souls' Day,* now in his collection at the Institute, has attracted much attention among theosophists, spiritualists, and neophytes and adepts in the faith of which Mme. Blavatsky is high priestess. . . . A quaint conceit cleverly depicted is this little picture, but not intended by the artist as the confession of a faith which he does not share. In spite of his reluctance, however, it is said that the spiritualists greet him as an unconscious medium and write him enthusiastic letters welcoming him to their ranks.[29]

While a few critics objected to the "childish sentimentality" and "phantasmagoric" nature of the subject, none criticized the painting's execution.[30] *The Absent One* was awarded the First Class Gold Medal in Berlin in 1891.

During the 1890s, MacEwen made a few prominent departures from Dutch subject matter, including *A Magdalen* (fig. 36), exhibited at the Salon of 1894. The painting depicts a fashionable but repentant "kept" woman, kneeling fervently in prayer in a candlelit church, surrounded by older, plainer women who survey her with surprise. MacEwen described the painting in a letter to Paul Leroi, the French critic who had so often championed his work, confiding that he had "tried to do

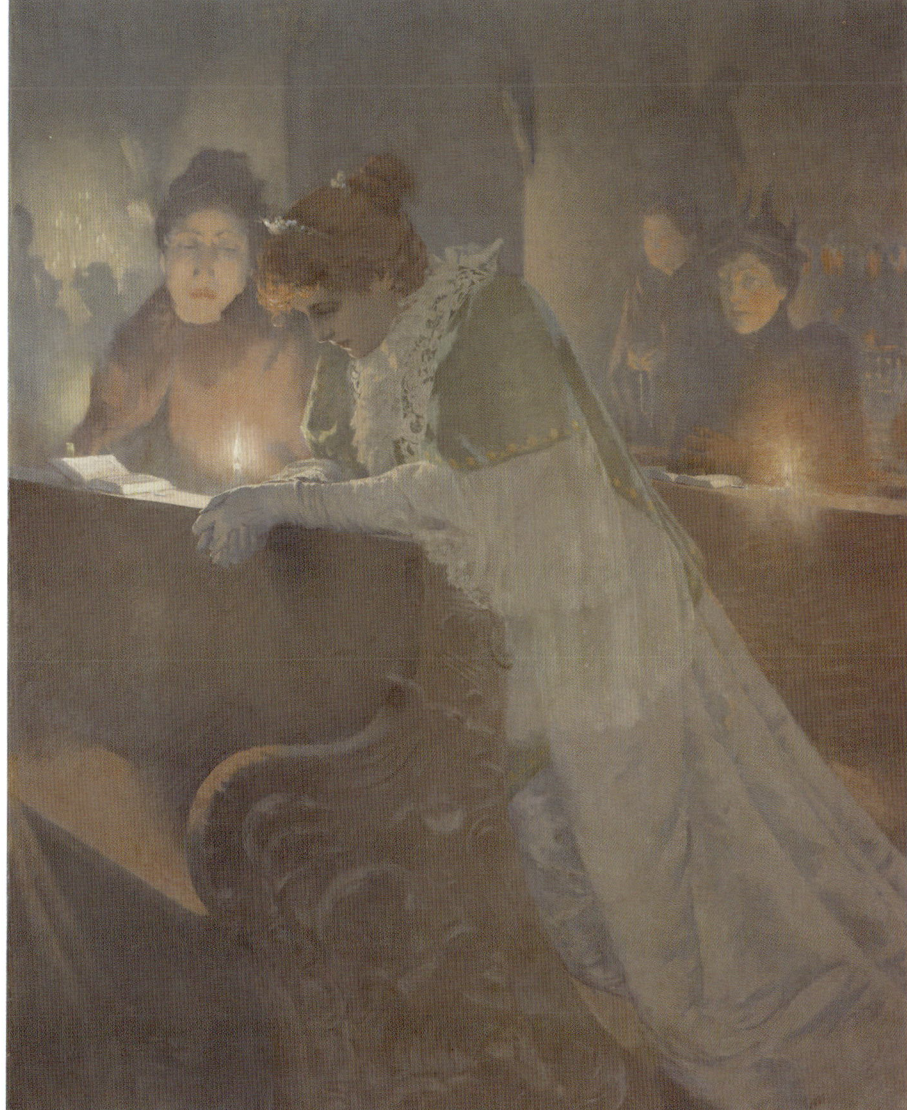

Fig. 36. Walter MacEwen, *A Magdalen,* 1894, oil on canvas, 54½ × 42", Art Institute of Chicago, Illinois, Gift of James Deering, 1925.705.

something entirely different from what I have done thus far." This comment suggests that MacEwen was perhaps either responding to a personal need to treat new subject matter, or to some critical plea that he should. If this was his intention, however, Mr. Leroi's published reply could not have pleased him: "I persist in thinking that this intelligent American artist was on a more seriously pictorial track when he painted *The Ghost Story*, done with a most successful modern execution. Mr. MacEwen is far too talented not to return to this style."[31]

It is impossible to know how this response may have affected MacEwen's subsequent production, except that his entries in the next several Salons were once again Dutch subjects. *Dutch Family* of 1895 initiated a series of three stylistically related works, including *Sunday in Holland* (fig. 37) and *Baby and Grandmother* (c. 1895–1900, originally Budapest Museum), all of which display a drab palette, dimly lit interior, and a strong portrait quality in the primary figures. The best known of these, the sizeable *Sunday in Holland*, portrays three somberly dressed women posed against a dark background. Only the face of the central figure and the white caps of

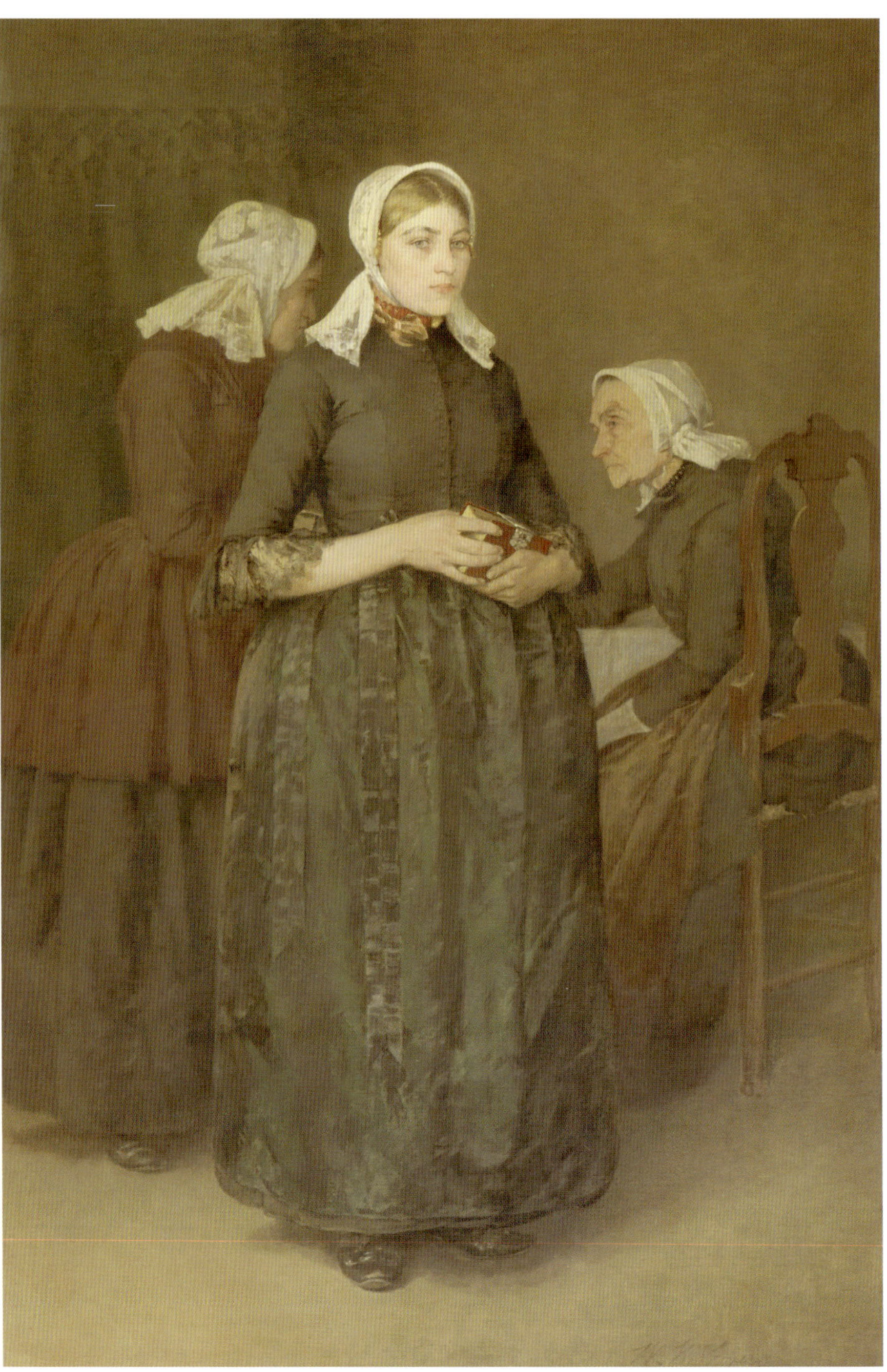

Fig. 37. Walter MacEwen, *Sunday in Holland*, c. 1898, oil on canvas, 74¾ × 47¼", Musée d'Orsay, Paris, France.

the three women create areas of brightness in the composition—a technical challenge that was appreciated by contemporary critics. Characteristically, MacEwen synthesized stylistic influences ranging from Frans Hals to the elegant full-length portraits of his contemporaries, Whistler and Sargent, to create a style appropriate to his theme—pious, plain-speaking, clean-living Protestant villagers. One Dutch observer who viewed the painting was profoundly moved: "This work is so much an image of a pious life, that it is almost a mystery how this stranger could penetrate into the soul of our people to such an extent and how he made his painting a striking example of the deep religious serenity that characterizes our church time on Sunday mornings."[32] MacEwen himself was very pleased with the painting; on a list of his principal works compiled for the National Institute of Arts and Letters, he ranked it as his most important.[33] In 1900, MacEwen sold *Sunday in Holland* to the French government for Luxembourg. He had previously sold *Dutch Family* to the Belgian government for Ghent in 1895, the first acquisition of a work by an American artist to be purchased by Belgium. The following year the Belgian government acquired

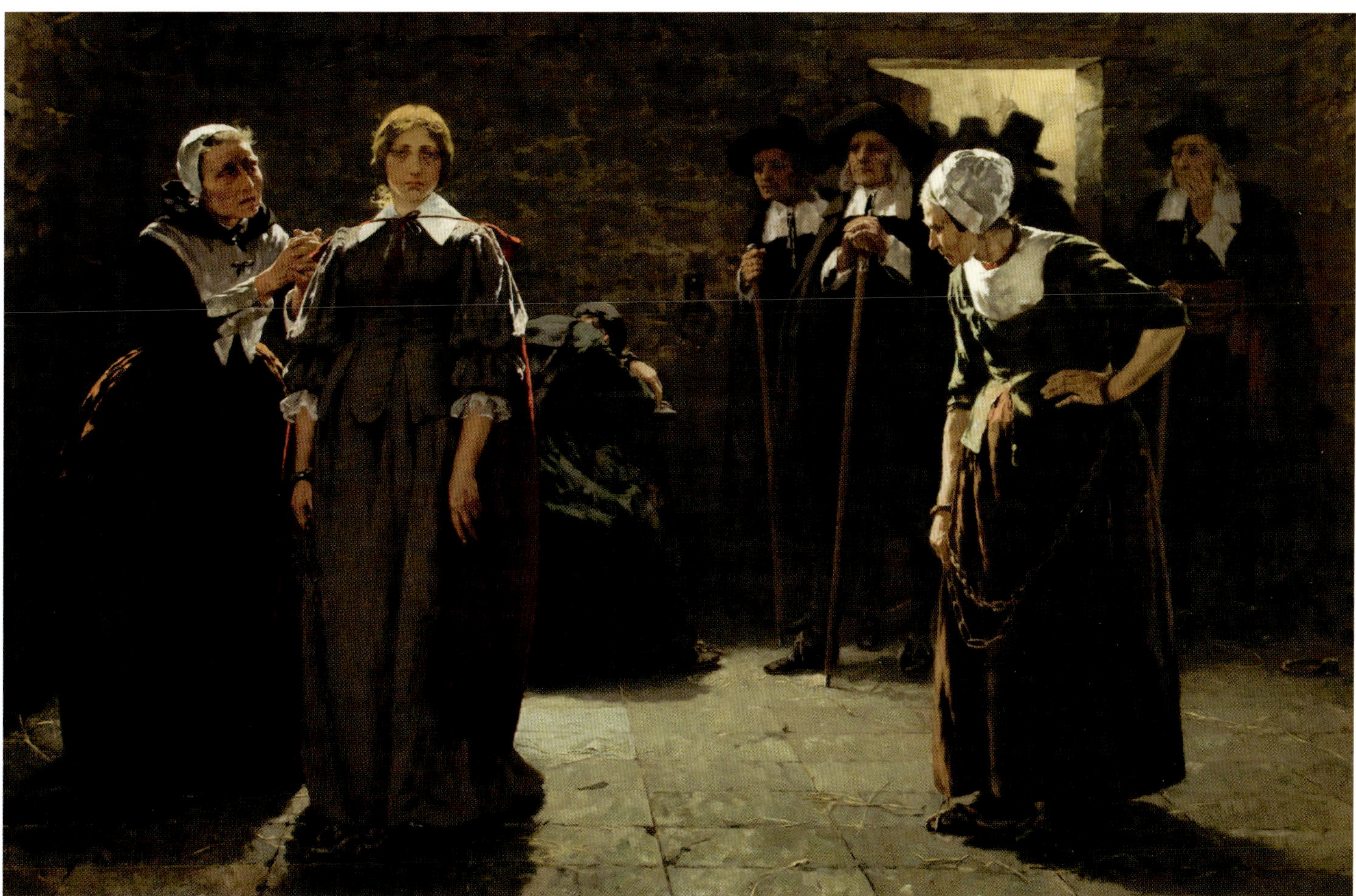

Fig. 38. Walter MacEwen, *The Witches*, c. 1892, oil on canvas, 79 × 118¾", Collection of The Jean and Graham Devoe Williford Charitable Trust.

The Absent One on All Souls' Day for Liège.[34] These important purchases amounted to an official European sanction of MacEwen's work.

As MacEwen achieved ever-greater success with his Dutch themes, calls for American artists to address subjects from the history of their own country grew more numerous. Early in his career, MacEwen had treated Puritan subjects, and in 1892 he sent *The Witches* (fig. 38), portraying an episode from the infamous Salem trials, to the Salon.[35] MacEwen's depiction of early American subjects was doubtless related to the Colonial Revival, a resurgence of interest in the founding of America sparked by the celebration of the country's centennial in 1876. For MacEwen, this impulse culminated in a series of New Amsterdam paintings begun in the 1880s.[36] In treating the early Dutch founders of New York, the artist was able to conflate

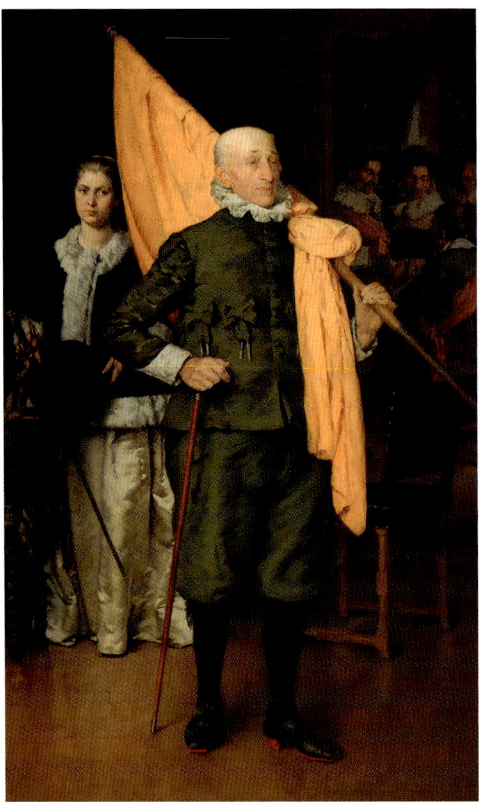

Fig. 39. Walter MacEwen, *Old Guard of the House of Orange*, c. 1895–1900, oil on canvas, 46 × 27", private collection, Philadelphia, Pennsylvania.

the Dutch types and historic interiors he had already perfected with native subject matter that would be appreciated by American critics and audiences. Like many of his contemporaries, MacEwen's foray into Dutch-American colonial history was filtered through a popular fictional literary source, Washington Irving's *A History of New-York from the Beginning of the World to the End of the Dutch Dynasty* (1809), written under the pseudonym Dietrich Knickerbocker. Inspired in part by Irving, MacEwen produced several canvases including *The Trumpeter of New Amsterdam; Cabaret New Amsterdam; The Council of New Amsterdam, Puzzled by a Cabbalistic Message from Rensellaerstein;* and *Tavern in the Old Stadt Haus, New Amsterdam, 1650*, which was awarded a second-class medal at the Paris Universal Exposition of 1889. One critic, reflecting upon this series of paintings, noted approvingly that MacEwen was "a marvelous exponent not only of modern Dutch life, but also of its earlier phases in New York," making explicit the connection between Dutch and American histories.[37] The New Amsterdam series offered MacEwen the opportunity to draw direct parallels between Holland and America, and his conflation of the histories of the two countries may be one of the reasons the artist was often noted for his sturdy Americanism, despite the preponderance of Dutch scenes in his oeuvre.[38] MacEwen also produced other Dutch historical narratives such as *Old Guard of the House of Orange* (fig. 39), which would presumably have resonated among the millions of Protestant Anglo-Scottish settlers to America, such as MacEwen's own father.[39]

MacEwen's American citizenship, combined with his artistic success in Europe, placed him at the crossroads of the contemporary American debate surrounding the development of a national artistic identity. To the oft-voiced concern that so many of America's talented artists were living abroad as expatriates, MacEwen offered a counterpoint. "Americans," he said, "have forced their artists to gain a reputation abroad. It is unfortunate, but as yet they will hardly touch pictures that do not bear the stamp of foreign approval." In the same breath, he defended the tradition of training and painting abroad, declaring, "The one thing a painter can't help doing . . . whether he wants to or not, is to put himself in his pictures; and in the same way he can't help putting his nationality into them. You can tell an American abroad as far as you can see him; and you can spot the American pictures as far as you can see them in any gallery."[40] Despite his lengthy residence overseas, MacEwen emphasized his American citizenship, and made it a point to return home to vote during presidential election years.[41]

Yet MacEwen's success in Europe was also a source of pride amongst Americans, particularly in his hometown of Chicago. David Neal, an American artist living in Munich, wrote to the *Chicago Tribune* after viewing MacEwen's work at the Munich Art Union in 1883:

> This exhibition . . . supports what has long been freely assented to by the whole corps of artists upon this side of the water—namely: that Americans are now prepared to successfully enter the field with Europeans on their own ground, notwithstanding the disadvantages we labor under from the want of early training and the absence of proper surroundings in early youth.[42]

Discussing the performance of American artists at the Salon of 1894, a more effusive critic declared, "If America is ever grateful to the foreign efforts of her children, Walter MacEwen has *bien merité de sa patrie*."[43] In France, upon whose shores so many Americans received their training, once-dismissive critics, inspired by the works of MacEwen and his contemporaries, also began to comment on the development of an American art. Paul Leroi, discussing the American works in the Paris Universal Exposition of 1889, observed, "I do not see any one among our own youth who will be strong enough to keep up with [the Americans]. Today, if you are frank with yourself, you will seek in vain a painter of genre who rivals Mr. McEwen, for example."[44]

As an artist, Walter MacEwen was a consummate and highly decorated professional. His work won awards at major exhibitions throughout Europe and America; he frequently served on juries for expositions and art institutions; he was elected to membership in numerous auspicious professional organizations; and he was decorated with honors by the French, Belgian, and German governments.[45] At home, he was selected to complete major murals for the Liberal Arts Building at the 1893 World's Columbian Exposition in Chicago and for the new Library of Congress in Washington. By all measures, he was one of the foremost American artists of the late nineteenth century. As the new century emerged, however, MacEwen's work began to garner a less enthusiastic critical reception. As early as 1891, one critic lamented the repetitiveness of the artist's oeuvre:

> It must be admitted that there is a tendency in MacEwen's work, as in that of Melchers and other men of the same school, to repeat the same effects, the same methods, the same problems, until there is danger that these may be reduced to a mere formula, and their painting becomes as much of a convention as that of the older generations against whose academic formality it was in the beginning an expression of revolt.[46]

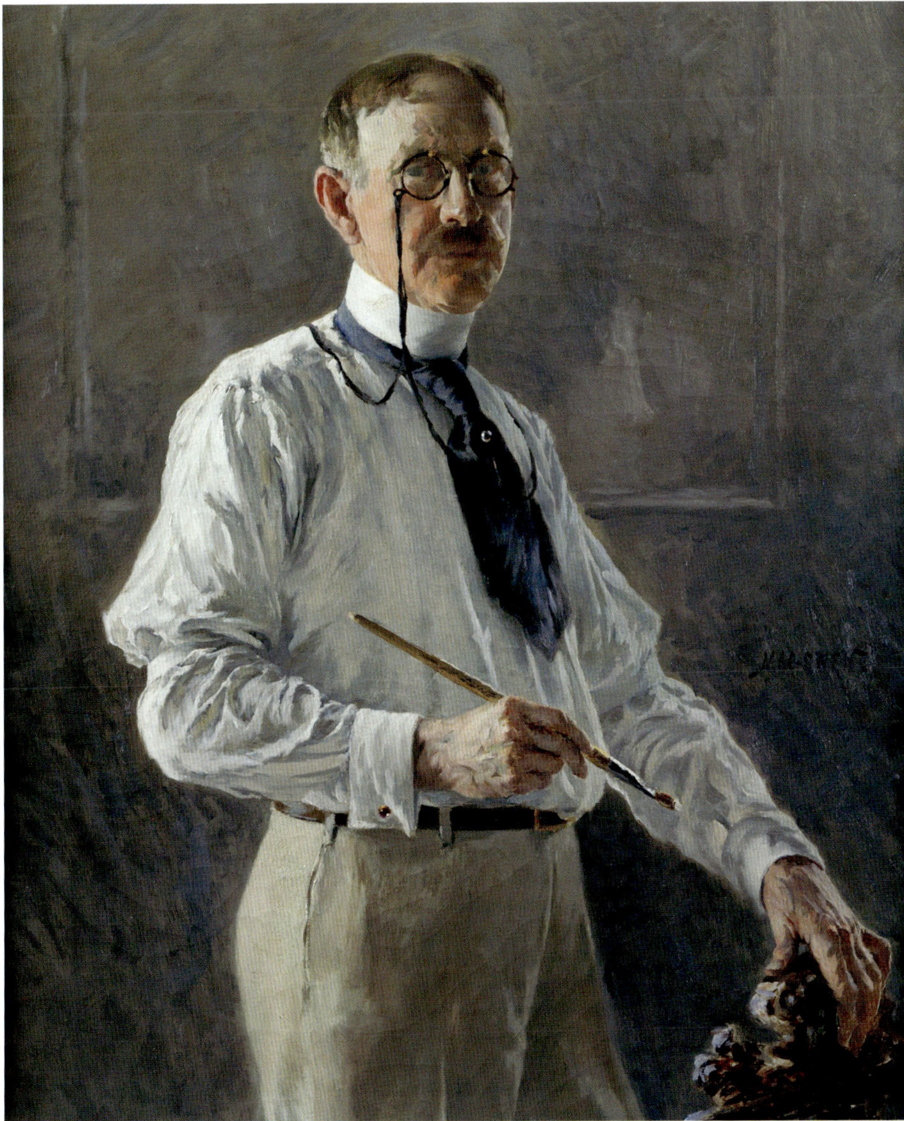

Fig. 40. Walter MacEwen, *The Painter,* 1919, oil on canvas, 41 × 32", private collection, New York.

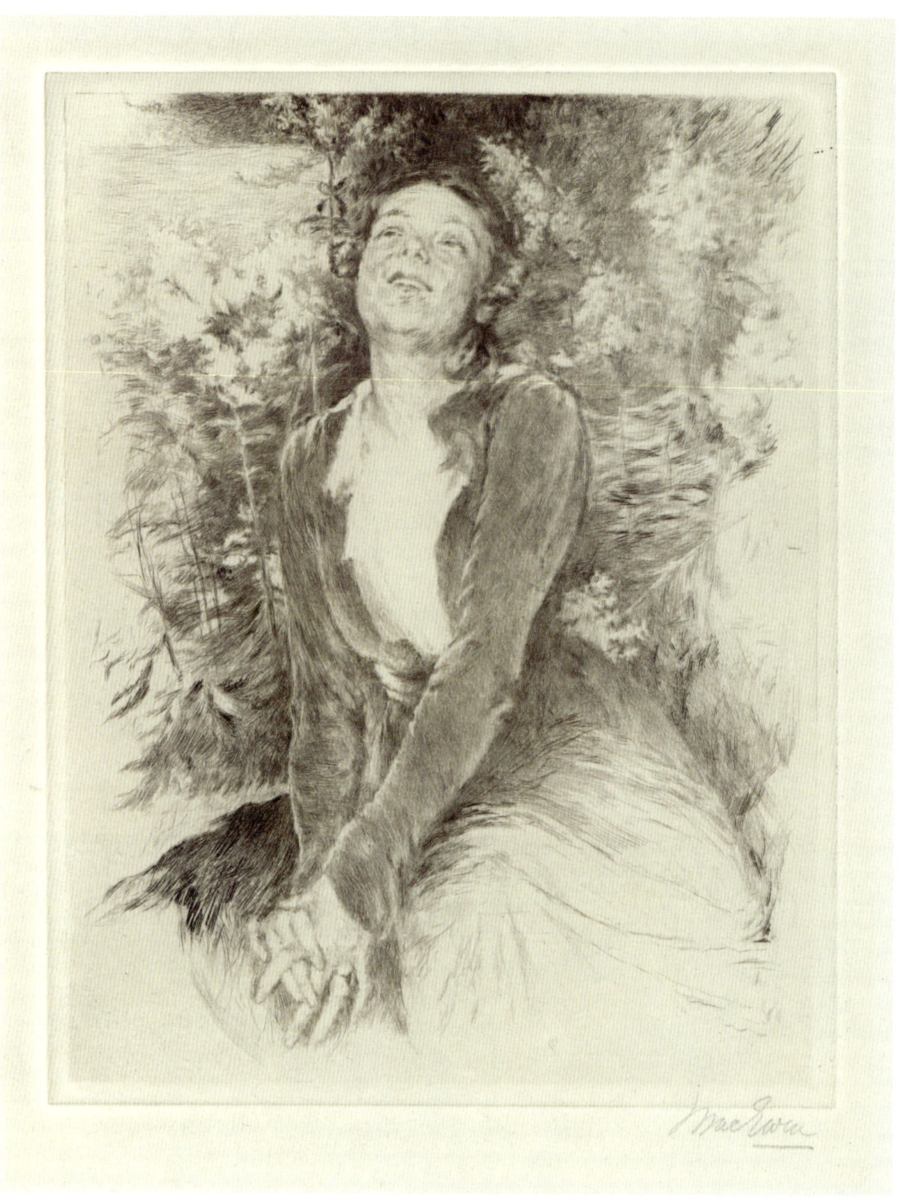

Fig. 41. Walter MacEwen, *Ecstasy,* c. 1934, etching on paper, 9⅛ × 7", Starke Family Archives.

By the second decade of the twentieth century, MacEwen's work had begun to be perceived as *retardataire.* In a critical guide to the galleries published in conjunction with the Panama-Pacific Exposition of 1915, the artist's work received the following blasé comment: "Walter MacEwen arouses memories of times gone by, technically and otherwise, in a huge storytelling Salon picture."[47]

Five years later, in what must surely have been a painful episode, MacEwen failed to be elected a full member of the National Academy of Design, falling short of the required twenty-four votes. The artist had been an associate member of the academy since 1903, and had been awarded the Proctor Prize at the National Academy annual exhibition in 1919 for his self-portrait, *The Painter* (fig. 40). The work had received a strong review in the *New York Times:* "Mr. MacEwen's *The Painter* is an exceptionally real thing, with emphasis laid upon those qualities in the subject which can be interpreted satisfactorily only in painting. Industry of the hand is not asked to take the place of mental industry. The mind has been at work all over the canvas."[48] This success did little to mitigate MacEwen's position at the Academy, however, and in December of 1920 the artist resigned his associate membership in protest.

MacEwen continued to paint through at least 1925, mainly producing portraits and decorative panels for domestic interiors. He even continued to paint Dutch subjects, although in smaller numbers. In 1935, in response to a query from the American Institute of Arts and Letters, he wrote, "The confusion existing in painting decided me a few years ago to devote myself to working on copper (etching and drypoint.)."[49] It is clear that MacEwen felt out of step with developments in modern painting, and shifted his energies to printmaking. By 1939, the artist had made forty to fifty plates, a group of which had been exhibited at the Corcoran Gallery of Art in 1934.[50] Ever the technician, MacEwen aimed to produce what he termed "painter's etchings" or "silver prints," delicately rendered impressions printed on a variety of English, Dutch, French, and antique papers to lend varied surface effects.[51] Many of MacEwen's prints repeat the compositions of earlier paintings—for instance, *An Ancestor, The Painter, The Absent One,* and *The Ghost Story* all reappear as etchings. However, MacEwen also created some delicate and possibly original print compositions of contemporary subjects, such as *Ecstasy* (fig. 41).

By 1940, MacEwen had returned to New York City, fleeing the war in Europe. He died there on March 20, 1943, at the age of 85. There is little doubt that at the time of his death, MacEwen's reputation had declined in the wake of new stylistic trends and as a result of the cultural changes wrought upon American society over the course of two world wars and a major economic depression. Nevertheless, MacEwen's significance was evidenced by the prominent obituaries run by the *New York Times* and the *New York Herald Tribune* upon his death. The artist's polished, graceful images of Dutch life—whether hushed, silvery domestic interiors, children cavorting in sunny meadows, or workers returning from the fields—helped to construct an image of Holland as a preindustrial, agrarian respite from the hurried modern world. While MacEwen's vision of Dutch life appealed to audiences both at home and abroad, for Americans his canvases may have suggested connections between the histories of the United States and Holland, engendering a sense of shared heritage and values. Among the many American artists who worked in Holland, MacEwen was perhaps the most committed to exploring these connections through paintings that evoked memories of colonial America or explored the role of Dutch settlers within it. Today, MacEwen's meticulously composed images stand as a testament to the American infatuation with traditional Dutch life and the cultural legacy of Holland during the late nineteenth century. Through his skillfully wrought depictions of Dutch life, MacEwen helped to establish an enduring presence for American art on the international scene.

NOTES

1. *The National Cyclopaedia of American Biography*, vol. 15 (New York: James T. White, 1916), 166–67, cites MacEwen's birth year as 1860, which is maintained by later sources. However, according to MacEwen's death certificate, he was 85 at the time of his death in 1943. Moreover, the artist listed his year of birth as 1858 on his 1920 and 1921 passport applications.

2. See *The National Cyclopaedia* and "New Fame for M'Ewen, Cross of the Legion of Honor," *Chicago Times-Herald*, January 1, 1896. At some point, the artist adopted "MacEwen" as an alternate spelling of his surname, but did not necessarily use it consistently. The only explanation for this curious shift is found in the artist's obituary in the *New York Herald Tribune*, "McEwen Dies: Noted as Artist for 60 Years," March 20, 1943. Describing MacEwen's early exhibitions in Munich, it states, "It was in one of these shows that an exhibition clerk insisted that the artist's name, which was McEwen, required a vowel in the first syllable, and supplied an 'a,' which Mr. MacEwen retained the rest of his life." The use of "MacEwen" on passport and census documents as well as the preponderance of that form by the late 1880s suggests that the artist chose that spelling as the primary one.

3. "Artist McEwen's Triumphs in France," *Philadelphia Evening Post*, January 12, 1900.

4. "New Fame for M'Ewen, Cross of the Legion of Honor," *Chicago Times-Herald*, January 1, 1896.

5. Janet Olson, assistant university archivist at Northwestern University in Evanston, Illinois, confirmed that MacEwen was enrolled at that institution in 1874 or 1875 (the records are inconsistent) for only two terms. Janet Olson, email to the author, September 15, 2008.

6. Information on MacEwen's training and awards in Munich is drawn from *The National Cyclopaedia*. The author's training in Munich is also briefly addressed in Paul Leroi, "Salon de 1894," *L'Art* 57 (1894). Also see Walter MacEwen, "List of Principal Works," curatorial file, Art Institute of Chicago, an unpublished list of his principal works and awards. (The author gratefully acknowledges both Annette Stott and Denise Mahoney at the Art Institute of Chicago for forwarding copies of this list.) Regarding sales of MacEwen's work, see the *Chicago Tribune*, untitled, undated clipping from 1887, contained in a scrapbook in the possession of MacEwen's great-nephew, George Starke, hereafter referred to as "MacEwen scrapbook." The article notes the sale of *The Judgment of Paris* to Mr. A. A. Munger for $3,000 and additional works for a sum of $10,000.

7. *Chicago Tribune*, "Art Notes," February 18, 1884, and *Chicago Tribune*, "Art Notes," May 11, 1884. The New York exhibition is noted in an untitled newspaper clipping from the *New York Daily Times*, March 16, 1884. For a list of some of MacEwen's early Dutch works, see MacEwen, "List of Principal Works," curatorial file, Art Institute of Chicago.

8. Annette Stott, "Documentation of American Artists' Activities in Holland from Dutch Archives," in *Holland Mania: The Unknown Dutch Period in American Art and Culture* (Woodstock, N.Y.: Overlook Press, 1998), 272. According to *The National Cyclopaedia*, MacEwen opened a studio in Hattem in 1881. His lengthy presence there is verified in a letter from Walter MacEwen to Louise H. Burchfield of the Cleveland Museum of Art regarding one of his paintings, *The Ghost Story* (1887; cat. 34), held in the curatorial files of the Cleveland Museum of Art.

9. *The National Cyclopaedia* notes that MacEwen was in Paris by 1881, but by the time of the 1883 International Exposition in Munich, the artist still provided his address as Munich. According to Annette Stott, the artist was still an active member of the American Art Club in Munich in 1884. MacEwen's move to Paris in 1886 is supported by a publication produced by the Art Institute of Chicago, *Catalogue of Paintings Exhibited at the Opening of the New Galleries, February 24, 1890* (Chicago: S. W. Cor., 1890), 16. By 1888, the artist had settled into a long-term studio at 11, place Pigalle, Paris.

10. "New Fame for M'Ewen: Cross of the Legion of Honor," *Chicago Times-Herald*, January 1, 1896. See Lois Marie Fink, *American Art at the Nineteenth-Century Paris Salons* (Washington, D.C.: Smithsonian Institution and New York: Cambridge University Press, 1990), 367–68, for a list of MacEwen's Salon entries prior to 1900.

11. Paul Leroi, "The American Salon," *The Magazine of Art* (November 1886): 488. Also see Annette Stott, *Holland Mania*, 57. As Stott had pointed out, MacEwen departed from convention in portraying his pastoral goddesses fully clothed.

12. For a general discussion of the subject, see Mary Anne Goley, *The Hague School and Its American Legacy* (Washington, D.C.: Federal Reserve, 1982).

13. Girard, *L'Ami du Peuple*, undated clipping (c. 1886) in the MacEwen scrapbook.

14. For a discussion of MacEwen's *Returning from Work* in relation to naturalism, see Gabriel P. Weisberg, *Beyond Impressionism: The Naturalist Impulse* (New York: Harry N. Abrams, 1992), 162. Weisberg has concluded that MacEwen, who was more influenced by the Hague School than the naturalist developments in France, "offered a new direction for American artists in Paris to follow—away from the craze surrounding [Jules] Bastien-Lepage."

15. *Chicago Tribune*, "M'Ewen's Pictures," February 23, 1890.

16. *Chicago Record Herald*, untitled clipping, October 22, 1905, from a scrapbook of articles chronicling Chicago artists, Ryerson Library, Art Institute of Chicago (hereafter AIC scrapbook), vol. 21: 93.

17. This work was purchased by the well-known Potter Palmer of Chicago. A photo of the work prominently installed in the Palmers' picture gallery is found in David Garrard Lowe, *Lost Chicago* (New York: Watson-Guptill, 2000), 38. Palmer lent the painting to an exhibition of MacEwen's work at the Art Institute of Chicago in 1890, where it was displayed under the title *Dutch Urchins Calling*.

18. Untitled clipping, *Chicago Tribune*, February 16, 1890, MacEwen scrapbook.

19. Untitled clipping, *L'Art*, May 1, 1888, MacEwen scrapbook.

20. Thanks to Annette Stott, Emke Raassen-Kruimel, and Jannig Kwakman for confirming the origin of the costumes.

21. Harriet Monroe, "At the Chicago Art Institute," *Art Amateur* 22 (March 1990): 114. Thanks to Annette Stott for sharing this source.

22. "M'Ewen's Pictures," *Chicago Tribune*, February 23, 1890.

23. Michael Quick, *American Expatriate Painters of the Late Nineteenth Century* (Dayton, Ohio: Dayton Art Institute, 1976), 108.

24. "M'Ewen's Pictures," *Chicago Tribune*, February 23, 1890.

25. Untitled clipping, *American Register*, March 1888, MacEwen scrapbook.

26. Untitled clipping, *Chicago American*, November 25, 1905, AIC scrapbook, vol. 21: 107.

27. MacEwen, quoted in "Progress of Mural Art," *Chicago Sunday Tribune*, December 15, 1895.

28. "Walter M'Ewen, 'The Madeleine' Hung at the Academy," *Philadelphia Inquirer*, January 4, 1896.

29. Untitled clipping, *Chicago Tribune*, March 12, 1890, MacEwen scrapbook.

30. Pondrou, *Gil Blas*, May 1, 1890, and Bousseriot, *La Revue du Monde Latin*, June 1890, MacEwen scrapbook.

31. Both MacEwen's statement and Leroi's reply were published in Paul Leroi, "Salon de 1894," *L'Art* 57 (1894): 21.

32. Untitled clipping, *Nieuwe Rotterdamse Courant*, May 4, 1898, MacEwen scrapbook.

33. MacEwen, "List of Principal Works," submitted to the National Institute of Arts and Letters (now the American Academy and Institute of Arts and Letters), New York.

34. Jennifer Martin Bienenstock, *The Forgotten Episode: Nineteenth Century American Art in Belgian Public Collections* (Brussels: The American Cultural Center, 1987), 50–52.

35. Early in the artist's career, he completed at least four paintings of Puritan girls, currently unlocated. See MacEwen, "List of Principal Works," curatorial file, Art Institute of Chicago.

36. See Stott, *Holland Mania*, 107–10. Regrettably, none of these works could be located for the *Dutch Utopia* exhibition.

37. *New York Times*, "Nothing Striking," June 9, 1890.

38. See Annette Blaugrund et al., *Paris 1889: American Artists at the Universal Exposition* (Philadelphia: Pennsylvania Academy of the Fine Arts and New York: Harry N. Abrams, 1989), 182–83. Also, as Annette Stott has observed in *Holland Mania*, MacEwen forged another connection between Dutch and American histories in *Making the Flag* (unlocated), a domestic scene featuring an elderly grandmother sewing a Dutch flag while her husband paints the gilt top for the flag pole. Stott surmises that this scene may have been perceived as a "Dutch prototype" of the Betsy Ross legend.

39. It is unclear how many works MacEwen may have produced in this vein; the series included *Old Guard of the House of Orange* and other unlocated works. One MacEwen descendant by marriage, George Starke, vividly recalled a large canvas depicting William and Mary, which hung in the home of a relative and was tragically destroyed by fire. MacEwen's father, John McEwen, was a native of Scotland who moved to Chicago in 1851. George Starke, phone interview with the author, May 2008.

40. Untitled article, *Chicago American*, November 25, 1905, AIC scrapbook.

41. "Artist McEwen's Triumphs in France," *Philadelphia Evening Post*, January 12, 1900.

42. David Neal, "Walter M'Ewen: A Collection of His Paintings to be Exhibited Here Soon," *Chicago Tribune*, June 20, 1884.

43. "The Old Paris Salon: Foreigners Lend Interest to the Dull Old Band," *New York Times*, June 17, 1894.

44. Paul Leroi, as paraphrased in the *Tribune Art Supplement*, June 9, 1890.

45. MacEwen served on the juries of the Chicago World's Columbian Exposition (1893) and the Paris American Committee for Fine Art for the Paris Universal Exposition (1900); he chaired the European advisory committee (chairman of Paris jury) for art selection jury of the Panama-Pacific Exposition (1915); and was a member of the Paris Jury of Selection for the American art section at the Louisiana Purchase Exposition, St. Louis (1904). In addition to his numerous exhibition and Salon medals, he was awarded the Legion of Honor by France in 1896 and the Order of King Leopold II of Belgium in 1909.

46. Untitled clipping, *New York Evening Post*, June 25, 1891, MacEwen scrapbook.

47. Eugen Neuhaus, *The Galleries of the Exposition* (San Francisco: Paul Elder, 1915), 84.

48. "Some of the Pictures at the Academy," *New York Times*, December 21, 1919.

49. "Contribution for the News Bulletin of the Institute," American Academy and Institute of Arts and Letters archive, New York, February 11, 1935. Thanks to Annette Stott for sharing this material.

50. MacEwen, letter to Daniel Rich, October 6, 1939, curatorial file on MacEwen's *A Magdalen*, Art Institute of Chicago.

51. "Items for the News Bulletin of the National Institute of Arts and Letters," American Academy and Institute of Arts and Letters archive, New York, February 1, 1938. Thanks to Annette Stott for sharing this material.

I am grateful to a number of individuals who provided information and assistance important to the development of this essay. Diane Rixon, former curatorial associate at the Telfair, carefully documented many MacEwen works in public and private collections. Likewise, a subsequent former curatorial associate, Johnna Gluth, helped search for documentation on minute aspects of MacEwen's life and work. Telfair intern Josephine Warshauer spent hours deciphering the nearly illegible handwriting in Walter MacEwen's personal letters. I was made aware of these letters through Jona Vieta, a descendant of the artist by marriage, who provided significant details on his life. I am also grateful to Craig Holbert of the archives at the University of Akron, Ohio, who supplied me with copies of the letters deposited there by Jona Vieta's family. Stephen Bennett Phillips, director of the fine arts program for the board of governors at the Federal Reserve System, offered important information on the MacEwen works at that site, and Mary Ann Goley, who formerly held his position and acquired the MacEwen work, set a wonderful example with her exhibition, *The Hague School and Its American Legacy* (1982, Federal Reserve Gallery), and gave me valuable leads on additional MacEwen works. Joanna Catron at the Gari Melchers Home and Studio provided copies of interesting letters from MacEwen to Melchers, as well as important information on works in their collection. H. Barbara Weinberg of the Metropolitan Museum of Art confirmed critical facts about MacEwen's training in Munich and Paris. Denise Mahoney of the Art Institute of Chicago supplied valuable assistance with the MacEwen works in their collection, and important documentation was provided by their Ryerson Library. Karen Cassard and Inge Brasseler generously translated foreign-language texts related to MacEwen, and Margaret Williams translated information from a relevant German archive. Ann O'Brien Fuller helped me to access official documentation on the artist available online, including ship's passenger registries and passport applications. Hanneke van Zuthem, curator at the Open Air Museum in Arnhem, the Netherlands, helped identify regional costumes in some of MacEwen's Dutch genre scenes. Jannig Kwakman at the Hotel Spaander, Volendam, also provided important insight. Annette Stott was a wise and generous advisor on this essay's finer points as well as general content. Courtney McGowan and Kate Hoernle at the Telfair were early and thoughtful proofreaders. Finally, thanks are due to Mr. and Mrs. George Starke, who, in addition to donating a lovely Dutch genre scene by MacEwen to the Telfair's collection, generously shared memorabilia and work by the artist that had descended in their family, inspiring me to learn more.

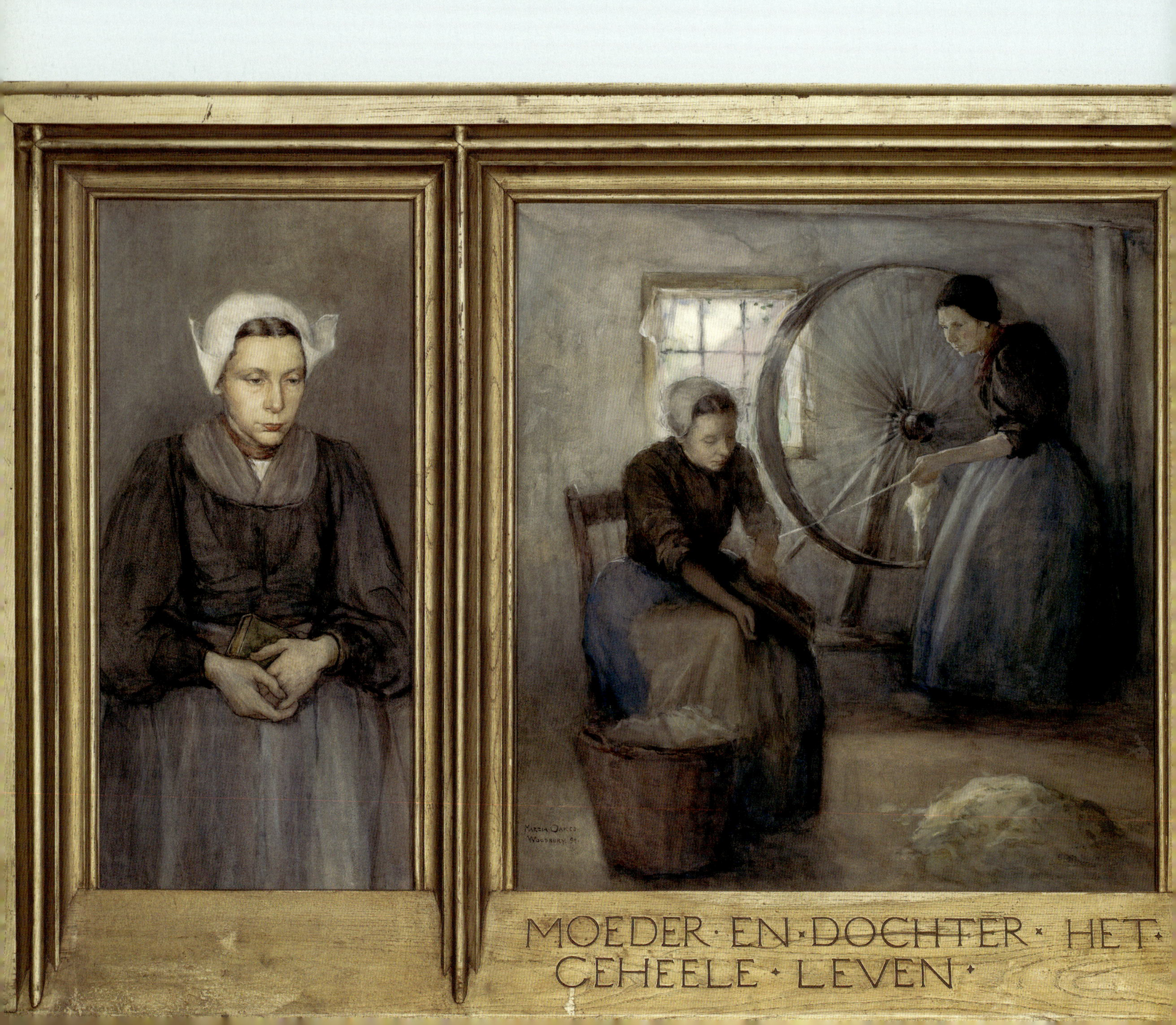
MARCIA · OAKES
WOODBURY
MOEDER · EN · DOCHTER · HET ·
GEHEELE · LEVEN ·

Catalog

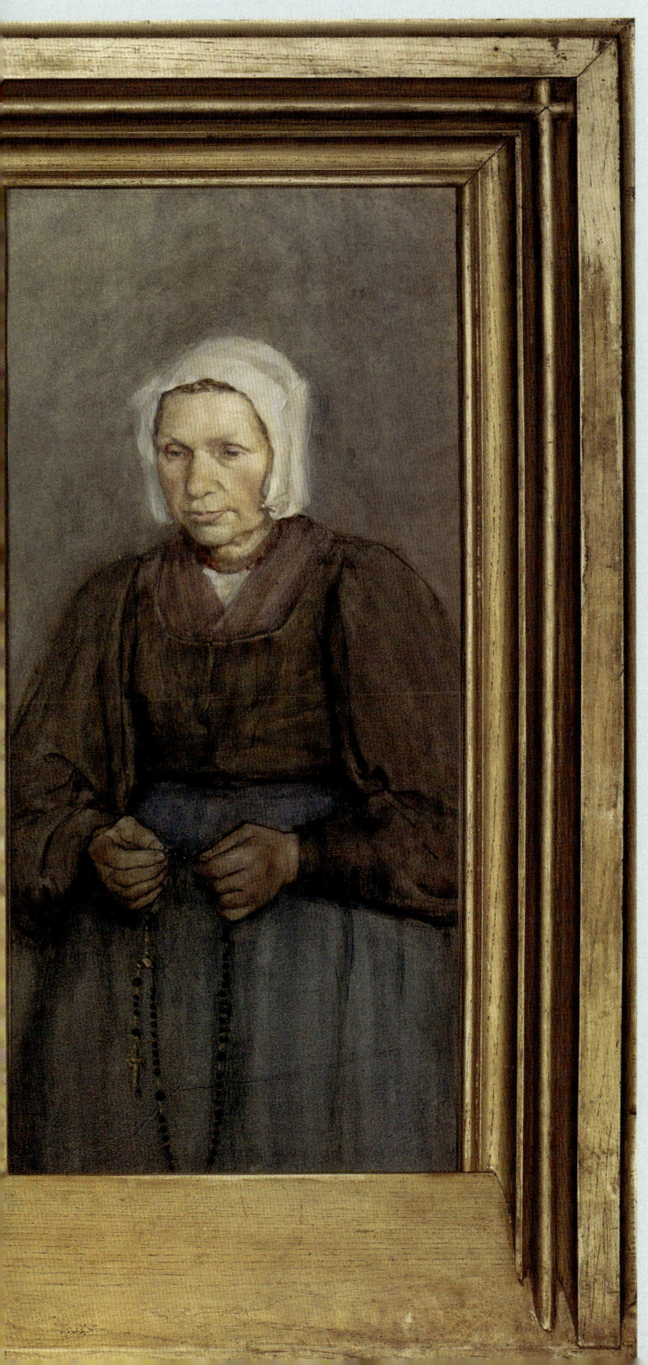

AUTHORS

AB	Alison Bowman
AvD	Alexandra Gaba-van Dongen
AS	Annette Stott
CM	Courtney McGowan
ERK	Emke Raassen-Kruimel
HKM	Holly Koons McCullough
JC	Joanna Catron
KH	Kaitlyn Hogue
LG	Lori Grecco
MG	Meagan Goddard
MM	Micah Messenheimer
MR	Miku Rager
MW	Maya D. Wright
NB	Natasha Brandstatter
ON	Olivia Nagel
RM	Renee Miller

VENUES

TMA	Telfair Museum of Art, Savannah, Georgia
TAFT	Taft Museum of Art, Cincinnati, Ohio
GRAM	Grand Rapids Art Museum, Michigan
SL	Singer Laren Museum, the Netherlands

Unless otherwise noted, works will be exhibited at all four venues.

Mathias J. Alten 1871–1938

1

The Broken Mast, 1910–11

Oil on canvas, 32 × 42"
Signed: "M. Alten"
Grand Rapids Art Museum, Michigan
Gift of Peter C. and Pat Cook, 1998.1.2

IN AUGUST 1910, THE THIRTY-NINE-YEAR-OLD MICHIGAN ARTIST Mathias J. Alten made his second trip to Holland, taking his family and a student with him. Alten spent about a year in Katwijk and other Dutch coastal towns, producing seascapes and beach scenes at a tremendous pace.[1] Among the results was *The Broken Mast,* which depicts a crippled Dutch fishing boat pulled in from the sea by a team of horses. The composition was influenced by the Hague School artists Hendrik Willem Mesdag and Willem Maris, but the palette is typical of Alten's 1910 Holland views in its suggestion of the higher key color of French impressionism. Alten was particularly skillful in his depiction of animals, and it is the horses in *The Broken Mast* that are the true sympathetic subjects of the piece as they strain against the weight of the damaged vessel. Meanwhile, the human laborers in the painting seem more relaxed, as if they are going through the motions of a task so familiar it has become second nature. This painting is about humankind's reliance on and relationship with a powerful natural world. The sea gives the village its food and economy, but also breaks ships. The horses aid the fishermen in their quest, while requiring care and direction.

NB

1. William H. Gerdts, et al., *Mathias J. Alten: Journey of an American Painter* (Grand Rapids, Mich.: Grand Rapids Art Museum, 1998), 37–38.

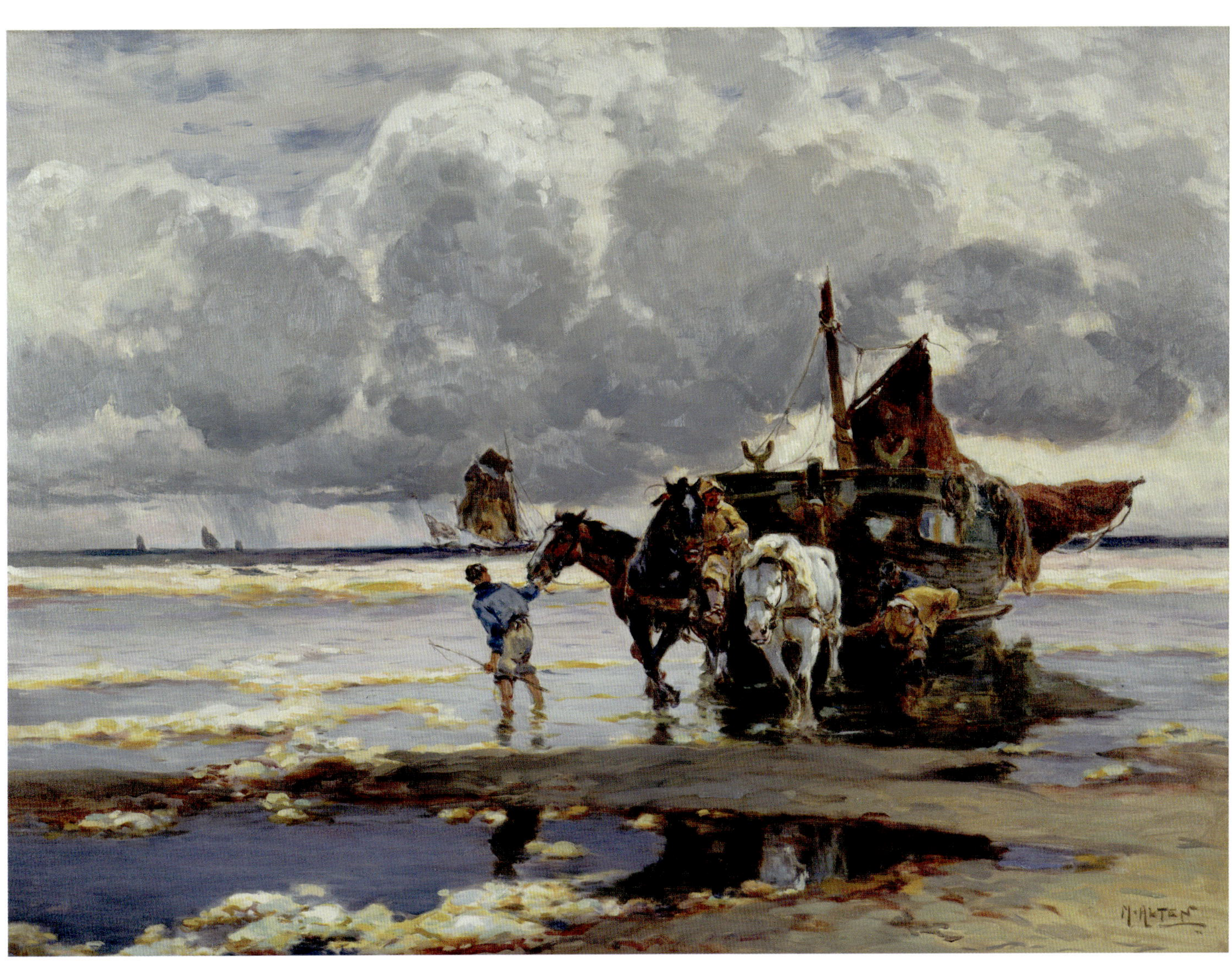
M·ALTEN

Martin Borgord 1869–1935

2

Portrait of Japie Wiegers, 1903

Oil on canvas, 21⅞ × 18⅜"

Signed: "M. Borgord. 1903"

Singer Laren Museum, the Netherlands

IN 1902 MARTIN BORGORD TRAVELED TO LAREN WITH HIS FRIENDS, the painter William Henry Singer Jr. (cat. 60–62) and Singer's wife, Anna Spencer Brugh. They had met in Allegheny City near Pittsburgh in the 1890s. Borgord—originally "Borgard" in Norwegian—was born in Gausdal, Norway, and emigrated to the United States around the age of fifteen, after the death of his parents. Borgord studied at the Académie Julian in Paris in the early 1890s and subsequently received instruction from William Merritt Chase (cat. 8–9) in New York. Besides being a painter he was also a sculptor. He became director of the Allegheny School of Art in 1898. Following a second period of study at the Académie Julian together with William Singer, he worked in Laren from 1902 to 1905. Little is known about his art prior to this time other than that he painted landscapes and figures. A few color sketches made while he was still in America feature charmingly attired ladies. In Laren, the romantic atmosphere of this early work gave way to a more realistic vision. In 1903 he exhibited Laren interiors with figures at the J. J. Gillespie gallery in Pittsburgh. A reviewer wrote in *The Pittsburg Index:* "Mr. Borgard's treatment of Dutch subjects is said to be very faithful and at the same time somewhat more vivacious than is usually the case."[1] Borgord certainly achieved greater realism in his portraits of farmers than most other painters in Laren. He not only accurately limned Japie Wiegers's countenance, he also expressed something of her inner self. Her life's travails are reflected in her careworn face. Knowledge of seventeenth-century Dutch portraiture undoubtedly underlay Borgord's likenesses, as is further discussed in the entry on *Lammert Wortel, a Laren Farmer* (cat. 3).

ERK

1. "Dutch Paintings by Martin Borgard," *Pittsburg Index*, January 31, 1903.

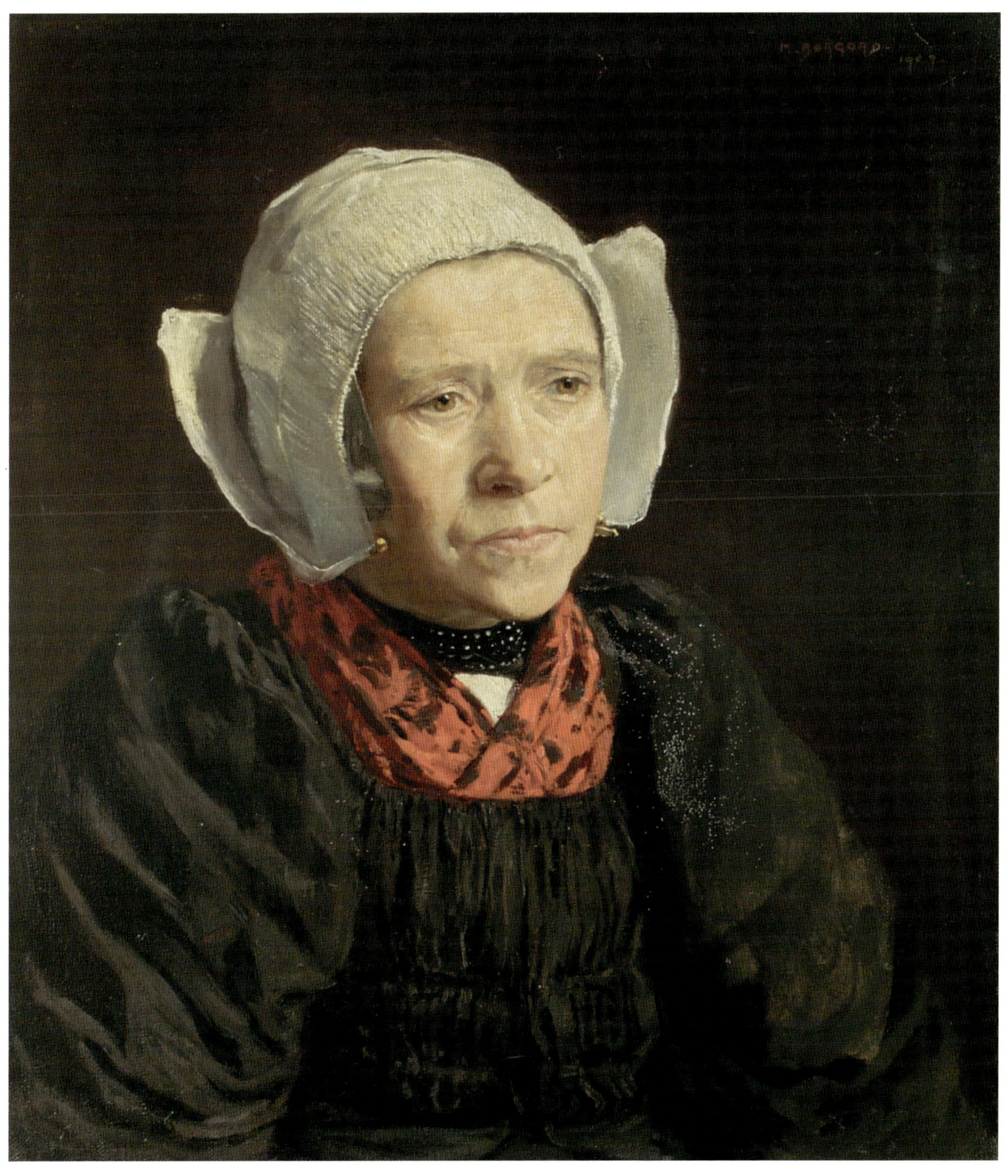

Martin Borgord 1869–1935

3

Lammert Wortel, a Laren Farmer, 1905

Oil on canvas, 21⅞ × 18⅜"

Signed: "M. Borgord. 1905."

Singer Laren Museum, the Netherlands

MARTIN BORGORD'S INTEREST IN SEVENTEENTH-CENTURY ART can be deduced from the fact that in 1903 and 1904 he visited the Rijksmuseum in Amsterdam to copy paintings, including *The Merry Drinker* by Frans Hals and the *Jewish Bride* by Rembrandt; he also visited the Frans Hals Museum in Haarlem on several occasions for the same purpose. In addition to such ebullient canvases as *The Merry Drinker,* Hals painted portraits of affluent burghers, evidencing great insight into their character. Rembrandt, too, rendered his models with compassion and an understanding of their emotions. A sense of this empathy can also be discerned in Borgord's portraits of Laren sitters. The face of Lammert Wortel is not idealized, but is portrayed quite naturalistically. On the other hand, the striking profile view of the sitter lends him a certain status. The retiring and honest character of this portrait is reminiscent of likenesses by the Laren painter Ferdinand Hart Nibbrig, but whether Borgord had seen them is not known. In the period 1911–19 Borgord was officially registered at William Singer's address in Laren and worked in his studio. He gradually abandoned realism and painted dreamlike scenes with figures in pastel shades. He also made quite a few bronzes, mostly of female figures, betraying the influence of Auguste Rodin. In 1924 a large exhibition of these paintings and sculptures was held in Galerie de Marsan in Paris. Borgord enjoyed traveling; he spent time in Paris occasionally or worked in Norway with William Singer, with whom he always remained friends. He returned to America in the mid-1920s, and died in Riverside, California, in 1935.

ERK

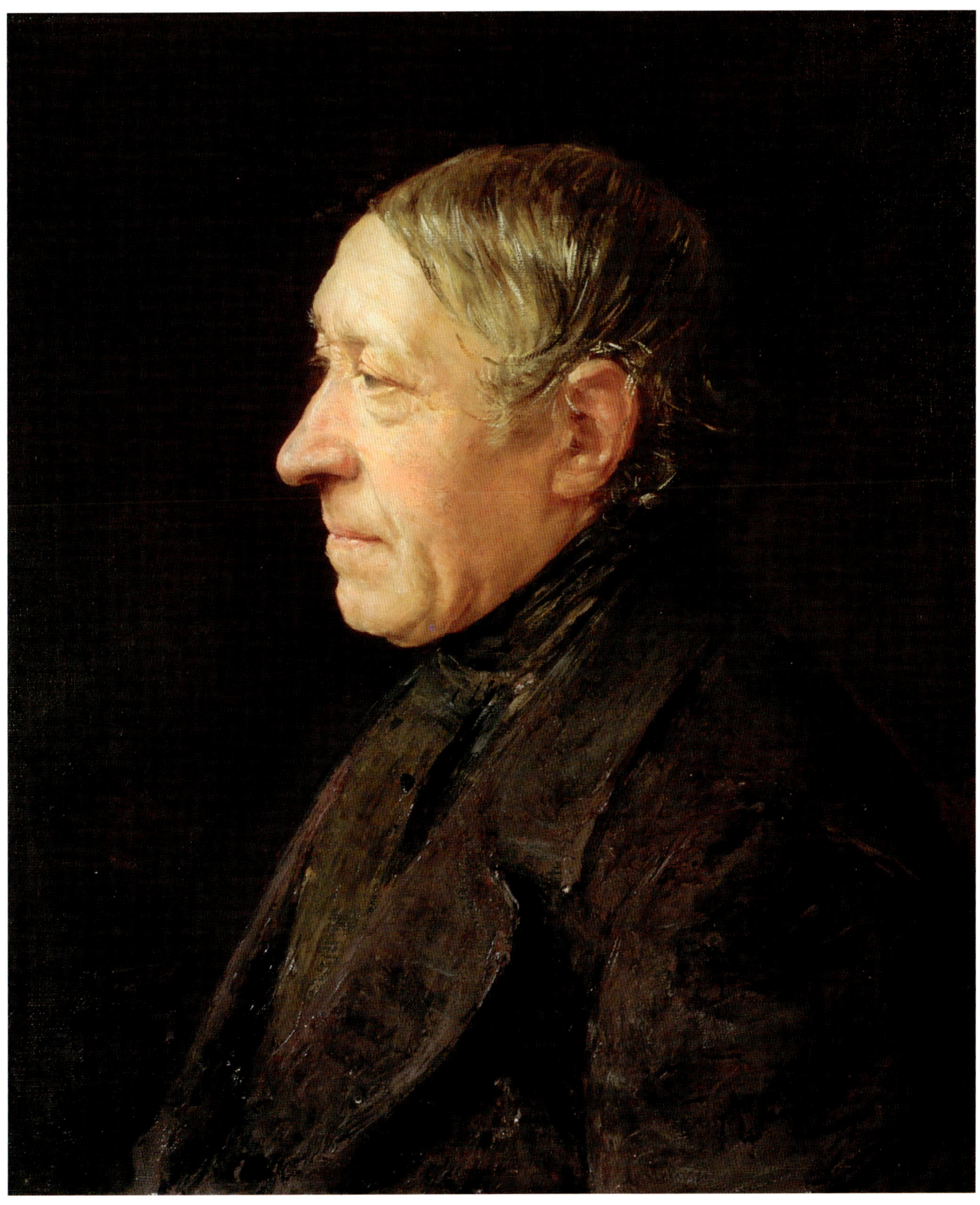

George Henry Boughton 1833–1905

4

The Edict of William the Testy, 1877

Oil on canvas, 43½ × 67¼"
Signed: "G. H. Boughton 1877"
Westmoreland Museum of American Art,
Greensburg, Pennsylvania
Gift of M. Knoedler & Company and Victor D. Spark

BORN IN ENGLAND, BOUGHTON MOVED TO ALBANY, NEW YORK, with his parents when he was a small child. He grew up there, surrounded by reminders of the region's colonial Dutch origins, and then moved to New York City where he opened a studio. He experienced some success as a self-taught illustrator and painter, but went to Paris around 1860 for further study. From there he traveled to England where he continued to study seventeenth-century costume and artifacts, eventually becoming an expatriate. Given this background, it is not surprising that Boughton specialized in historical pictures, many of which represented colonial New England and New Netherland. Often the same figure served both capacities with a simple change of dress or setting from one canvas to the next.

Boughton sought inspiration for his pictures in literature. *The Edict of William the Testy* illustrates an event in Washington Irving's humorous *Knickerbocker's History of New York*, in which Irving explains that William the Testy, a governor of New Netherland, issued an unpopular decree banning smoking. The irate Dutchmen, "armed with pipes and tobacco-boxes and an immense supply of ammunition, sat themselves down before the governor's house and fell to smoking with tremendous violence," wrote Irving. "The testy William issued forth like a wrathful spider, demanding the reason of this lawless fumigation." Boughton chose that moment for this painting. William clutches his edict in one hand and shakes his walking stick at the smokers with the other. He and the woman behind him are dressed in costumes taken straight from the paintings of the Dutch Golden Age. A supply of clay pipes and loose tobacco sits on a barrel at the ready, and citizens of all classes raise a cloud of smoke that hovers in the air. The painting, at one time in the collection of the Metropolitan Museum of Art, was very popular. Boughton made at least one copy of it, and it was reproduced in prints and journals on both sides of the Atlantic. It is one of several scenes Boughton drew from this source; in 1886 the Grolier Club of New York commissioned a new edition of Irving's *History of New York*, illustrated by Boughton.

Comparison with an earlier painting of the same subject by John Quidor, which has a similar compositional organization but more wildly active caricatured figures, throws into relief the relative solemnity and respect with which Boughton treated his subject. That change can be attributed in part to Boughton's study of the old masters and to the greater regard that Americans developed for the Dutch and for their own Dutch history in the late nineteenth century. Boughton's later Dutch historical genre pictures would continue this trend, informed by his travels in the Netherlands, where he sketched pictures at a great rate. Working in his London studio, he turned them into illustrations for a travelogue that was serialized in *Harper's New Monthly Magazine*. Soon, he was combining details from his sketches of contemporary Holland with his images of colonial New Netherland.

AS

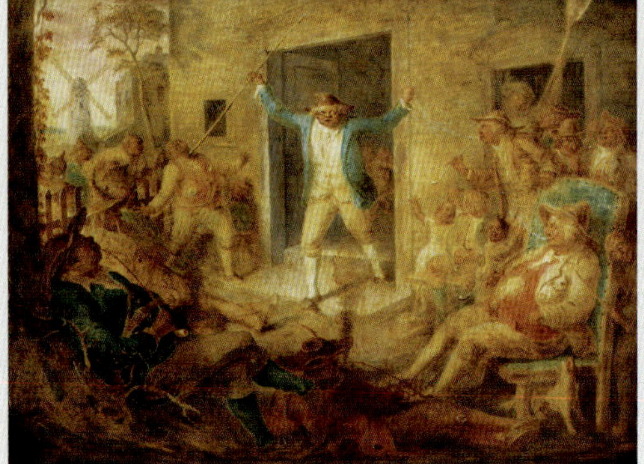

John Quidor, *Edict of William the Testy against Tobacco*, c. 1865, oil on canvas, Shelburne Museum, Vermont.

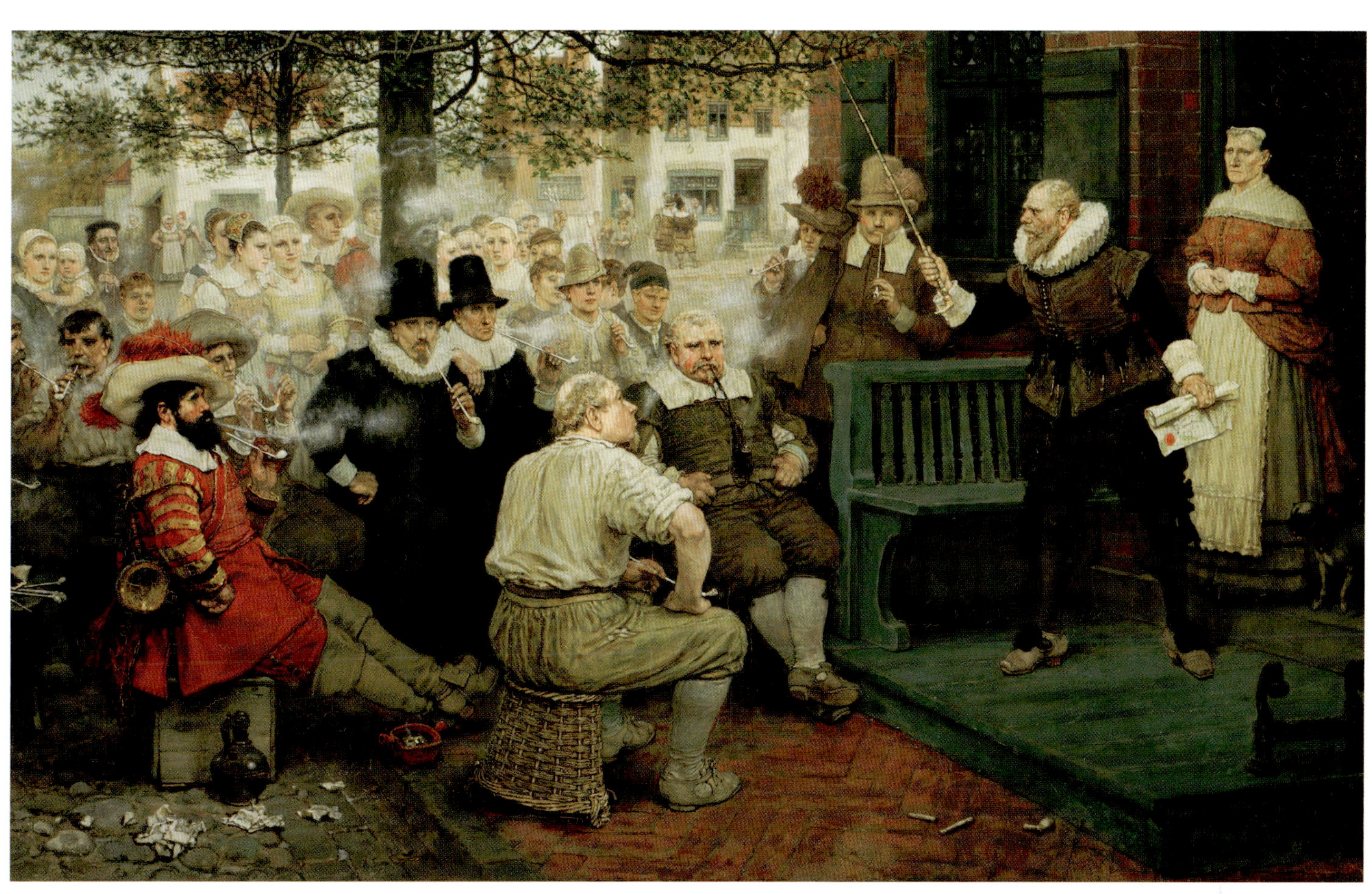

George Henry Boughton 1833–1905

5

Weeding the Pavement, 1882

Oil on canvas, 36 × 60"
Signed: "G. H. Boughton 1882"
Tate, London, England
Presented by Sir Henry Tate 1894

FUNDED BY THE NEW YORK PUBLISHING FIRM HARPER AND BROTHERS, George Henry Boughton traveled to the Netherlands in the summers of 1880 and 1881 to sketch and write about the inhabitants of rural Dutch villages. He painted *Weeding the Pavement* in 1882 from his sketches and exhibited it at Grosvenor Gallery in London that year as *The Weeders of the Pavement—A Grass Grown Port, North Holland.* The scene takes place in Hoorn on the Zuider Zee and shows the remarkable task of women in traditional Dutch dress pulling weeds from a cobbled quay. Boughton reproduced it as an illustration in *Harper's New Monthly Magazine* in 1883 and in his 1885 book *Sketching Rambles in Holland*, where it gained an American audience. The painting was purchased by British sugar magnate Sir Henry Tate, who appreciated the work so much that he presented it to the nation as one of the first pieces in the National Gallery's founding collection.

The popularity of Boughton's Dutch imagery among British and American audiences revealed a desire for utopian scenes of Holland that could stand in direct opposition to the chaos of an increasingly industrialized West.[1] It also suggests a pressing need to capture and preserve what was considered both picturesque and morally sound in the Dutch way of life, before it was razed by Holland's own advancing industrialization. In his preface, Boughton states his intent to "give the impression day by day of . . . one of the most quaint and artist-beloved countries in the world," while his description of women weeding emphasized the honored Dutch stereotypes of honest labor and impeccable cleanliness: "They don't let the grass grow in the streets so long as they can prevent it. If you stroll out in some of the less frequented parts in early morning, you will see a bevy of women, young and old, sitting on little, low stools, or kneeling on folded sacks, picking out the grass and herbage from between the stones of the street and quays. It is all so orderly, and they look so neat and prim . . ."[2]

In *Weeding the Pavement*, Boughton created a picturesque scene of what American audiences considered typically and admirably Dutch. The traditional architecture and neat figures create a quaint picture not of backbreaking labor but of communal gathering. Boughton's composition—tightly organized horizontal bands of quay, water, and sky—reinforces the tidiness of his subject. Signs of industry appear in the hazy distance across the water, but rather than impede the viewer's experience of a preindustrial Holland, they gently underscore the importance of preserving a vanishing culture against encroaching industrialization. Hoorn had seen economic decline in the eighteenth century, but was experiencing steady commercial growth at the time of Boughton's stay. He described the return to the harbor of the small commercial steamers, but in *Weeding the Pavement* he chose to highlight the unique qualities of a fading utopia. His image served as both a visual record of Holland's folk culture and an antidote against the growing din of industry.

RM

1. Annette Stott, "Dutch Utopia: Paintings by Antimodern American Artists of the Nineteenth Century," *Smithsonian Studies in American Art* 3, no. 2 (Spring 1989): 47–61.

2. George H. Boughton, *Sketching Rambles in Holland* (New York: Harper and Brothers, 1885), preface, 160–61.

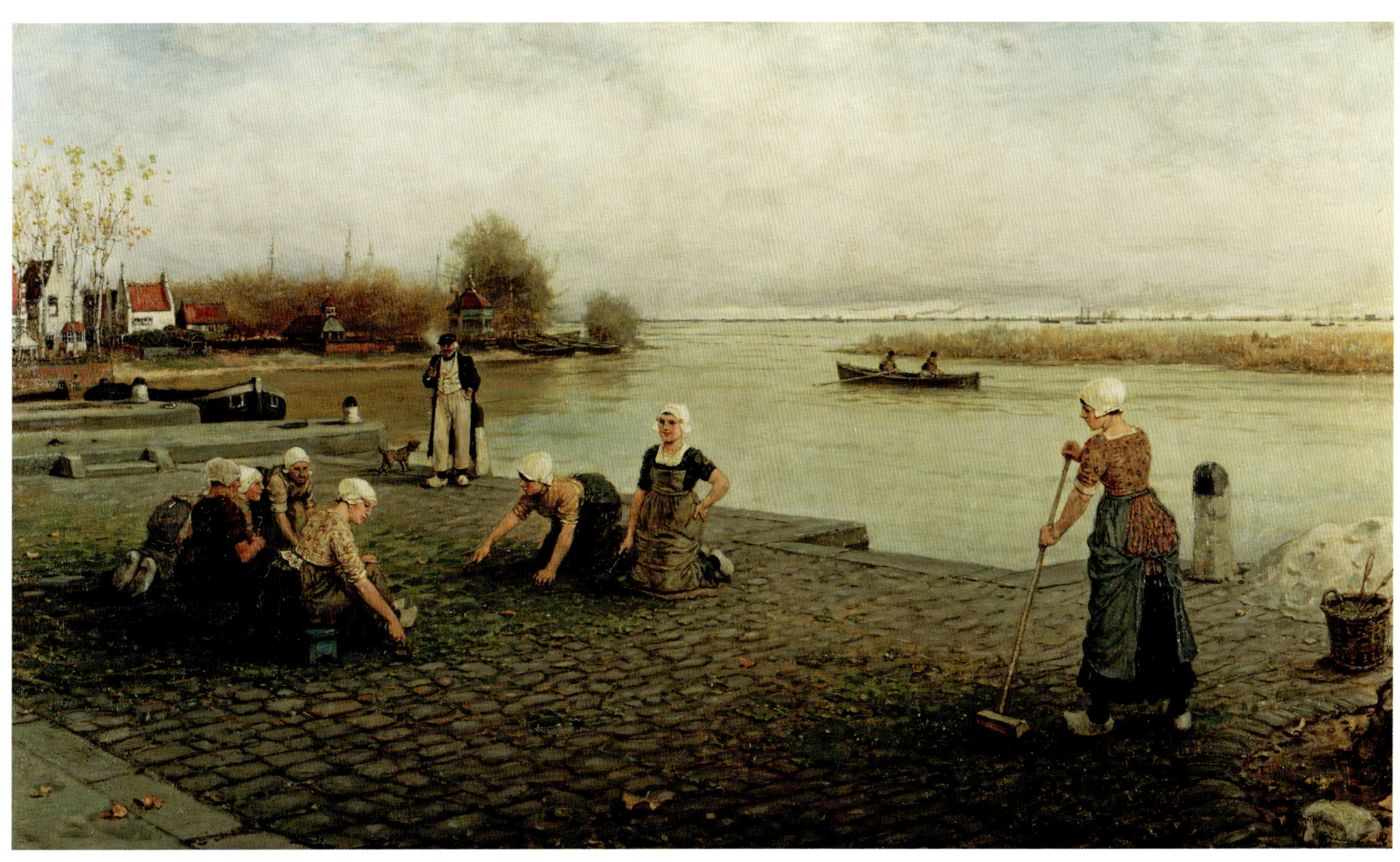

Anna Richards Brewster 1870–1952

6

Wharf at Volendam, 1908

Oil on canvas, 20 × 30"

Signed: "A Richards 1908"

Huntsville Museum of Art, Alabama

DURING HER PROLIFIC CAREER OF MORE THAN SIXTY YEARS, Anna Richards Brewster created more than two thousand oil sketches. According to her husband, William Tenney Brewster, her painting sessions took no more than a couple of hours and she sometimes painted two sketches a day, one in the morning and one in the afternoon.[1] Her rapid working method contrasted sharply with the painstaking Pre-Raphaelite inspired technique of her famous father and first teacher, William Trost Richards. Brewster used her small oil sketches to paint larger-scale works that often retain the vigor of her rapid sketches, despite their size.

Brewster painted *Wharf at Volendam* in 1908 from sketches she had made on a trip to Holland with her friend and fellow painter, Helen Simpson Whittemore, six years earlier. Although the painting measures twenty by thirty inches, Brewster's rapid and loose brushstrokes sustain the instantaneous quality of the smaller sketches on which she based the painting. Brewster's chief concern here was to capture a moment in time as she observed it with her own eyes. While the title and traditional costumes with tall fur hats disclose the location as the Dutch fishing village of Volendam, what Brewster captured was time itself. The squatting Volendam fishermen simply pass the time, waiting for the tide and winds to be right to sail. A woman in local dress ambles unhurriedly along the dyke that protects the village from inundation. *Wharf at Volendam* embodies Brewster's quick method of painting and her ability to recognize a moment worthy of capturing, while conveying the attraction to a slower, simpler life.

Brewster went on to found the Scarsdale Art Association in Scarsdale, New York. She continued to travel frequently, visiting regions in Europe, Africa, the Middle East, and the United States, where she gathered more raw material for her paintings.

MR

1. Susan Brewster McClatchy, "A Biographical Sketch," in *Anna Richards Brewster: American Impressionist*, ed. Judith Kafka Maxwell (Berkeley: University of California Press, 2008), 16.

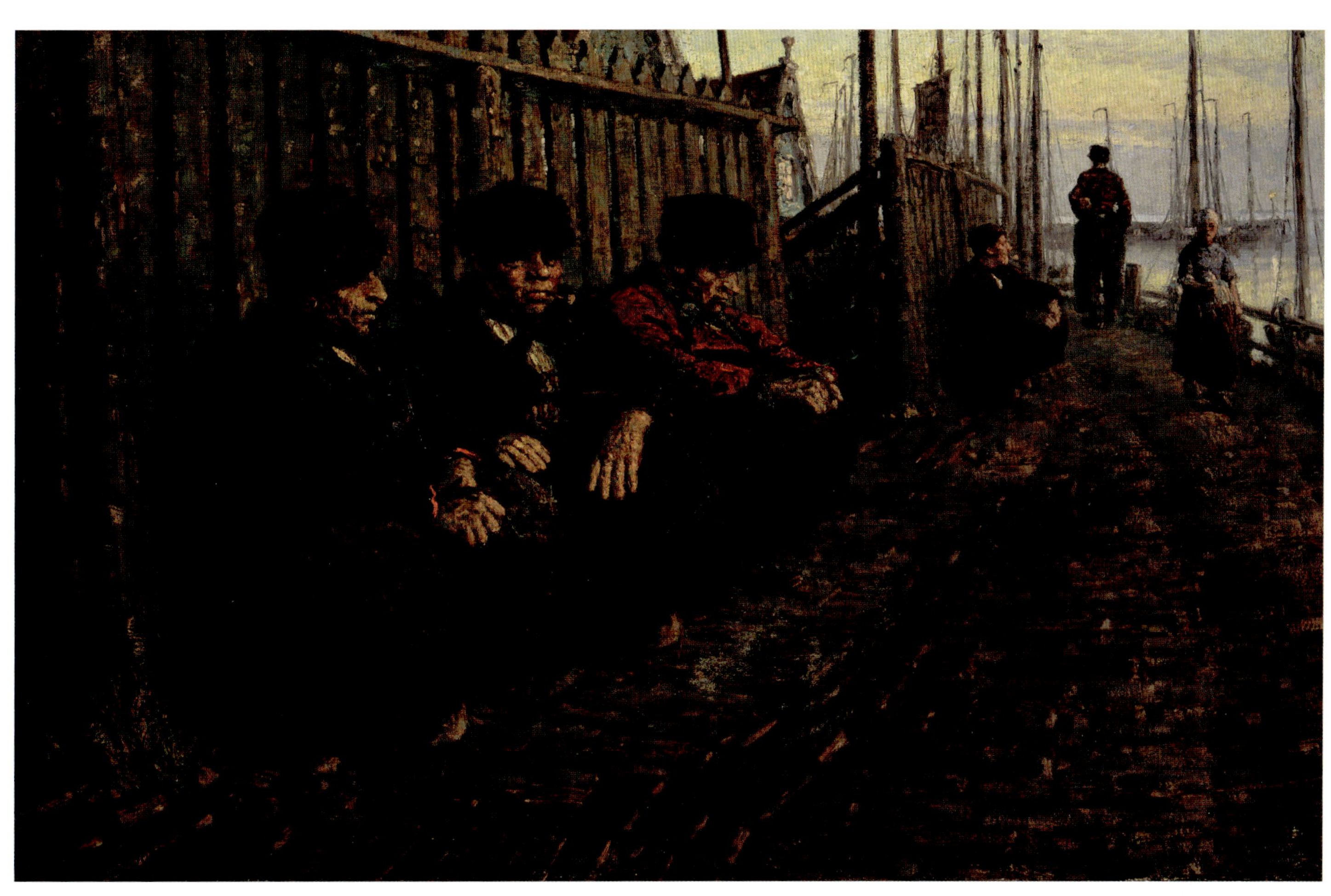

George Elmer Browne 1871–1946

7

City of Leiden, c. 1901–10

Oil on canvas, 31¾ × 39"

Signed: "Geo Elmer Browne"

Peabody Essex Museum, Salem, Massachusetts

BORN IN GLOUCESTER, MASSACHUSETTS, George Elmer Browne first studied art in Boston at the School of the Museum of Fine Arts and at the Cowles Art School in the 1890s. About 1898 or 1899 he traveled to Paris to finish his education at the Académie Julian with Jules Lefebvre. Browne traveled extensively in Europe from that time forward. He benefited considerably from the study of Dutch art, making a copy of Frans Hals's *The Merry Drinker* at the Rijksmuseum in 1901. He had several successes at the Paris Salons between 1900 and 1910, including his *Dutch Hay Ship*, an image of farmers loading a canal boat with loose hay, accepted to the 1906 Salon of the Société des Artistes Français. Primarily a landscape painter, Browne frequently painted coastal views, harbor imagery, and cityscapes. He took a studio in New York City around 1900 and thereafter painted the life and scenery along the New York waterfront, on the canals of Holland, and along the rivers of France and England.

City of Leiden fits into this genre. It was probably created during the period from 1901 to 1910, when Browne was most active in the Netherlands. He chose a perspective with part of the old city moat, called the Rijnsburgersingel, in the foreground. The top of the windmill De Valk—now a museum—can be seen on the right, the ornate tower of the famous Leiden town hall in the center, and the dome of the Hartebrugkerk—a Catholic church—on the left.[1] The artist may have taken some liberties with this scene to create the effect of an old Dutch town dominated by sunlit moist atmosphere and cloud-filled sky. A contemporary journalist wrote in 1904 that "Browne has painted much in Holland, and has undoubtedly profited by the study of the modern Dutch painters; his temperament is like theirs. . . . His composition is always pleasing, his color good, and his brushwork adequate, but the charm of his pictures is the tender elusiveness of their somewhat somber air tones."[2] Leiden carried special meaning for some Americans as the city that gave shelter to the Pilgrim Fathers before they set sail for America. It was also widely admired for standing fast against a terrible Spanish siege during the Eighty Years' War until the dykes were cut, the surrounding land flooded, and Dutch boats carrying food to the starving citizens broke the siege on October 3, 1574. For their steadfastness, Prince William of Orange granted the people of Leiden a university.

For many years, *City of Leiden* hung in the living room of the artist's brother Ralph C. Browne, an electrical engineer and inventor from Salem, Massachusetts. This painting and a portrait of Ralph Browne by George Browne are the only objects that Ralph cited separately in his will; he bequeathed them to the Essex Institute of Salem.[3]

AS

1. With great gratitude to Arti Ponsen of Leiden for identifying the canal and all the buildings in this painting.

2. W. Lewis Fraser, quoted in David C. Preyer, "George Elmer Browne, Painter," *Brush and Pencil* 14 (May 1904): 112.

3. Copy of the will of Ralph C. Browne, curatorial file, Peabody Essex Museum, Salem, Massachusetts.

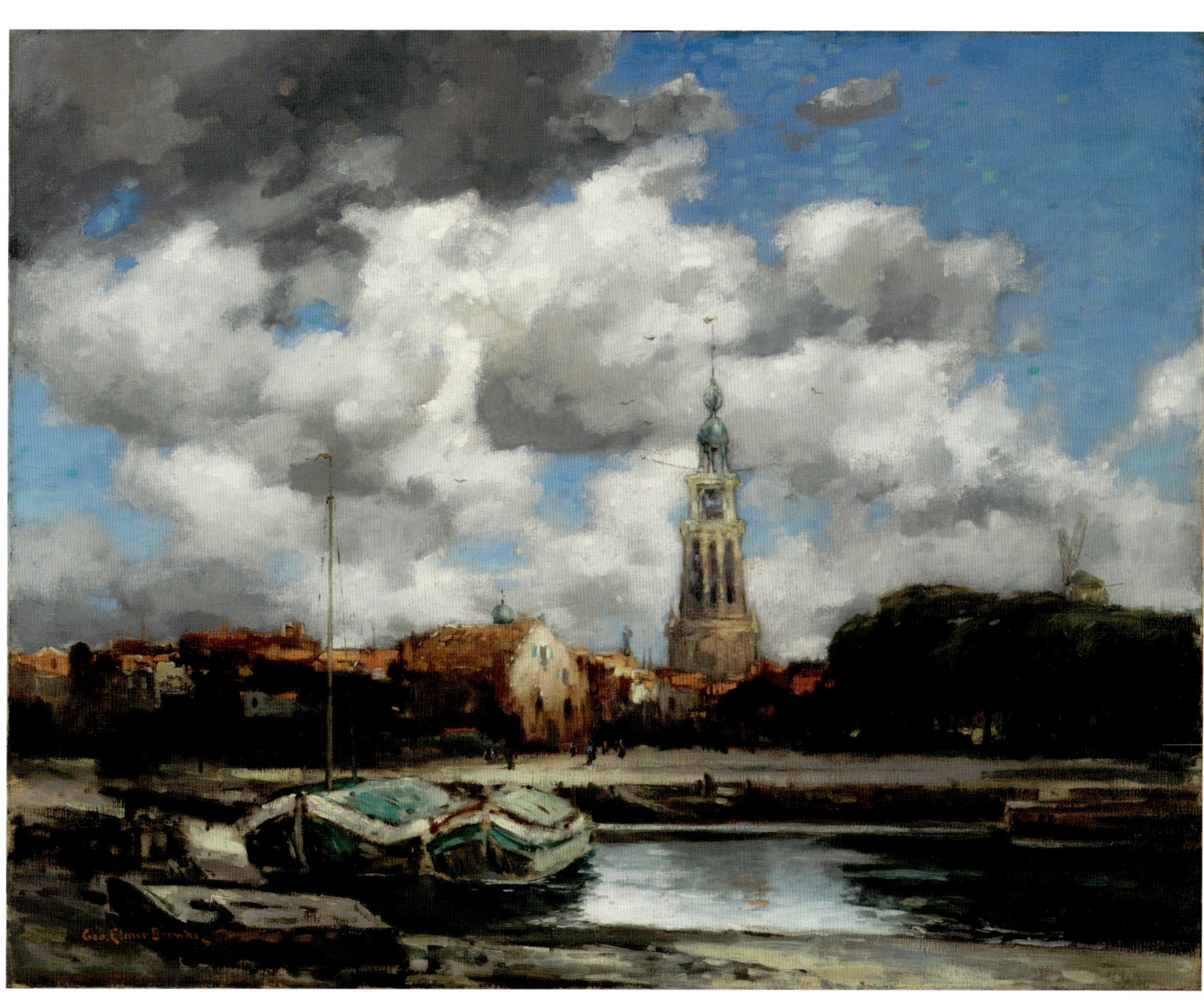
Geo. Elmer Browne

William Merritt Chase 1849–1916

8

Along the Canal (Haarlem, Holland), c. 1884

Oil on wood panel, 10 × 13½"
Signed: "W M Chase"
Memorial Art Gallery,
University of Rochester, New York
Gift of a Friend of the Gallery

WILLIAM MERRITT CHASE WAS BORN IN INDIANA and received his initial training with little-known artists there and in New York before entering the National Academy of Design. After attracting some patronage in St. Louis, where his family had moved, he was able to go to Germany for a period of study. Chase visited Haarlem briefly for the first time to pay tribute to the old Dutch masters, signing the Frans Hals Museum register in August 1878, on his way home from Munich. He returned for the summer of 1883 where, according to the *New Amsterdam Gazette,* "he spent his time chiefly in copying the works of Frans Hals in the museums."[1] Settling in for a new summer of work in 1884 with the painter Robert Frederick Blum, Chase finally began to focus on the scenery around Zandvoort, where he was staying, and nearby Haarlem. *Along the Canal (Haarlem, Holland)* may have been painted during that summer and reflects Chase's new interest in painting in the open air. A canal with small moored boats leads the eye back through a grassy plain to the massive towers of a fourteenth-century gate in the old walled city of Haarlem. Called the Amsterdam Gate because the road through it led to Amsterdam, this landmark of Haarlem anchors the left side of Chase's picture.[2] The somewhat experimental application of paint to a wood panel using broad swaths of quickly applied pigment reflects Chase's continued study of Hals. When he returned to New York he began to paint open-air park scenes and applied the lessons of his European experience. Chase returned to Holland in 1885 with James Abbott McNeill Whistler, but the two men fought from London to Haarlem and parted ways. Chase stayed to work, visiting the Hals Museum in September with landscape painters Walter Launt Palmer and John Henry Twachtman (cat. 68–69).

The view of a Dutch city across a waterway was also a theme painted by contemporary Hague School painters, with whom Chase was on the best of terms. He visited his Dutch artist friends when he traveled in Europe and they came to see him when they traveled in the United States. He owned paintings by Anton Mauve, Hendrik Willem Mesdag, and Willem Maris, possibly obtained in trade or as gifts, but it is also possible that he purchased them. Chase became one of the most successful and sought-after American painters in New York by 1890, commanding high prices for his portraits and furnishing his studio and home with the luxury items he accumulated on his many travels.

AS

1. *New Amsterdam Gazette,* September 29, 1883, 14.
2. Identification of the Amsterdam Gate by Frans Tames and Emke Raassen-Kruimel.

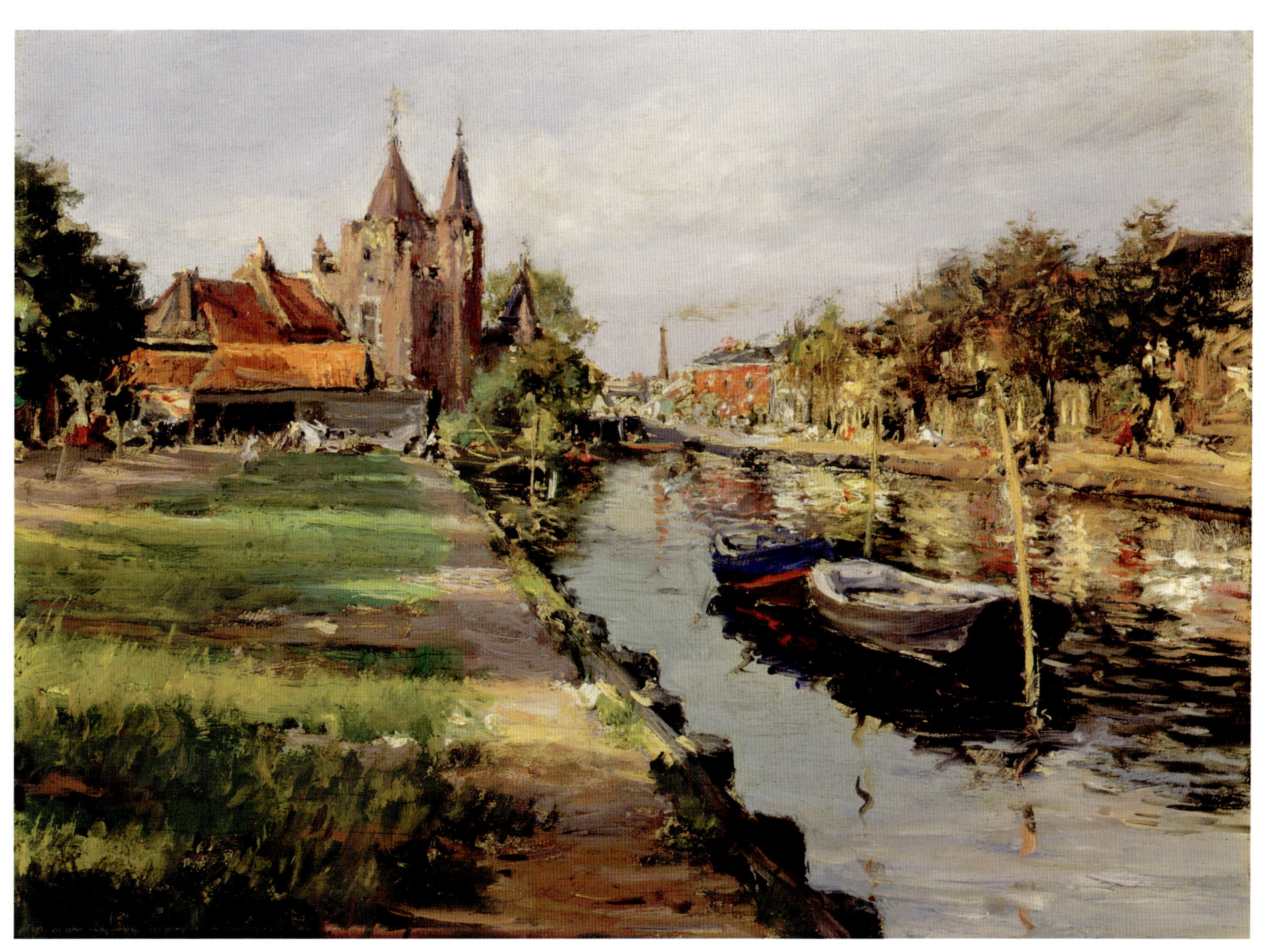

William Merritt Chase 1849–1916

9

Coast of Holland (Beach Scene, Zandvoort, Holland), 1884

Oil on canvas, 59 × 80"
Signed: "W M Chase"
Frye Art Museum, Seattle, Washington

WILLIAM MERRITT CHASE SPENT MUCH OF THE SUMMER OF 1884 with fellow painter Robert Frederick Blum in the coastal village of Zandvoort, where they shared a cottage. The artists painted Zandvoort women, landscapes, interior genre scenes, and portraits of each other. Both Chase and Blum experimented widely during that summer, testing mediums such as watercolors, egg tempera, and pastels against a variety of supports. Only a few paintings, like this one, were completed in the more traditional oil on canvas. Chase had met Édouard Manet through his friend and teacher Wilhelm Leibl in 1881. As he experimented with materials, he also experimented with style. *Coast of Holland* resembles certain landscapes by Manet. The quick brushwork, flattened space, and lack of narrative all reflect the aesthetic sensibility of the French impressionists in the 1880s.

Despite the fact that Chase was originally drawn to Holland because of his admiration for Frans Hals, many of the scenes he painted during the summer of 1884 do not look particularly Dutch. *Coast of Holland*, for example, shows a group of Hollanders walking or resting along a grassy dune and a single tossing mast off the shore. Yet the people on the beach are not the subject of the painting. Instead, Chase captures the chilly, blustery sensation of the wind and the soft, insubstantial quality of the dunes shifting beneath his feet. While this scene was certainly painted in Zandvoort, the atmosphere it conveys is familiar to anyone who has visited a similar type of coastline, not just those acquainted with Holland. Chase had little interest in painting the characteristic subjects that formed the core of Dutch work by his contemporaries George Hitchcock (cat. 22–26), Walter MacEwen (cat. 31–36), and Gari Melchers (cat. 37–45). For Chase, a commonplace corner of a meadow, some tree trunks, or an unidentifiable stretch of beach satisfied the desire for paintable subjects.

Throughout the 1890s Chase was occupied with commissions in New York, teaching, establishing a school at Shinnecock on Long Island, and conducting the business of the various artists' associations with which he was engaged. Not until 1903 did he return to Holland for a summer's work, this time with a class in tow. They made copies at the Rijksmuseum and the Hals Museum, painted landscapes and figures *en plein air*, and visited contemporary artists' studios in The Hague. Nine years later he made his last Dutch foray. Chase's style had advanced far from his 1883 copy work and his 1884 experiments, but that earlier Dutch period had proved pivotal in his development as an artist. Perhaps because of its experimental nature, the *Coast of Holland* was still in Chase's possession when he died. The McDonough Galleries purchased it from the 1917 sale of the Chase Collection for $210.[1]

NB and AS

1. "Paintings Sold at Auction 1916–1917," *American Art Annual*, 14 (1917): 345.

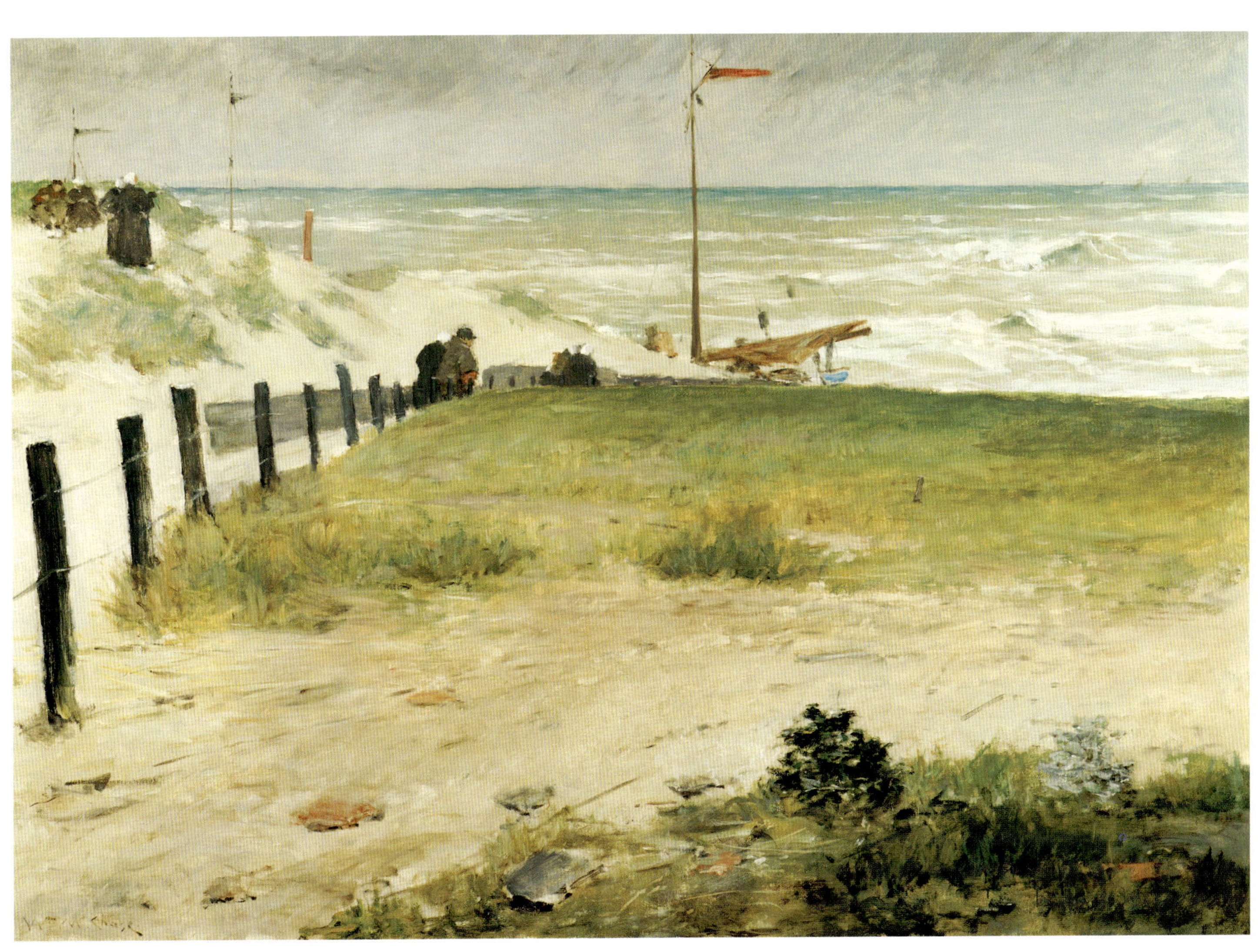

Colin Campbell Cooper 1856–1937

10

Dordrecht Harbor, c. 1898

Oil on canvas, 32 × 24"
Signed: "Colin Campbell Cooper"
Payton Family Collection

COLIN CAMPBELL COOPER SPECIALIZED IN HARBOR AND CITY VIEWS, painting in both oil and watercolor. With his wife, Emma Lampert Cooper (cat. 11), he traveled to the Netherlands several times, often working in Laren and Dordrecht. Whereas his wife portrayed the impoverished country folk, Colin preferred the urban scene. His view of Dordrecht harbor features the medieval Dordrecht Minster with its distinctive clocks on top of the fourteenth-century square tower. Yet it is not that structure's age nor the history-laden city from which the Counts of Holland once ruled that most strikes the viewer in this light-filled colorful painting, but the modernity of the artist's vision. Steeped in American impressionism and fascinated with skyscrapers, Cooper brought a fresh perspective to a subject that had been painted by European artists from the seventeenth century forward. Famous views of Dordrecht harbor by the seventeenth-century Dutch artists Jan van Goyen and Aelbert Cuyp, the English master Joseph Mallord William Turner, the nineteenth-century Hague School artist Jacob Maris, and the French impressionist Charles François Daubigny preceded Cooper's effort. Even his countryman Charles Yardley Turner had already painted a Dordrecht scene (cat. 67) in a manner almost the opposite of Cooper's—one reminiscent of the tradition of Dordrecht's Golden Age artists. Cooper ignored those precedents and instead rejoiced in sunlight on old brick, whitewash, slate, and painted wood. He made several versions of this view of Dordrecht harbor, as well as painting other views of the city.

Cooper was born in Philadelphia and studied at the Pennsylvania Academy of the Fine Arts before traveling to Paris to complete his training at the Académie Julian. He traveled throughout the world seeking inspiration for his paintings. By the end of the century he was based in New York City, where he was elected to full membership in the National Academy of Design in 1912. He is perhaps best known for his paintings of New York's tall buildings.

AS

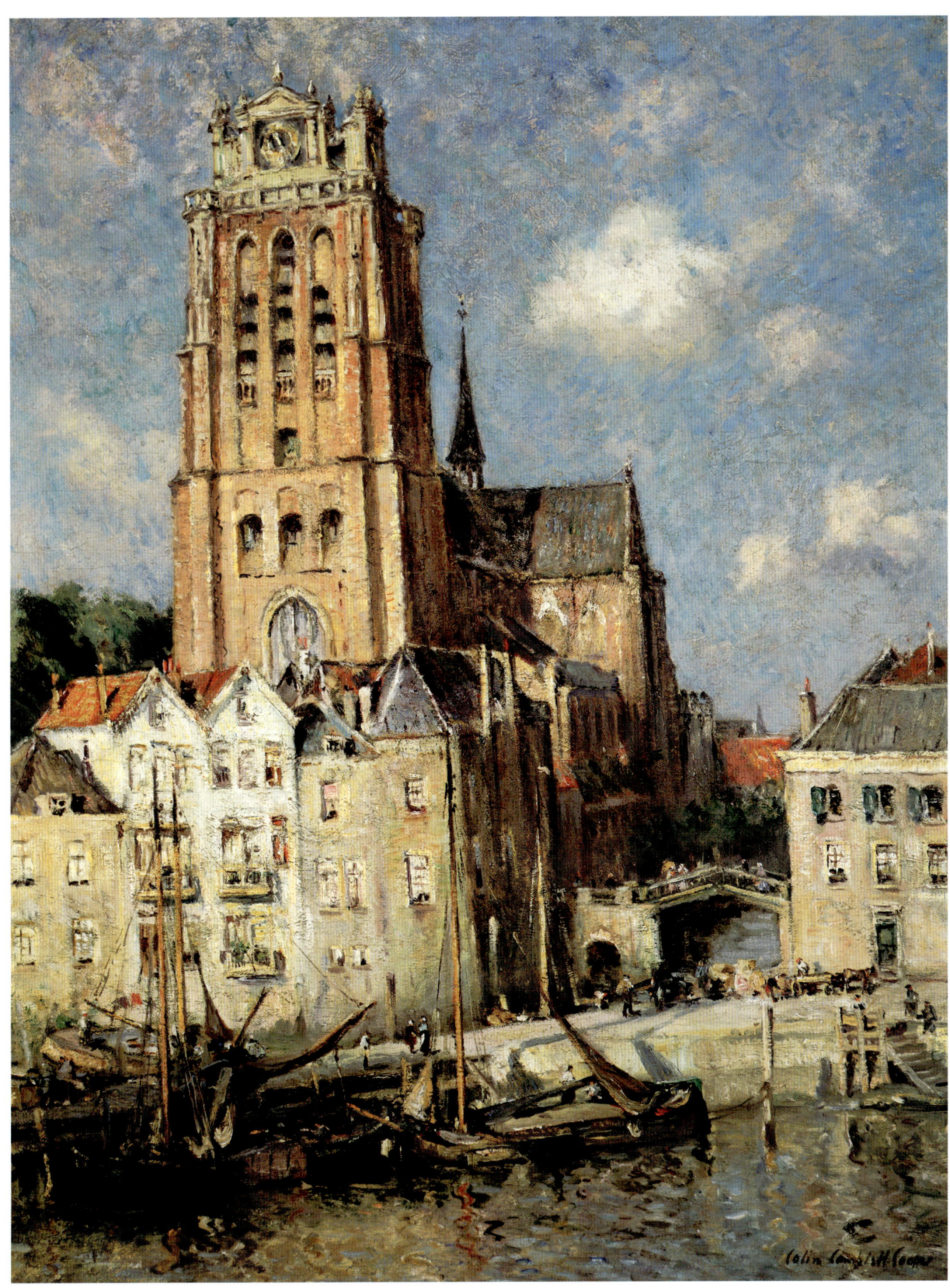

Emma Lampert Cooper 1855–1920

11

The Breadwinner, 1891

Watercolor on paper, 20 × 24"
Signed: "E. E. Lampert 1891"
Memorial Art Gallery,
University of Rochester, New York

EMMA LAMPERT WAS BORN IN NUNDA, NEW YORK, IN 1855 and received her art training at several institutions in New York City before traveling to the Netherlands where she studied with the Hague School painter Jacobus Simon Hendrik Kever. She took her studies very seriously, intent on becoming a professional artist. It was during this time studying in the Netherlands that she first visited Laren. Her painting *The Breadwinner* is set in that village and depicts a theme commonly painted by the Hague School artists and others who worked there. See, for example, Marcia Oakes Woodbury's *Moeder en Dochter* (cat. 73). In *The Breadwinner* a young woman sits at her spinning wheel working by the faint light of a window. Balls of yarn attest to her industriousness in this impoverished brown interior. The woman's blue apron and red kerchief provide the only color, similar to the dress worn by Amy Cross's Laren model in *The Holland Vegetable Vendor* (cat. 12). Like Cross, Lampert was most interested in the Dutch artists' watercolor techniques, which were both more painterly and more substantial than the watercolor paintings typically seen in the United States. Lampert began exhibiting at the National Academy of Design in 1883 and the Paris Salon in 1887. She also taught art, heading the art department of a school in Clifton Springs, New York, and teaching at the Mechanics Institute, the principal design school in Rochester. She won medals at the 1893 Chicago World's Columbian Exposition, the 1895 Atlanta Exposition (for a Dutch dunes landscape), and the 1904 Louisiana Purchase Exposition in St. Louis, in addition to various prizes in other exhibitions. At both the 1889 and the 1900 Paris Universal Expositions, she exhibited a painting titled *The Breadwinners.* The plural form suggests that it was not the same painting as *The Breadwinner* in the present exhibition, but it may have been quite similar. She married the artist Colin Campbell Cooper (cat. 10) in 1897 when she was a well-established artist with no fear of being overshadowed by her husband.

AS

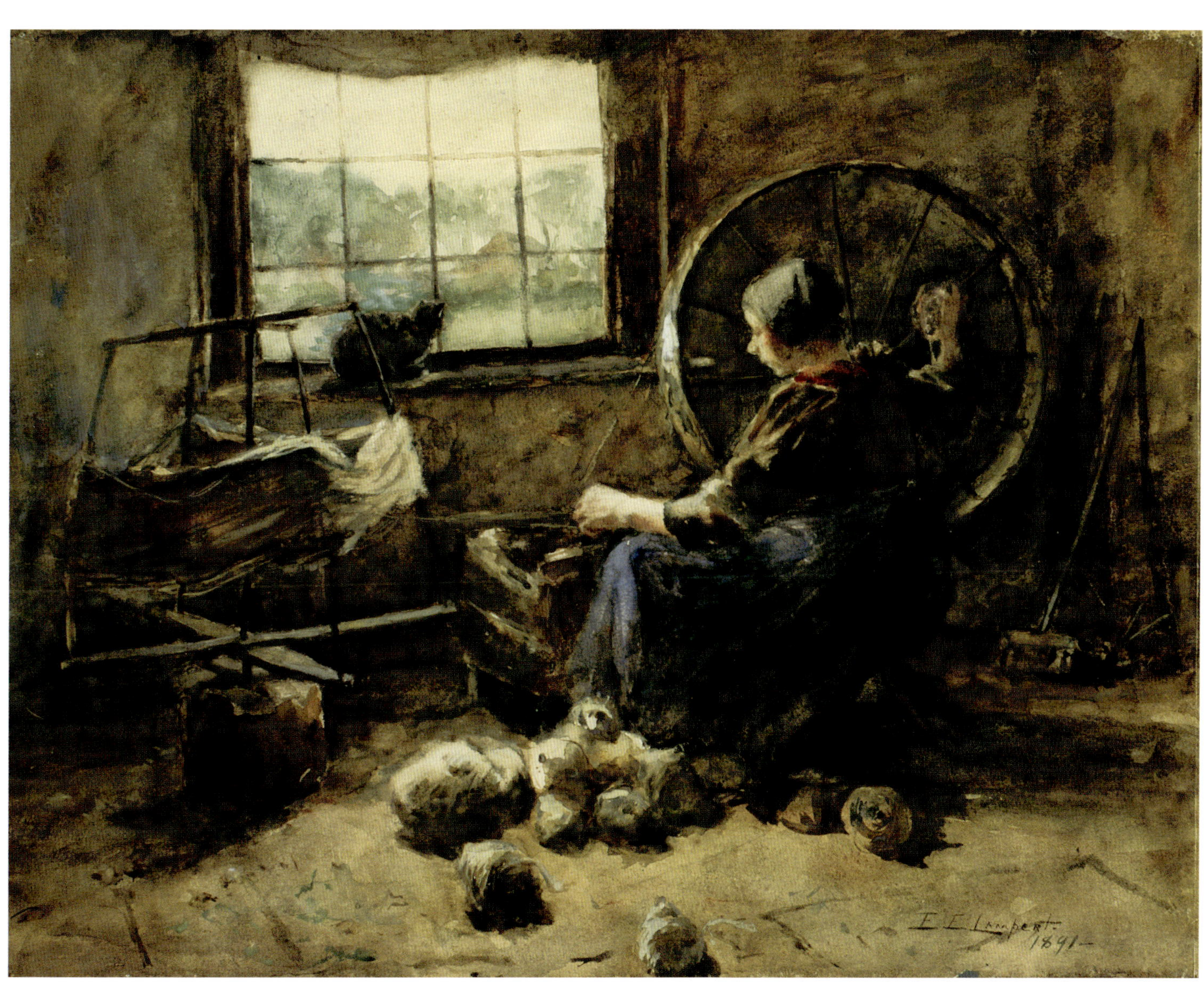
E E Lampert.
1891-

Amy Cross 1856–1939

12

The Holland Vegetable Vendor, c. 1890s

Gouache on paper, 20 × 26"
Signed: "Amy Cross"
Danforth Museum of Art, Framingham, Massachusetts
Gift of Mr. and Mrs. Eliot F. Bartlett

AMY CROSS IS ONE OF THE FEW AMERICAN ARTISTS who pursued formal academic training in the Netherlands. Born in Milwaukee in 1856, she began her studies with local landscape painter Henry Vianden, continued them at Cooper Union and the Art Students League in New York, and maintained a professional studio where she taught watercolors. At the age of thirty-three she moved to The Hague with her mother, enrolled in painting classes at the Royal Academy of Art, and entered Dutch art life. She studied with Albert Neuhuys for two seasons, probably going to Laren for the first time with her teachers and fellow students. Among her new circle of friends, she became particularly close to the lesser-known Dutch artist Tony Offermans, who painted a portrait of her mother as a gift to Cross in 1890. Like other Hague School painters, Cross spent many seasons in Laren painting landscape, floral still lifes, and local farm folk such as those depicted in *The Holland Vegetable Vendor.* Set in the street in front of a typical thatch-roofed cottage, this bucolic genre scene conveys the relaxed atmosphere of a friendly chat over the carrots and cabbages while a child plays happily in the dirt. The blue and brown palette is typical of Cross's Dutch training, as is her way of using watercolor to create solid effects. Cross is one of a handful of American artists who studied Dutch watercolor techniques in preference to the better-known English methods and introduced them to American audiences as part of the late-nineteenth-century watercolor revival. Her love of premodern subjects did not interfere with the business of being an artist. The weekly newspaper *Gooi en Eemlander* noted that the first telegraph ever received in Laren arrived from New York art dealer Knoedler & Company on December 8, 1892, for Cross and her mother, who were in residence at Hotel Hamdorff. Cross exhibited in the annual Dutch *Exhibition of Artwork by Living Masters* in 1893 and 1896, winning a medal in the first and attracting attention for her painting, *Weighing the Bread,* now lost, in the second. She belonged to the Dutch artists association Pulchri Studio as a foreign member from 1893 to 1897, when she left The Hague to establish a studio in New York. Cross never married, but devoted herself instead to painting the East Coast landscape, floral still lifes, and additional Dutch pictures. She made at least one return trip to the Netherlands in 1907.

AS

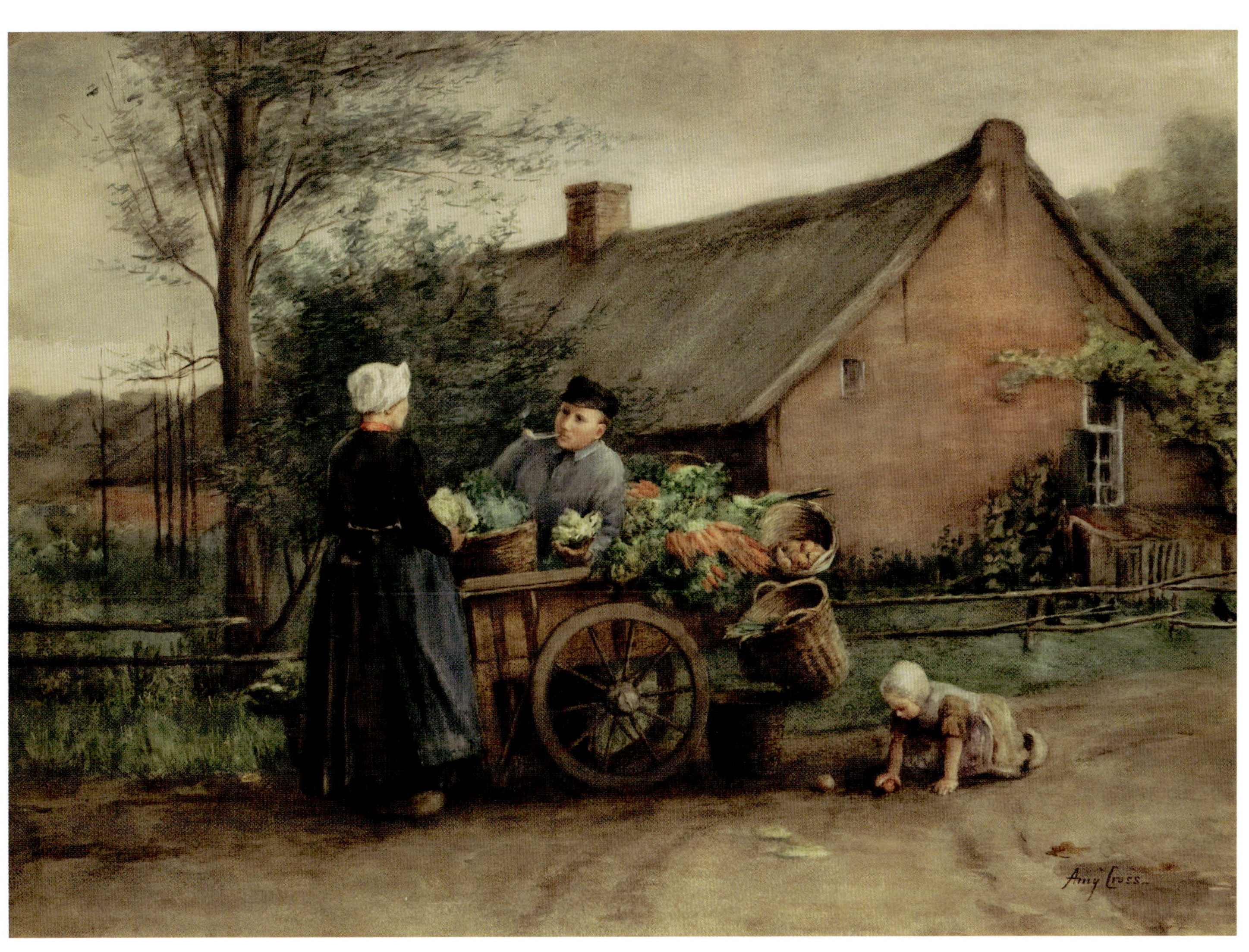
Amy Cross

Cass Gilbert 1859–1934

13

Tower of the Cathedral of Utrecht, Holland, 1898

Watercolor and pencil on paper mounted on paperboard, 18¼ × 11⅞"
Signed: "Cass Gilbert 1898"
Smithsonian American Art Museum, Washington, D.C.
Bequest of Emily Finch Gilbert through Julia Post Bastedo, executor

CASS GILBERT IS PRIMARILY KNOWN AS THE ARCHITECT who designed such Beaux-Arts gems as the St. Louis Palace of Fine Arts and who contributed to the birth of the modern Gothic skyscraper with his Woolworth Building. Yet he was also recognized throughout his career for the detailed, expressive quality of his rendering, especially his watercolors. In 1880 Gilbert embarked for Europe on his first grand tour with the purpose of gathering sketches of building motifs and decorations. The quality of his European watercolor sketches secured him his first position as a draftsman in the office of McKim, Mead, and White upon his return. After establishing himself as an architect, first in St. Paul, Minnesota, then in New York, Gilbert continued taking frequent sketching trips to Europe. His 1897–98 tour of the Low Countries, when he painted this image of the Dom Tower of the Cathedral of Saint Martin in Utrecht, appears to have been the architect's only visit to the Netherlands. However, a number of additional watercolors from that trip attest to its importance.[1] Furthermore, the works garnered an enthusiastic reception upon their display at the 1899 Exhibition of the Chicago Architectural Club at the Art Institute: "How often do the well-known down-town windows or galleries contain more fascinating, 'juicy' water-colors than Cass Gilbert's delightful, foreign sketches? . . . The architect and artist, who is never in the least labored or fussy . . . makes pure dripping color tell its architectural story, grave or gay."[2]

Gilbert synthesized numerous elements of European design into his own architectural vocabulary. The Woolworth Building, in particular, took great influence from the civic and cathedral architecture of the Netherlands. Yet the strongest correlation between *Tower of the Cathedral of Utrecht, Holland* and any building that Cass Gilbert designed may be found on a piece of hotel stationary from 1933 in the collection of the Library of Congress.[3] By encircling a drawing of the Utrecht Dom Tower next to the Broadway Chambers Building (1899–1900), constructed soon after his excursion, Gilbert suggests the influence of the columnar structure of the lower two-thirds of the tower and its transom details. This is especially evident as the archival drawing is dated well after the construction of the Broadway Chambers Building. While earlier authors have noted a dissimilarity between Gilbert's watercolor and the Broadway Chambers Building, it has recently come to light that *Tower of the Cathedral of Utrecht, Holland* and another Gilbert painting, *St. Martin's Church, Utrecht, Holland,* were accessioned under each other's titles.[4] This exhibition marks the first instance that *Tower of the Cathedral of Utrecht, Holland* is being shown with its proper title, which should clarify its impact upon Gilbert's architecture.

MM

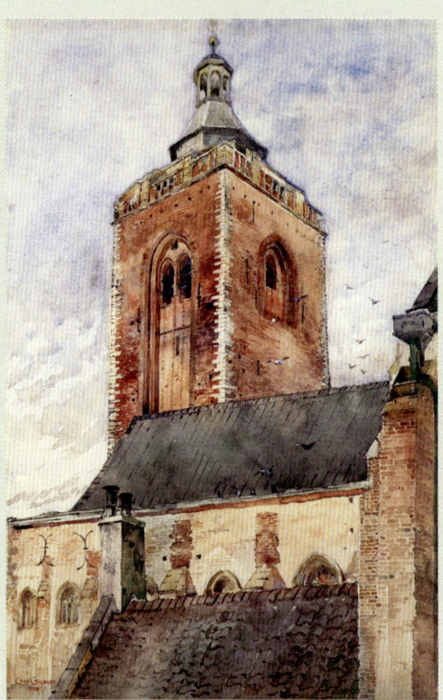

Cass Gilbert, *St. Martin's Church, Utrecht, Holland* (Previously labeled *Tower of the Cathedral of Utrecht*), 1898, watercolor, Smithsonian American Art Museum, Washington, D.C., Bequest of Emily Finch Gilbert through Julia Post Bastedo.

1. See, for example, *Mint Tower, Amsterdam* (1962.13.7; SAAM lists this as *Minttown*), *Tower at Enkhuisen, Holland* (1962.13.27), and *St. Martin's Church, Utrecht, Holland* (1962.13.33), all Smithsonian American Art Museum, Washington, D.C.

2. Robert C. Spencer Jr., "The Architectural Club's Annual Exhibition at the Art Institute, Chicago," *Brush and Pencil* 4, no. 2 (May 1899): 90–91. *Tower of the Cathedral of Utrecht* was also exhibited at the Fourteenth Annual Exhibition of the Architectural League of New York, February 11–March 4, 1899.

3. See illustration in Sharon Irish, *Cass Gilbert, Architect: Modern Traditionalist* (New York: Monacelli Press, 1999), fig. 41.

4. This assertion was made in Annette Stott, *Holland Mania: The Unknown Dutch Period in American Art and Culture* (Woodstock, N.Y.: Overlook Press, 1998), 180–81.

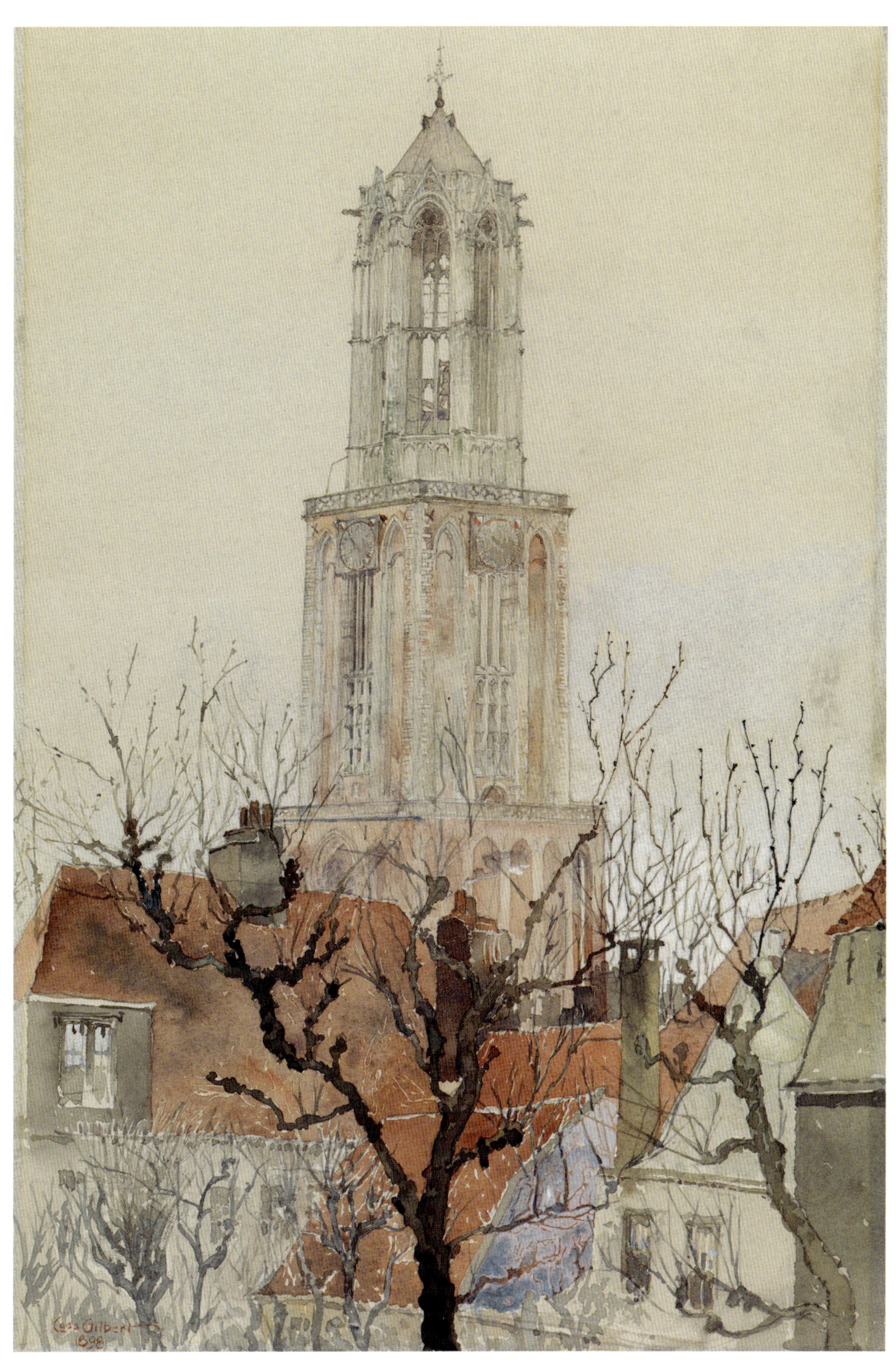

Charles Paul Gruppe 1860–1940

14

October Skies, Holland, Near Voorburg, 1890s

Oil on canvas, 28 × 36"

Signed: "Chas. P. Gruppé"

Strong National Museum of Play, Rochester, New York

BORN IN CANADA IN 1860, CHARLES PAUL GRUPPE came to the United States when he was ten and became an American citizen. He may have gone to Holland earlier in the 1880s, but definitely was there in 1890, taking classes at the Royal Academy of Art in The Hague. Throughout the 1890s he traveled between his home in Rochester, New York, and the Netherlands. In Holland he traveled extensively, often including the name of the place where he painted and the weather or subject in the titles of his paintings. *October Skies, Holland, Near Voorburg* is a typical example of this. The emphasis on the billowing clouds, the smoke drifting up from a cottage chimney, and the reflections on the water's surface impart the atmosphere of a brisk fall day. Gruppe's paintings generally suggest the Hague School, of which he was a member of the younger generation. He focused on animal paintings, landscapes, town views, and harbor and river scenes. Beginning in 1892, he exhibited these subjects in the annual *Exhibition of Artwork by Living Masters* held in a different Dutch city each year. He lived in Dordrecht in the mid-1890s, The Hague in 1897, Katwijk in 1898 and 1899, and moved to The Hague again in September or October 1899. He returned to Rochester at least three times during the 1890s for the birth of a child, the first of whom he named for the Dutch marine painter Hendrik Willem Mesdag. Gruppe was elected to the Pulchri Studio artists' association in The Hague in 1898, became a working member of the more progressive Haagse Kunstkring in 1899, and joined the national artists' group Arti et Amicitiae in Amsterdam in 1900. The Dutch Queen Mother purchased his painting *In the Rain* that year. Gruppe also experienced some success in international exhibitions, showing regularly in the Paris Salons beginning in 1899. He moved between Katwijk and The Hague until 1910 when he moved his principal domicile back to New York. Nevertheless, he continued to exhibit Dutch subjects all his life, painting them from his stock of sketches, memory, and the occasional return trip to the Netherlands.

AS

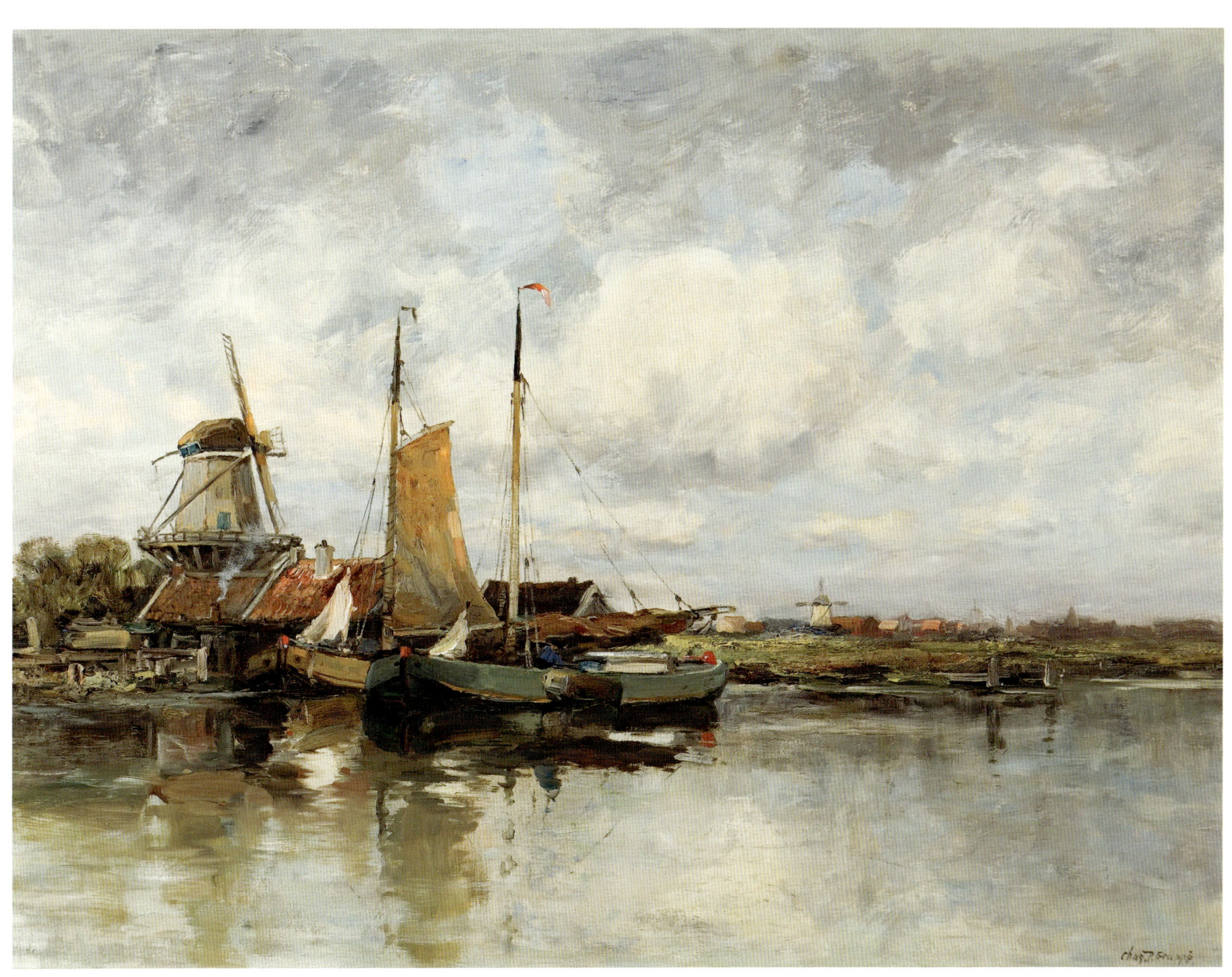

William Stanley Haseltine 1835–1900

15

Dutch Coast, 1885

Oil on canvas, 14 × 25"
Signed: "W S Haseltine 85"
Currier Museum of Art, Manchester, New Hampshire
Gift of Helen Haseltine Plowden, 1953.1

WILLIAM STANLEY HASELTINE'S WORK WAS DEFINED BY A LIFE that bridged two continents. He began studying art in Philadelphia, but his style would be most heavily influenced by his tutelage in Düsseldorf under the renowned landscape painter Andreas Achenbach. By the 1880s, Haseltine had achieved success both in America and abroad. He permanently settled in Rome, becoming a distinguished member of the expatriate community there; yet he never relinquished his ties to the United States. He selected works by American artists living in Italy for the Chicago World's Columbian Exposition in 1893, which he attended, and helped establish the American Academy in Rome in 1894. Reflecting on Haseltine's life, an Italian newspaper remarked: "He belonged to that set of American artists who, although they pass the greater part of their life 'abroad', still preserve to the end the characteristics of their race: rapid conception of ideas, accurate reproductions of what they see and thorough knowledge of what they undertake."[1]

With Rome as his base, Haseltine traveled throughout Europe and the United States. He spent several summers in Holland between 1875 and 1885, sketching the towns of Scheveningen and Dordrecht.[2] On his 1885 trip he gathered the idea and sketches for *Dutch Coast*, which he signed and dated. In *Dutch Coast*, Haseltine incorporated the composition and techniques used by seventeenth-century Dutch painters in their seascapes. The Golden Age artists lowered the horizons in their works in order to emphasize the impressive cloud formations common to the region, and applied transparent layers of glazes to increase the luminosity of their paintings. Fishing villages such as Scheveningen had been depicted in art for centuries, but saw a rise in popularity in the late nineteenth century as they developed into tourist destinations that catered to The Hague's elite as well as visitors from across Europe. Artists such as Haseltine ignored these developments in their work and chose to romanticize the local fishing culture instead. Herring fishermen would moor the characteristic flat-bottomed boats seen here by dragging them onto the beach. This laborious process had been common practice for several hundred years, and the fishermen symbolized a preindustrial existence and slower way of life to patrons of art. After a series of bad storms ravaged the coast, a protective harbor was built in Scheveningen in 1904, and the old-fashioned fishing boats were quickly replaced by newer ones.[3]

LG

1. "The Late William Stanley Haseltine," *Evening Post* (New York), April 28, 1900, originally published in *Il Giorno* (Rome), February 11, 1900.

2. Marc Simpson, Andrea Henderson, and Sally Mills, *Expressions of Place: The Art of William Stanley Haseltine* (San Francisco: The Fine Arts Museums of San Francisco, 1992), 192, 197.

3. See related works at Florence Griswold Museum, "Dutch Fishing Boats Off Shore by William Henry Howe," Florence Griswold Museum, www.flogris.org/learning/insitu/html/east/howe.php, accessed February 20, 2009.

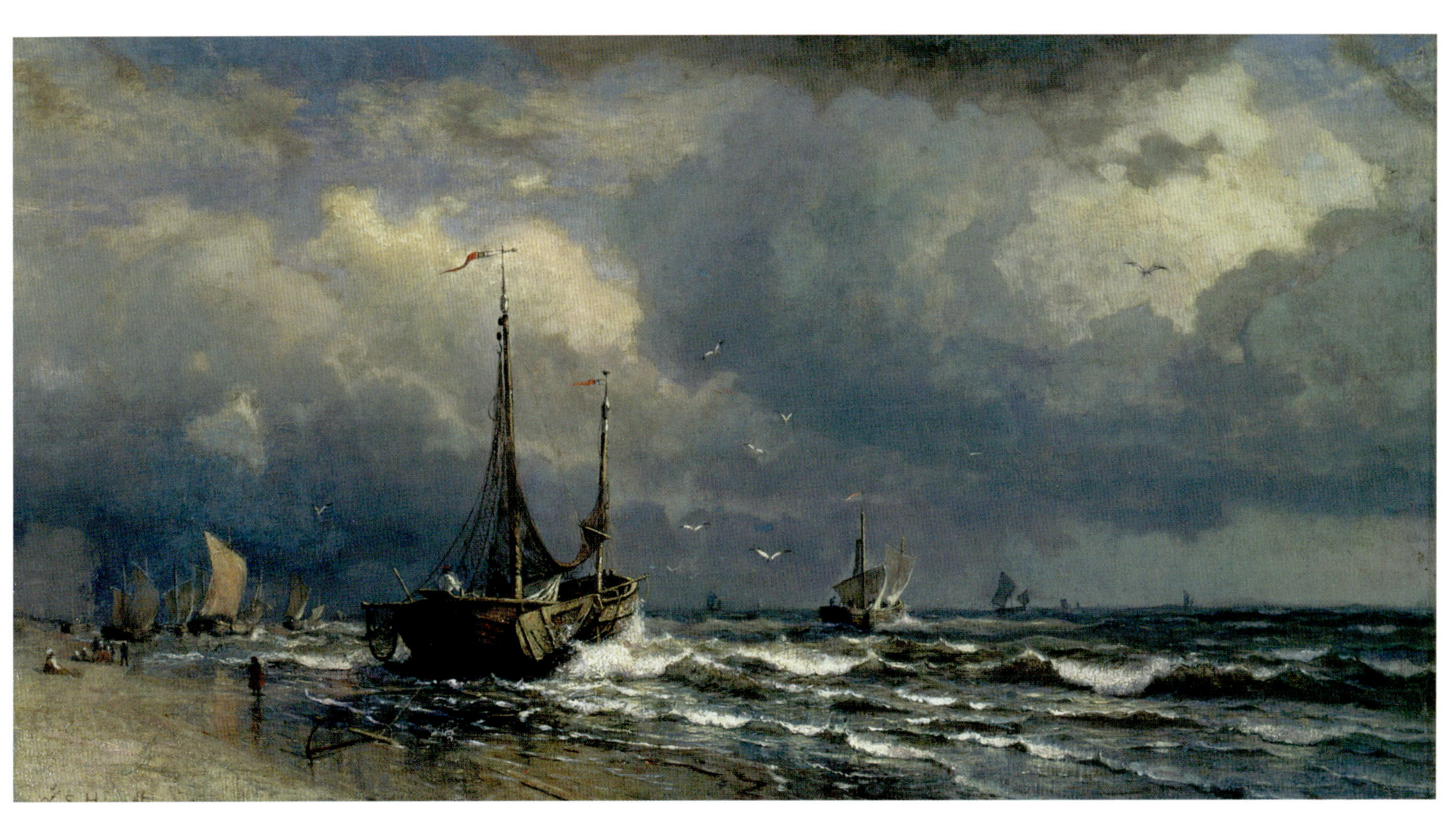

Wilhelmina Douglas Hawley 1860–1958

16

Two Women near the River Waal, 1894

Oil on canvas, 29 × 24"
Signed: "W. D. Hawley '94"
Collection of William van Dongen, Utrecht, the Netherlands

BORN IN PERTH AMBOY, NEW JERSEY, IN 1860, Wilhelmina Hawley grew up in New York City. In 1879, she began her art career at the Cooper Union School of Art under Julian Alden Weir (cat. 71). The next year, she decided to move to the more independent Art Students League, and took lessons from James Carroll Beckwith, William Merritt Chase (cat. 8–9), Charles Yardley Turner (cat. 67), and Kenyon Cox. In 1886 Hawley was elected vice-president of the Art Students League and worked in her studio in New York until she moved to Paris in the summer of 1892. In the French capital, she continued her studies at the Académie Julian under Adolphe William Bouguereau, Gustave Boulanger, Jean-Paul Laurens, and Jules Lefebvre. According to Hawley's journal, she visited Holland and the artists' colony of Rijsoord shortly after her arrival in Paris, before the new academy season started. In 1893, *Holland Peasant Girl*, which Hawley made in Rijsoord, was shown at the National Academy of Design in New York. Dutch-American artist John Vanderpoel, student, teacher, and eventually director at the Art Institute of Chicago, also taught at the Académie Julian. In 1888, he was the first to introduce art students from Paris to the Dutch village of Rijsoord, where he still had contacts with some of his Dutch relatives. His cousin Volksje Noorlander consequently built a new farmhouse in Rijsoord in 1889, which served as a shelter for foreign art students during the summer months. Pension Noorlander was located directly behind the old Hotel Warendorp, which also housed many of the visiting artists.

In the summer of 1894, Hawley returned to Rijsoord for the second time. Of the seven located oil paintings by Hawley, all depicting Rijsoord themes, *Two Women near the River Waal* is the only dated example. The two young women are depicted in traditional local dress, wearing elegant *krullenmutsen*. This type of everyday bonnet, also known as *keuvel*, made of white batiste or gauze, was fixed to the head, using a distinctive golden or gilded set of *krullen*, a spiral-shaped headdress ornament. The *kantemus*, a bonnet with lace frill, was primarily for Sundays or special occasions. Hawley portrayed a number of Rijsoord women wearing their bonnets.

AvD

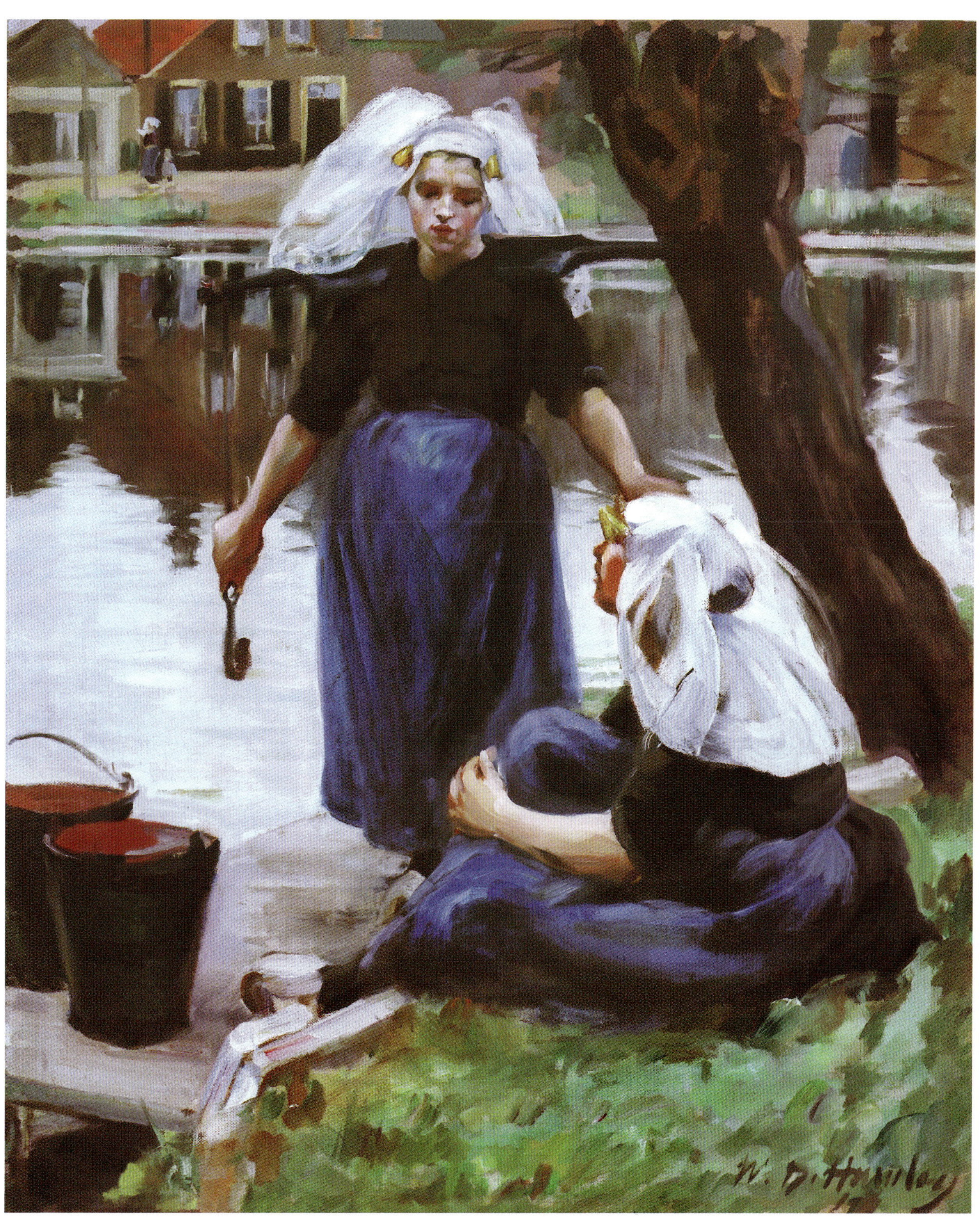

Wilhelmina Douglas Hawley 1860–1958

17

The Cold Bath, 1897

Watercolor on paper, 26 × 18"
Signed: "W. D. Hawley '97"
Collection of Frank van Dongen, Amstelveen, the Netherlands

IN THE SPRING OF 1897, WHILE STUDYING AND TEACHING ART CLASSES in Paris at the Académie Julian and the Académie Colarossi, Wilhelmina Hawley moved from 111, rue Notre-Dame-des-Champs to her new studio at 9, rue des Fourneax. In that same period, she received a letter from the Société Nationale des Beaux-Arts, informing her that four of her watercolors had been selected by the jury of the Salon for the exhibition at the Champ de Mars. One of the selected watercolors was *The Cold Bath*, which she made in Rijsoord. The first version of this watercolor is only known through a black-and-white reproduction in the illustrated Salon catalog (no. 1498). The second version of the same subject in a very similar composition—a mother and child by a washtub in a backlit interior—is presented here. The left part of the composition seems to have been cut off. In 1898, the first version of *The Cold Bath* (present whereabouts unknown) was exhibited at the Trans-Mississippi and International Exposition in Omaha, Nebraska, and in 1899 at the Art Gallery in Toronto, Canada. In 1899, Hawley went back to Rijsoord again and made the acquaintance of Bastiaan de Koning, eight years her junior. He was the son of an old Rijsoord peasant and flax merchant family. Hawley is thought to have met him during a boat trip on the river Waal. A number of villagers regularly rowed the visiting foreign artists from Hotel Warendorp or Pension Noorlander, which were located near the river Waal, to the artist's location of the day. In 1901 Hawley married de Koning, and they had one daughter in 1904. The popularity of painted images of village life in Holland is reflected in the Parisian exhibitions where Hawley showed her Rijsoord models. New approaches to time-honored themes, inspired by seventeenth-century Dutch genre painters such as Frans Hals, were very well received in Paris and the international art market. In her work, Hawley observed the daily lives of the local inhabitants of Rijsoord, eschewed historical or narrative events, and endowed her figures with a sense of individuality.

AvD

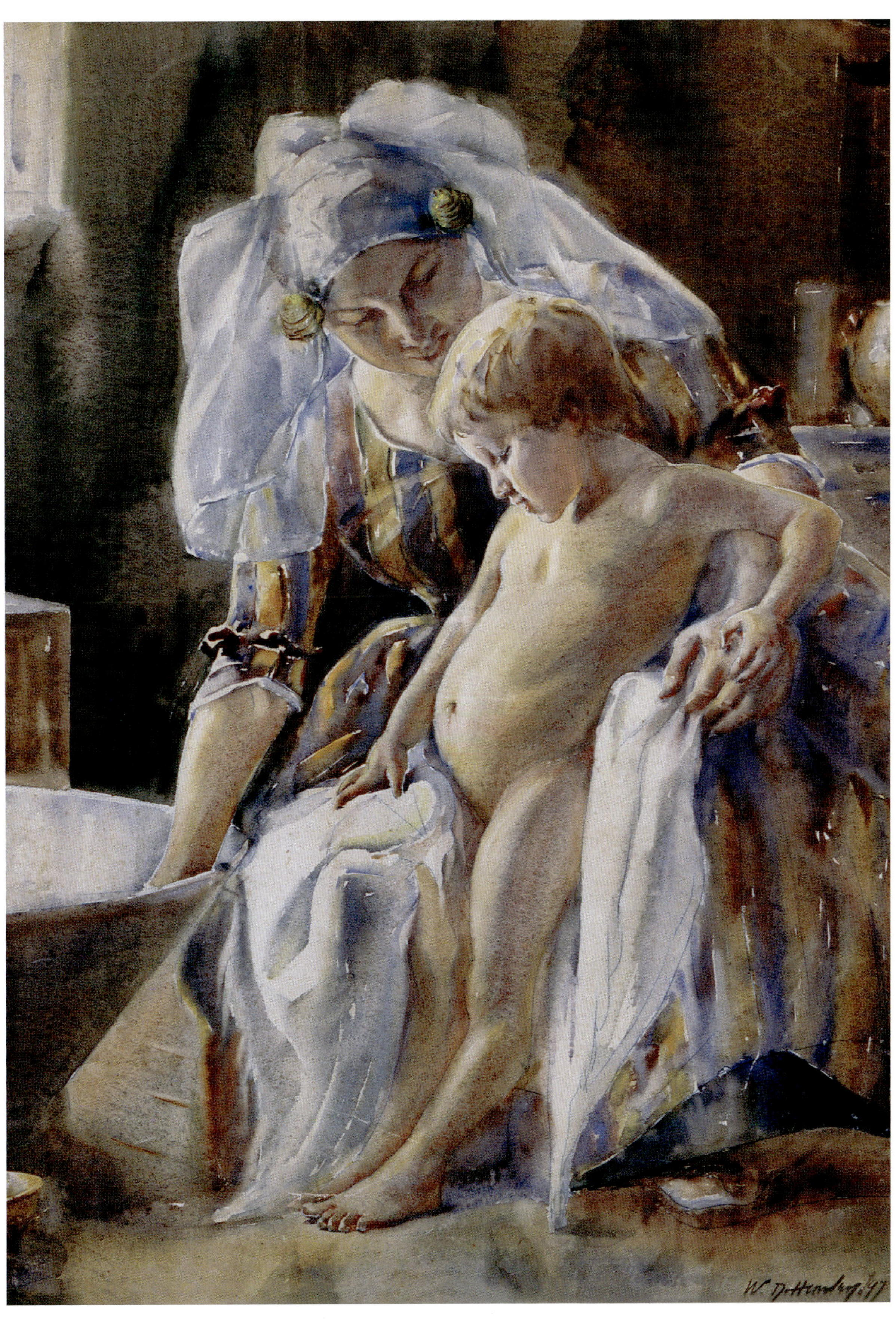

Robert Henri 1865–1929

18

Dutch Girl Laughing, 1907

Oil on canvas, 32 × 26"

Signed: "Robert Henri"

Dallas Museum of Art, Texas

Dallas Art Association Purchase

BORN ROBERT HENRY COZAD, ROBERT HENRI CHANGED HIS NAME when he was a young teenager, as did his father and brother. Henri's father had been accused of murder in Cozad, Nebraska, and decided to leave the town he had founded to seek refuge in a new name and other places. The family moved often; Henri became a realist and a rebel in his approach to life and art. Henri is best known as a member of the Ashcan School, a group of young artists who rebelled against pretty pictures and embraced modern urban subjects in all their gritty realism. The roots of at least part of Henri's modernism are to be found in his admiration for the work of Frans Hals, which he discovered in the 1890s. Since the best examples by Frans Hals resided in the museum in Haarlem, Henri traveled to the Netherlands and worked in Haarlem for several summers, including 1907 when he painted this picture of a Dutch girl laughing. Henri befriended a group of children who lived in an alley near his Haarlem studio and painted many pictures of them, usually one child at a time in head-and-shoulders portraits. He often employed the other children to entertain the one posing and as a result, many of the children are laughing or smiling brightly in his pictures of them. They have many of the qualities of the informal portraits that Hals made of his own children. Broad brushstrokes retain their identity as paint, even as they imitate a piece of cloth, an eyebrow, or a mouth. In some, Henri appears to have slashed the paint on the canvas, and in all, the sense of urgency, of bravura brushwork, is strong. Unlike most of his American contemporaries in Holland, Henri showed no interest in rural Dutch costumes, but painted modern urban children as he found them.

AS

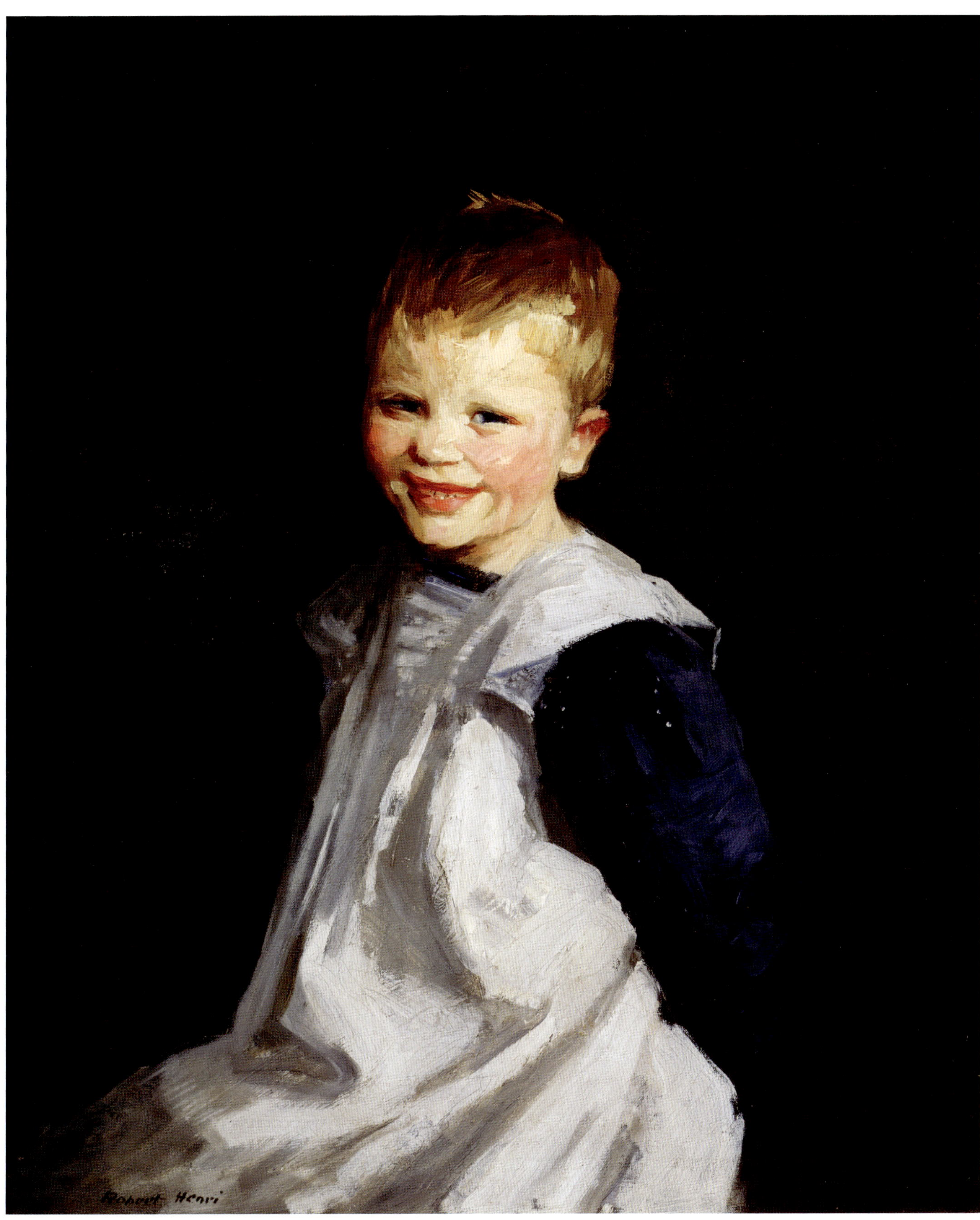
Robert Henri

Robert Henri 1865–1929

19

Dutch Soldier, 1907

Oil on canvas, 32⅝ × 26⅛"
Signed: "Robert Henri"
Munson-Williams-Proctor Arts Institute,
Utica, New York

ROBERT HENRI'S *Dutch Soldier* IS STRONGLY REMINISCENT of the seventeenth-century tradition of military portraiture in the Netherlands. Frans Hals painted many group portraits of militias; Henri not only reveals his careful study of Hals's bravura brushwork in this portrait, but has also chosen a military subject, unusual in his oeuvre. The serious demeanor and pose of this figure contrasts with the informality of Henri's numerous depictions of Haarlem children. The composition is carefully considered, with the white lines of braid trim and the white glove sharply standing out against the black background and dark uniform. Red decorations on the soldier's jacket and hat balance the ruddy tones in his face. This palette of red, black, and white is one of the most dramatic he could have chosen, contrasting with the stillness of the subject. Henri exhibited *Dutch Soldier* at the Cincinnati Art Museum's fifteenth annual exhibition of American art in 1908.

AS

TMA, TAFT, GRAM

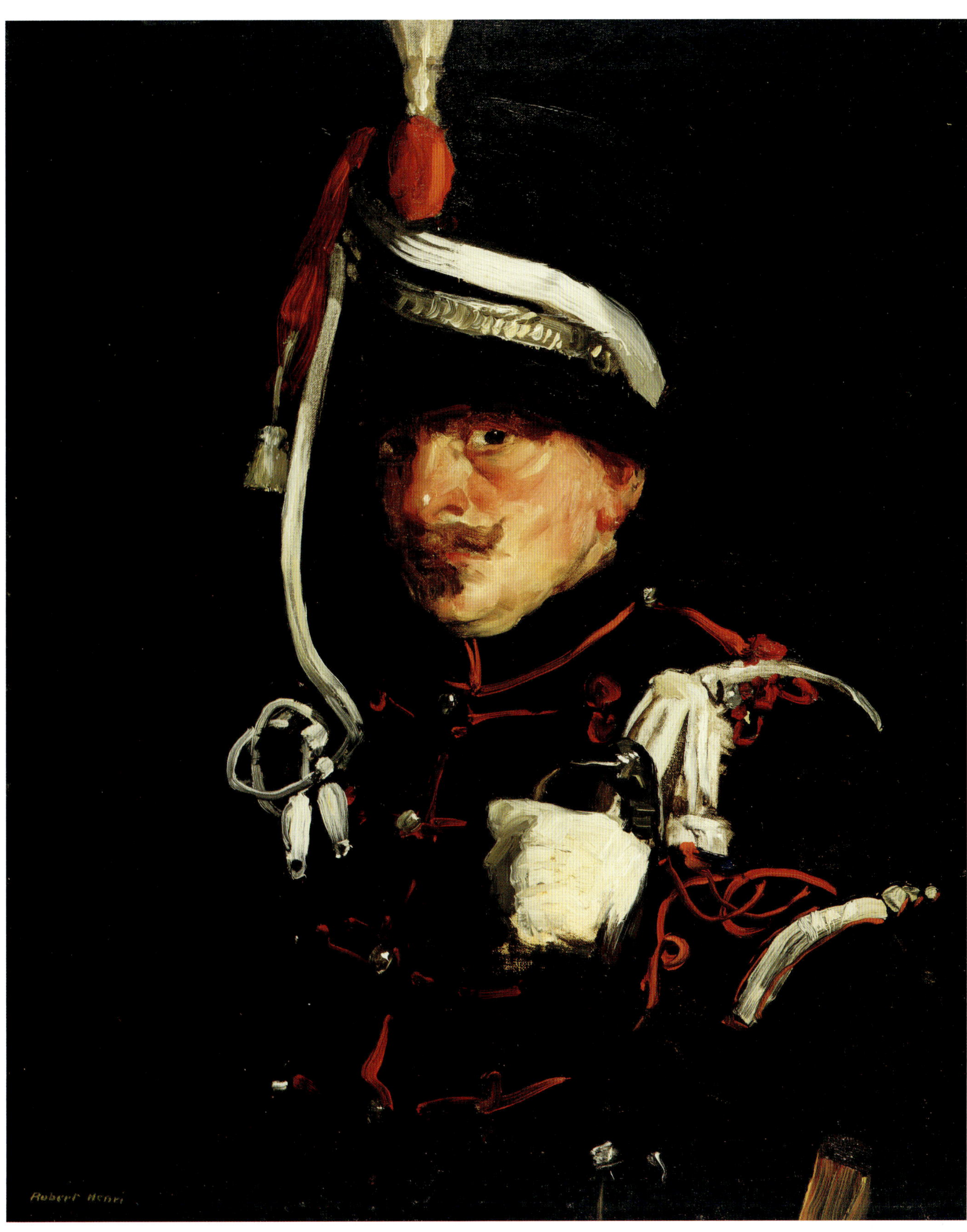
Robert Henri

Robert Henri 1865–1929

20

Volendam Street Scene, 1910

Oil on canvas, 20 × 24"
Signed: "Robert Henri"
National Gallery of Art, Washington, D.C.
Gift of Mr. and Mrs. Gerard C. Smith

ALTHOUGH PRINCIPALLY A PORTRAIT PAINTER, Henri left his New York City studio each summer to seek out more remote communities around the world. He saw the international artists' and tourists' village of Volendam through different eyes than most earlier American painters. The subject of *Volendam Street Scene* is the activity on the town's main thoroughfare, which was built on top of a dyke with the harbor on one side and the houses on the other. The tall masts of the fishing fleet are visible at anchor on the left. A woman carrying baskets, perhaps of fish, and a group of men in baggy Volendam pants occupy the stage. The impression of haste is conveyed by Henri's brushwork, rather than the subject. This is not a sleepy village, as he describes it, but a vibrant, living place. He shared this modern vision of Volendam and modernist style with his countryman Charles Herbert Woodbury (cat. 72), the German painter Hans von Bartels, Dutchman Willem Bastiaan Tholen, and the Belgian Maurice Sijs, all of whom painted in Volendam at the beginning of the twentieth century. At that time they were in the minority among artists with a more traditional approach to this much-painted village. The painting's exhibition history is dominated by its use in decorating federal government offices, including five years in the U.S. Embassy residence in The Hague (1987–92).

AS

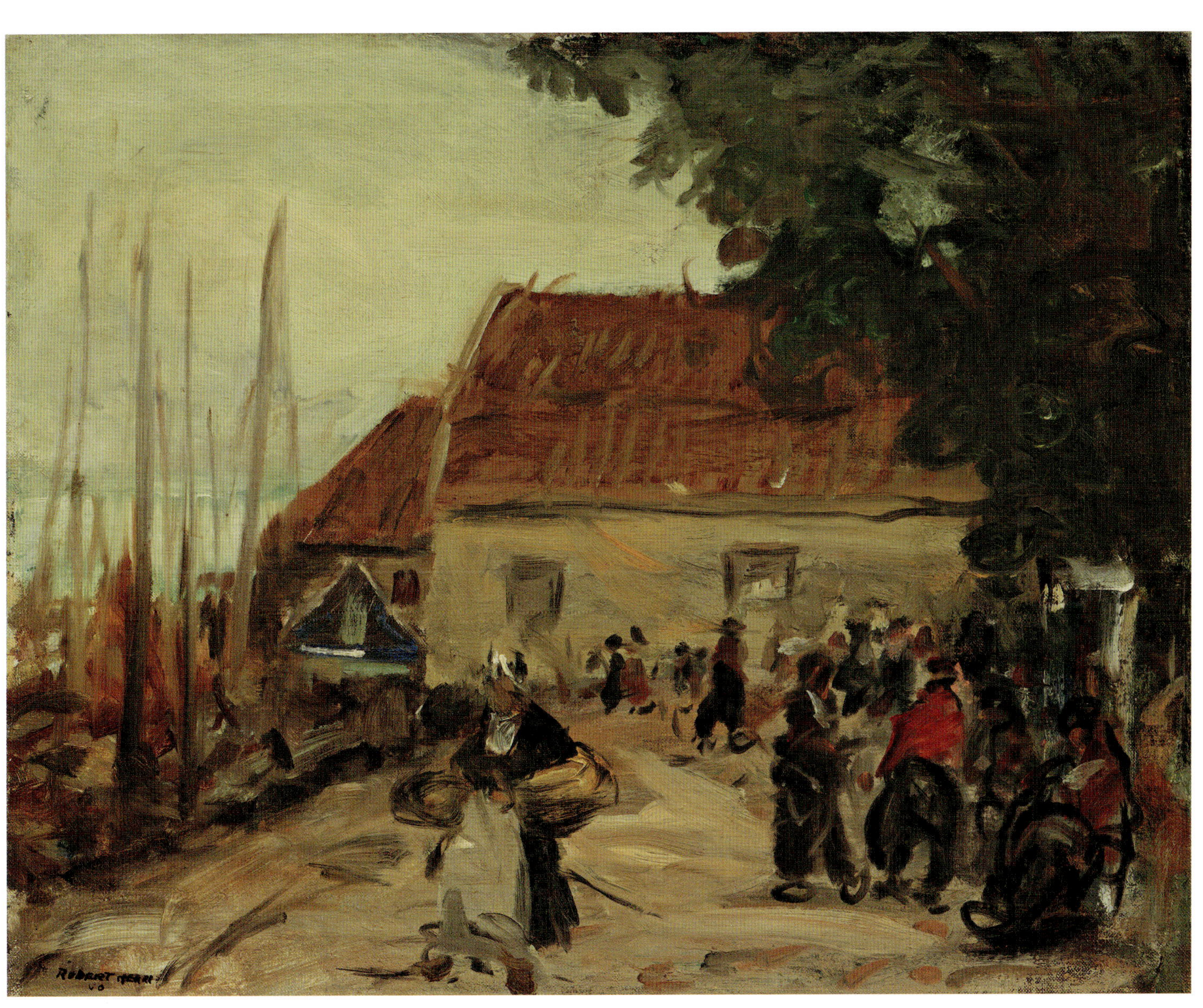

Herman Herzog 1831/32–1932

21

Moonlight in Holland, n.d.

Oil on board, 22 × 26"
Signed: "H Herzog"
Private Collection,
Kiawah Island, South Carolina

Moonlight in Holland IS ONE OF WELL OVER A THOUSAND undated paintings produced by Herman Ottomar Herzog during a prolific one-hundred-year lifetime. He was born in Bremen before it became part of Germany, in either 1831 or 1832, and began studying art at the Düsseldorf Academy as a teenager. Strongly influenced by his teachers Andreas Achenbach, Johann Wilhelm Schirmer, and the Norwegian landscape painter Hans Gude, he traveled throughout Europe for the next two decades, painting landscapes in which he manipulated effects of light and atmosphere to attain particular moods. In the 1860s he extended his travels to the United States, settling permanently in 1869, first in New Jersey and soon after in Philadelphia. Born "Hermann," he may have dropped the second *n* in his name after becoming a naturalized American citizen. In the United States, Herzog continued his extensive travels in search of paintable subjects, working in California, the Yosemite, Florida, and along the East Coast, as well as in Mexico.

Despite his great success in Europe, where he sold paintings to royalty in England, Germany, and Russia, Herzog stopped marketing his work after becoming independently wealthy from his investments in the Pennsylvania Railroad. He did not stop painting, however. Herzog continued to return to Europe, where *Moonlight in Holland* was set. It contrasts with many of his other Dutch scenes, which depict fishing boats along the North Sea coast, either beached or fighting stormy seas. *Moonlight in Holland* reveals a quiet, orderly harbor. Herzog has experimented with the effects of lighting from a full moon partially hidden behind clouds, lamplight shining from a window, a small fire on the shore, and the reflections in the water of all these light sources. He may have been inspired by the moonlit landscapes of the seventeenth-century Dutch painter Aert van der Neer, whose work many American artists admired.

AS

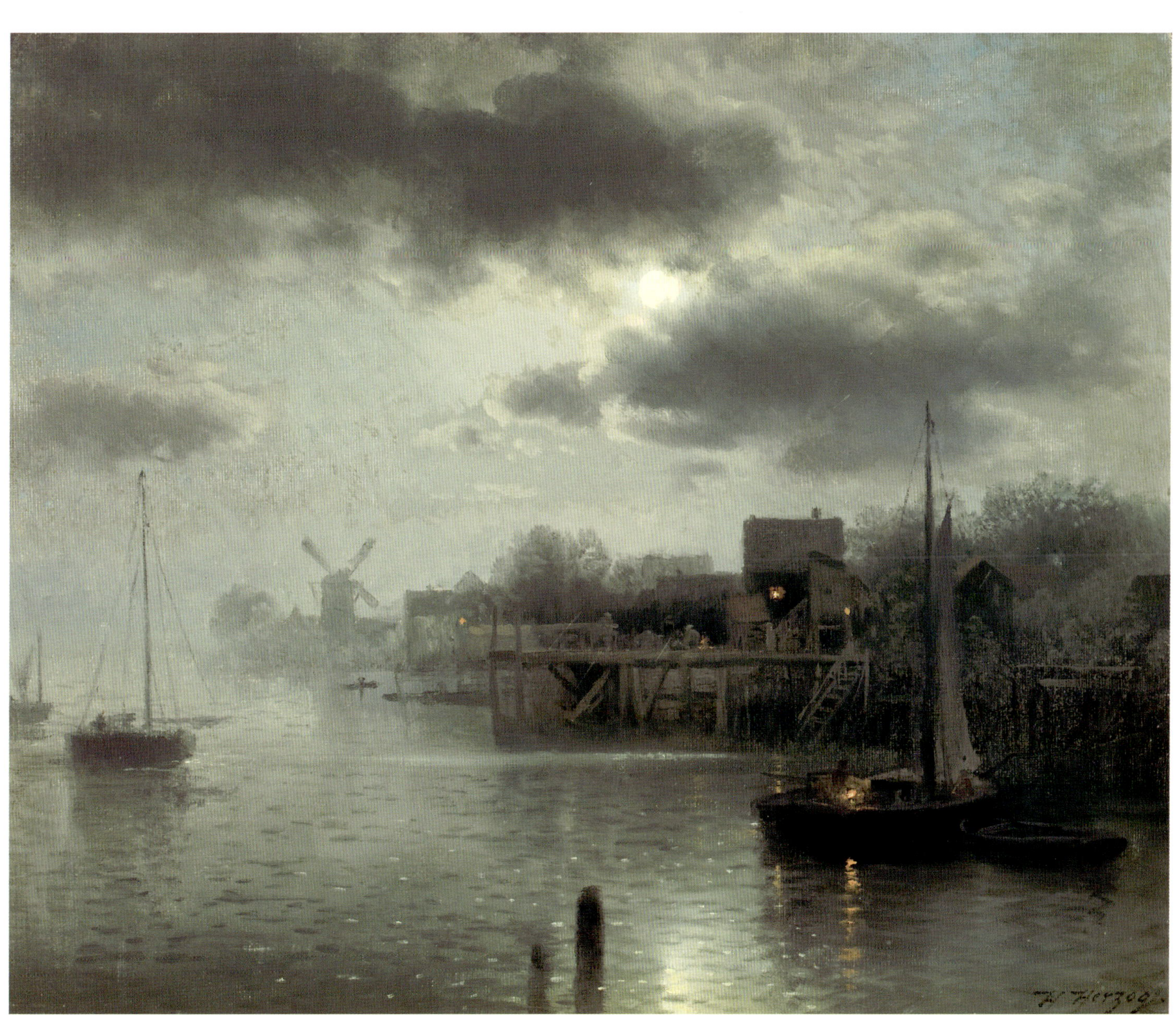
H. Herzog.

George Hitchcock 1850–1913

22

Early Spring in Holland, c. 1890–1905

Oil on canvas, 35⅞ × 51¼"
Signed: "G. Hitchcock"
Telfair Museum of Art, Savannah, Georgia
Museum purchase, 1908

BORN INTO A PATRICIAN FAMILY IN PROVIDENCE, RHODE ISLAND, George Hitchcock graduated from Brown University in 1872 and then attended Harvard Law School. After a few years, he decided to pursue a career in art and moved to London. In 1882 he enrolled at the Académie Julian in Paris under the tutelage of Gustave Boulanger and Jules Lefebvre. He also spent one winter studying at the Düsseldorf Academy before settling in Egmond aan Zee, where he began to develop his own style. At the 1887 Paris Salon he won an honorable mention for *La Culture des Tulipes* (*Tulip Culture*, private collection), a vibrant, sun-drenched rendering of a Dutch woman in a tulip field. The success of this painting inspired Hitchcock to produce a series of colorful, flower-filled landscapes.

With its high-key colors, broad brushstrokes, and sensitivity to natural light, *Early Spring in Holland* reveals the influence of impressionism on Hitchcock's mature work. The artist portrays row after row of colorful tulips, ranging in hue from purple to yellow to pink, interspersed by gleaming white. The painting's horizontal format emphasizes the long rows of bulbs and the flatness of the Dutch terrain. Bordering the tulip field is a tree-lined stream traversed by a bridge leading to a cottage in the distance. The lavender-gray sky reflects Hitchcock's deep appreciation for the special light of the Netherlands. The artist remarked, "That which in other lands is a cold grey, uninteresting, often repellant, here becomes an indefinable harmony, containing a depth and richness or a pearly brilliancy, opalescent, sad—an infinite variety, each effect apparently more beautiful than the last."[1]

George Hitchcock established a summer art school in Egmond where young artists, including Corinne Lawton Mackall, came to study.[2] Mackall married Gari Melchers in 1903 and initiated Melchers's long association with the Telfair Museum of Art in Savannah through her maternal uncle, Alexander R. Lawton, who was president of the Telfair's board. Lawton petitioned Corinne's aid in enlisting Gari Melchers as the museum's fine arts advisor, a position he held from 1906 to 1916, during which time he purchased *Early Spring in Holland* for the Telfair's collection.

Hitchcock lived abroad the remainder of his life. He died on the Dutch island of Marken in 1913. Although his career was largely based in Europe, Hitchcock was elected an associate member of the National Academy of Design in 1909. He was the first American member of the Akademie der Bildenden Künste, Vienna, and the first to receive the Officer's Cross of the Order of Franz Joseph of Austria. Like Melchers, he was made a chevalier of the French Legion of Honor.

HKM

1. George Hitchcock, "The Picturesque Quality of Holland," *Scribner's Magazine* 2, no. 2 (August 1887): 160.

2. See Annette Stott, "The Holland Years," in *Gari Melchers: A Retrospective Exhibition*, ed. Diane Lesko and Esther Persson (St. Petersburg, Fla.: Museum of Fine Arts, 1990), 69. Corinne Mackall's handwritten journal from 1902 (archives, Gari Melchers Home and Studio) documents her studies with Hitchcock.

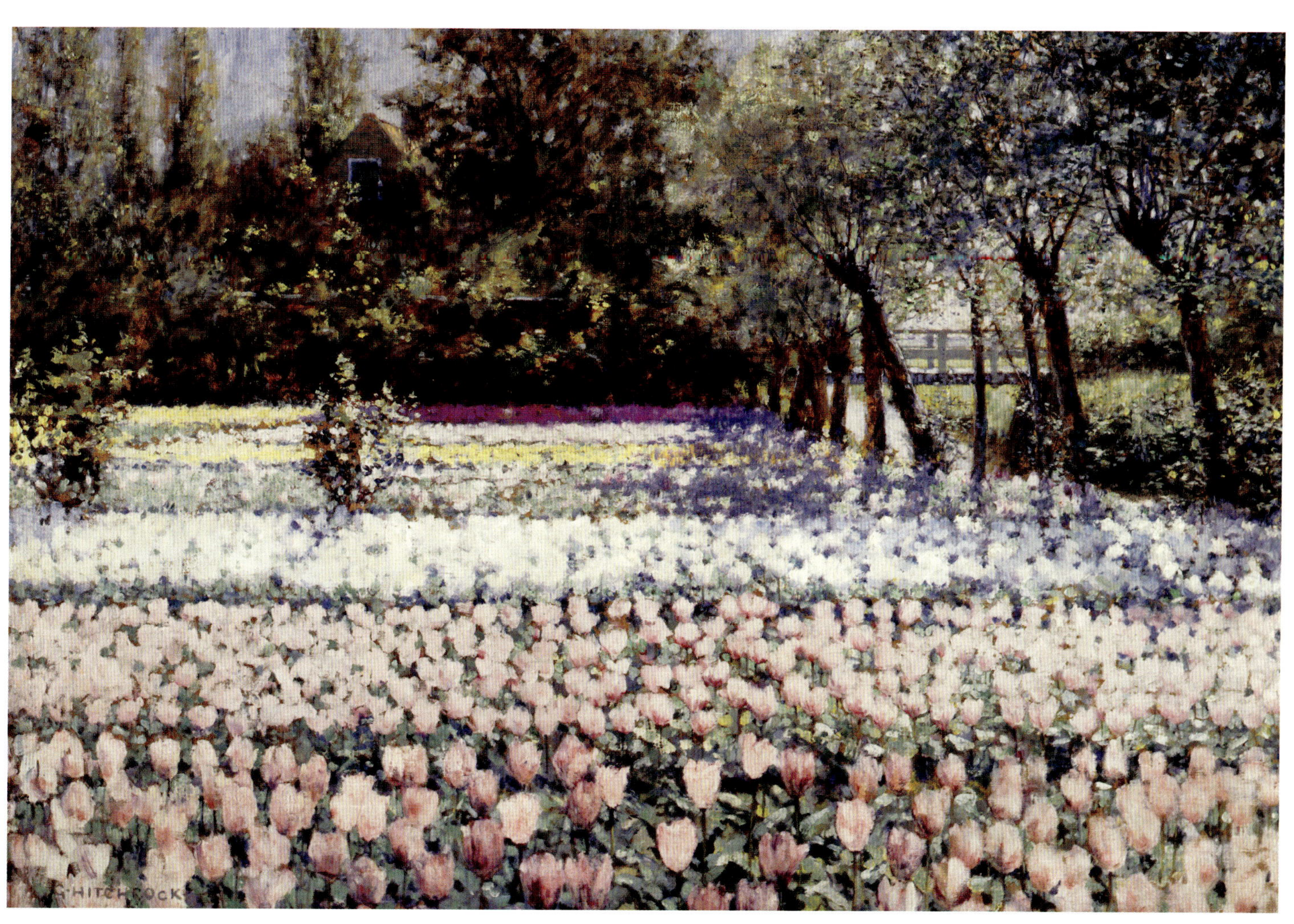
G·HITCHCOCK

George Hitchcock 1850–1913

23

The Stork's Nest, c. 1890–1906

Oil on canvas, 22¼ × 17¼"
Signed: "G Hitchcock"
Private Collection,
Kiawah Island, South Carolina

The Stork's Nest IS AN INTRIGUING EXAMPLE of American expatriate George Hitchcock's flower field paintings of the Netherlands, where he lived for most of his adult life. The painting was exhibited in 1906 and 1910 at Knoedler & Company, fine-art dealers in New York City. It was also one of thirty-three paintings shown at a joint exhibition with Hitchcock's second wife, Cecil Jay (fig. 31, p. 60), at the Art Institute of Chicago in 1911.

Hitchcock advocated painting *en plein air* and came to be known as the "Painter of Sunlight."[1] *The Stork's Nest* is a good example of his ability to combine open-air observation of nature with symbolism. Tulips have been an iconic image of the Netherlands since "tulip mania" overtook the country in the mid-1600s, causing a financial crisis. The white stork with an eel in its mouth is the official symbol of the city of The Hague and is featured on its coat of arms, which was adopted in 1861. *The Stork's Nest* shares common traits with many Hitchcock paintings of flowers, but is unique in its depiction of a stork.

White storks have inhabited Europe and Africa since ancient times. They migrate twice a year by soaring on thermal air currents, and the Netherlands is one of many European countries where they gather in the spring to mate and nest. Storks were regarded as a symbol of good luck; they ate the leftover fish after street markets closed, lessening the chance of infectious disease from the rotting fish. Male storks often use the same nest year after year and have adapted to building their nests on man-made structures. They stay in loyal family units for the mating season, and may or may not reunite with the same mate the following season. Despite this, the birds have become a symbol of fidelity, good parenting, and good luck. The expectation of return and the sense of the bird as a good omen may have contributed to the building of structures on roofs and in fields to support stork nests, such as the one painted by Hitchcock. With the proud stork standing atop his nest, a bright field of Dutch flowers, and arms of windmills just visible over the horizon, Hitchcock created an iconic image of the country that was his home.

MW

1. Christian Brinton, "George Hitchcock, Painter of Sunlight," *International Studio* 26, nos. 101–4 (July–October 1905): i–vi.

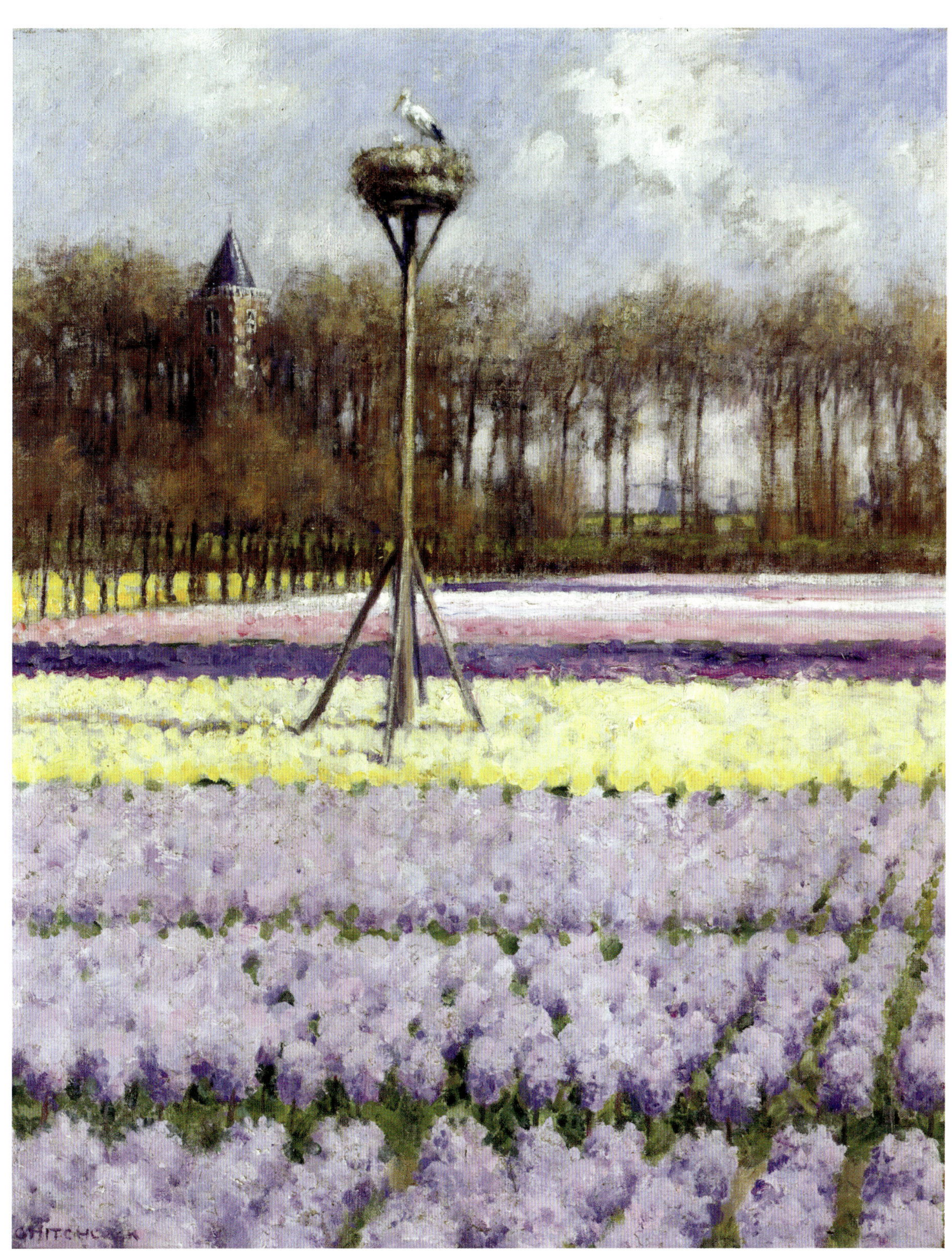

George Hitchcock 1850–1913

24

Maternité (Maternity), 1889

Oil on canvas, 69 × 98"
Signed: "Geo. Hitchcock 1889"
Aberdeen Art Gallery & Museums,
Aberdeen, Scotland

GEORGE HITCHCOCK PAINTED *Maternité* FROM SKETCHES made on the dunes near Egmond aan Zee. Ostensibly a representation of a Dutch mother carrying a shallow basket nestled in a heavier woven basket on her back, a baby in her arms, and a young boy behind her, the image alludes quite obviously to Mary, Jesus, and John. It was the precursor for a series of pictures that Hitchcock created in the early 1890s representing the flight of the Holy Family into Egypt. All use the same setting, palette, and basic composition, but in some images in this series Mary rides a donkey, a long cape covering the child in her arms, and in others Joseph strides along behind them. As with most of Hitchcock's thematic series, they vary in size and focus.

Maternité was generally well received when it appeared publicly for the first time in the Paris Universal Exposition in 1889. One reviewer wrote that this "new picture of Dutch figures in pale and pearly landscape . . . is charming in aspect and most delicate in tone; the landscape is exquisite; the figures alone betray the inevitable weakness of opsimathy, . . . Nevertheless, you feel that this picture is the work of a singularly artistic temperament."[1] The reviewer's reference to opsimathy, or late-life education, was a veiled disparagement of Hitchcock's relatively late entry to art as a profession. He did not make his break on the international art scene until he was thirty-seven, two years before this painting appeared.

Most reviewers commented on the picture's most striking feature, its pale silver-blue atmosphere. In an essay of 1912, the writer Charles Henry Meltzer claimed that George Hitchcock had once explained to him:

> And the Dutch sunlight is not yellow, brown or golden. Sunlight, as I have discovered, is pale blue in tone. That is why I put so much blue and so much violet into my pictures. At times, I admit, sunlight may seem golden. But that is due, I think, to the small glittering particles of cosmic dust in the atmosphere. The atmosphere itself is really blue—a faint, tender blue. Not cobalt or deep blue, as the "Impressionists" would have us believe; but blue in quality.[2]

Hitchcock went on to explain that he had discovered this by observing light streaming through a stained glass window. He realized that the blue color reflected on the floor was coming through a clear piece of glass and concluded that the atmosphere must be blue. Nowhere does he carry this conviction further than in his painting *Maternité*. In 1891 he exhibited *Maternité* at the Royal Academy exhibition in London, and it was purchased by a private collector before entering the Aberdeen Art Museum in 1913.

AS

1. *Harper's New Monthly Magazine* 79 (September 1889): 508.
2. Charles Henry Meltzer, "A Painter of Sunlight," *Hearst's Magazine* 22, no. 7 (July 1912): 132.

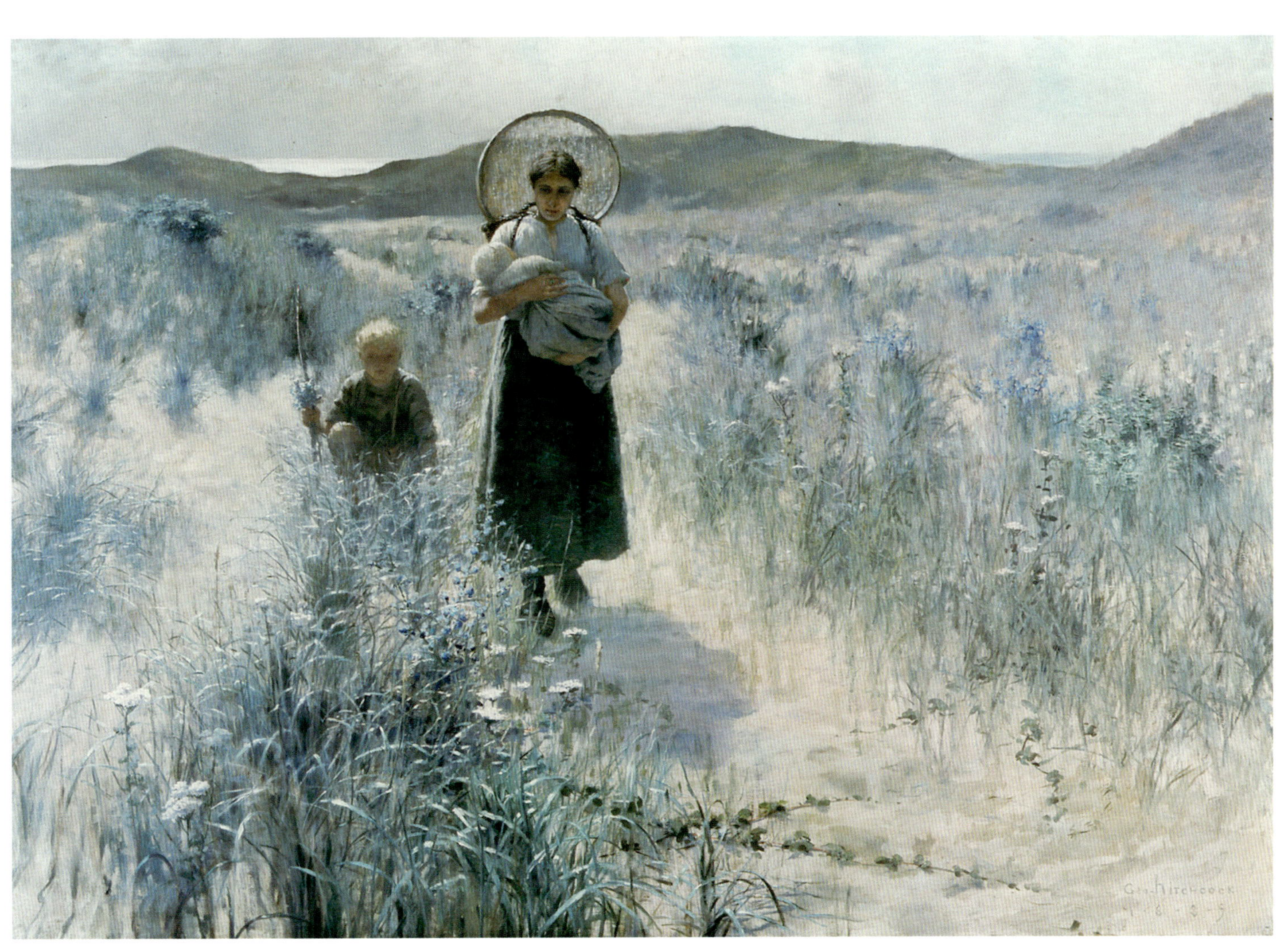

George Hitchcock 1850–1913

25

Magnificat (Annunciation), 1894

Oil on canvas, 63 × 38"
Signed: "G. Hitchcock 1894"
Gari Melchers Home and Studio,
Fredericksburg, Virginia

Magnificat RECEIVED A BRONZE MEDAL WHEN EXHIBITED at the Paris Universal Exposition in 1900. Like *Maternité* (cat. 24), it was part of a series of related pictures. The first in this series was *The Annunciation* (1887, Art Institute of Chicago) which was exhibited at the 1888 Paris Salon, the Jubilee Exhibition at the Royal Bavarian Academy in Munich the same year, and at the Universal Exposition in Paris in 1889, before entering the Potter Palmer collection in 1890. When Hitchcock returned to this theme with his painting *Magnificat* around 1894, he depicted the same veiled and haloed figure against an even higher, denser hedge with the same white "annunciation lilies" in front of her. Where the thinly disguised Virgin Mary in *The Annunciation* demurely gazes downward, ready to learn how she can serve the Lord, in *Magnificat* she casts her reverential gaze upward in praise. She also now holds a lily in the opposite hand to the one she raises to her breast. The composition of *Magnificat* is tighter than the Chicago version, with the figure dominating the picture's surface. Pansies and other flowers contribute to the floral garden setting of this *hortus conclusus*, or enclosed garden, a symbolic reference to Mary's virginity that is traditional in paintings of Mary.

A third painting, almost identical to *Magnificat* but without the modest cape and with the blouse unbuttoned, was published in the *Art Journal* in 1895 under the title *Mary at the House of Elizabeth*. This title refers to an event recorded in the Gospel of Luke where Mary visits her cousin Elizabeth, who is pregnant with John the Baptist. At Mary's appearance, Elizabeth feels the child leap in her belly and praises Mary, who responds by singing the song of praise known as the "Magnificat." This song, beginning "My soul magnifies the Lord," was a common part of liturgy in many Christian traditions, and Hitchcock's European and American audiences would have recognized the reference in his title *Magnificat*. That Hitchcock enjoyed reworking themes and imagery is well demonstrated in these paintings. *Magnificat* was part of the Stroh family collection in Detroit, descending to the Louise S. and John W. Stroh family, who gave it to the Gari Melchers Home and Studio with the title *Annunciation*.[1]

AS

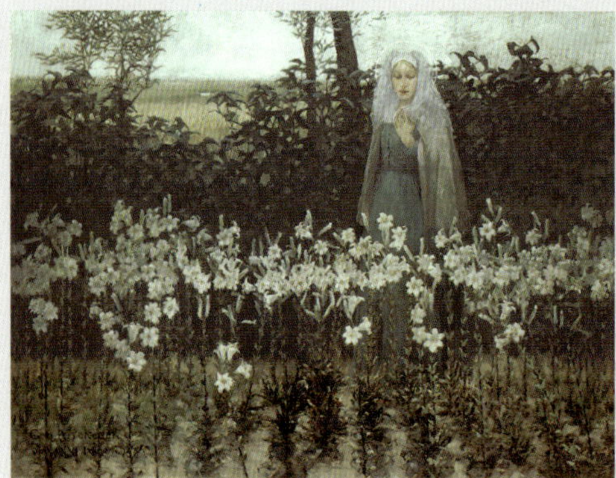

George Hitchcock, *The Annunciation*, 1887, oil on canvas, 62½ × 80½", Art Institute of Chicago, Illinois, Potter Palmer Collection, 1930.1289.

1. I am grateful to Joanna Catron for identifying this painting as *Magnificat* through comparison with an old print in the Melchers archive.

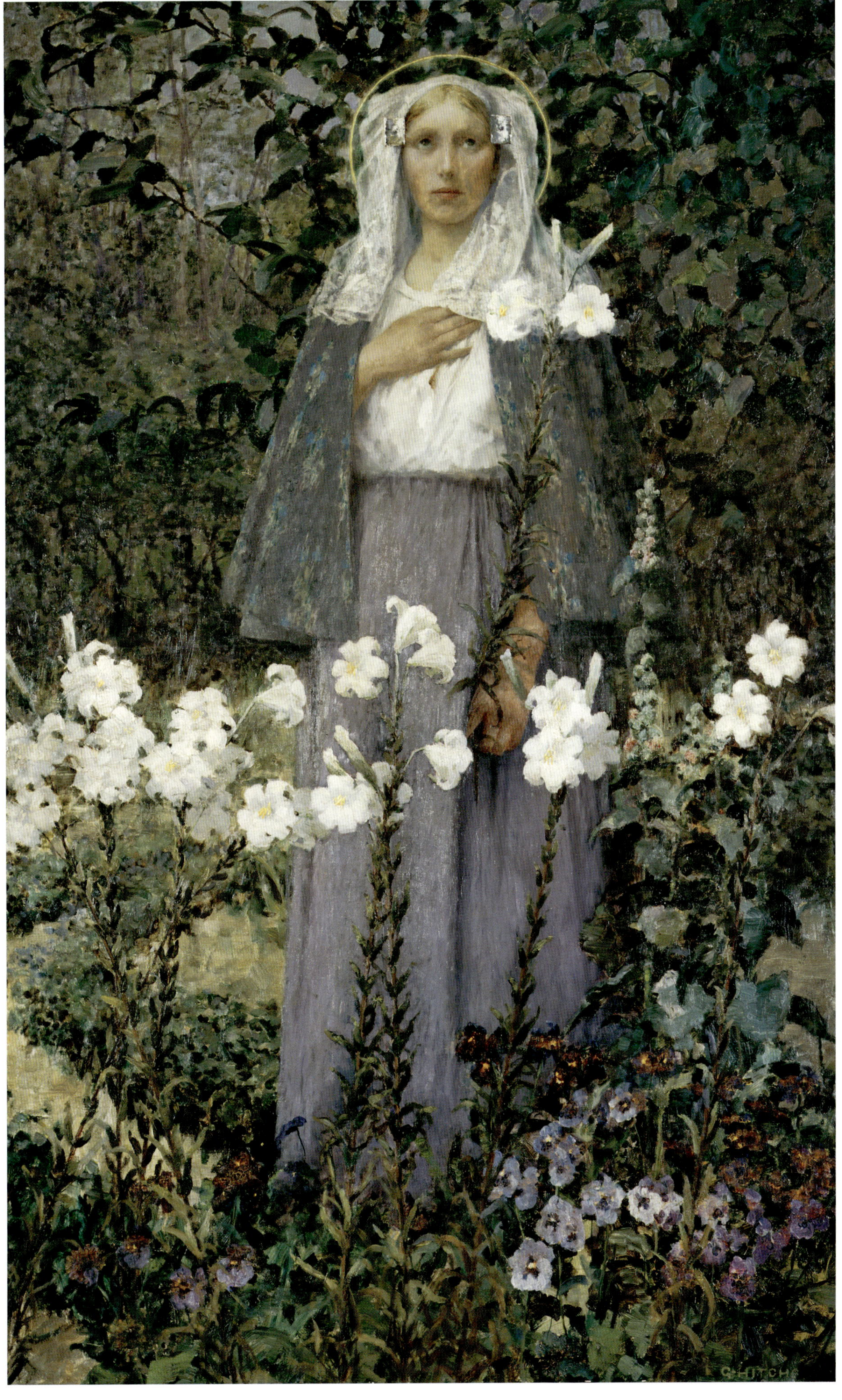

George Hitchcock 1850–1913

26

In Windmill Land, n.d.

Oil on canvas, 44 × 35¼"
Signed: "G. Hitchcock"
Heckscher Museum of Art,
Huntington, New York
Gift of the Baker/Pisano Collection

GEORGE HITCHCOCK PAINTED SEVERAL PICTURES OF DUTCH WINDMILLS, another iconic representation of Dutchness in the touristic view of Holland that developed during the nineteenth century. Although this mill looks like the one in the background of Gari Melchers's *In Holland* (cat. 38)—identified by Egmond historian Ron van Vleuten as a mill on the road between Egmond aan Zee and Egmond aan den Hoef—the broad stream, flat land, and line of distant mills suggest a different location for the subject of *In Windmill Land*.[1] It could have been painted almost anywhere in the Dutch countryside, which Hitchcock traveled extensively. The low horizon line and cloud-filled sky remind the viewer of similar compositions by Dutch painters of the seventeenth through the nineteenth centuries. This windmill is of a type sometimes called a smock mill. The entire cap can be pivoted using the long tail pole so that the sails will catch the wind. Canvas was unfurled along the wooden sails in various configurations to control the speed of the turning sails, which in turn worked the gears and powered the machinery inside the mill. These windmills were commonly used for grinding grain. They represented a premodern, pre-mass-production era of industry and one that suggested a more healthful environment to educated late-nineteenth-century American audiences than the often crowded, urban factories of American industrial life. For residents of Long Island, however, Dutch windmills such as this may have held special meaning as the precursors to the mills that Dutch Americans built on the island in the eighteenth and early nineteenth centuries.

In Windmill Land was part of the personal collection of Ronald G. Pisano, art historian and director of the Parrish Art Museum of Long Island, and his partner, Fred Baker. After Pisano's death in 2000, the painting was given to the Heckscher Museum of Art, where he had served as curator of American art in the 1970s. It has been shown at least once as *In Windmill Lane*, but is thought to be properly titled *In Windmill Land*. A painting of that title was included in the 1914 memorial exhibition of Hitchcock's work, held at the Buffalo Fine Arts Academy (now part of the Albright-Knox Art Gallery).

AS

1. Ron van Vleuten, letter with maps, pictures, and publications given to Annette Stott at Schuylenburg, George Hitchcock's Egmond aan den Hoef home, during a visit in 2006.

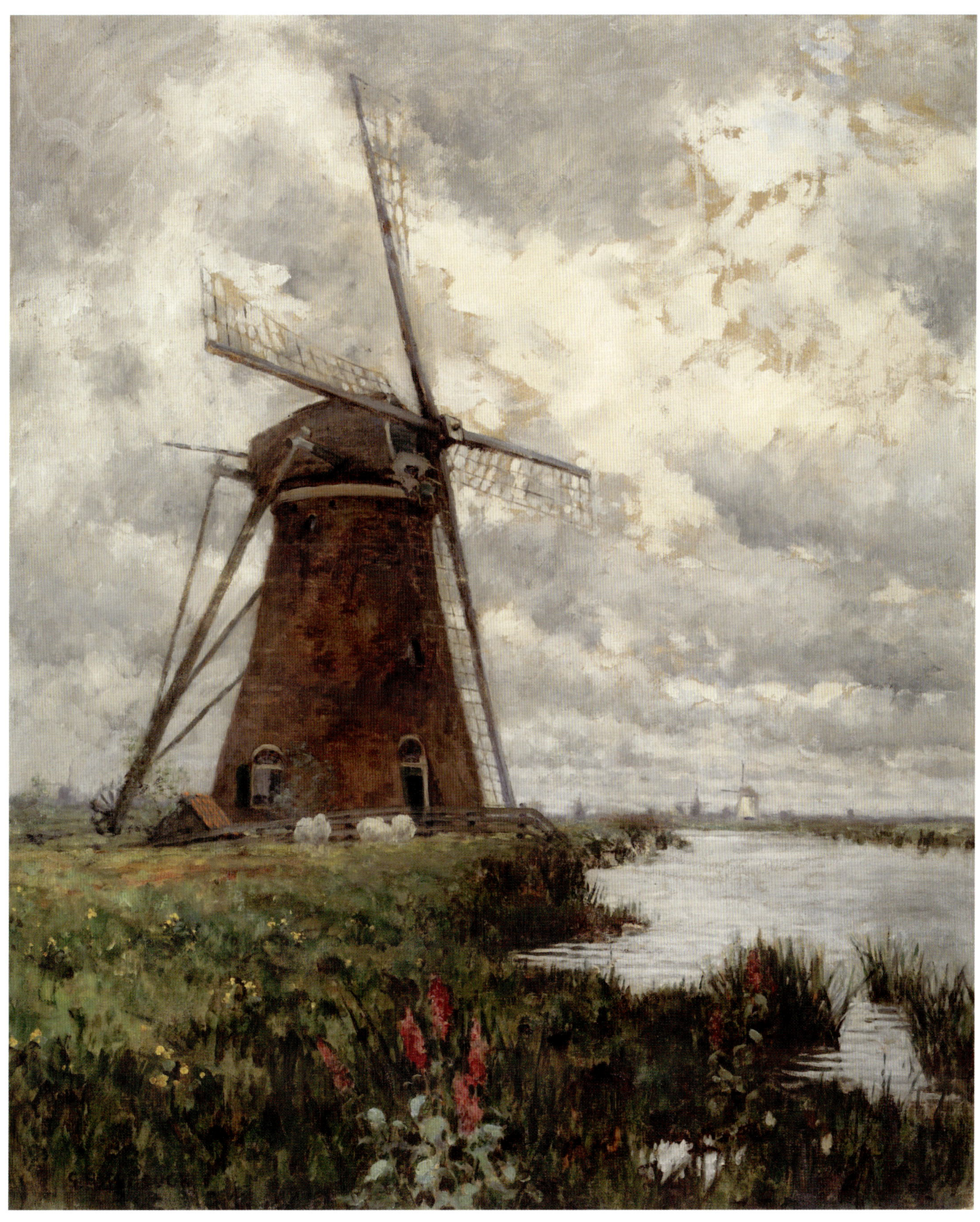

William Henry Howe 1846–1929

27

Reclining Cow in the Stall, 1890

Oil on paper on panel, 14½ × 20"
Signed: "Howe À mon ami Hamdorff Laren Oct '90"
Art Collection of the Municipality of Laren, the Netherlands

BORN IN RAVENNA, OHIO, IN 1846, WILLIAM HENRY HOWE did not decide to study art until he had first tried business and found it did not suit his temperament. Attracted to animal painting, which had become the rage in the 1860s, he traveled to Paris to study with Felix Dominique de Vuillefroy and to Düsseldorf to work with Otto von Thoren. He became steeped in the French Barbizon style and then looked to Holland for further inspiration. He admired the work of the great Dutch animal painter Paulus Potter, whose *Young Bull* in The Hague (fig. 7, p. 10) figured prominently in nineteenth-century guidebooks and was generally considered a must-see by European and American audiences for its great naturalism. Howe won honorable mentions at the New Orleans Exposition in 1885 and at the Salon of 1886, but he made his major entry on the international animal painting scene in the 1888 Paris Salon with a very large painting of four Dutch cows on their way to market with the Zuider Zee in the background. This gained him a medal and much positive press. Critics and audiences praised the lifelikeness of his cattle, noting the nonchalance of their poses and the individual expressions on their faces.

Settling in Laren in 1890 at the inn of Jan Hamdorff, Howe followed in the footsteps of Anton Mauve, painting pictures of sheep on the heath, gray dunescapes, and cattle herded along the country lanes in the rain. His work covered a range of animal subjects, but it was as a painter of cattle that he became particularly adept and he was by this time known as America's foremost cattle painter. *Reclining Cow in the Stall* was painted as a gift for the innkeeper and Howe inscribed it (in French) "to my friend Hamdorff Laren Oct '90." Hamdorff gave it a place of honor in the dining room where many of Laren's artists took their meals and gathered to talk in the evenings. This was an important year for Howe, who won a gold medal in Boston, the Temple gold medal at the Pennsylvania Academy, and the grand gold medal at the Crystal Palace in London. He would go on to win many more medals and honors with his paintings of Dutch and French landscapes and animals.

AS

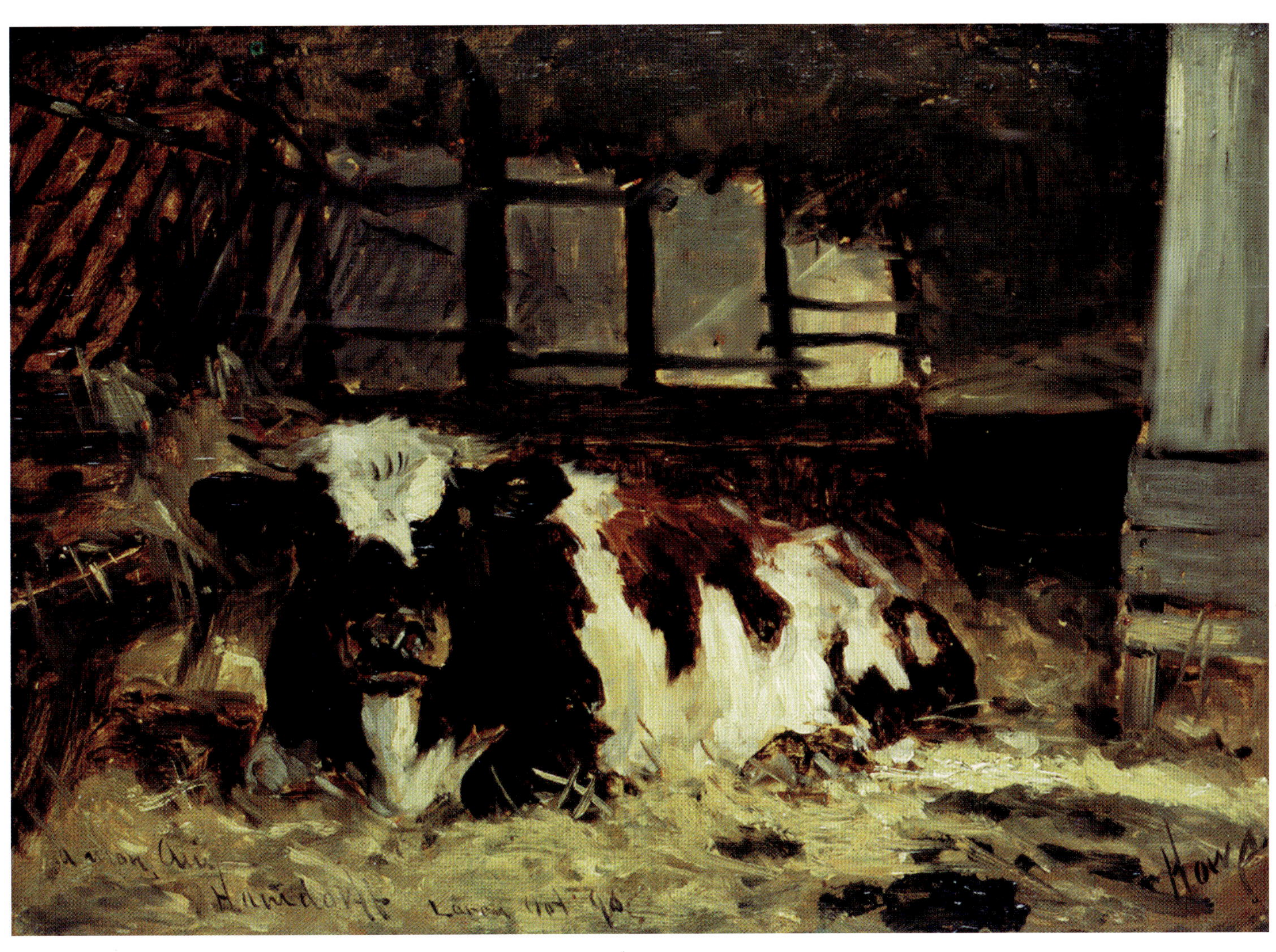

William Henry Howe 1846–1929

28

Evening at Laren, the Meadows—Cattle (Evening—Laren Meadows), 1890

Oil on canvas on panel, 33 × 42½"
Signed: "William H. Howe 90"
Collection of the Union League Club of Chicago, Illinois, UL1908.4

TITLED *Evening—Laren Meadows* WHEN IT WAS PURCHASED IN 1908 by the Chicago Union League Club's art committee, this painting demonstrates the artist's versatility despite painting hundreds of pictures of the same subject—cows. In this version of cows lying in the meadow, the moon is rising over a broad twilight pasture and the animals in the foreground seem to peer out of the picture at the viewer. It was William Henry Howe's ability to convince the viewer of the warmth and intelligence of his animals that made his paintings so much in demand. Nostalgia for the agrarian way of life that was slowly eroding under the forces of American industrialization, recognition of the healthfulness of fresh country air, appreciation for the Dutch dairy cattle that had helped found America's herds, and a desire for the calmness embodied in still scenes like *Evening at Laren, the Meadows—Cattle,* in contrast to the increasingly frantic pace of American life, all contributed to the popularity of Howe's lifelike cattle.

A visitor to Howe's American studio in 1900 explained his technique:

> His pictures are all laid in and three-quarters finished while in the field, leaving but little to be done in the studio. This little is, however, not always undertaken at once, for there are, for instance, some canvases left from the painter's years in Holland which need yet the final brush.[1]

Not only did Howe continue to paint Dutch pictures along with his American cattle pictures after returning to the United States, but he maintained his close association with the artists of the Hague School. When he helped jury art into the 1904 exhibition for the World's Fair in St. Louis, it was not as an American, but "as a Dutchman on the Holland jury, having been invited and commissioned by Mesdag to act with them."[2] In his later years, Howe saw the market for cattle pictures dissipate, but he continued to paint the subject he knew best.

AS

1. *The Collector and Art Critic* 2 (February 1, 1900): 115–16.
2. William Henry Howe, Old Lyme, Conn., letter to William MacBeth, New York City, September 25, 1904, MacBeth Papers, Smithsonian Institution, Archives of American Art, microfilm McB 8, frames 209–10.

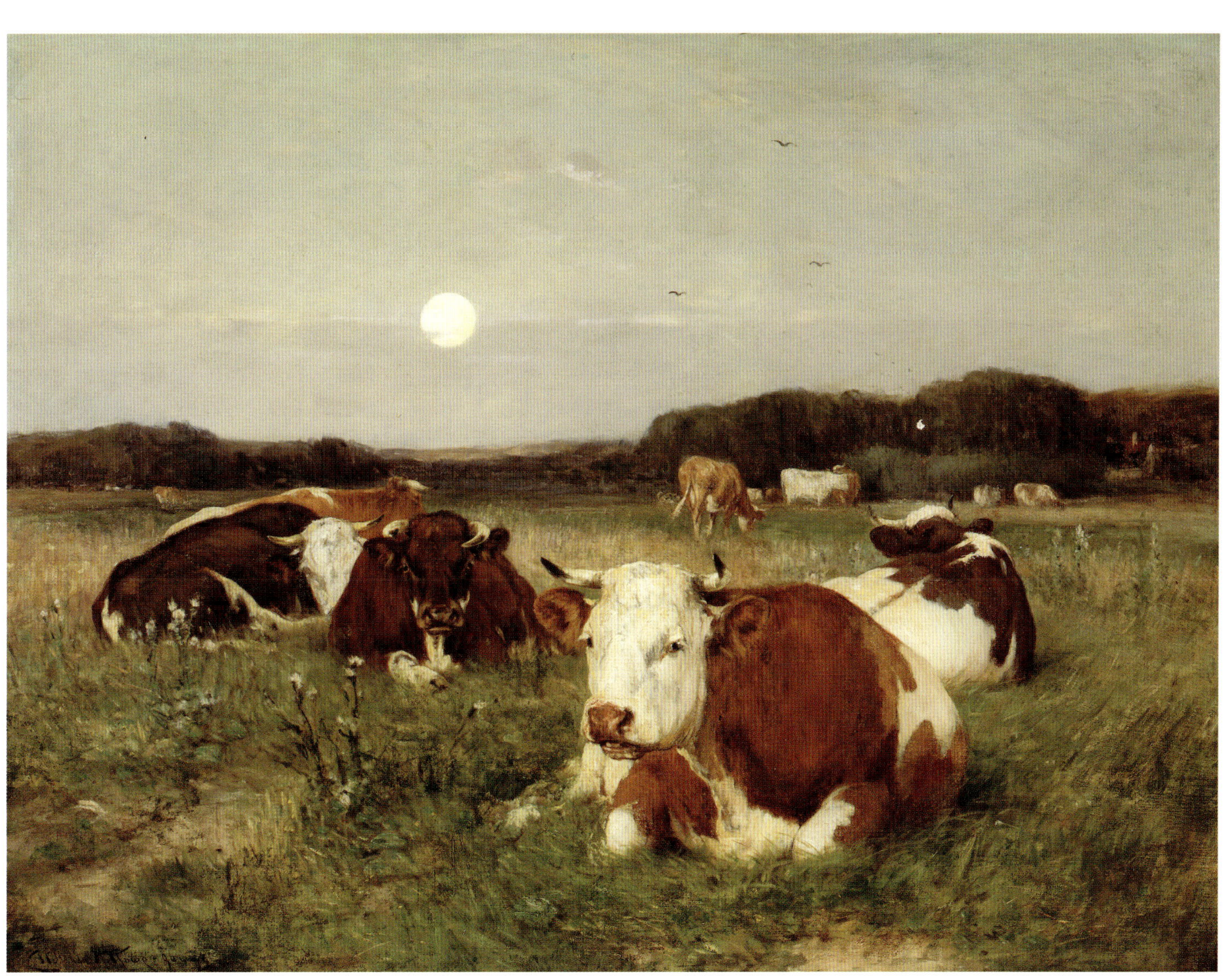

Walter Castle Keith 1863–1927

29

Beach Scene, 1905

Oil on canvas, 29½ × 35⅜"
Signed: "Castle Keith"
Katwijks Museum,
Katwijk, the Netherlands

BORN IN DETROIT ON FEBRUARY 18, 1863, WALTER CASTLE KEITH preferred to be known by his middle name. He went to Europe to study art in 1889, working first in London and then for two years in Munich. Beginning in 1895, when he visited Dordrecht from Germany, he made regular sketching and painting trips to the Netherlands from his home in Syracuse, New York. He filled his sketchbooks with ideas for paintings in Laren, Volendam, Katwijk, The Hague, Voorburg, Loosduinen, Rijnburg, and many rural villages. His subjects ranged from farmers milking their cows to woodlands, farm houses, canal boats, cottages, hay ricks, mothers with children, cityscapes, and beach scenes. He moved permanently to the Netherlands in 1901, living alternately in Katwijk, Laren, and The Hague. In 1912 he moved to Amsterdam, then in 1914 back to Laren, and finally in 1917 to Heeze, as recorded in the various registers of residency in these cities. Not until 1921 did he return to spend his last few years in the United States.

It was in Katwijk that Castle Keith painted this beach scene, the original title of which has been lost. It typifies the "unfinished" appearance of many of his finished paintings, which he blocked in with large areas of local color in light or shade, rendering only a few areas of the canvas in any detail. The strong composition of this picture, with its cropped boats and figures clustered on the left and the open sky and sea on the right, reveals his study of photography. His was a modern view of an old subject, but a very different modern view from that produced by Paul King in the same summer on the same beach (cat. 30). Keith exhibited primarily in the Netherlands, where his dealers and some of his patrons were located. Frans Buffa and Sons of Amsterdam held a memorial exhibition of his work shortly after his death in 1927.

AS

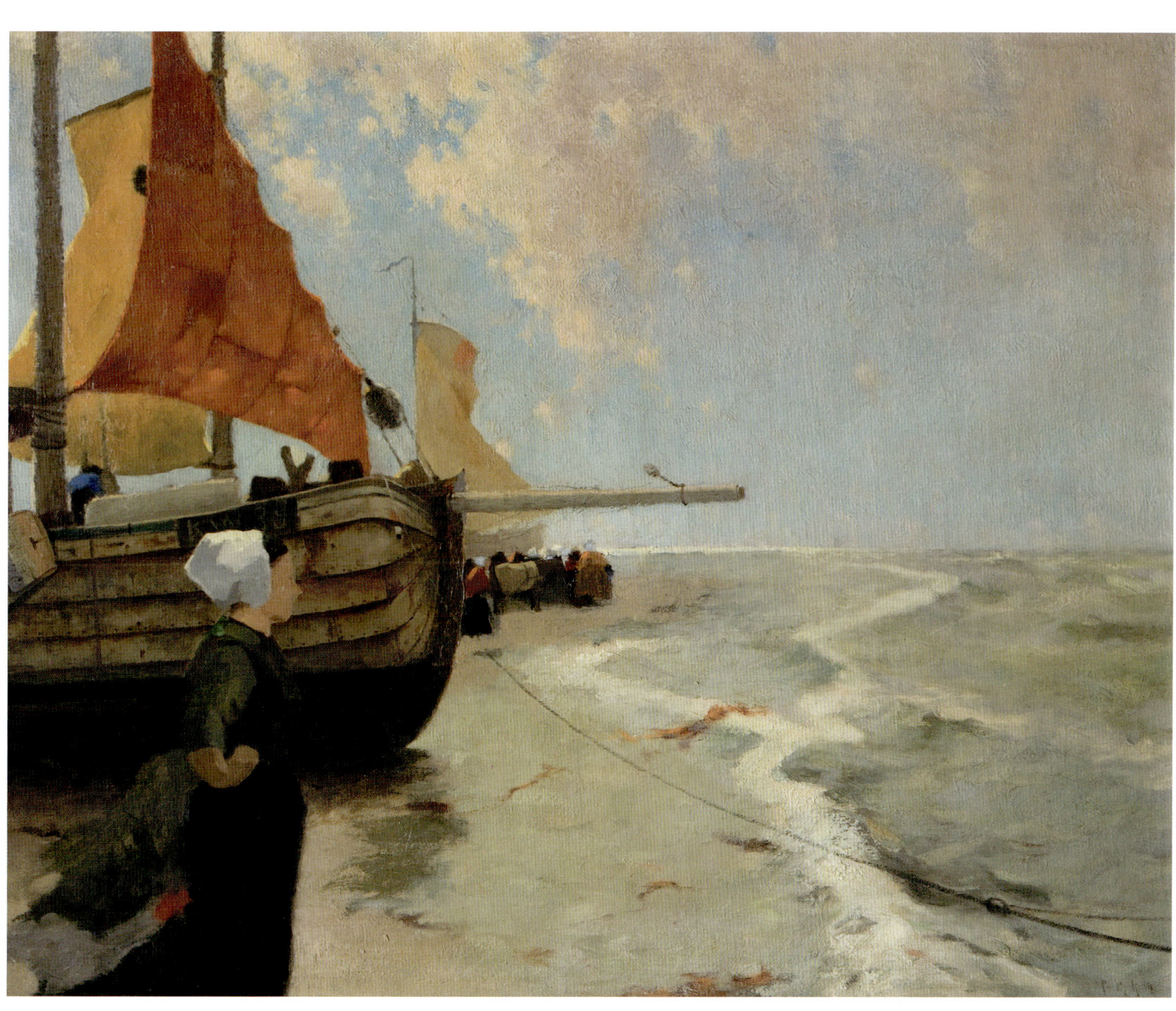

Paul Bernard King 1867–1947

30

Hauling in the Anchor Line, 1905

Oil on canvas, 25 × 31"
Signed: "Paul King Katwyk 05"
Collection of Alice Miles,
Providence, Rhode Island

THE MOST NOTEWORTHY OF PAUL BERNARD KING'S DUTCH PAINTINGS, *Hauling in the Anchor Line* was painted in Katwijk during the summer of 1905. The painting earned King both the Inness prize and the Samuel T. Shaw purchase prize at the Salmagundi Club in 1906. It was exhibited at the National Academy of Design and was reproduced in *International Studio* in March 1906. The artist's high opinion of this work is evidenced by the fact that, shortly before his death, he purchased it back from Samuel T. Shaw; the painting has since remained in the collection of the artist's descendants.[1] The work utilizes vigorous brushwork, scattered spots of bright color, and a dynamic composition to glorify an ordinary moment in the lives of average Dutch fishermen and villagers: two men on horseback robustly tow to shore a flat-bottomed fishing boat as a crowd gathers to watch their efforts. Most unusual is King's chosen viewpoint for the painting, which places the viewer on the bow of the ship, looking at the backs of the men on horseback, rather than on land.

King began his career as an apprentice at a lithographic printing firm in Buffalo, New York, where he was listed in the Buffalo city directory as "lithographer" from 1884 through 1898. He received his earliest artistic training at the Art Students League of Buffalo, and went on to study under Henry Siddons Mowbray at the Art Students League of New York from 1901 to 1904. King began making regular trips to Holland to study and paint, coming into contact with Dutch artists Willy Sluiter, Evert Pieters, and noted Hague School painter Bernardus Johannes Blommers. King developed a particularly close friendship with Willy Sluiter. Although King's visits to Europe ceased with the onset of World War I, he and Sluiter continued to correspond regularly during the war—King's letters accompanied by packages of food and clothing, Sluiter's by small watercolors that he had painted.[2] King served on the board of directors of the Philadelphia School of Design for Women from 1908 to 1921, holding the position of acting president from 1915 to 1918. He was a member of and regularly exhibited at the Salmagundi Club, National Academy of Design, Pennsylvania Academy of the Fine Arts, and many other establishments.

CM

1. This information was kindly provided by the artist's granddaughter, Alice Miles, during an interview with the author, May 28, 2007.

2. Ibid.

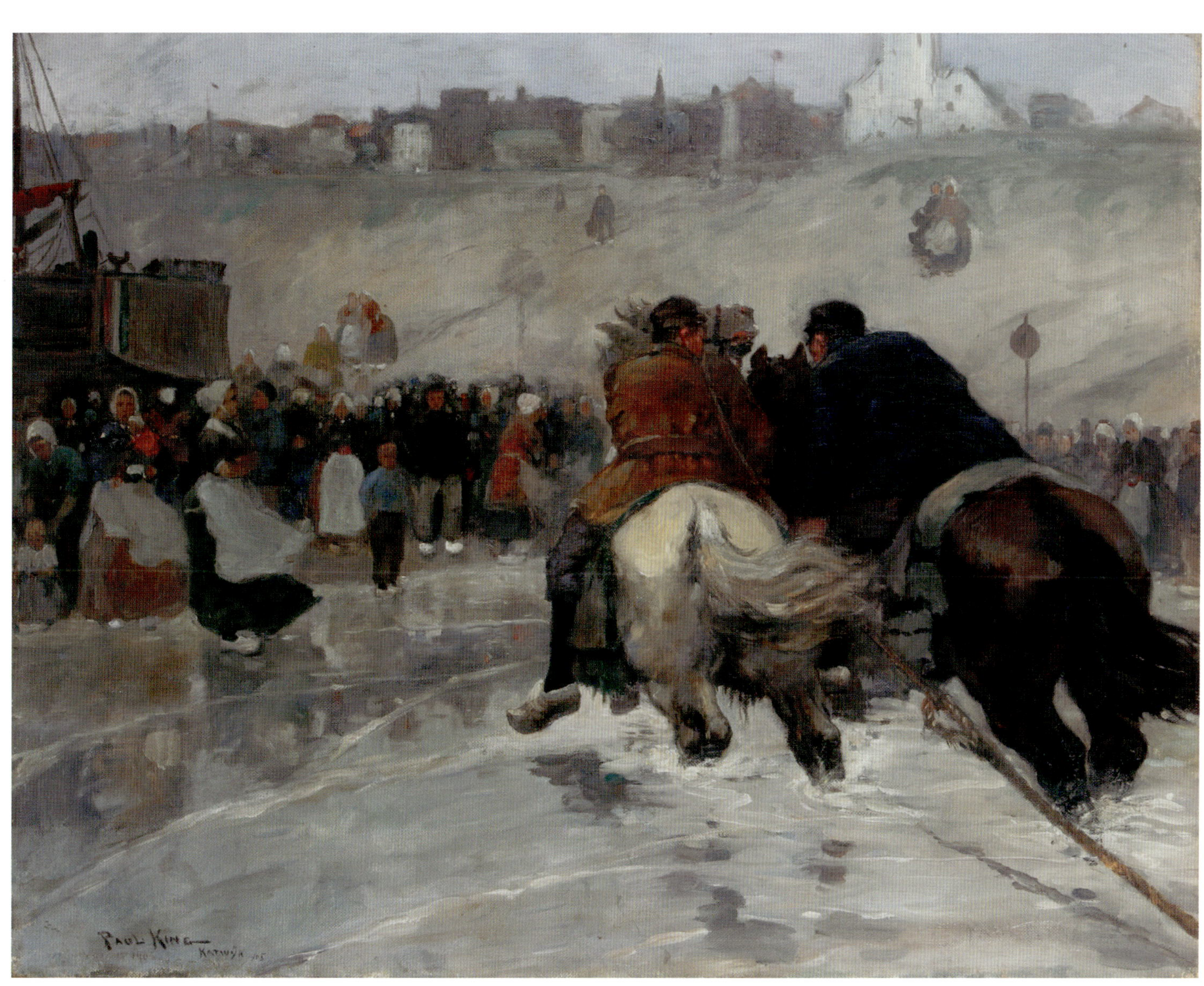

Walter MacEwen 1858–1943

31

The Notary, 1884–85

Oil on canvas, 20 × 17¼"
Signed: "MacEwen"
Collection of Dr. Edward T. Wilson, Bethesda, Maryland

WALTER MACEWEN WAS BORN AND RAISED IN CHICAGO. After a year at Northwestern University, he went to the Royal Academy of Fine Arts in Munich, where the curriculum included study of the old Dutch masters. He made his first trip to the Netherlands by 1878 and began spending his summers in the Dutch town of Hattem around 1881. Here he specialized in interior genre scenes, in some of which contemporary figures wear the traditional Dutch costume of the region and in others the raiment of Volendam. He also painted many historical figure pieces, relying on the art of an earlier era to provide models for his figures' satin dresses, lace collars, and velvet jackets. He admired the little Dutch masters such as Vermeer and Terborch, absorbing their lessons and recasting them in his own terms. MacEwen's first Salon picture, *The Letter* (Indianapolis Museum of Art, believed destroyed), represented four members of a typical rural Dutch family seated around a table listening to a letter read out loud by the youngest daughter.[1] A lightly curtained window behind them stands open to let a stream of sunlight fall upon the old woman at the end of the table. This general composition would be repeated by MacEwen throughout his lifetime with a variety of narrative schemes.

The Notary is part of a series that includes MacEwen's 1891 Salon picture *At the Burgomaster's*.[2] MacEwen painted at least three pictures with that title, distinguishing the later versions in his "List of Principal Works" with the added notations "*(blue curtain)*" and "*(white satin dress)*."[3] Since he also listed two works titled *Dutch Interior (at table)*, and many others with equally vague titles, it is difficult to associate any given painting with a specific title or exhibition record. Nevertheless, *The Notary* most closely resembles *At the Burgomaster's*, which shows the same woman seated at the same table with the same windows and flowers behind her. The same older man takes his place behind the carpet-covered table. In fact the two pictures continue a single narrative. In *At the Burgomaster's*, the woman consults with the seated man who holds his quill pen above a large piece of paper on the table, evidently a contract. They appear to be discussing what he should write. In *The Notary*, the document is complete and the standing notary points to the place where the young woman signs it with the quill pen. A date of 1641 is embroidered into the table cloth instead of the coat of arms in the earlier picture, and a map now decorates the wall à la Vermeer.

To judge by the number of variations, these intimate interiors showing figures at a table near a window reading, sewing, consulting maps, and writing constitute some of MacEwen's most popular pictures. Another series hints at romance, with titles that include *The Betrothed, Broken Contract, Dutch Courtship, Wedding Presents*, and *Making the Trousseau*. These narrative interior genre scenes found a ready market in the United States.

AS

1. Kirstin Krause, Indianapolis Museum of Art, email to Annette Stott, November 3, 2008, included an old photograph.

2. Illustrated in John D. Trask, ed., *Catalogue de Luxe of the Department of Fine Arts, Panama-Pacific Exposition*, vol. 1 (San Francisco: Paul Elder, 1915), 354.

3. Walter MacEwen, "List of Principal Works," curatorial file, Art Institute of Chicago. Arranged in five-year increments, it does not include the title *The Notary*, nor is it clear when this painting acquired that title.

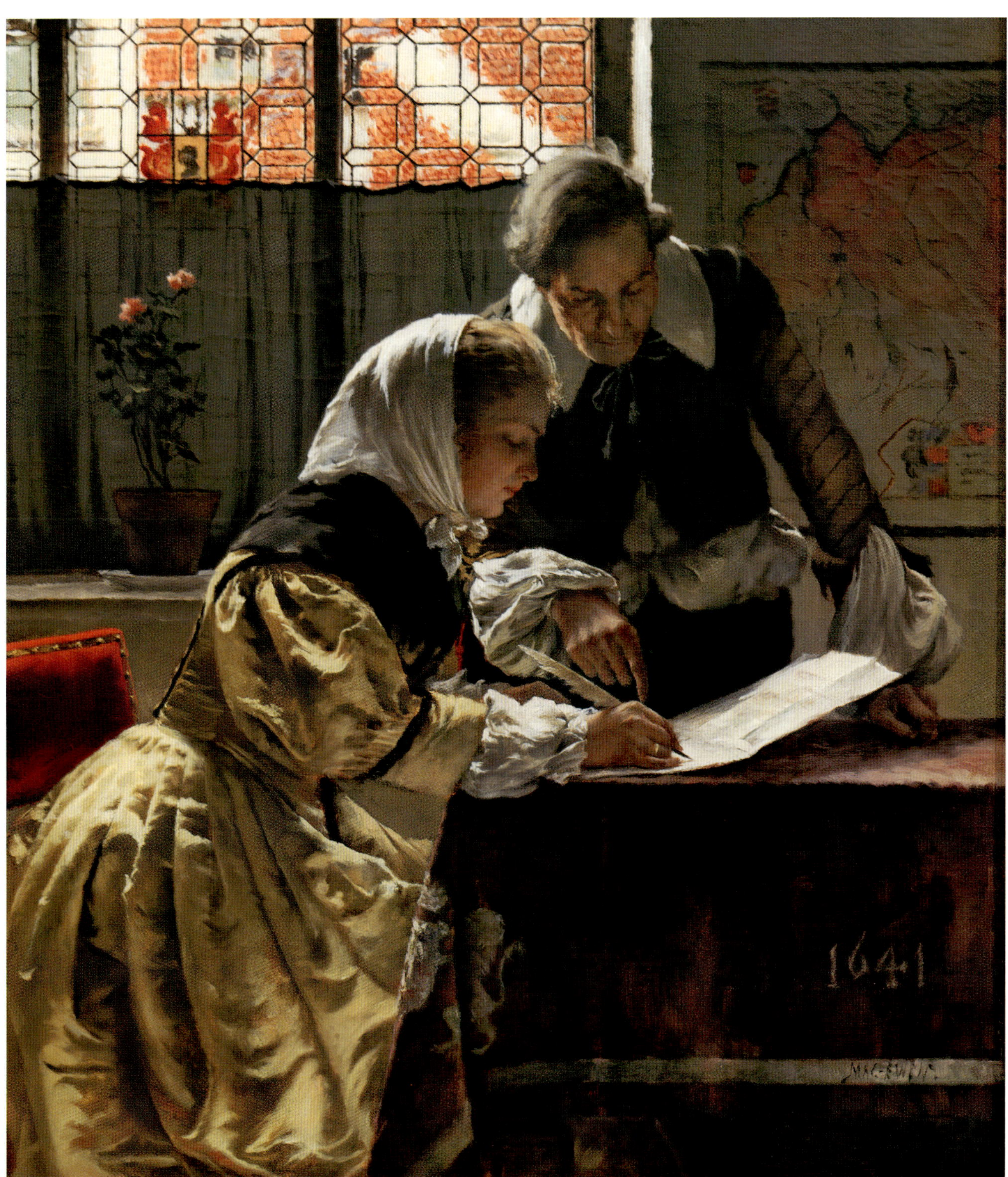
1641

Walter MacEwen 1858–1943

32

Kite Flying, c. 1885–1905

Oil on canvas, 37 × 51"
Signed: "MacEwen"
Private Collection,
Courtesy of Garzoli Gallery,
San Rafael, California

ALTHOUGH MACEWEN WAS BEST KNOWN FOR DUTCH INTERIORS, he completed a number of outdoor scenes beginning in the late 1880s. The largest and best known of these, *Returning from Work* (cat. 33), portrays villagers trudging home under a vast and gloomy sky. In contrast to the somber tone of this work, MacEwen produced numerous paintings of Dutch children, particularly boys cavorting in the sunlight, beginning in the late 1880s. One of these, *Eh! Eh! les autres, allons jouer! en Hollande* (fig. 35, p. 69), portrays four fair-haired boys in a meadow bellowing to their companions. The work received significant critical attention after it was exhibited in the Salon of 1889, and was eventually purchased by the major Chicago collector Potter Palmer. It was probably this painting that inspired a story included in a short biography of MacEwen published in 1913: "While painting in Holland he once saw a number of round-face, flaxen-haired boys staring at him and making sport of the stranger. The sun shone through their fair hair, making glowing halos. He instantly saw the opportunity of painting the faces of the boys against the sunlight."[1] Thereafter, portrayals of Dutch children became a minor specialty for the artist.

MacEwen painted a series depicting small Dutch boys, clad in colorful smocks and wooden shoes, flying kites in open meadows. The theme so attracted the artist that he continued to produce paintings of boys flying kites through 1905.[2] *Kite Flying* portrays a group of children, all boys but one, playing in a meadow on the outskirts of a small village. One child arranges a kite on the ground while another, positioned in the center of the canvas, appears to be directing the action. The radiance of sunlight, so different from the muted silvery light characteristic of MacEwen's interiors, is indicated by the strong shadows cast by the children and the bright glare on their hair and clothing. The seemingly haphazard, circular arrangement of these small figures reinforces the impression that MacEwen has presented an authentic and unvarnished slice of life. Many of MacEwen's contemporaries used photography to capture spontaneous compositions that would later inspire paintings, and it is certainly possible that MacEwen used photographic sources in these works.

Unlike his often meticulously detailed interior scenes, the treatment of outdoor light and the broad application of paint in these pictures reveal MacEwen's assimilation of impressionism. In its naturalistic depiction of ordinary rural life, the kite flying series also reflects the influence of the contemporary Hague School. Finally, these works can be linked to the widespread taste for charming images of children that existed during the latter half of the nineteenth century. Clearly, MacEwen was drawn to the comedy and pathos inherent in the animated facial expressions and social interactions of children, although he never had children of his own.[3]

HKM

1. Notice concerning reproductions for *The Judgment of Paris* from the Art Institute of Chicago, copyright 1913, printed by S. D. Childs, Chicago, and distributed by Brown-Robertson Co., New York; MacEwen file, American Academy and Institute of Arts and Letters, New York.

2. Walter MacEwen, "List of Principal Works," curatorial file, Art Institute of Chicago.

3. MacEwen's descendants confirm he had no children, but it is possible (but as yet undocumented) that he may have had a stepdaughter. His wife, Ella Ward Graham, had been previously married and widowed.

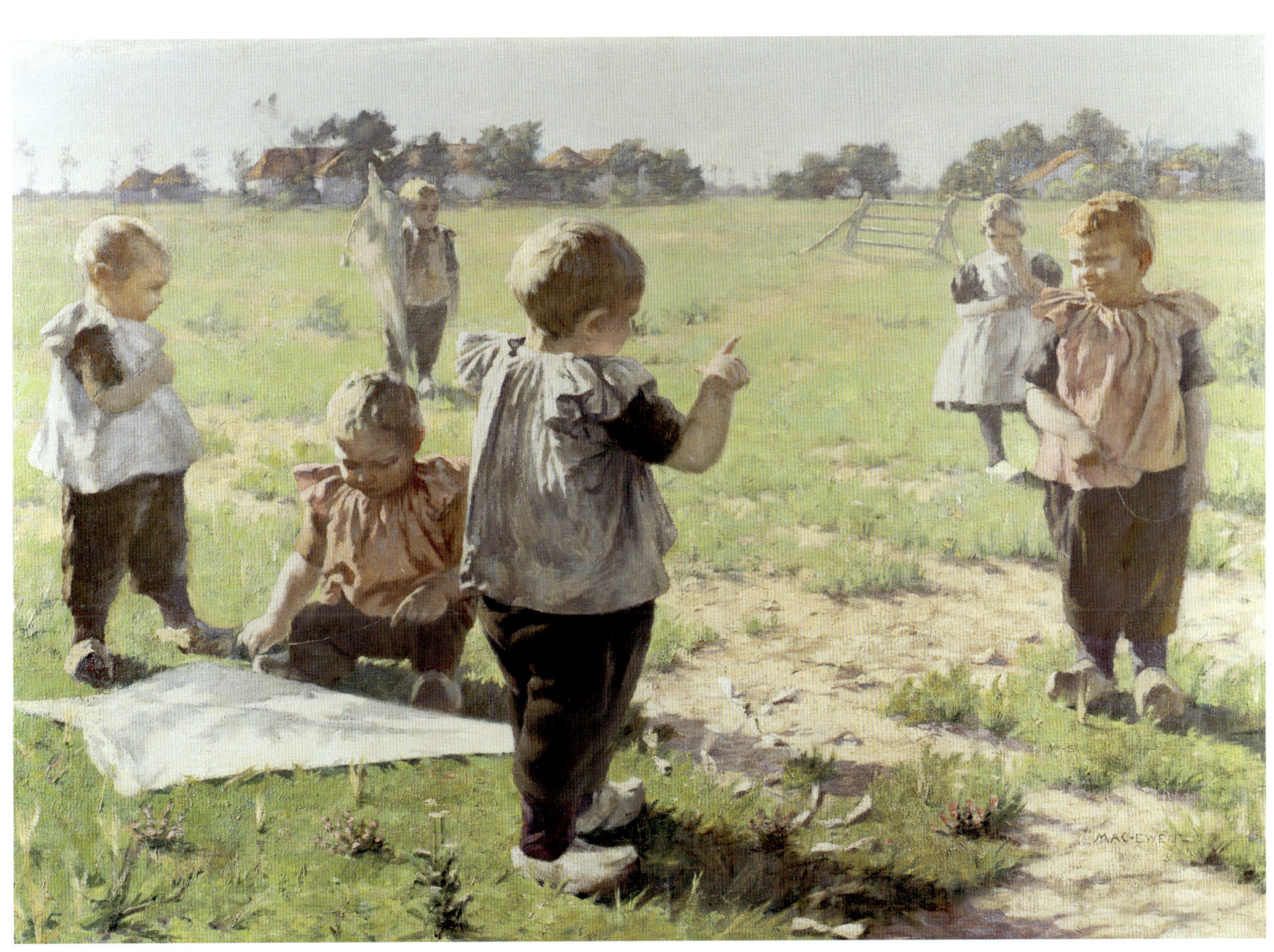
MAC-EWEN

Walter MacEwen 1858–1943

33

Returning from Work, c. 1885

Oil on canvas, 41½ × 75"
Signed: "W McEwen"*
Collection of George Haigh, Cambridge, Massachusetts

*MacEwen (McEwen) used two different spellings of his surname during his active period as an artist. See p. 78, note 2, for more information.

Returning from Work CAPTURES AN INSIGNIFICANT MOMENT IN TIME—a peasant woman pausing to retie her garter during the return from a typical workday. Ahead of her, her fellow laborers wearily trod a path through a rugged meadow toward a village in the distance. One young man pauses and looks back at the bending girl—an action that supplies what little narrative exists in this work. Yet the sizeable scale of the painting and the naturalistic treatment of the workers, garbed in humble and well-worn clothing, invest them with a dignity that was not lost on contemporary viewers. When the work was exhibited at the Salon of 1886, one French critic observed, "all these backs of men and women, these backs somewhat bowed down by work, these rounded and touching backs of decent people, all these backs move you."[1] The awkward pose of the woman in the foreground, combined with the mundane nature of the scene itself, present a convincing glimpse of an ordinary day in rural Holland. MacEwen produced pastel studies of a model in the seemingly unstudied pose of the bending woman, offering some insight into his working methods. The artist likely found his models around the agrarian town of Hattem in the northern badlands, where he maintained a studio. These laborers may have earned a subsistence living working in the peat bogs that provided fuel and employment in this impoverished region.[2]

Returning from Work is one of the most painterly and least overtly narrative of MacEwen's major works. Produced early in his career, the painting was linked to the naturalist movement that swept European art in the late nineteenth century. Naturalism advocated the unsentimental, sometimes unsparing depiction of rural peasant life at a time when traditional lifestyles were increasingly threatened by encroaching industrialization. In its matter-of-fact presentation of anonymous rural laborers, *Returning from Work* reveals MacEwen's involvement with naturalism, and in particular the contemporary Hague School, one manifestation of the naturalist movement.[3] Yet the painting was to remain something of an anomaly in the artist's oeuvre. In general, MacEwen avoided the gritty realism that characterized many naturalist canvases. His pictures, in fact, were often described as optimistic and uplifting, and his peasants were thought to be more refined and attractive than those typically represented in the canvases of the day.

HKM

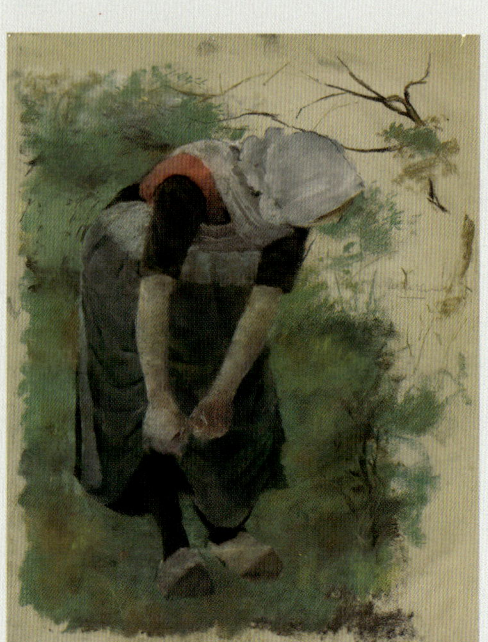

Walter MacEwen, Study for *Returning from Work*, c. 1885, pastel on paper, 24⅞ × 19¼", Starke Family Archives.

1. Untitled press clipping in MacEwen scrapbook, Starke Family Archives.

2. Annette Stott, *Holland Mania: The Unknown Dutch Period in American Art and Culture* (Woodstock, N.Y.: Overlook Press, 1998), 57.

3. See Gabriel P. Weisberg, *Beyond Impressionism: The Naturalist Impulse* (New York: Harry N. Abrams, 1992), 162, for a discussion of MacEwen's *Returning from Work* in relation to naturalism.

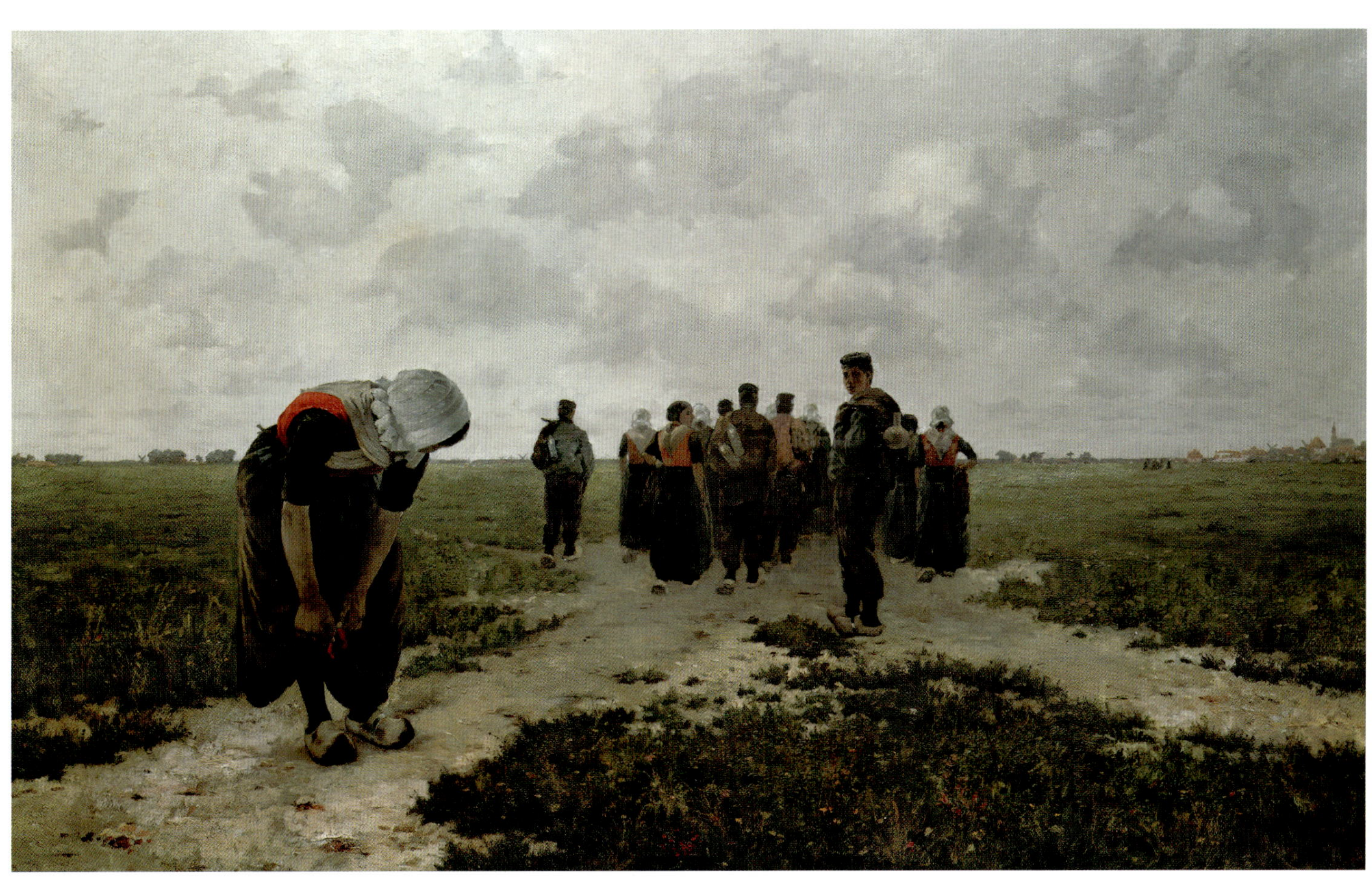

Walter MacEwen 1858–1943

34

The Ghost Story, 1887

Oil on canvas, 47⅝ × 75⅜"
Signed: "W McEwen"*
The Cleveland Museum of Art, Cleveland, Ohio
Gift of Mrs. Edward S. Harkness 1923.416

*MacEwen (McEwen) used two different spellings of his surname during his active period as an artist. See p. 78, note 2, for more information.

The Ghost Story WAS THE MOST CELEBRATED AND WIDELY REPRODUCED WORK of Walter MacEwen's career. The painting portrays a group of Dutch women in a domestic environment, who pause from their spinning and needlework to listen in rapt attention to one of their party telling a ghost story. The modest but comfortable setting, decorated with Delft tiles and illuminated by a large bank of windows in the background, is typical of the type of light-filled, orderly Dutch interiors that became a staple of MacEwen's work. The potted flowers on the windowsill and the bodices of the women's dresses add bright touches of red and pink to the otherwise muted palette. *The Ghost Story*'s critical success at the Salon of 1888 firmly established MacEwen's reputation as one of the most talented genre painters of his time.

This scene of rural community life—with women and children coming together to accomplish traditional labor—presents an idyllic vision of Dutch society in which communal work is enlivened by fellowship and a good story. The painting may also have resonated with viewers on a deeper level. One contemporary observer suggested that the three generations of women depicted in *The Ghost Story* alluded to the enduring cycles of rural life. The spinning wheel, meanwhile, underscored the preindustial lifestyle of these Dutch villagers, and would likely have evoked in American viewers a memory of their country's own colonial past.[1] The painting's broad appeal is evidenced by the many awards it received. At the Paris Universal Exposition in 1889, it won a silver medal, placing MacEwen *hors concours* (beyond awards). *The Ghost Story* later won the medal of honor at Antwerp (1896) and the large gold medal at Vienna (1902).

The painting was eventually acquired by the Cleveland Museum of Art, where, in response to a query from a curator, MacEwen provided some background on the work: "*The Ghost Story* was painted in 1887 in a small Dutch village in the center of Holland. Hattem, Gelderland, was the village where I spent a large part of twenty years. I carried the picture to Paris . . . and sent it to the Salon of 1888 the next spring where it had considerable success."[2] Although the work was painted in Hattem, the women wear the distinctive costume of Volendam, a picturesque fishing village on the coast that attracted scores of foreign artists. The domestic setting, however, is not typical of Volendam. Moreover, the painting's narrative—the telling of a ghost story—may have specifically referenced the Veluwe, the region in which Hattem is situated, which had a long tradition of folklore and storytelling.[3] This tendency to combine costumes from one region with settings and traditions from another reveals the artistry and poetic license in MacEwen's portrayal of rural Dutch life.

HKM

TMA only

1. Kathleen A. Pyne, "Walter McEwen," in David C. Huntington, *The Quest for Unity: American Art Between the World's Fairs 1876–1893* (Detroit: Detroit Institute of Arts, 1983), 236–37; and Annette Blaugrund, et al., *Paris 1889: American Artists at the Universal Exposition* (Philadelphia: Pennsylvania Academy of the Fine Arts and New York: Harry N. Abrams, 1989), 182–83.

2. Walter MacEwen, letter to Louise H. Burchfield, curator at the Cleveland Museum of Art, March 7, 1938, curatorial files, Cleveland Museum of Art.

3. The author acknowledges Annette Stott, Emke Raassen-Kruimel, and Jannig Kwakman for identifying the costumes. Regarding Veluwe storytelling, see Saskia de Bodt, *Schildersdorpen in Nederland* (Warnsveld: Terra and Laren: Singer Laren Museum, 2004), 64–71.

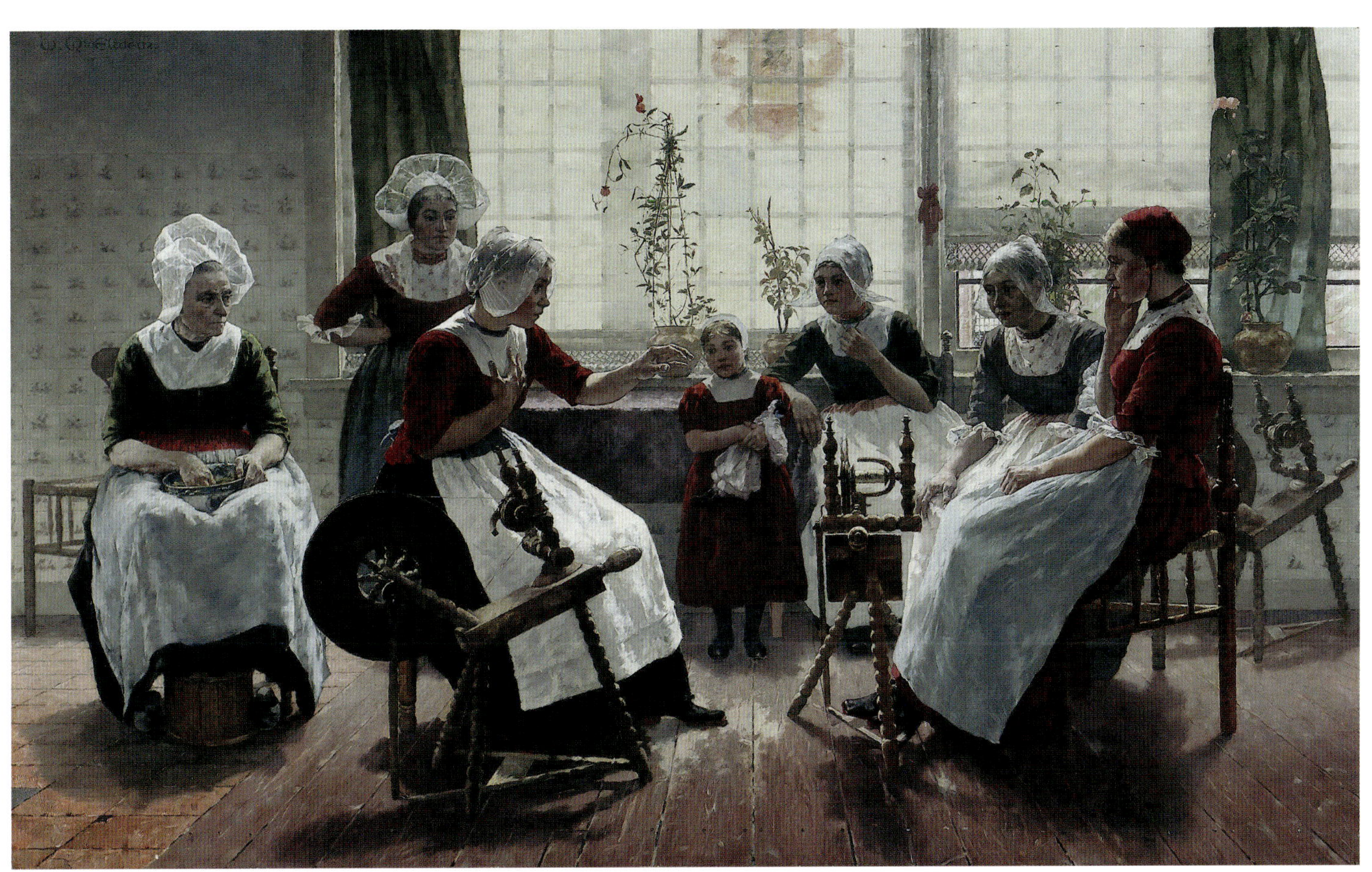

Walter MacEwen 1858–1943

35

L'absente (The Absent One on All Souls' Day), 1889

Oil on canvas, 63 × 49¼"
Signed: "W. MacEwen, 89-H"
Museum of Modern Art and Contemporary Art, Liège, Belgium

WALTER MACEWEN'S *The Absent One on All Souls' Day* WAS ONE of the most celebrated works of the Salon of 1890. The painting depicts a young woman and her father seated in a domestic interior. Formally and somberly dressed, they have perhaps recently returned from church services. The father inadvertently dozes while the daughter reads Scripture. A third figure—a ghostly, semitransparent specter representing the deceased mother—inhabits the room, completing the family circle. Is the apparition conjured by the nodding father, who dreams the presence of his departed spouse? Or by the daughter, whose piety summons her mother's spirit?

The daughter wears a *boomhul* cap, a part of the traditional costume worn by the villagers of Volendam. The remainder of her costume is not specific to Volendam, nor is that of her father.[1] This disparity reveals MacEwen's tendency to utilize provincial costumes for aesthetic impact rather than regional veracity. It is also a reminder that his paintings were created not for the rural Dutch he portrayed, but for international audiences in America, France, and other European urban centers, who were unlikely to quibble over details of regional costume. *The Absent One* may well have been completed in MacEwen's studio in Hattem in the Gelderland province. Unlike his friends Gari Melchers (cat. 37–45) and George Hitchcock (cat. 22–26) in the Egmond colony, who regularly produced paintings of religious ceremonies or scenes of daily life imbued with Christian symbolism, MacEwen rarely addressed sacred subjects. *The Absent One* was something of a departure, one that elicited critical debates ranging from MacEwen's supposed spiritualist connections to charges of sensationalism and sentimentality.

The work was first exhibited at the Paris Salon in 1890 under the simple French title *L'absente*. However, in the same year at an exhibition of MacEwen's works in the new galleries of the Art Institute of Chicago, a small study for the painting bore the title *All Souls' Day*. By the time the work was exhibited at the Berlin International Exposition in 1891, it was entitled *Die Abwesende am Allerseelentag* (*The Absent One on All Souls' Day*).[2] A religious observance instituted by the Catholic Church in the fourteenth century, All Souls' Day was not traditionally observed in the Calvinist Protestant sects dominant in Holland. This may, perhaps, have contributed to MacEwen's decision to place the daughter in the widely recognized cap of Volendam, a strongly Roman Catholic village.

The religious rituals and profound piety of rural peasants had been a fashionable subject among artists since the 1850s. Certainly, there were contemporary precedents for the portrayal of a ghostly figure. Jules Bastien-Lepage's enormously popular *Joan of Arc Listening to the Voices* (1879, Metropolitan Museum of Art), for instance, depicted the angel who appeared to Joan in her rural village as a hovering, otherworldly presence. In the case of *The Absent One*, contemporary observers were struck by MacEwen's meticulous rendering of the ethereal figure of the deceased mother. One French critic opined, ". . . this vision which is impalpable and without depth was not an insignificant difficulty to overcome: the artist has succeeded completely."[3] The painting was awarded the First Class Gold Medal at the Berlin International Exposition in 1891, and was purchased by the government of Belgium for Liège in 1896.

HKM

1. Thanks to Annette Stott, Emke Raassen-Kruimel, and Jannig Kwakman for lending their expertise on costume.

2. See Lois Marie Fink, *American Art at the Nineteenth-Century Paris Salons* (Washington, D.C.: Smithsonian Institution and New York: Cambridge University Press, 1990), 367; the Art Institute of Chicago, *Catalogue of Paintings Exhibited at the Opening of the New Galleries, February 24, 1890* (Chicago: S. W. Cor., 1890), 18; and Cornelius Gurlitt, *Die Internationale Kunstausstellung zu Berlin 1891* (Munich: Franz Hanfstaengl Kunstverlag, 1891), 126.

3. Untitled newspaper clipping notated *Brelan de Salons*, in MacEwen scrapbook, Starke Family Archives.

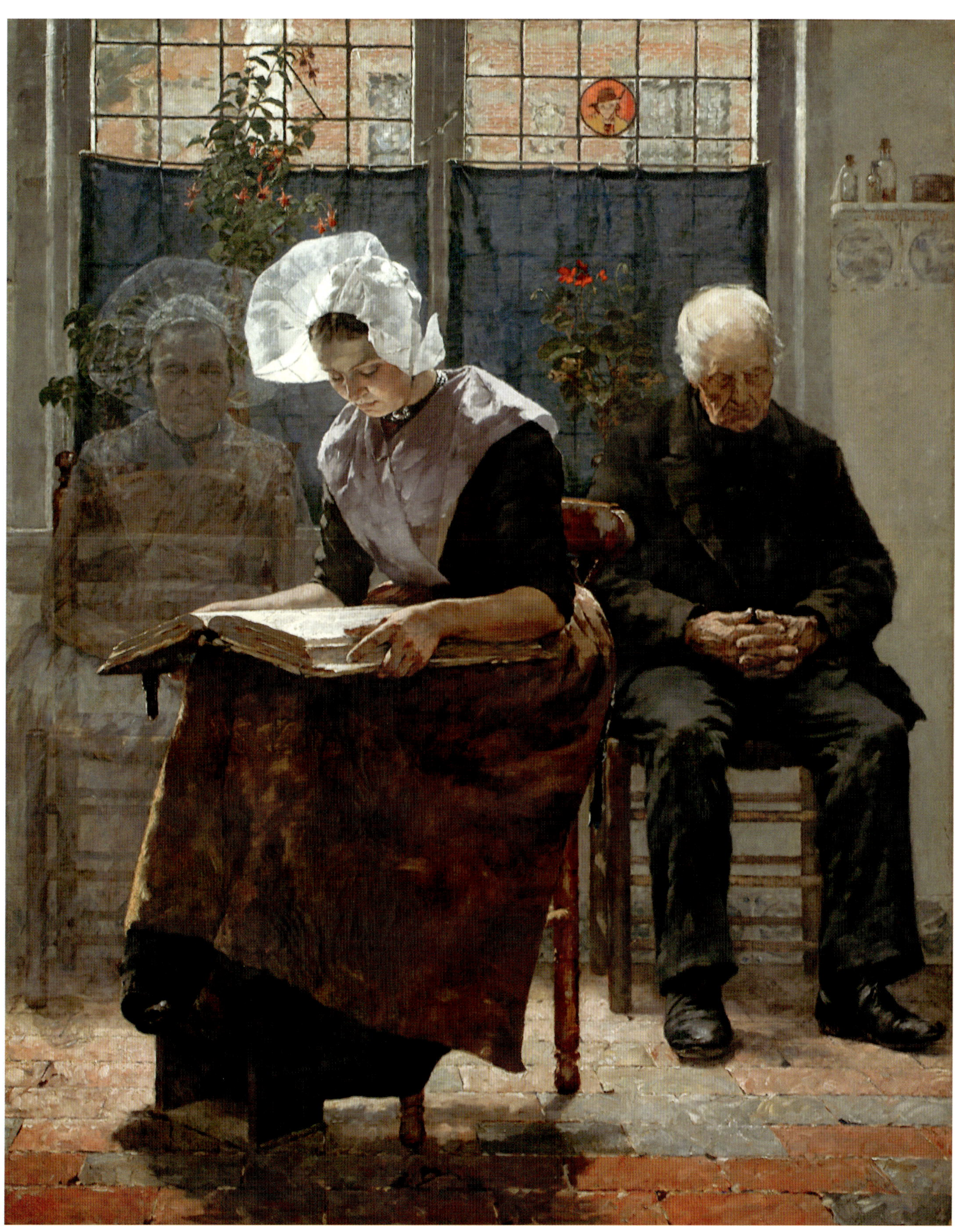

Walter MacEwen 1858–1943

36

The Lacemakers, c. 1885–1900

Oil on canvas, 22⅞ × 38¾"
Signed: "W. McEwen"*
Telfair Museum of Art, Savannah, Georgia
Gift of Mr. and Mrs. George A. S. Starke Jr. and family, 1992

*MacEwen (McEwen) used two different spellings of his surname during his active period as an artist. See p. 78, note 2, for more information.

LIKE HIS FRIEND AND FELLOW EXPATRIATE GARI MELCHERS (cat. 37–45), Walter MacEwen was attracted to the culture and scenery of rural Holland. Although MacEwen's primary residence and studio were in Paris, the artist spent summers in the small village of Hattem, a walled medieval town in the Veluwe region of Holland. The costumes of the female figures in the Telfair's work accurately reflect those worn by women in the province of Gelderland during MacEwen's residence there.[1]

The painting known as *The Lacemakers* depicts three seated women engaged in tatting the edges of a large piece of white fabric.[2] The setting, flooded with light emanating from two prominent window casements in the background, is quiet and introspective. Behind the women, a man stands by the window, his foot raised on the seat of a chair, smoking a long pipe and staring at the woman on the left. She seems to be lost in meditation, absentmindedly clutching the corner of the fabric. What little narrative exists here is supplied by this thoughtful figure and the man with the pipe. The work is representative of a specialty that MacEwen developed and pursued over the course of three decades: the Dutch interior with figures, typically female, engaged in daily tasks. Such paintings are characterized by the attractive, well-to-do appearance of the artist's peasant subjects; his meticulous treatment of surface details; and his handling of the silvery light that illuminates his canvases, typically originating from a window in the background. MacEwen rendered dozens of these interiors over the course of his career, many of them featuring repetitive elements such as Delft tiles, potted plants on windowsills, and large banks of heavily paned windows.

MacEwen's strong familiarity with genre scenes of the seventeenth century is evident here. Vermeer, in particular, exerted a strong influence upon his work, and contemporary critics often likened MacEwen's paintings to the works of the little Dutch masters. Vermeer's influence is evident in the Telfair's painting in details such as the open window at the top right and the small still life of a wine bottle and glass on the table. The traditional costumes of the women lend a timeless quality to the work; were it not for the more modern clothing of the male figure, a casual viewer might mistake this for a seventeenth-century painting. MacEwen's art was also influenced by the movements of his own time, including the Hague School, whose adherents captured rural Dutch life in straightforward, chromatically muted canvases. MacEwen has also been associated with the naturalist movement of the late 1870s through the early 1890s, which emphasized accurate, objective portrayals of regional life devoid of overt sentiment, narrative, or political content.[3]

HKM

1. Thanks are due Annette Stott for identifying the costumes in this picture. For further discussion of MacEwen's work in Hattem, see Annette Stott, *Holland Mania: The Unknown Dutch Period in American Art and Culture* (Woodstock, N.Y.: Overlook Press, 1998), 56–57.

2. This work descended in MacEwen's family and was given to the Telfair by the artist's great nephew. The family called it *The Lace Ladies*, whereas museum records indicate it may have been titled *The Lacemakers*. No conclusive evidence was found for either title. The attributed dates are based on the first appearance of MacEwen's Dutch genre scenes in the Paris Salon in 1885 and his change of focus to the costume series of around 1900.

3. Gabriel P. Weisberg, *Beyond Impressionism: The Naturalist Impulse* (New York: Harry N. Abrams, 1992), 7–9.

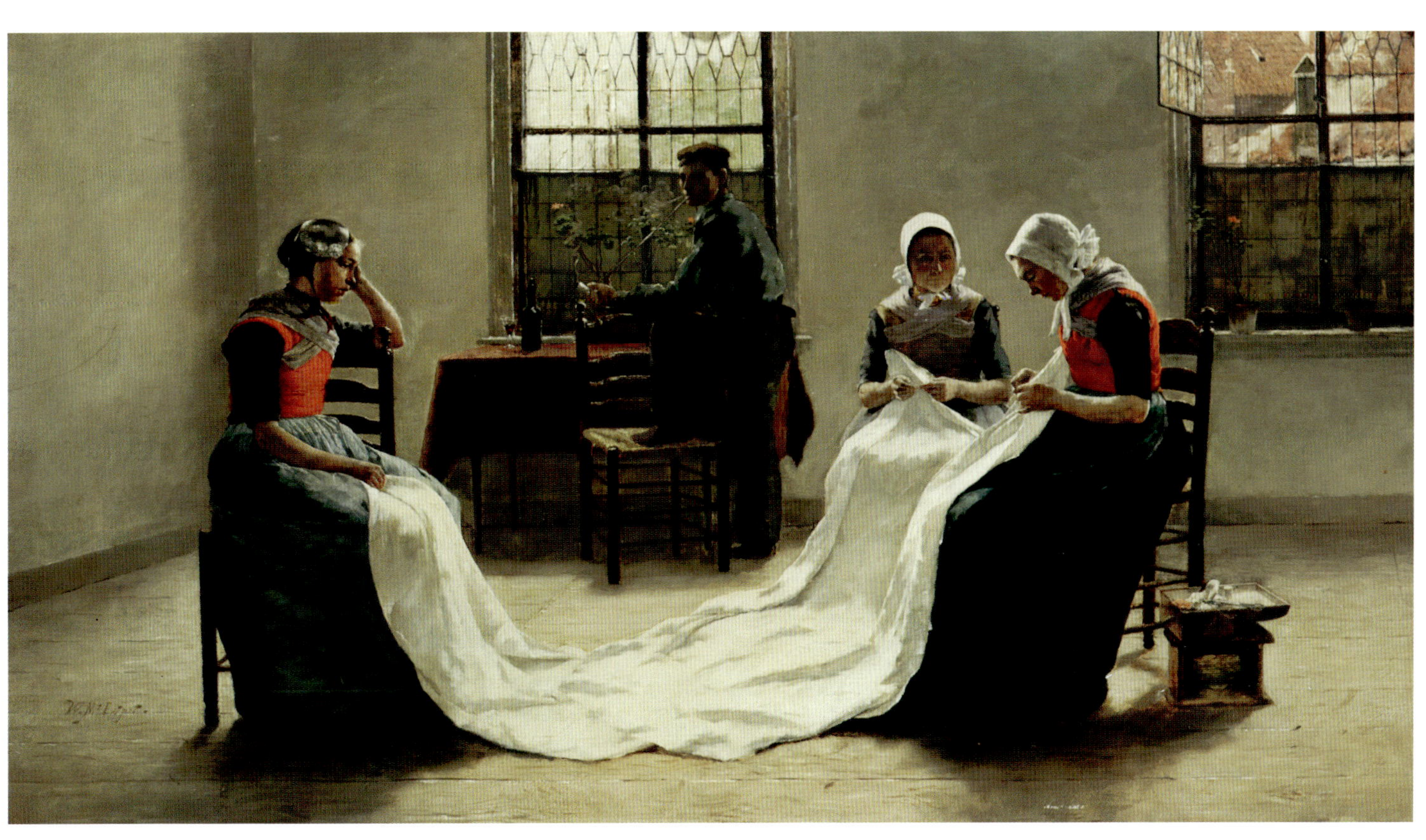

Gari Melchers 1860–1932

37

The Sermon, 1886

Oil on canvas, 62⅝ × 86½"
Signed: "Gari Melchers"
Smithsonian American Art Museum, Washington, D.C.
Bequest of Henry Ward Ranger through the National Academy of Design

IN WHAT WOULD BECOME HIS FIRST MASTERPIECE, Gari Melchers combined his observations of Dutch piety and old-world custom and costume to produce an insightful portrayal of working-class Protestantism that rivaled the seventeenth-century Dutch masters. *The Sermon* was also a commercial stroke of genius. Melchers had hit upon a scene that would embody the tastes and values of an audience hungry for pictures of a premodern, God-centered world.

Set in a Dutch Reformed Church in Egmond Binnen, Holland, two male parishioners sit in a raised stall overlooking nine women seated in straight-back chairs on the floor. The attention of the congregation is directed toward a minister just out of view, but the center of the narrative focuses on a sleeping peasant girl and her frowning neighbor. The soft, gray cloak of light that gently illuminates the figures and the muted gray-blue tonalities of the backdrop set the sober moral tone that underlies the subject matter.

In his effort to paint an authentic snapshot of the working class, Melchers allied himself with the era's most popular peasant painters, the naturalists, led by French painter Jules Bastien-Lepage. Because of the current rage for the work of Bastien-Lepage and his followers, Melchers hoped to find high praise and a ready market for *The Sermon* at the Paris Salon. From the start he painted with his audience in mind, and American collectors, a powerful new force on the scene, were eager to buy works that had the stamp of European training and style. What's more, they believed they shared a common historical past with Holland and had a passion for things Dutch.

Melchers painted his subjects with the utmost frankness and objectivity to underscore the virtues of honesty and sincerity that he believed typified the Dutch peasant. Not only did Melchers reproduce the scene with compelling realism, he rendered it on a monumental scale to enhance the illusion of life and the heroic significance of its hardworking and devout characters. Whether or not he fabricated the incident of the sleeping girl, the little drama smacked of reality. Audiences were sympathetic, if not amused, by the all-too-familiar narrative. This ambition to "paint the natives as they really are," to quote Bastien-Lepage, was echoed in the motto Melchers hung above his studio door: "Waar en Klaar," true and clear.

The Sermon was widely praised for its technical mastery and expressive power. More than one critic hailed it as a "sensation" at the Salon. It earned Melchers an honorable mention at the Paris Salon, First Class Gold medals in Amsterdam and Munich, and assured him the Grand Prize at the Paris Universal Exposition in 1889. The accolades he earned set in motion the meteoric rise of his career and established him as a leading American practitioner of rustic naturalism. The painting was purchased by the Chicago real estate developer and hotelier Potter Palmer and passed down through his family until it was acquired for the Smithsonian in 1931.

JC

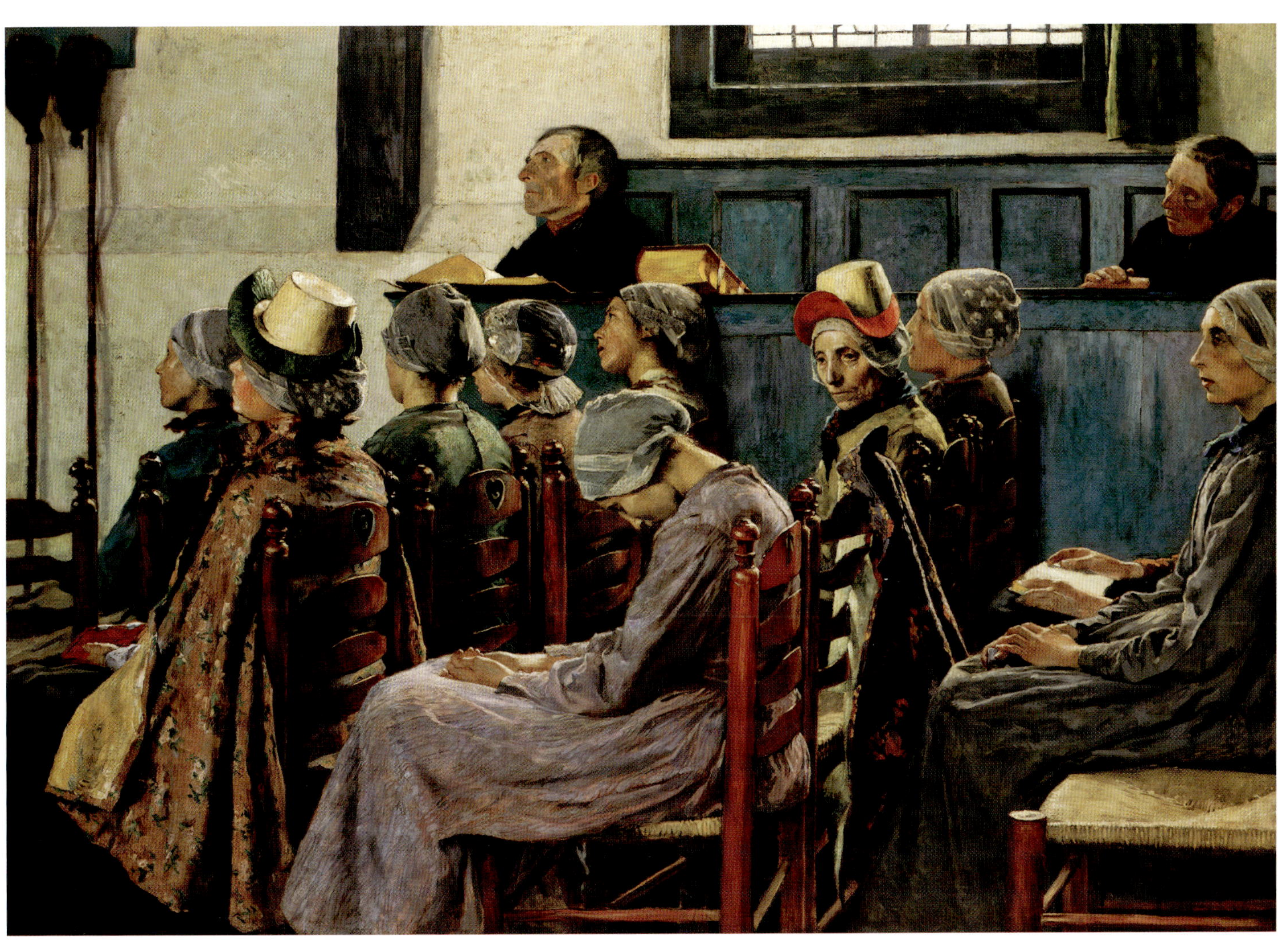

Gari Melchers 1860–1932

38

In Holland, 1887

Oil on canvas, 109 × 77¾"
Signed: "Gari Melchers"
Gari Melchers Home and Studio,
Fredericksburg, Virginia

THE SUCCESS OF *The Sermon* (CAT. 37) WAS A TURNING POINT in Melchers's career. The young artist was so eager to keep up the momentum that he submitted another figural composition large enough to guarantee notice at the spring Salon of 1887. Melchers portrayed two Dutch farm girls against the steep slope of a scruffy sand dune, one pausing to wait for the other as they head home with farm implements in hand. Their figures dominate the canvas. One, appearing in surprisingly fancy dress, carries a yoke with milk pails, reflecting the importance of the dairy industry to the Dutch economy. The other, who is more practically attired in work clothes, carries a rake and basket used for gathering potatoes. At the top of the slope is visible a windmill and the familiar red tile rooftops of Egmond aan Zee, although these structures were a later addition.

In emphasizing the sturdy wholesomeness of the natives in their customary pursuits, Melchers paid homage to the virtues of communal agrarian life, a popular late-nineteenth-century ideology. His life-size heroines were the antithesis of the modern city dweller, commonly viewed as being softened and corrupt, with little know-how or appreciation for manual labor and even less of a connection with the Almighty. The unusually high horizon line was a common device of contemporary French and Dutch peasant painters to symbolically unify the human figure with the land and to express man's dependence on it and reverence for its blessings.

Critical review of *In Holland* was mixed. Some admired Melchers's picture for the illusion of life and atmosphere he achieved and for his faithful characterization of the Dutch. Conversely, others thought its large-scale illusionism theatrical, and that the simple composition of two plain girls was unworthy of the scale afforded. Several found fault with the combination of the shrill blue buckets, intense lilac cape, and blue-green sea hollies. The most common complaint came from those who felt that Melchers's portrayal was too objective, that his models lacked the pretty and idealized appearance to which nineteenth-century audiences were accustomed. The irony here is that Melchers sacrificed truth in favor of the picturesque when he outfitted the milkmaid in an unlikely "Sunday best" dress. Melchers may have taken his "slice of life" realism too far. More and more he would be derisively viewed by critics for his adherence to the "cult of ugliness," because his peasants reminded them of the cloddish rustics of Gustave Courbet and Jules Bastien-Lepage.

Perhaps in response to its lackluster critical reception at the Paris Salon, Melchers reworked the picture in an effort to improve upon it. By 1890 he had painted out the crescent moon and the "J." in his signature, as well as the date. Where once was a featureless dune, he now added the windmill and surrounding buildings at the top margin of the painting. Melchers darkened the milkmaid's wooden shoes, modified the style of her cap to expose her hair, and reworked her face. He revisited the work at least one more time, reconfiguring the clouds, adding more vegetation to the fore- and middle ground, fussing once again with the milkmaid's face, and emphasizing the ties of her cap. In the end, Melchers succumbed to the temptation to construct a prettified, colorful pastiche of what his audience preconceived as Dutch life, thereby including the requisite wooden shoes, windmill, and blond maids.

JC

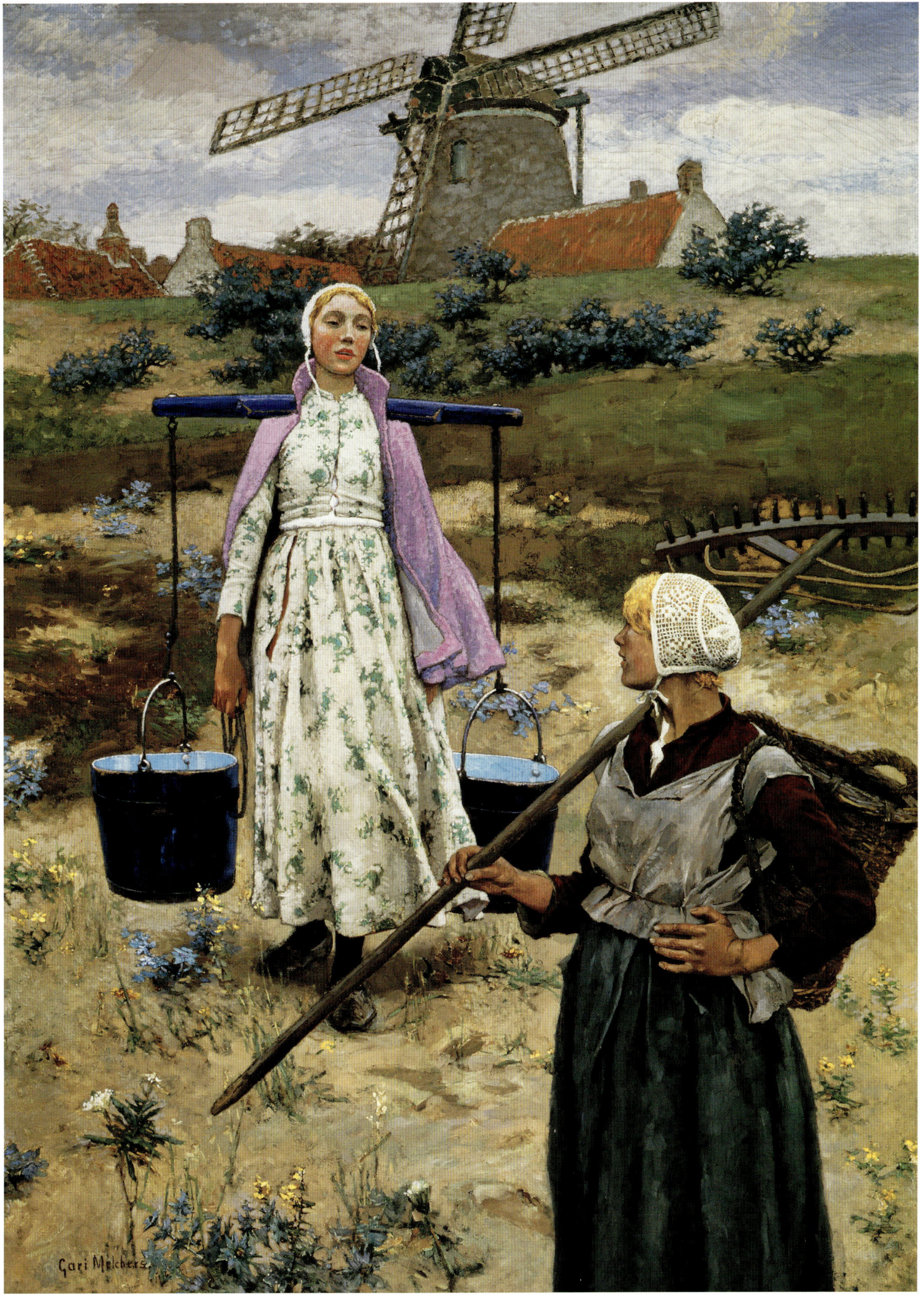
Gari Melchers

Gari Melchers 1860–1932

39

The Pilots, 1887–88

Oil on canvas, 67 × 83"
Signed: "Gari Melchers"
Frye Art Museum,
Seattle, Washington

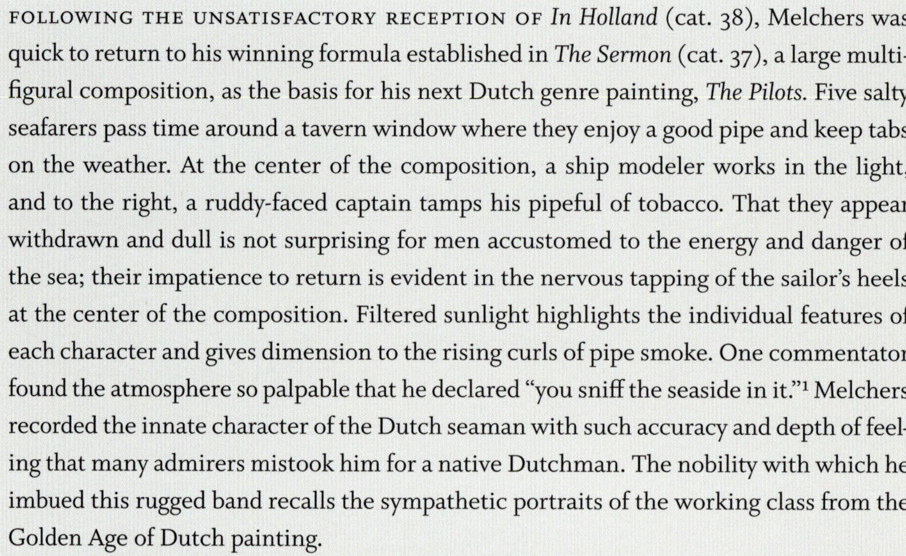

FOLLOWING THE UNSATISFACTORY RECEPTION OF *In Holland* (cat. 38), Melchers was quick to return to his winning formula established in *The Sermon* (cat. 37), a large multi-figural composition, as the basis for his next Dutch genre painting, *The Pilots*. Five salty seafarers pass time around a tavern window where they enjoy a good pipe and keep tabs on the weather. At the center of the composition, a ship modeler works in the light, and to the right, a ruddy-faced captain tamps his pipeful of tobacco. That they appear withdrawn and dull is not surprising for men accustomed to the energy and danger of the sea; their impatience to return is evident in the nervous tapping of the sailor's heels at the center of the composition. Filtered sunlight highlights the individual features of each character and gives dimension to the rising curls of pipe smoke. One commentator found the atmosphere so palpable that he declared "you sniff the seaside in it."[1] Melchers recorded the innate character of the Dutch seaman with such accuracy and depth of feeling that many admirers mistook him for a native Dutchman. The nobility with which he imbued this rugged band recalls the sympathetic portraits of the working class from the Golden Age of Dutch painting.

The Pilots may have been in progress when Melchers submitted *In Holland* to the Salon, for an early photograph of it in his papers shows that he originally dated it "1887" alongside his signature. We may never know whether *The Pilots* could not be completed in time for the 1887 Salon or whether it was born out of the disappointment of *In Holland*. Regardless, the date was later removed and with very slight reworking, the painting was submitted to the Paris Salon of 1888. *The Pilots* was widely admired at the Salon, where it was declared one of the "chief attractions" and "one of the most forceful paintings," earning a third-class Gold Medal.[2] It was especially popular in Germany, where it received additional medals and where Melchers's fondness for everyday types, overall blue-gray tonalities, and the precision of his descriptions reminded audiences of the working-class themes and "super realism" of celebrated painter Wilhelm Leibl. Following its exhibition at the Great Berlin Art Exhibition of 1900, where it found a buyer, *The Pilots* became the basis of a satirical political cartoon in the German magazine *Ulk*, entitled "A Session of the State Ministers," featuring caricatures of some of the Kaiser's best-known cabinet members.

JC

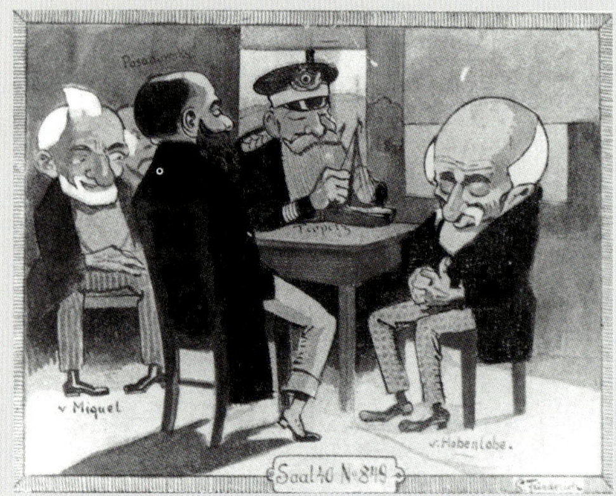

"A Session of the State Ministers (after the painting *The Pilots* by Gari Melchers, Paris, from the Great Berlin Art Exhibition, 1900)," published in *Ulk*, May 25, 1900, Courtesy of Gari Melchers Home and Studio, Fredericksburg, Virginia.

1. Untitled press clipping, *Nottingham* [United Kingdom] *Daily Express*, May 5, 1888, the artist's papers, Gari Melchers Home and Studio, Fredericksburg, Va.
2. Untitled press clipping, *Parti National*, June 9, 1888, and untitled press clipping, *Salon Illustré*, June 19, 1888.

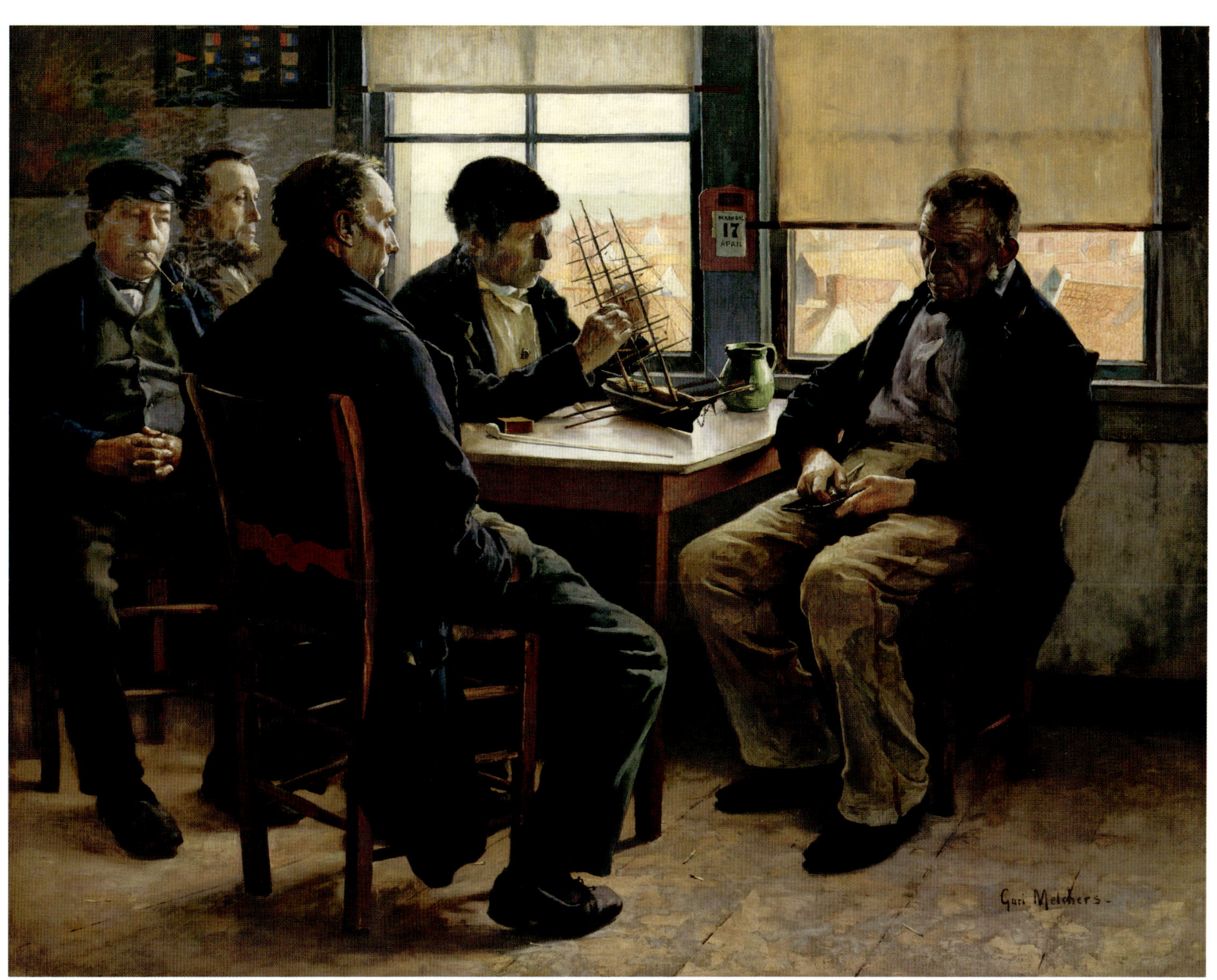
17
APRIL
Gari Melchers

Gari Melchers 1860–1932

40

Arranging the Tulips, late 1880s

Oil on canvas, 54⅝ × 28¾"
Signed: "Gari Melchers"
Smithsonian American Art Museum, Washington, D.C.
Gift of John Gellatly

AS FURTHER RESPONSE TO THE STRONG AMERICAN MARKET FOR DUTCH PICTURES, Melchers began to produce single figure portraits of "Dutch types," or what amounted to stereotypical constructs of how patrons expected Netherlanders to look and dress. *Arranging the Tulips* is an early example; a winsome maiden attired in an archaic costume and lace cap arranges flowers in a Delft vase. Images of shipbuilders, sailors, and shepherdesses would follow, some almost life size, but *Arranging the Tulips* possesses the strongest sense of "Dutchness" by virtue of the requisite props: tulips, a Delft vase, and the wainscot made up of hand-painted Delft tiles.

By presenting the girl in strict profile, her lowered face half-sheltered by her cap, and within an uncluttered and confined stage, Melchers formulated an icon of premodern ideals: simplicity, honesty, and purity. The outline of the girl's upper frame is replicated in the silhouette of an ancestor displayed on the wall. This subtle means of suggesting the continuum of family tradition and values is just another way in which audiences, Americans in particular, identified with Melchers's images. And finally, Melchers's emphasis on things hand-cultivated and hand-crafted (the tulips, tiles, vase, and the provincial chair with rush seat) reflects attitudes prevalent during the era of the Arts and Crafts and Colonial Revival movements.

JC

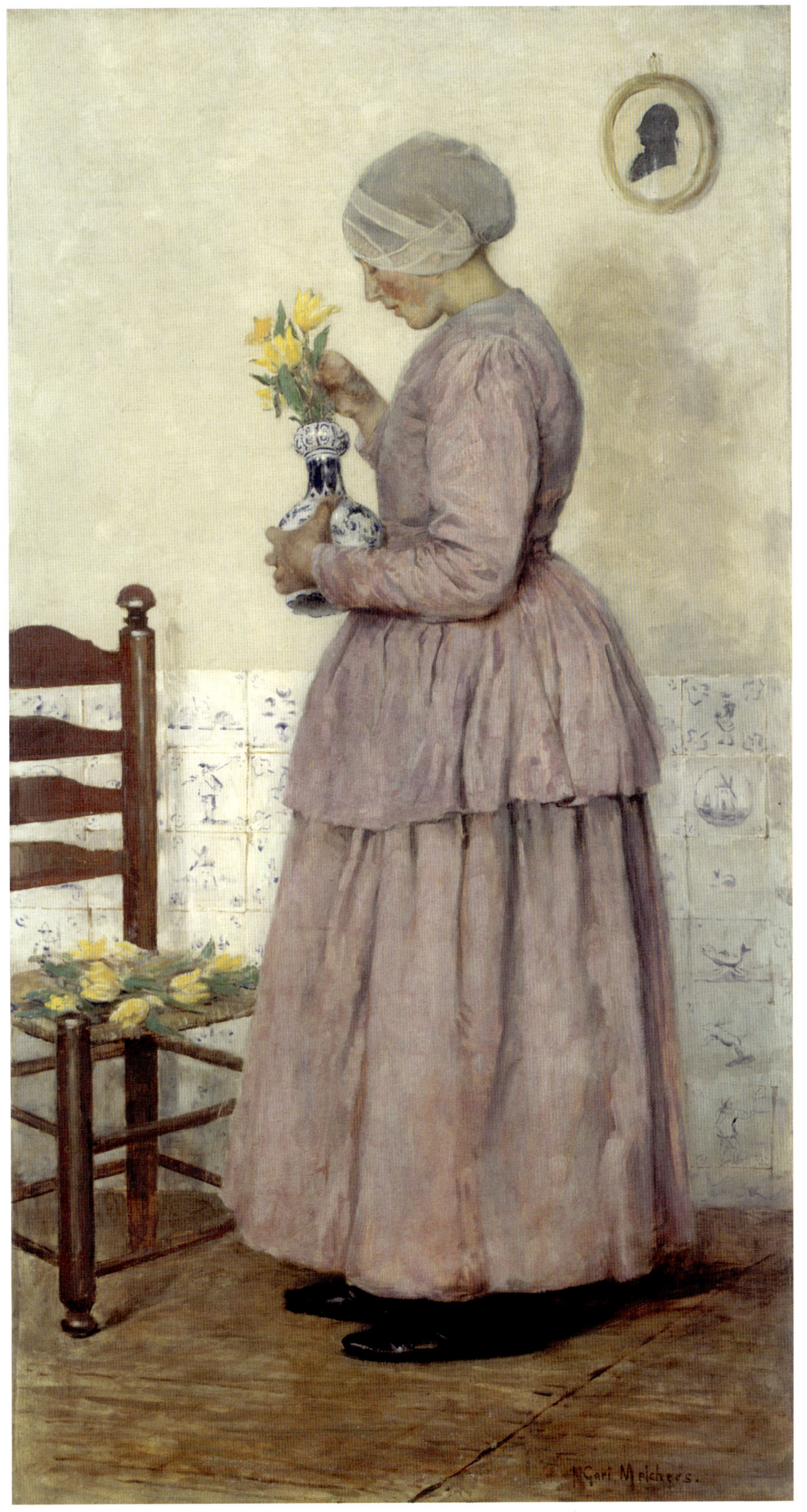
Gari Melchers.

Gari Melchers 1860–1932

41

Skaters, c. 1892

Oil on canvas, 43¼ × 27½"
Signed: "Gari Melchers"
Pennsylvania Academy of the Fine Arts,
Philadelphia, Pennsylvania
Joseph E. Temple Fund

"ONLY THAT WHICH HAS CHARACTER IS TRULY BEAUTIFUL."[1] Such was the position voiced by Gari Melchers, a painter grown accustomed to hearing what some critics termed the "meanness" of his models. Still, he was sensitive to contemporary tastes and as there was no shortage of the picturesque in Holland, he took up his brush with a new eye to the decorative concerns of color and pattern, which had less to do with narrative.

A favorite model of Melchers's in the early 1890s was a young woman named Anna. She and another model, Arie Zoon, pose as the youthful couple, skating stick and blades in hand, striding across a wintry landscape in *Skaters*. Melchers was in the habit of collecting old-fashioned costumes and bric-a-brac to beautify and "authenticate" his scenes of native life. One particular garment, a colorful and boldly patterned cape, made its debut in *Skaters:* the introduction of the cape was an efficacious response to the charge that his peasants were mean and coarse. So pleased was he with its decorative properties that he used the same cape again and again to enliven his paintings. Not surprisingly, the cape resurfaces in the paintings of George Hitchcock (cat. 22–26), the American painter with whom Melchers shared a studio on the dunes of the North Sea.

Melchers responded to the rising popularity of impressionism by gradually adopting many of its chief features, giving new vitality to his pictures. For *Skaters* he retained the accurate drawing and firm modeling of his academic training, but his handling of paint loosened and became thick with texture. He achieved a faithful rendering of northern light and atmospheric effects by incorporating the chalky pastel palette of impressionism. Finally, he utilized cropping, a modern device that gives the "impression" of a scene in the action of unfolding.

The annual exhibitions of the Pennsylvania Academy of the Fine Arts provided one of the most important showcases of emerging American impressionism, including the work of expatriates. Melchers was a regular contributor and his position within the impressionist movement was solidified when *Skaters*, submitted to the seventieth Annual Exhibition of Pictures in 1901, was bought by that institution. The Pennsylvania Academy loaned *Skaters* to the White House in 1978, where it was displayed on a wall outside President Carter's study.

JC

1. John W. Beatty, *The Relation of Art to Nature* (New York: William E. Rudge, 1922), introduction by Gari Melchers, n.p.

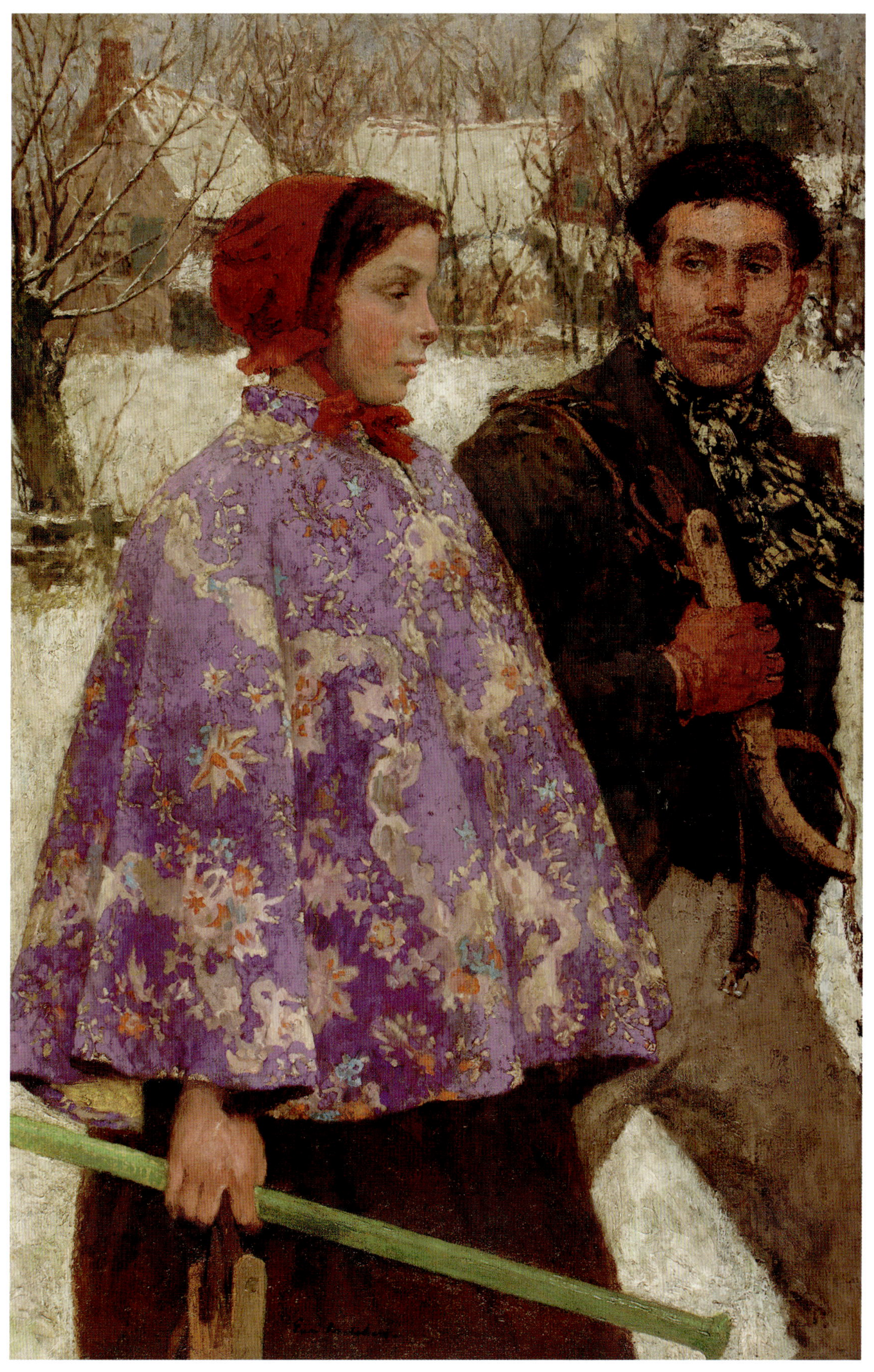

Gari Melchers 1860–1932

42

The Family, c. 1895

Oil on canvas, 73¾ × 53⅜"
Signed: "Gari Melchers"
Staatliche Museen zu Berlin (National Gallery), Berlin, Germany

GARI MELCHERS'S STYLISTIC EVOLUTION CANNOT BE SEEN as moving in a straight line from the academic to the progressive, for he often reverted back to earlier styles, as was the case with *The Family.* Melchers's fondness for the tender subject of a nursing mother and child was expanded here to include a proud and watchful father and a towheaded toddler, assembled at home *en famille* as if before the camera. The child has abandoned her doll in a dark corner and has sought out the protection of the towering patriarch, clutching onto his trouser leg and viewing the audience with suspicion.

The owner of a preparatory sketch for *The Family* recounted Corinne (Mackall) Melchers's explanation for how it came to be:

> And when [Melchers] was painting that picture, with the father standing by . . . and the mother nursing her baby, . . . a little three-year-old ran out and caught her father's trouser leg, and turned her head and looked at Gari; and he was so delighted, that he made a quick sketch, which he afterwards incorporated into the portrait.[1]

Despite Melchers's reputation as an objective commentator on everyday life, there were other motives emerging in his art. He often sought to convey something of the sacred underlying the secular, and in *The Family* he relies on historical precedent in order to accomplish this. The Dutch mother (wearing the same cape as appeared in *Skaters* [cat. 41]) is seated with the child at her breast and one foot elevated in the fashion of traditional enthroned Madonna imagery. The addition of the father completes the reference to the Holy Family and the triangular configuration, which unifies the group physically and psychologically, recalls the Holy Families of Raphael and other masters of the High Renaissance. The details of the marriage bed curtains, the Delft holy water font, and image of the Holy Family on the back wall also are emblematic of the sacred bond of family. The earthiness of the artist's characters and the homey domestic interior are evocative of the seventeenth-century Dutch masters Pieter de Hooch and Jan Steen, favorites of Melchers's, but while the earlier masters painted on a diminutive scale, Melchers painted *The Family* on a monumental scale. It was awarded the Temple Gold Medal by the Pennsylvania Academy of the Fine Arts in 1896.

JC

1. Virginia W. Mackall Bellamy (Mrs. Melchers's sister-in-law), reminiscences, February 1974, archives, Gari Melchers Home and Studio.

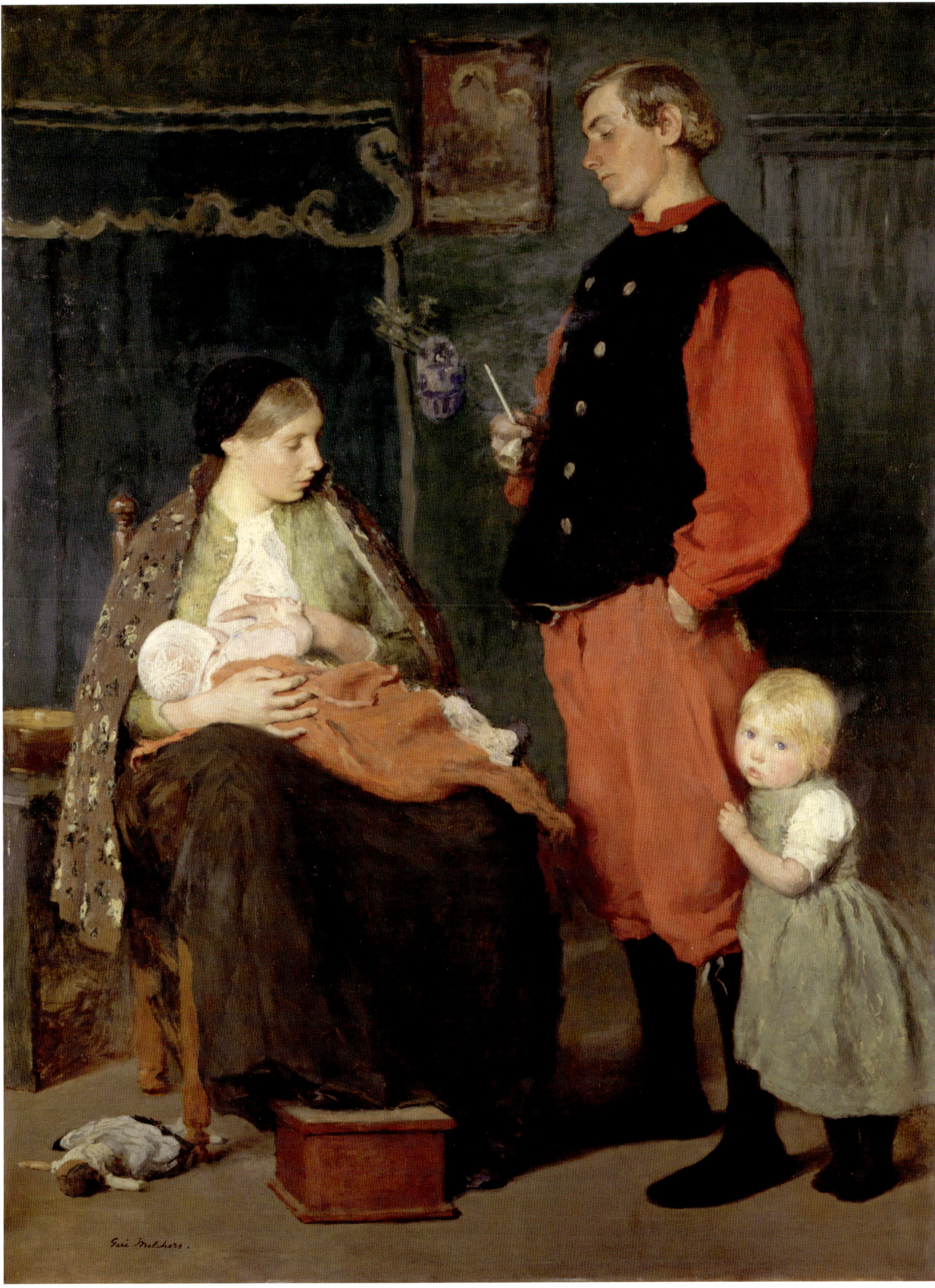
Gari Melchers.

Gari Melchers 1860–1932

43

The Sisters, c. 1895

Oil on canvas, 59 × 39½"
Signed: "Gari Melchers"
National Gallery of Art, Washington, D.C.
Gift of Curt H. Reisinger

ONE OF MELCHERS'S CHIEF INTERESTS IN THE FIRST HALF OF HIS CAREER was the subject of traditional family life—pictures of mothers and their babies, pairs of siblings, families at work and worship, the very old with the very young, and rites of passage, including baptism and marriage. It is worth noting that while he and his wife were childless, the welfare of the Dutch children who lived around them was always an important consideration, and Melchers was affectionately referred to by all ages as "Malle Melsie," funny or odd Melchers.

In *The Sisters*, also known as *The Doll*, two young girls stand, hand in hand, at the top of a dune overlooking the rooftops of the Dutch seaside village of Egmond aan Zee. Two white goats amble in the grass that separates the girls from the village. The older sister, displaying all the physical awkwardness of approaching adolescence, fixes her eyes protectively on her young sister, who intently studies the viewer, oblivious to her drooping black stocking.

On the face of it, *The Sisters* is another straightforward portrayal of the wholesome and unaffected Dutch type Melchers favored. One scholar, on the other hand, sees in *The Sisters* a modernist bent to Melchers's approach, contending that he relied not so much on the naturalist aesthetic of his earlier years, but on a symbolist-inspired one; the picture is a symbol of the "Eden of childhood" in which the little girl with the doll under her arm, innocent and reliant on the protection of an older sister, is the equivalent of the domestic animals in the background.[1] The painting appeared in at least two Belgian exhibitions, venues which had a reputation for a more progressive art climate. Its appearance there and Melchers's emphasis on formal design over narrative (seen in an intensified palette and lively pattern) seem to underscore his modernizing objectives. Still, Melchers's style is not one to be pigeonholed as strictly adhering to this "ism" or that. While it is true that he assimilated many of the progressive tendencies circulating around 1900, he did so in the service of old-fashioned, time-honored themes, coalescing the old and the new into something uniquely his own.

The Sisters was acquired by the wealthy German businessman and art collector, Hugo Reisinger, a founder of the Busch-Reisinger Museum at Harvard University. Reisinger worked with Melchers between 1909 and 1910 to organize exhibition exchanges between American and German artists. Reisinger's son gave the painting to the National Gallery of Art in Washington, D.C. in 1957. *The Sisters* has enjoyed a rather distinguished diplomatic career, traveling for extended loan to the Blair House, the guest house of foreign dignitaries to Washington, D.C., from 1970 to 1984; for display in the official residence of Ambassador Swanee Hunt, Vienna, Austria, from 1993 to 1997; and for use by Vice President and Mrs. George H. W. Bush in Washington, D.C., from 1987 to 1989.

JC

1. Jennifer A. Martin Bienenstock, "Gari Melchers and the Belgian Art World: 1882–1908," in *Gari Melchers: A Retrospective Exhibition*, ed. Diane Lesko and Esther Persson (St. Petersburg, Fla.: Museum of Fine Arts, 1990), 92–95.

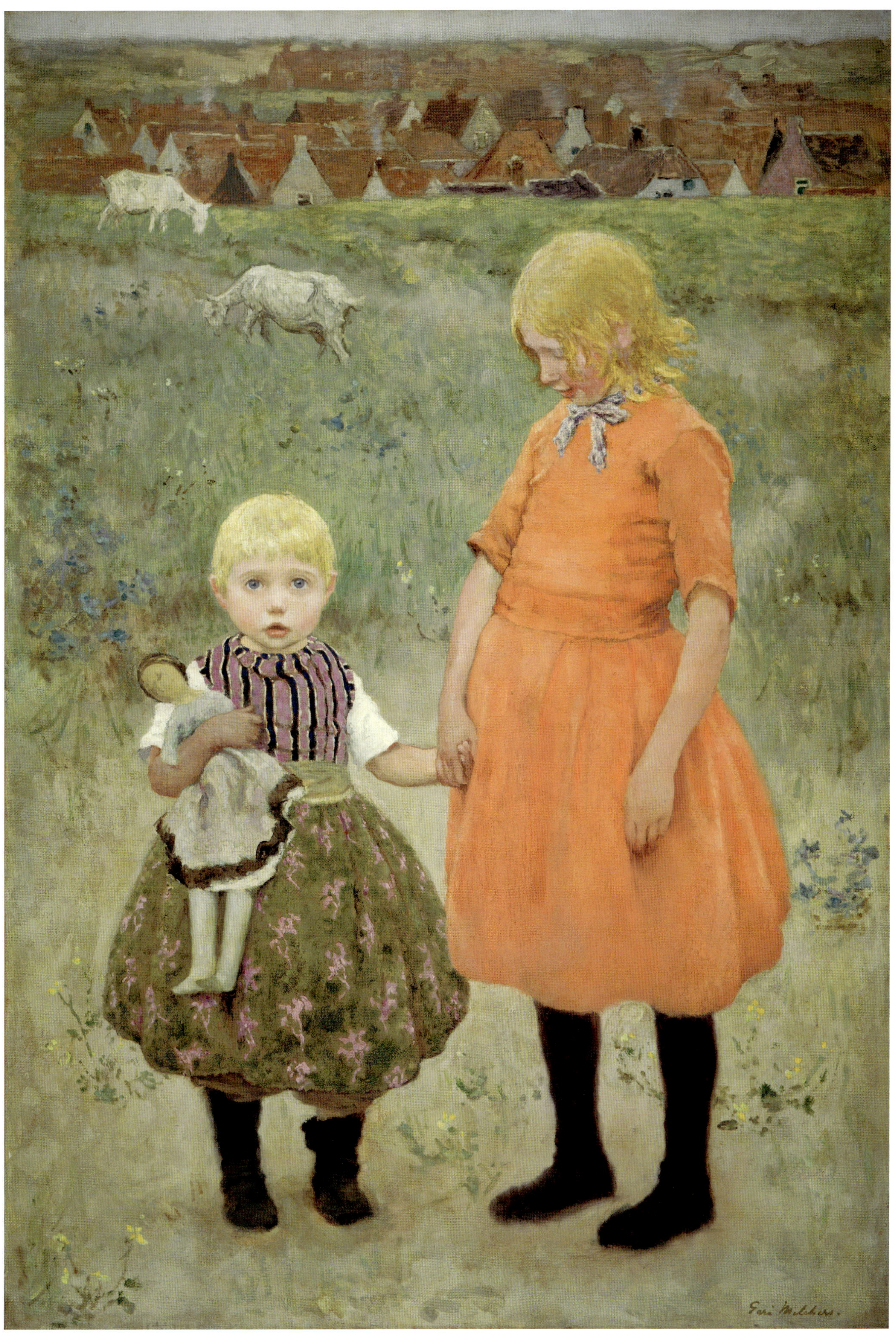
Gari Melchers.

Gari Melchers 1860–1932

44

The Unpretentious Garden, c. 1903–15

Oil on canvas, 33⅝ × 40½"
Signed: "G. Melchers"
Telfair Museum of Art, Savannah, Georgia
Museum purchase, Button Gwinnett
Autograph Fund, 1916

FROM 1884, MELCHERS SPENT A GOOD PART OF EACH YEAR IN HOLLAND, where he found his chief inspiration in the bucolic countryside and its picturesque inhabitants. In 1903 he set his roots deeper, acquiring his first home, a seventeenth-century dwelling in the village of Egmond aan den Hoef, to share with his young American bride, Corinne Mackall. Melchers happily embraced his authentic Dutch experience and encouraged his wife to learn the language, observe tradition, and live as the Dutch did. The couple outfitted their cottage with antique Dutch bric-a-brac, china, linens, and furniture; employed locals to serve as domestics; and attended the local markets, fairs, and house parties of artists and local gentry.

With his new marital status, growing respectability, and cosmopolitan attitude, Melchers now took up the subject of modern women in stylish interiors and gardens—an aspect of his oeuvre that is not recognizably Dutch. To suit his new emphasis on the domestic sphere of women, he turned away from the dark and factual approach of his earlier years toward the bright and decorative idiom of impressionism.

The Unpretentious Garden is set in the lush backyard of the couple's house at 8 School Street. The artist's wife sits at the left of the composition in the dappled shade, her head bent over her needlework. A rose arbor at dead center, perhaps a metaphor here for a highly cultivated, well-ordered life, perfectly frames a first floor window. To its right, a maid, whose presence serves to establish the household's affluence, stands in the sun with her back to us, watering can in hand. The strong horizontal of the pink brick house and the careful balance of the compositional elements establish a restful setting, enhancing the air of domestic tranquility. Melchers's breezy and broken brushwork (there are actually areas of exposed canvas) produces a soft, flickering effect of unmixed points of harmonious color, enlivening the whole and making it easy to understand why *The Unpretentious Garden* is the most-often-reproduced image by Gari Melchers.

JC

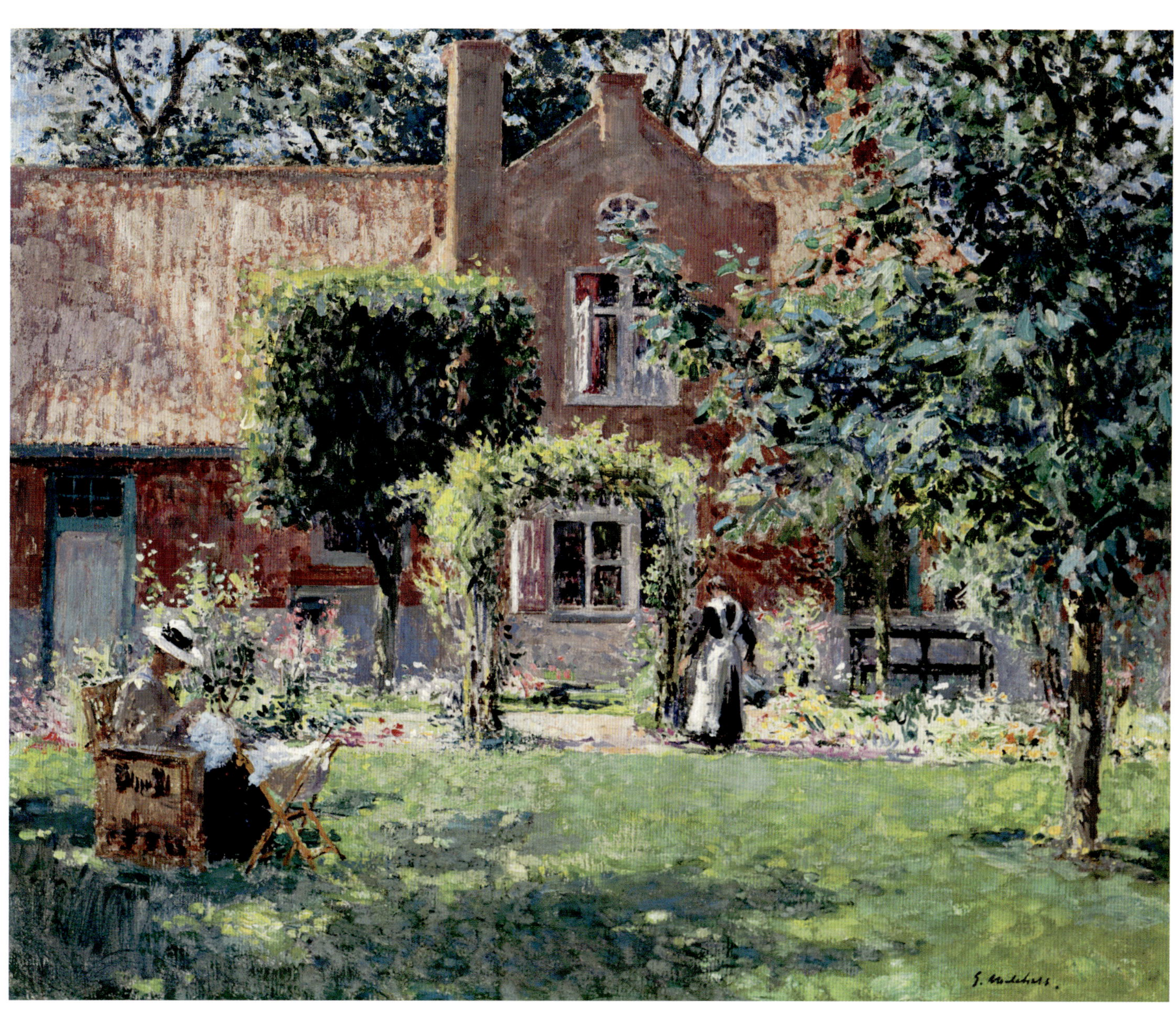

45

Easter Sunday, 1910–11

Oil on canvas, 52 × 56"
Signed: "Gari Melchers"
Toledo Museum of Art, Toledo, Ohio
Gift of Florence Scott Libbey, 1923.21

MELCHERS REVISITED A FEW FAVORITE THEMES OVER A CAREER spanning fifty years. While we might recognize a familiar setting, model, or title, it is in his formal approach that we witness the greatest change. *Easter Sunday* is just such an example. It is the direct descendant of *The Sermon* (cat. 37), painted nearly twenty-five years earlier. Where narrative and factual reportage were the goals of the original version, here Melchers shifted his focus to a greater pictorial effect, intensifying his palette and the prismatic effects of sunlight and modifying his title to reflect the more festive tenor of the picture.

Fourteen members of a congregation fill the lower half of a church nave. The men are seated in side pews, segregated from the women seated in chairs in the foreground. Their attention is fixed on the preacher, who remains out of view to the left. Melchers has arbitrarily outfitted the ladies in a variety of regional Dutch dress to heighten the visual interest. Sometime after 1912, he improved the compositional balance by adding a third figure to the second row, dressed in the traditional dark costume of Egmond. The young woman in the lacy Dutch cap in the last row, farthest from the picture plane, is the artist's wife, Corinne (Mackall) Melchers. The men at the middle ground are merely incidental to the decorative role played by the women and the other important focus of the painting, the brightly illuminated stained-glass windows and the play of light, worked up in thick daubs of paint, on the neutral back wall.

In place of the sober church setting at Egmond Binnen depicted in *The Sermon,* Melchers chose the cheerier, grand space of the Slotkapel or Castle Chapel, built in 1633 in his own village of Egmond aan den Hoef. The artist faithfully reproduced the details of the windows, as well as the hanging oil lamps and brass wall sconces. In a 1925 letter presented to the Toledo Museum of Art, the owner of the painting, Melchers stressed that the scene was laid out in the first Protestant church ever built in North Holland, a point of history he must have assumed Americans, the spiritual heirs of Dutch Protestantism, would well appreciate.

JC

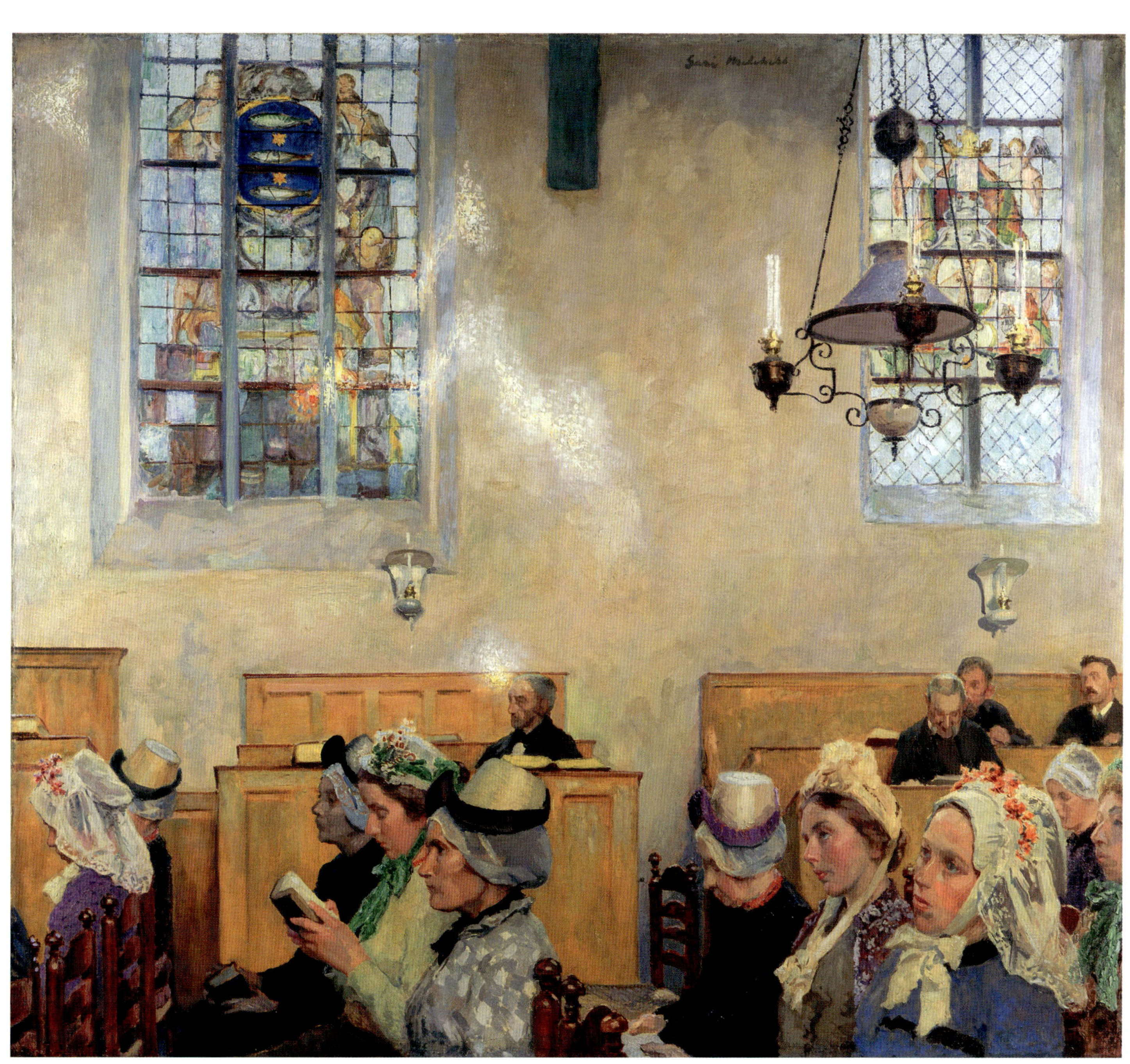

Richard E. Miller 1875–1943

46

Woman at the Table, before 1908

Oil on canvas, 28 × 22"
Royal Museum of Fine Arts,
Antwerp, Belgium

RICHARD MILLER IS PRIMARILY KNOWN FOR HIS ATTRACTIVE DEPICTIONS of female figures in the colorful palette of American impressionism. However, at the beginning of his career he painted sober works in dark shades, such as *Woman at the Table* (previously called *The Old Woman*). Miller's artistic training took place at the Washington University School of Fine Arts in his native St. Louis. In 1899 and 1900 he attended the Académie Julian in Paris, studying under Jean-Paul Laurens and Benjamin Constant. He subsequently taught in St. Louis but returned to Paris in 1903. Dating from that year is his oil painting *Woman Knitting in an Interior,* depicting a girl wearing the traditional costume of Walcheren in the province of Zeeland. Miller must therefore have been in the Netherlands, which is also suggested by paintings of a harbor scene and a landscape with mills. Miller was successful early on; he took part in important exhibitions and even won a prize at the Paris Salon of 1904. The French state then acquired his *Les vieilles demoiselles,* an interior scene of two older women drinking tea, which is now in the Musée d'Orsay, as well as *La tasse de thé* or *Vieille Hollandaise* from the same period. The atmosphere and tonality of these genre scenes are related to the work of James Abbott McNeill Whistler, whose *Arrangement in Grey and Black: Portrait of the Artist's Mother* (1871, Musée d'Orsay) had been on view in the Musée du Luxembourg in Paris since 1891. *Woman at the Table,* which also recalls Whistler, was exhibited in Antwerp in 1908 and acquired for the Royal Museum of Fine Arts. In this case, Miller not only portrayed an older woman, he also included an elaborate still life on the table. The attention lavished on the objects and the serenity radiating from the woman performing her simple task is related to the work of Johannes Vermeer.

ERK

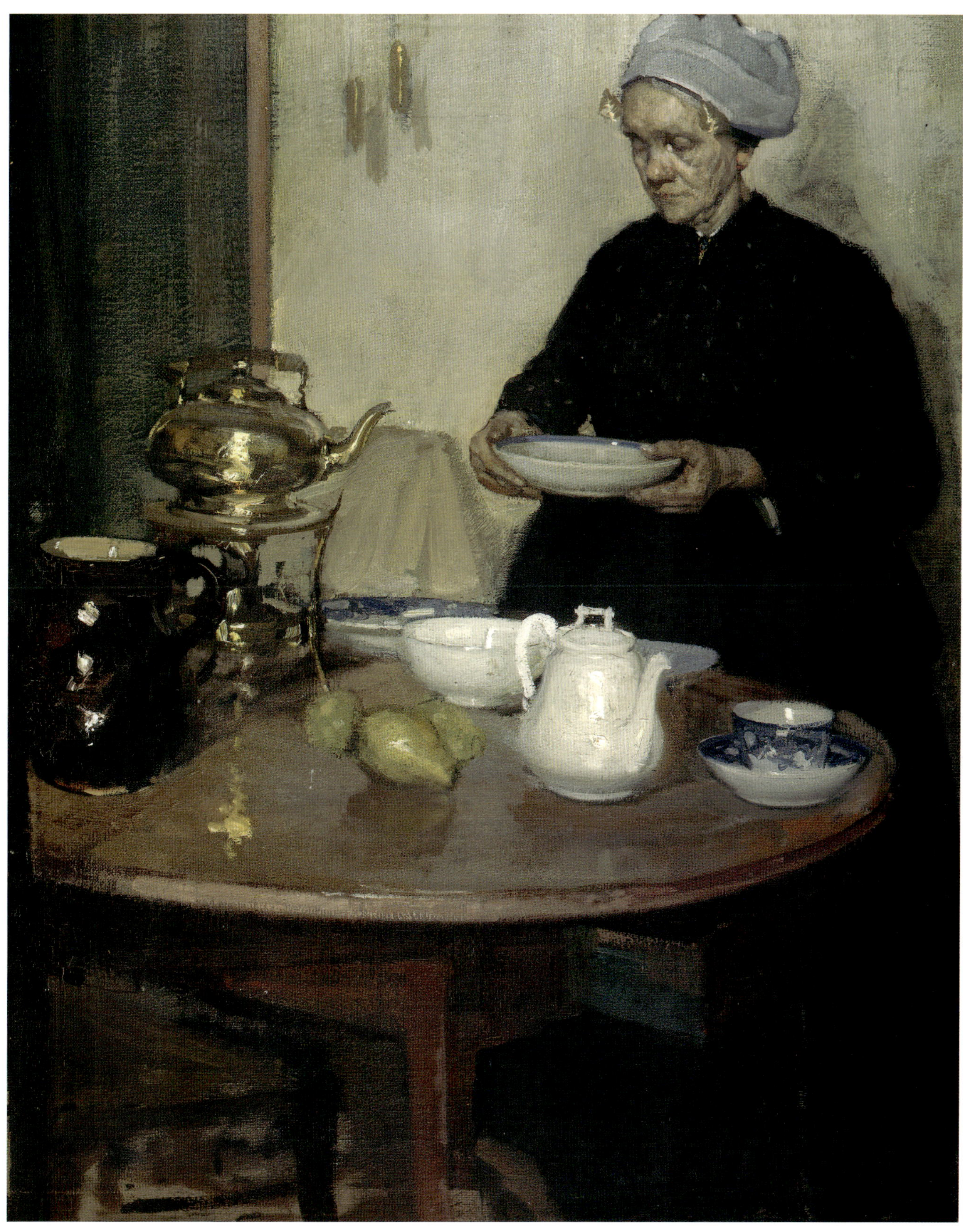

Richard E. Miller 1875–1943

47

Portrait of Martin Borgord, before 1912

Oil on canvas, 40½ × 32"

Signed: "Miller"

Singer Laren Museum, the Netherlands

IN THE YEARS WHEN RICHARD E. MILLER WAS PAINTING DEMURE OLDER WOMEN, he also treated elegant themes, such as richly dressed ladies in their boudoirs, and café scenes—subjects that intrigued many artists at the time. Under the influence of French impressionism, Miller's palette became more colorful and his brushwork coarser. His contact with other American painters, such as Frederick Carl Frieseke and Lawton Parker, surely stimulated this development. They all worked in Giverny during the summer, regularly joined there by Miller as of 1907. Miller's success also secured him numerous portrait commissions, including eleven of prominent St. Louis individuals in 1906. He presumably painted the *Double Portrait of Anna and William Singer with a Palette* (West Norway Museum of Decorative Art, Bergen, Norway, on loan to the Singer Laren Museum) and the *Portrait of Martin Borgord* before or around 1912. Both of these large canvases were hanging in the Singers' mansion in Laren in 1912/13. And we know that Miller, who had probably met the Singers in Paris, visited them in 1912, at which time he may well have painted both works. That affluent individuals were eager to have themselves portrayed by Miller is understandable when looking at Borgord's portrait. The painter-sculptor is characterized as a genteel and distinguished man. The size and monumental format of the canvas contributes to the status of the sitter. He poses together with the plaster model of his sculpture *The Kiss,* which is also in the collection of the Singer Laren Museum. In 1914 Miller returned for good to America, where he long continued to paint women and female nudes.

ERK

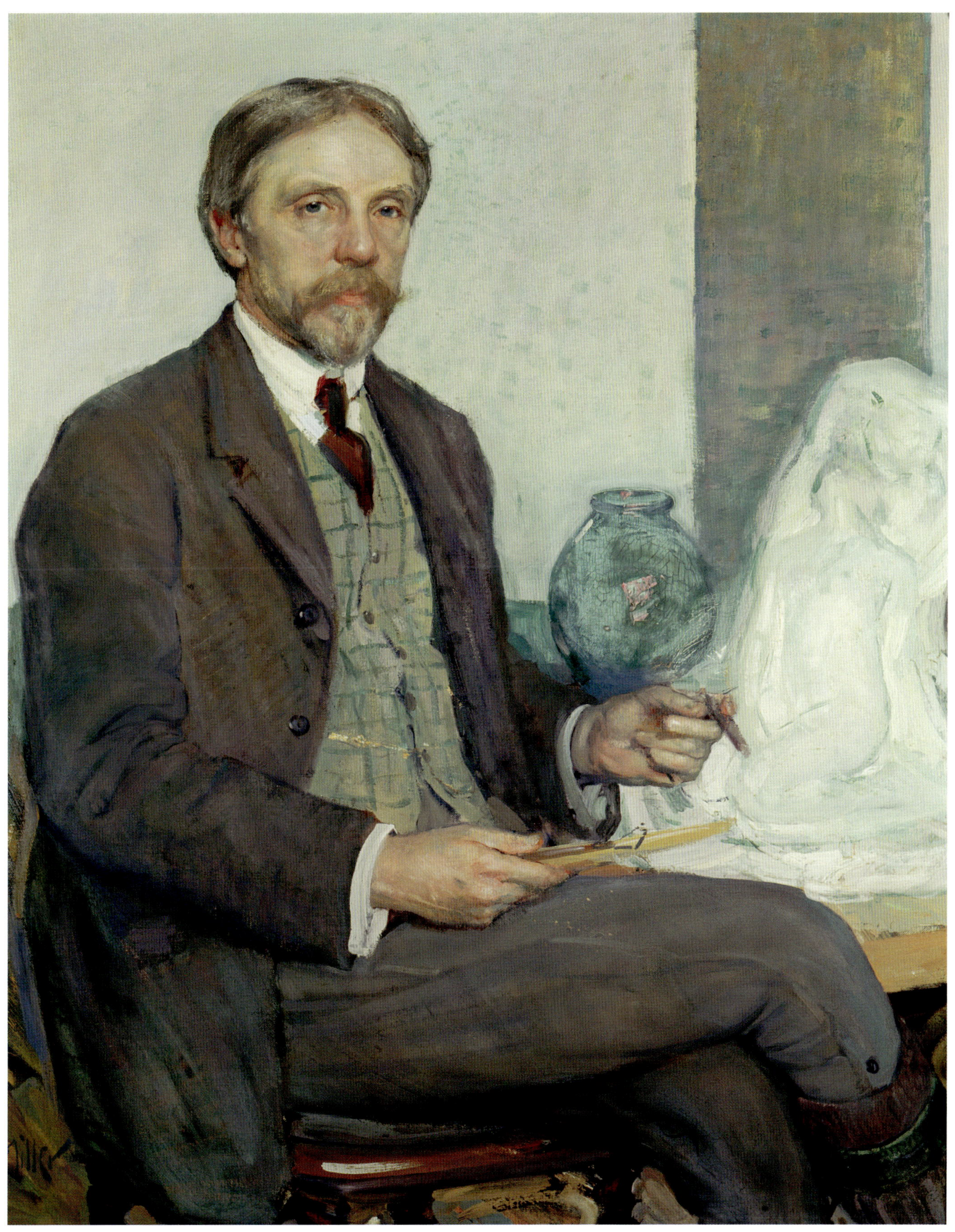

Carl Eugene Mulertt 1869–1925

48

Fishergirl by the Old Church, Katwijk, 1910

Pastel on paper, 20⅞ × 18⅛"
Signed: "Eugene Mulertt Katwijk. 1910."
Patrimony Dutch Jesuit,
The Hague, the Netherlands

EUGENE MULERTT BELONGS TO THE SMALL GROUP OF AMERICAN ARTISTS who lived in the Netherlands for a long time; he lived in Katwijk from 1904 to 1920. Born in Braunschweig in Germany, Mulertt emigrated with his mother to the United States in 1882. After studying at the Académie Julian in Paris, he went to Katwijk in 1904. He was primarily inspired by the village women and children, whom he painted either in interiors or in the dunes. These genre scenes originated in part under the influence of the Hague School painter Bernardus Johannes Blommers, whose work was popular in America and who was active in Katwijk as of 1900. Mulertt's scenes reflect the same charming simplicity as Blommers's. His Katwijk works also include depictions of fishermen and portraits that are closer to daily reality. In his pastel *Fishergirl by the Old Church, Katwijk*, he drew a serious portrait of a young girl in traditional Katwijk costume. The composition's center of gravity is at the right. The viewer's eye is led along her profile via the two women to the striking church tower in the background. The artist might be telling a story in a symbolic fashion, though this is not clear from the title. Mulertt painted a similar composition of an old Katwijk woman with the sea in the background. Known as an amiable man, the artist was nevertheless somewhat feared by Katwijk inhabitants because he could hypnotize them, as described in the book *Katwijk in de Schilderkunst* (Katwijk in Painting) from 1995. As of 1910 he was chairman of the local tourist office and he also wrote articles for German and English periodicals. Mulertt owned a house along the seaside promenade for some time.

ERK

SL only

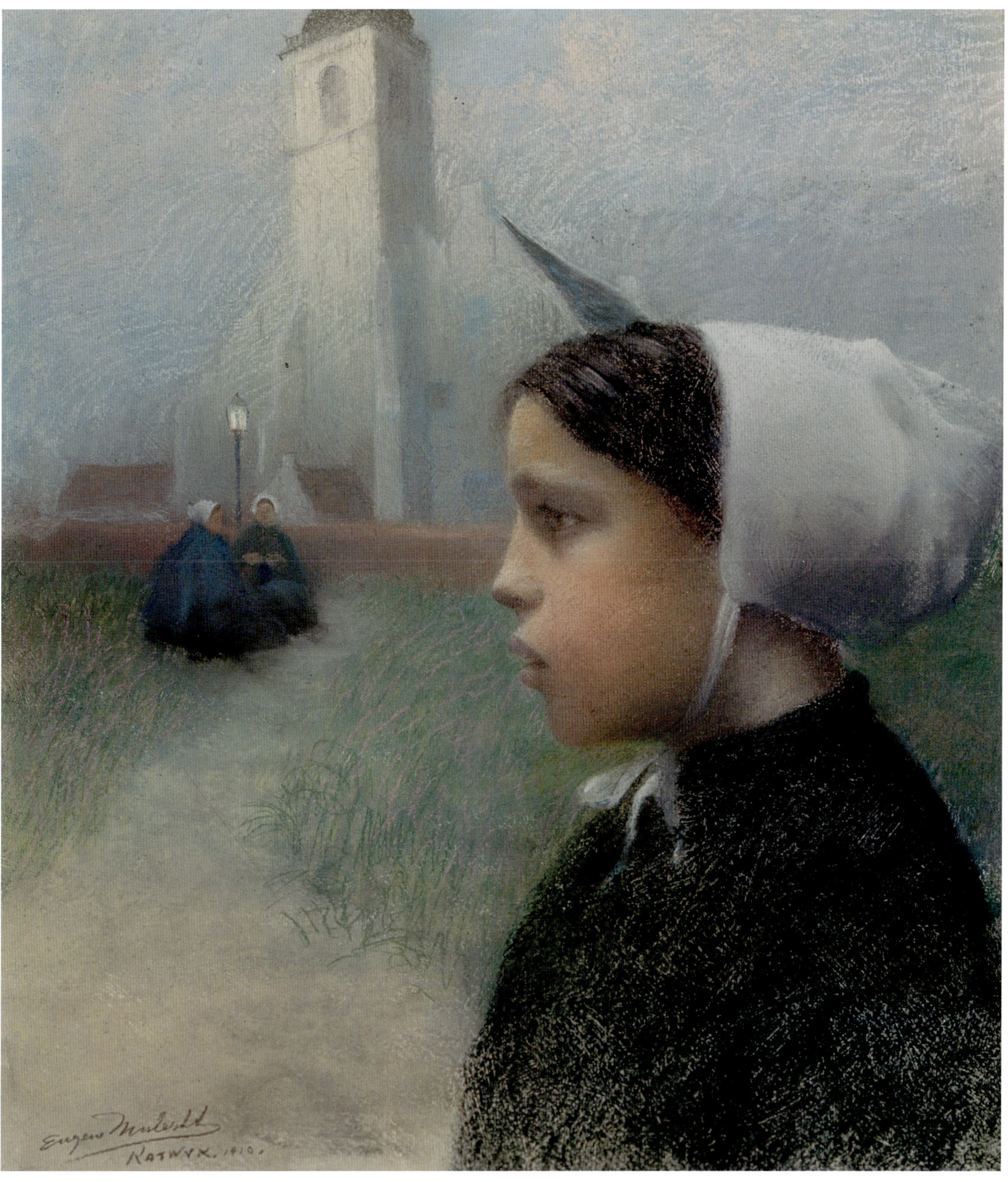
KATWYK. 1910.

William Edward Norton 1843–1916

49

A Moment's Rest, 1892

Oil on canvas, 48½ × 64¾"
Smithsonian American Art Museum, Washington, D.C.
Gift of Dr. Morris F. Wiener

IN *A Moment's Rest,* WILLIAM EDWARD NORTON PORTRAYS an intimate anecdotal scene of Dutch fishermen at work on the North Sea coast. Primarily known as a marine painter, Norton began his career as a housepainter in Boston, studying to be an artist at night at the Lowell Institute and with the noted American landscape painter George Inness. In the late 1870s he moved to Paris to study painting with Antoine Vollon and Louis Jacquesson de la Chevreuse, and remained in Europe, living primarily in London for the next twenty-five years. Norton was a frequent exhibitor at the Royal Academy of Arts in London (1878–1901), at the Paris Salon (1895–98) where he received an honorable mention in 1895, and at exhibitions in New York, Boston, Philadelphia, Chicago, and St. Louis.

On several occasions beginning in the 1880s, Norton visited the Dutch coast to paint. He set *A Moment's Rest* in Katwijk, a picturesque Dutch fishing village with a substantial artists' colony. Art historian Gabriel P. Weisberg views the painting as exhibiting a naturalist's interest in recording the day-to-day realities of rural European peasants.[1] Norton, however, also captured a sense of nostalgia for the slower pace of rural life that extends beyond the naturalist's examination of reality in his carefully composed depiction of two men, a boy and their horses taking a quiet break from the job of pulling a fishing boat into or out of the sea. This traditional task was strenuous, requiring teams of sturdy horses and logs to maneuver the heavy flat-bottomed boats over the flats leading to deeper water. Rather than depicting the difficulties of the task, Norton selected an unhurried moment when the large vertical mass of the ship is at rest on the beach and the men and their powerful draft horses droop in relaxed poses before the strain of work begins again. The large horses are at rest with the focus on their enormous hindquarters, subtly suggesting the grueling job ahead. Norton's subject and the artistic approach create a romanticized view of the rural traditional pace of Katwijk.

The slower pace of rural life was also the subject of an earlier painting by Norton entitled *A Moment's Rest, Dieppe, France* (1882, private collection).[2] It portrays a Frenchman seen from behind with a woman partially obscured by the drooping head of a large, white work horse carrying baskets on its back. Similar to his later version, the figures are at rest on a wide calm beach, and the horizontal bands of beach, sea, and sky in neutral tans, blues, and grays create a sense of tranquility that stands in sharp contrast to the frenetic pace of contemporary urban life.

A Moment's Rest is one of five paintings Norton exhibited at the 1893 Chicago World's Columbian Exposition. Looking back on his career in 1910, Norton placed this painting fourth in a list of his most important pictures.[3] From 1922 to 1966, the painting was on loan from the artist's daughters to what is now the Smithsonian American Art Museum. In 1966 Dr. Morris F. Wiener acquired it from Norton's daughters and gifted it to the Smithsonian.

AB

1. Gabriel P. Weisberg, *Beyond Impressionism: The Naturalist Impulse* (New York: Harry N. Abrams, 1992), 159–61.

2. Lot 72, sale catalog, May 21, 1996, Christie's East, New York.

3. William Edward Norton, New York, letter to George Washington Stevens, Toledo, Ohio, May 19, 1910, Stevens Collection, Smithsonian Institution, Archives of American Art.

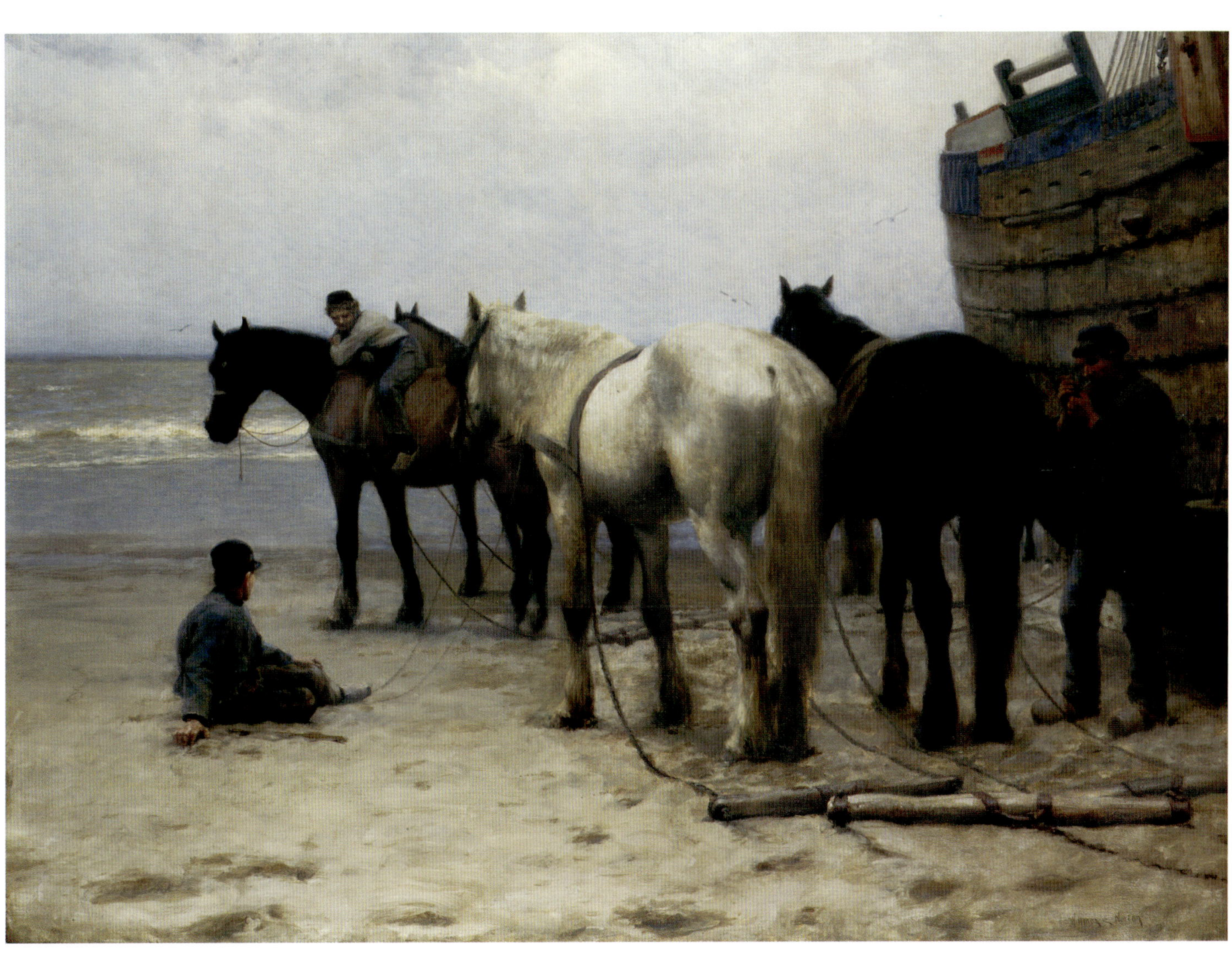

Elizabeth Nourse 1859–1938

50

On the Dyke at Volendam, 1892

Oil on canvas, 62 × 49"
Signed: "E Nourse 1892"
Collection of Mr. and Mrs. Stephen G. Vollmer, Cincinnati, Ohio

If all the world could see her as I have, walking along the Volendam dykes, her eyes searching the faces of man, woman and child . . . could see her delicate hand touch lovingly the cheek of child or mother, as if to say, "This I love. This will I paint.". . . then all the world would want to possess the pictures which tell the story.[1]

AN AMERICAN CRITIC WROTE THIS PASSAGE ABOUT ELIZABETH NOURSE, a Cincinnati-born painter who lived most of her life in France. Famous and beloved in her time, Nourse was best known for her paintings of peasant women and children. She spent the summer of 1892 in Volendam, Holland, and found the popular artists' colony to be an inspiring setting. Its citizens still wore the traditional costume, including the women's distinctive winged lace bonnet.

As a devout Catholic and member of the Third Order of St. Francis, Nourse felt an affinity with the Catholics of Volendam and admired their lives of worship and hard work. In *On the Dyke at Volendam,* Nourse painted a group of these stalwart women and children as they await the return of the fishermen. The solidity of their diagonal forms shows their strength and fortitude in the face of the harsh wind and sea. The notoriously wet and windy weather of Volendam inspired Nourse to build a platform out of her studio window so that she could pose her models while remaining sheltered from the damp. She told her sister, Adelaide, that she was determined to "stand anything in order to paint this heavenly place."[2]

Nourse did most of her training in Cincinnati at the McMicken School of Design, and studied with Gustave Boulanger and Jules Lefebvre at the Académie Julian in Paris, but the muted palette of *On the Dyke at Volendam* shows the influence of the Hague School. The large painting was exhibited in 1893 at the Société Nationale des Beaux-Arts in Paris, and again in a major exhibition of her paintings at the Cincinnati Art Museum, where it was offered for sale for $700.[3] It was not purchased from the exhibition, although Nourse enjoyed hometown patronage throughout her career. Nourse spent only one summer in Volendam, but her loving and respectful attitude toward her models is seen in her portrayal of them as spiritually triumphant, elevated above the moral failings of industrial Europe and America.

KH

TMA and TAFT

1. "An American Woman Painter Who Has Been Honored in Paris." *Current Literature* 48, no. 1 (January 1910): 90.

2. Elizabeth Nourse, letter to Adelaide Nourse Pitman, Volendam, July 2, 1892, Cincinnati Historical Association, Cincinnati, Ohio.

3. Cincinnati Art Museum. *Catalogue of the Work of Elizabeth Nourse* (Cincinnati, Ohio: Cincinnati Museum Association, 1893).

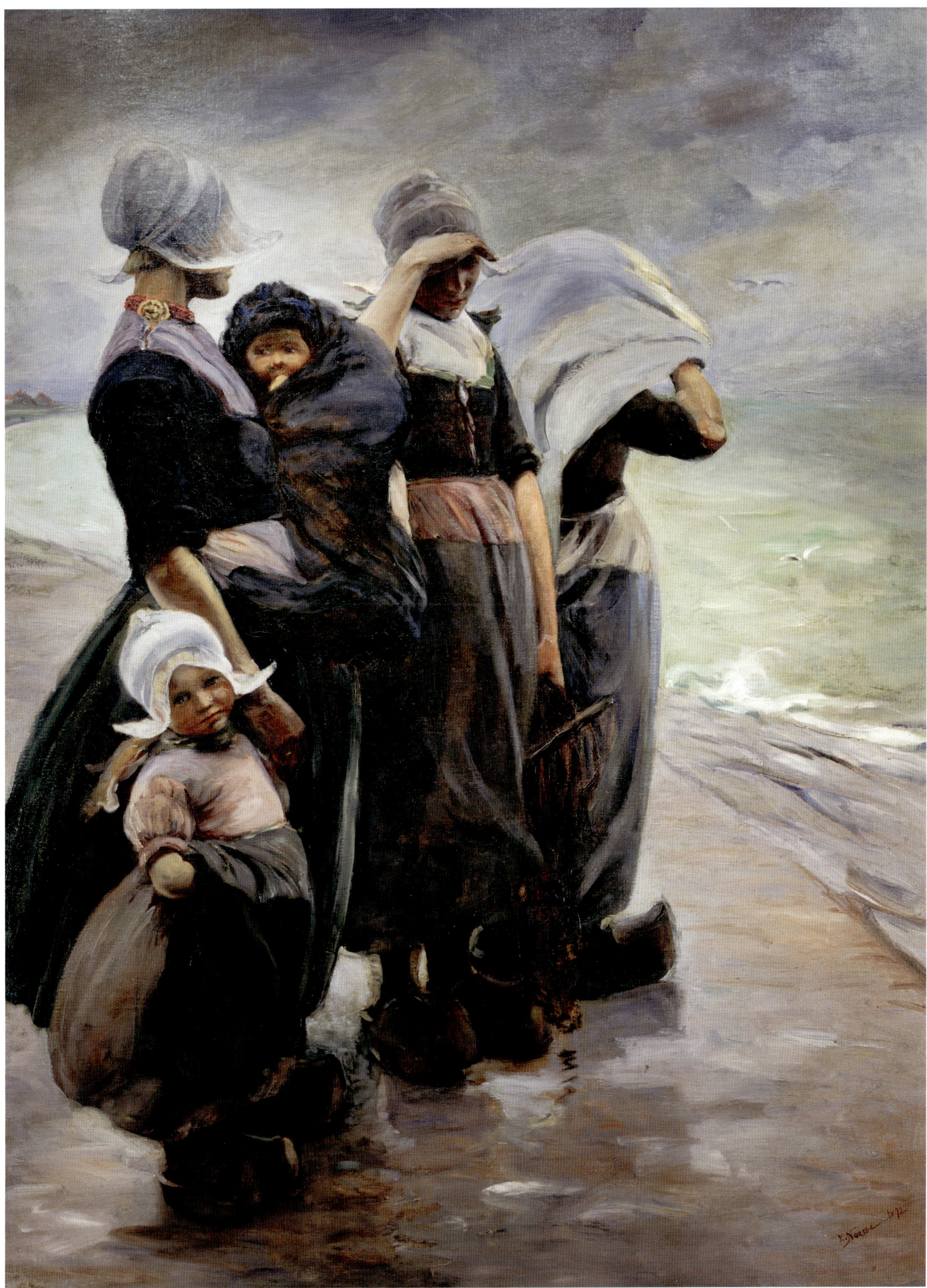

Henry Ward Ranger 1858–1916

51

Dutch Harbor, c. 1890

Oil on fabric, 24 × 30¾"
Florence Griswold Museum,
Old Lyme, Connecticut
Purchase, 1970.4

HENRY WARD RANGER WAS BORN AND RAISED IN SYRACUSE, NEW YORK. He entered the Académie Julian in the early 1880s, specializing in landscape painting under the strong influence of the Barbizon School. The Hague School paintings that he had seen in the United States and Paris impressed Ranger as extending the Barbizon idea, so he sought out Anton Mauve and Jozef Israëls in their native land. His biographer, Ralcy Husted Bell, described Ranger's life in Laren, where he mixed with the artists who gathered at the local inn, the Vergulde Postwagen, discussing art matters. Most of the pictures he produced in and around Laren are landscapes with small figures and convey various moods of weather. He also depicted the herds of sheep made famous by Mauve. Ranger painted in oils and studied the Dutch watercolor techniques, which he later wrote about in American art magazines. He admired the moist hazy atmosphere of the Low Countries that softened hard outlines, what he called the "soft charming effects that lend themselves so well to a poetic interpretation."[1] His painting of a Dutch harbor provides just such a poetic interpretation of a leaden gray day. He minimized the tonal range, keying the whole palette to a single slate-blue note. The place is not identifiable, although the Amsterdam harbor has been suggested. Ranger did not believe in strict *plein air* methods, but preferred to combine his outdoor studies with memories and imagination to produce finished paintings in his studio.

AS

1. Henry Ward Ranger, "Mr. H. W. Ranger on Sketching in Holland," *Art Amateur* 28 (1893): 132.

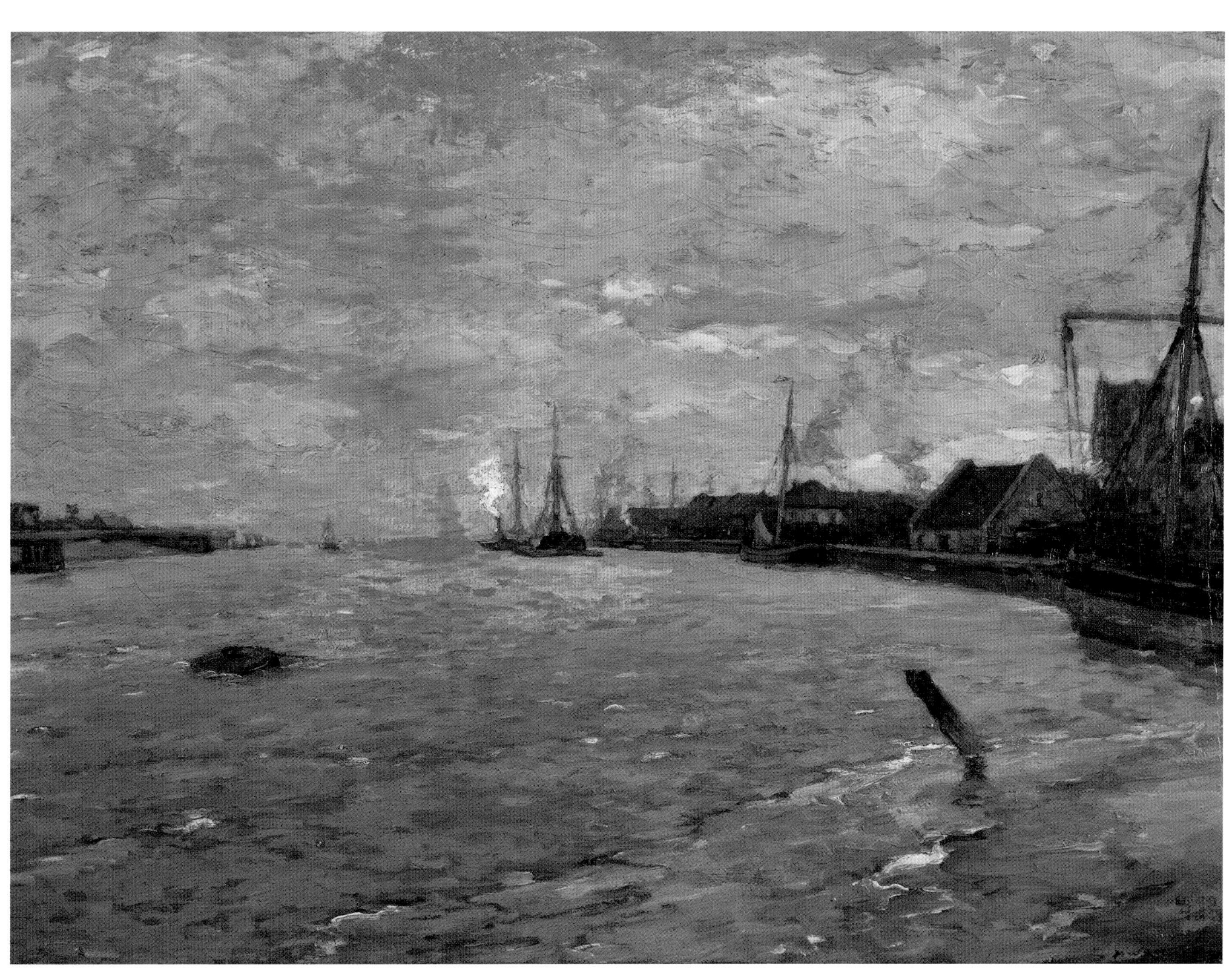

Joseph Raphael 1869–1950

52

The Town Crier and His Family, 1905

Oil on canvas, 78 × 64⅝"
Signed: "Jos. M. Raphael"
Montgomery Gallery,
San Francisco, California

TRAINED AT THE MARK HOPKINS INSTITUTE OF ART under Arthur Mathews in San Francisco, Joseph Raphael would maintain close ties with California his whole life, even as he became an expatriate in Holland and Belgium. He first moved to Paris in 1902 to continue his art studies and from there began visiting Laren in the summer of 1903. There he was inspired to paint this large group portrait around the central figure of Jan de Leeuw, Laren's town crier. De Leeuw's profession is evident from the rattle he carries, a wooden instrument that made a terrible racket when twirled on its pole above the crier's head to draw the attention of all within hearing. Raphael learned from the group portraits of Frans Hals and Rembrandt how to create an interesting composition from multiple models without obscuring any faces. In this instance, he chose to arrange the pale heads of his subjects in a circular composition against a dark background, with each face tilted at a different angle. The bent arms of the eldest daughter, father, and youngest daughter create a pinwheel effect that ties them to the center while keeping the viewer's eye moving. The effect is of a vibrant group in a snapshot moment of rest that will, in the next moment, burst into movement again.

This painting is typical of the compromise made by many portrait painters between actual portraiture and genre painting when working with peasant subjects. The swaggering stance of the crier in his wooden shoes, his slight paunch, distinctive features, and single earring create a sharply individualized portrait of De Leeuw. Likewise the four children grouped around him, each clutching a favorite toy or pet, assume poses and expressions indicative of unique personalities. However, the placement of the group in such obvious poses and the presence of the unseen portrait painter whom they regard suggest an interior genre scene in which the shared activity of posing for a family portrait becomes the subject. A narrative element is supplied by one of the boys, who mischievously peers around his father's elbow to see what expression his father wears. Raphael granted this rural family the status more often reserved for those who could afford to commission group portraits, but at the same time the painting can be interpreted as anecdotal genre—the amusing response of a peasant family to having their picture painted.

The Town Crier and His Family received an honorable mention when Raphael exhibited it at the Salon of the Société des Artistes Français in 1905. Chicago chose it for their annual exhibition of American paintings and sculpture later that year and from there it went to an exhibition of the San Francisco Art Association at the Mark Hopkins Institute in March 1906. The San Francisco department store owner and collector Raphael Weill probably saw this picture at one of its first two exhibitions and purchased it. By January 1906 he had announced that he would donate it to the city for the M. H. de Young Memorial Museum in Golden Gate Park (Fine Arts Museums of San Francisco). There it remained until it was deaccessioned in 2004.

AS

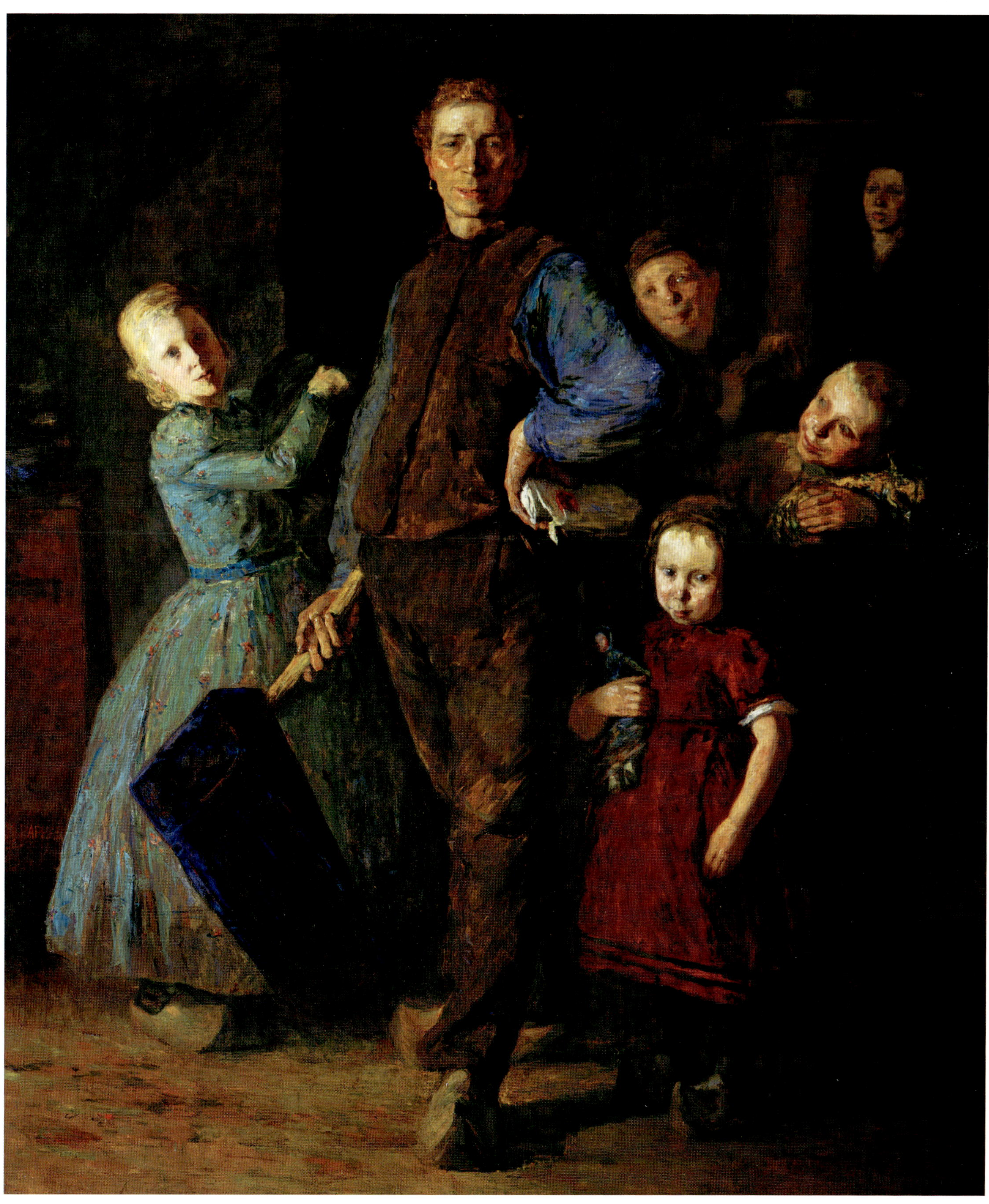

Joseph Raphael 1869–1950

53

Holland Tulip Fields, 1913

Oil on canvas, 29½ × 29½"
Signed: "Jos Raphael 1913"
Iris & B. Gerald Cantor Center for the Visual Arts
at Stanford University, Stanford, California
Gift of Morgan Gunst

THE STUNNING CHANGE IN RAPHAEL'S STYLE BETWEEN THE FIRST and second decades of the twentieth century is well demonstrated with this impressionistic view of a tulip field. Before 1910 the artist painted large, rather dark figure pictures in Laren such as the *Town Crier and His Family* (cat. 52), but he made many trips to France, where he was gradually influenced by the well-established impressionist and postimpressionist movements. After a return trip to San Francisco in 1910, he settled in at Laren again, sharing a studio with the American painter Wilder Darling, whose paintings bore some resemblance to Raphael's at that time. Raphael's life took an abrupt change of direction beginning in the spring of 1911 when he married Johanna Jongkindt, a native of Dordrecht whom he met in Laren where she, too, was visiting. He had a difficult time adjusting to married life and spiraled into a depression. This turbulent time altered his relationship with the town where he had painted his Salon pictures and experienced his first major artistic successes. He wrote to a patron in California: "I have been away for three weeks to north Holland and north Belgium in search of new material—for me Laren is sickening, but in Belgium I found the place in which I will work for the next few months . . . I am working now outdoors rather moderne-luminous portraits."[1] He had left his wife, now expecting a child, in Laren but within a few months of this letter they both moved to Ukkel, a suburb of Brussels. There he continued with his new direction, painting landscapes outdoors. Several months later he wrote: "With my work I have experimented and really studied and progressed not in the way of doing big things (it's not in me) but in the outdoor work."[2] The couple made return trips to the Netherlands, on one of which he apparently painted *Holland Tulip Fields* in this new manner. Its bright colors, sunlit effects, and broken brushwork reflect the changes in his life and in his perspective on art.

AS

1. Joseph Raphael, Laren, to Albert Bender, July 12, 1911, Bender Papers, Mills College Library, Oakland, California.

2. Joseph Raphael, Laren, to Albert Bender, n.d. [before January 1912], Bender Papers, Mills College Library, Oakland, California.

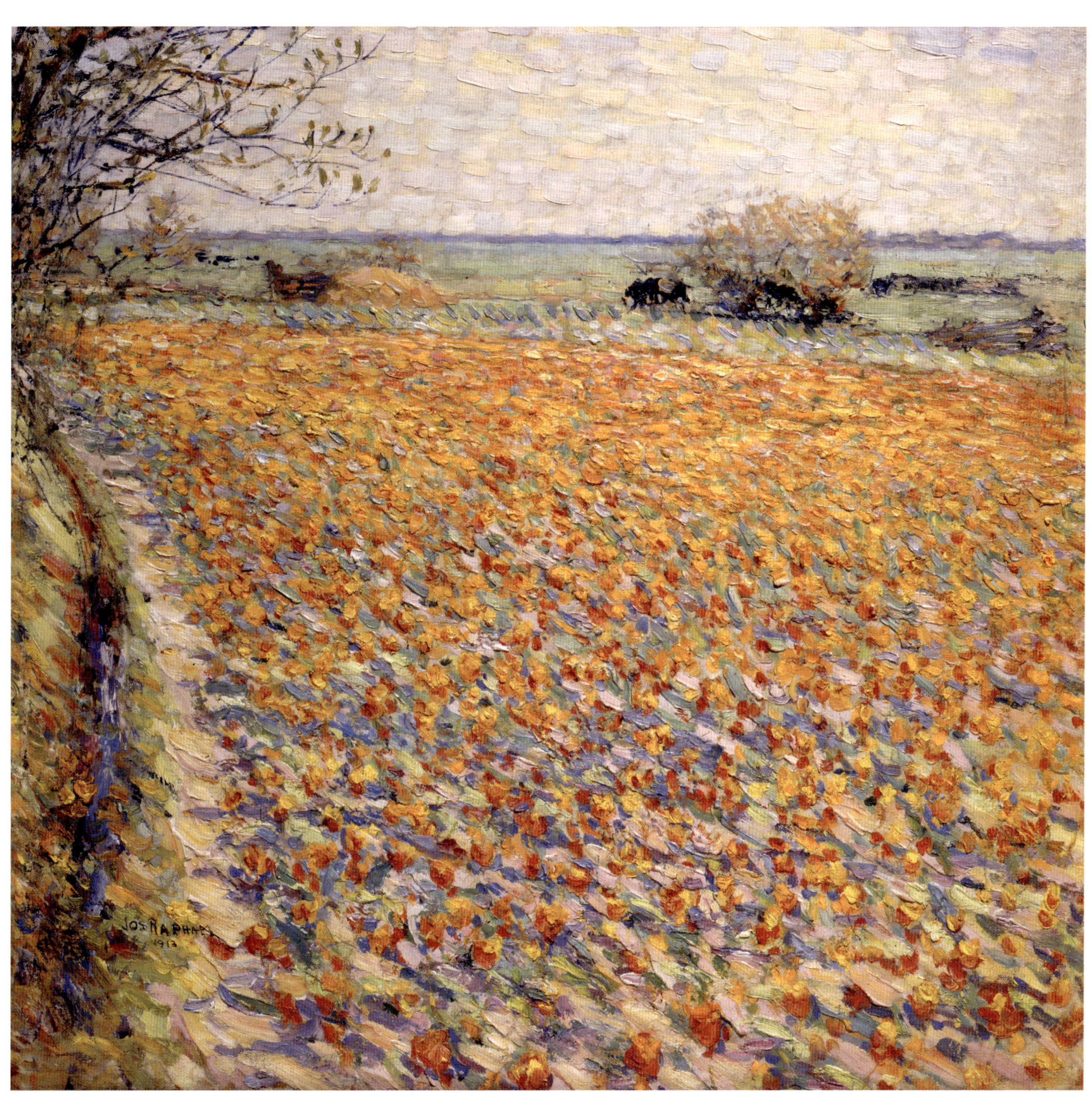

John Rettig 1858–1932

54

The Red Interior (Maartje), 1906

Oil on canvas, 23⅜ × 19⅜"
Signed: "John Rettig. V.D. 1906"
Collection of Jan Smit,
Volendam, the Netherlands

VOLENDAM'S FAME IN AMERICA DURING THE LATE NINETEENTH CENTURY is partly due to John Rettig. He was trained at the School of Design in Cincinnati, among other places, and initially made a name for himself as a designer, writer, and producer of theater and opera. He traveled throughout Europe and first visited the Netherlands in 1903, discovering Volendam. He and his wife stayed there annually for protracted periods of time both before and after World War I. They lodged at the Spaander Hotel, where virtually all the artists stayed, and Rettig rented a studio above a fish warehouse. He painted the village, its inhabitants, and the surroundings. He also worked elsewhere in the Netherlands, including Veere and Dordrecht. When the Rettigs returned to Cincinnati they took with them large quantities of Volendam costumes, Dutch furniture, and other objects, with which they furnished a "Dutch" room that John used as a setting for his paintings. At home they promulgated Volendam in a variety of ways to such an extent that for many residents of Cincinnati it became synonymous with the Netherlands. He was a famous personality in his place of residence.

The couple befriended the children in Volendam—they became some of Rettig's favorite models—and organized outings and parties for them. One of his Volendam models, Maartje Koning, posed for *The Red Interior*, as emerges from his notes.[1] Maartje is knitting, and the room affords a good image of a Volendam interior, with painted red wood walls. At the left can be seen the doors of a cupboard bed and, next to it, a wall shelf on which stands the image of a saint. Some implements, a kettle, and a cat complete the scene. For the rendering of these domestic details, Rettig may well have derived inspiration from seventeenth-century Dutch interior painters. Rettig exhibited his Dutch works primarily in Cincinnati and New York, where they sold well. He kept a notebook listing all his patrons, in which he recorded the sale of *The Red Interior (Maartje)* in 1917 to Cincinnati matron Mrs. Thomas H. Graydon for $300.[2]

ERK

1. John Rettig Papers, Smithsonian Institution, Archives of American Art, Washington, D.C.
2. Ibid.

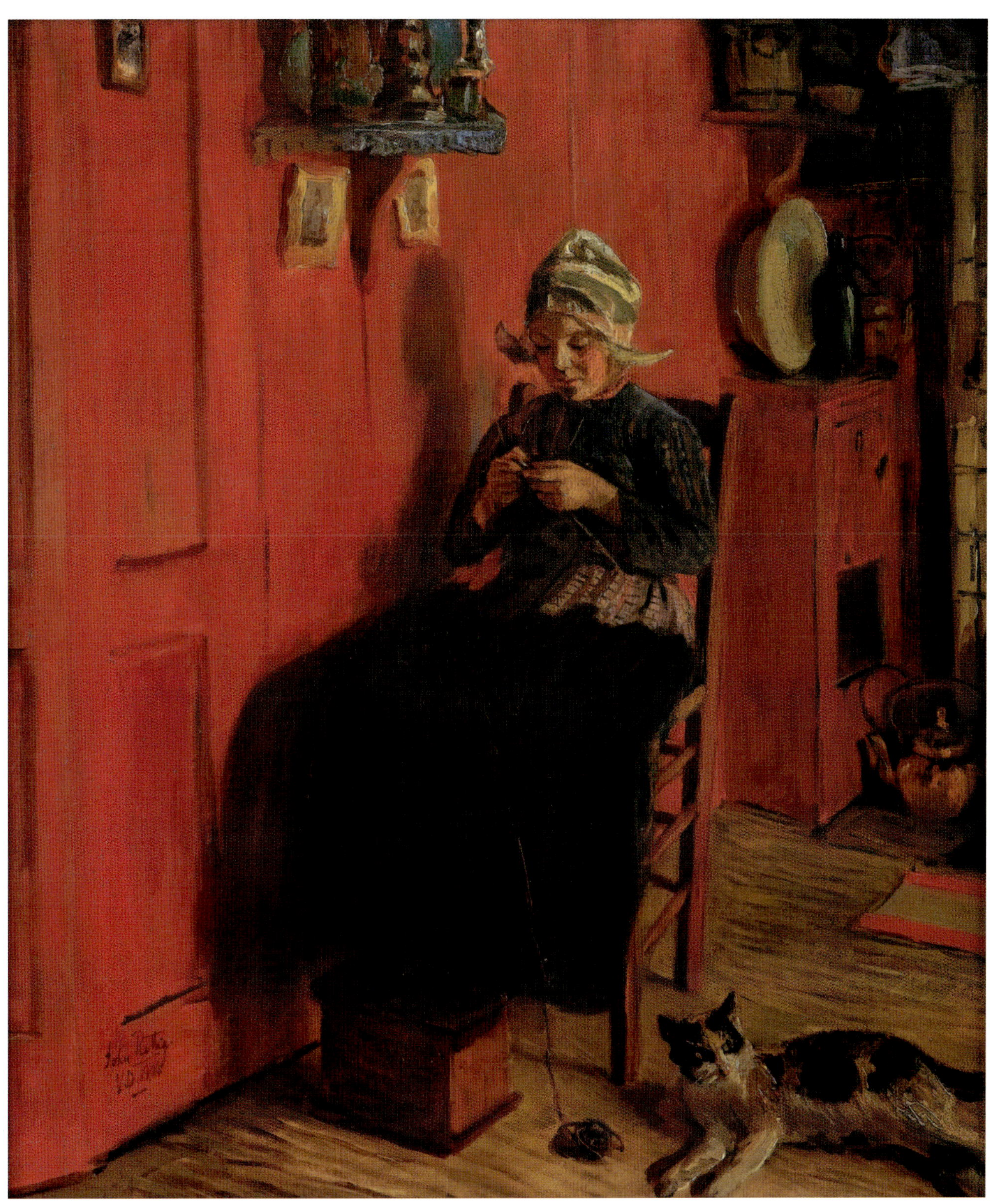

Alice Blair Ring 1869–1947

55

Morning Sunshine, 1906

Oil on canvas, 39 × 52"

Signed: "A B Ring"

Collection of Robert and Connie Constant, Los Angeles, California

BORN IN KNIGHTSVILLE, MASSACHUSETTS, ON MAY 4, 1869, Alice Blair Ring was educated at Oberlin College, graduating with a degree in art in 1890. After further study at the New York Art Students League and a summer sketch class with Frederick Gottwald in Zoar, Ohio, in 1897, she went to Paris and then to George Hitchcock's summer school for artists in Egmond. An inheritance made her financially independent, so she was able to travel fairly freely with the chaperonage of her mother. *Morning Sunshine* is set on a street in Egmond aan den Hoef in front of Bult's Inn—the white building on the corner with a painted inn sign over the door. The models have been identified as the Bakkum sisters by Bart Bult, a descendant of the original innkeeper who now uses the building as a private residence. Ring captured the dappled effect of sunlight filtered through the leaves in this bright impressionistic picture, typical of the mature Egmond style. The scene shows the companionship of two women talking in the street on a quiet Sunday morning, just the kind of antidote to dirty city streets and crowded slums that many Americans most valued at that time. Ring painted large oils with Dutch subjects during the period 1904 to 1908, of which her view of two women preparing cheeses the day before the market in nearby Alkmaar was accepted to the Paris Salon in 1906, the same year she painted *Morning Sunshine.* One of the figures appears to be the same model in both pictures. She exhibited *Morning Sunshine* in the *First Exhibition of Paintings by Alice Blair Ring* at William Taylor and Son in Cleveland in the fall of 1910. Ring later became a specialist in landscapes and miniature paintings. Looking back on her art life in 1938, she wrote to Naatje Bult, "I will not again go to Holland. It is a beautiful country and the Egmond corner of it is especially beautiful. I enjoyed so much the summers I spent there painting."[1]

AS

1. Alice B. Ring, Pomona, California, letter to Naatje Bult, Egmond, January 24, 1938, copy sent to Annette Stott by Ron van Vleuten.

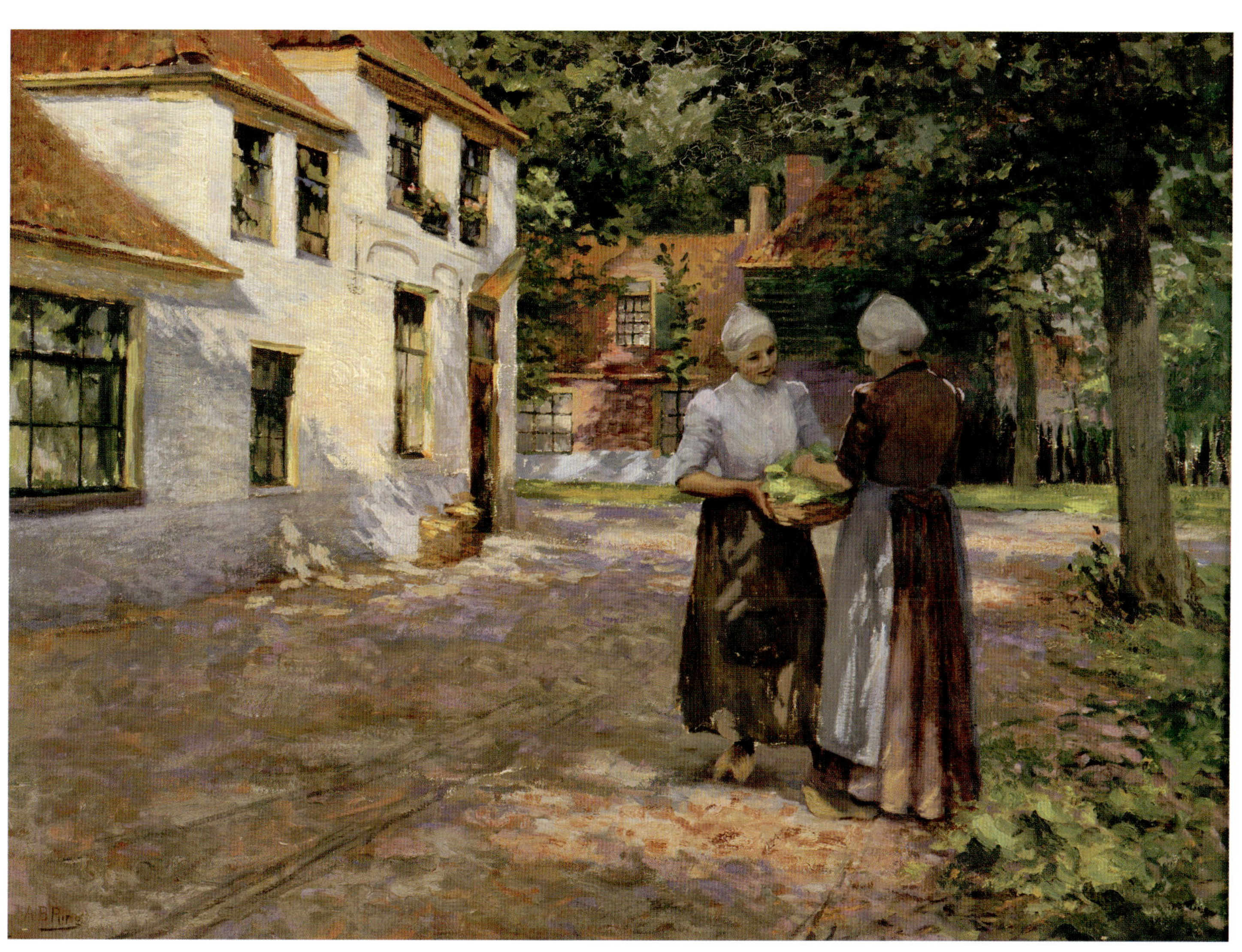

William Ritschel 1864–1949

56

Dutch Fishermen at Katwyck, n.d.

Watercolor and gouache on paper board, 20 × 28"
Signed: "W. Ritschel Katwyk"
Reading Public Museum, Reading, Pennsylvania
Gift of Mrs. Amelia S. Abercrombie

William Ritschel worked in Katwijk from 1904 through 1907 and again in 1908 and 1909. He exhibited the results of the time he spent in his Katwijk studio in the Salmagundi Club exhibitions in New York City, the Boston Art Club, the Art Club of Philadelphia, and the Indianapolis Art Museum, among other venues. Among his most unconventional works was a picture of Dutch boats on a beach, which Ritschel painted on a mug for the annual auction of the Salmagundi Club in 1904—it brought $180. A member of both the New York Water Color Club and the American Watercolor Society, Ritschel mastered this medium, of which his *Dutch Fishermen at Katwyck* is a good example. Painting with wet pigments on water-soaked paper, he was able to reproduce the feeling of a heavy wet day at the beach. Men and women stand in several inches of water covering a broad expanse of sand as the tide rolls in under gray clouds. A blowing mist slowly drenches the figures, who work to unload the day's catch from the beached fishing boats. A choppy surf is visible in the distance. The red, blue, and yellow clothing of the Katwijkers appears the more colorful for this uniformly gray setting.

Ritschel was born in Nuremberg, Bavaria, in 1864, and studied art in Munich before coming to the United States and establishing a studio in New York City about 1895. His work was well received in America. His colleagues elected him to associate membership in the National Academy of Design in 1910 and to full membership in 1914.

AS

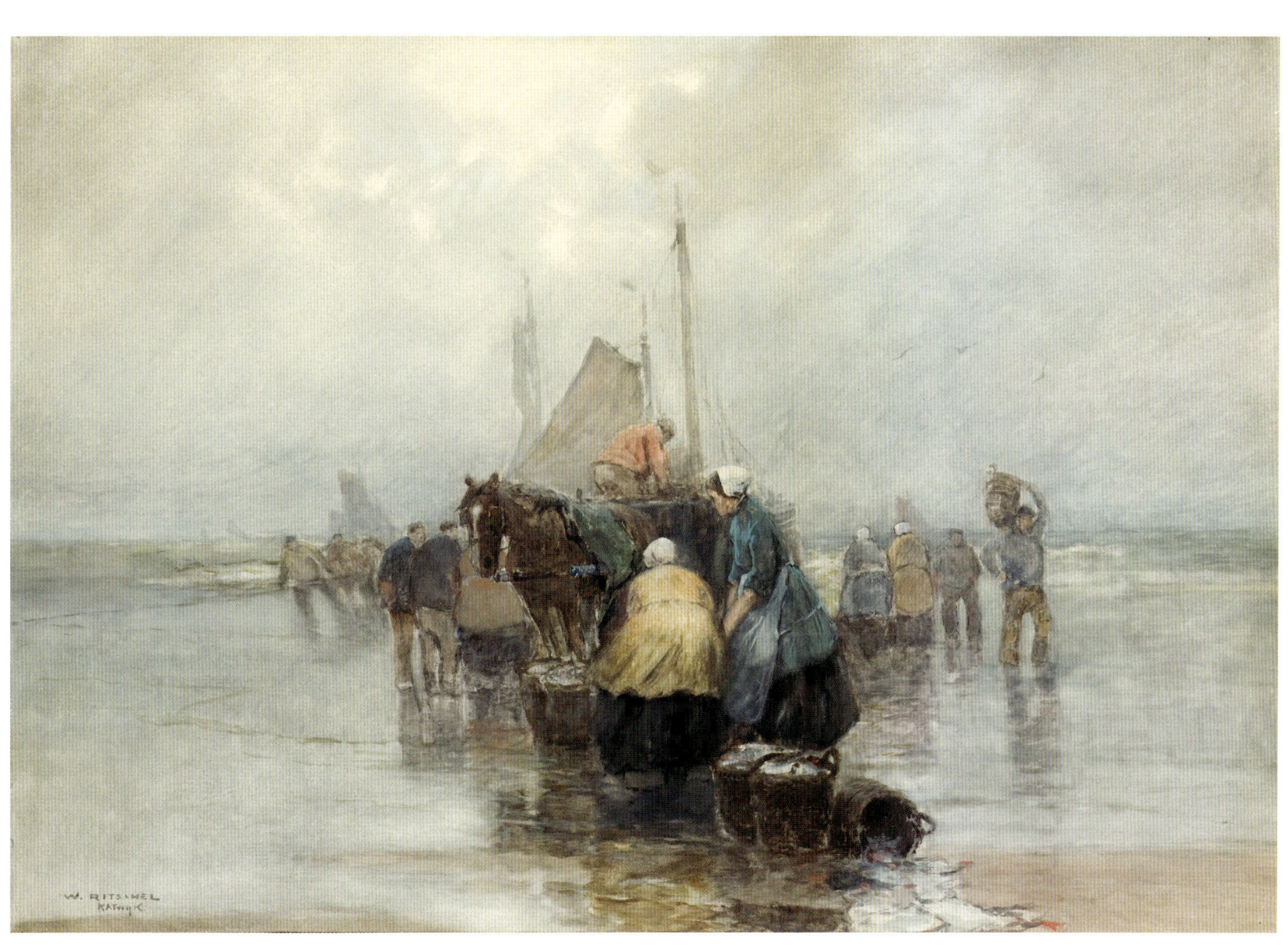
W. RITSCHEL
KATWYK

John Singer Sargent 1856–1925

57

Portrait of Ralph Curtis on the Beach at Scheveningen, 1880

Oil on panel, 10½ × 13⅛"
Signed: "J. S. Sargent Scheveningen 1880"
High Museum of Art, Atlanta, Georgia
Gift of the Walter Clay Hill and Family Foundation, 73.3

THE CIRCUMSTANCES OF JOHN SINGER SARGENT'S BIRTH SET THE COURSE of his later life. He was born to an American couple in Florence, Italy, and although he would call himself an American, he spent very little of his life in the United States. His childhood was passed in erratic wanderings with his family through Europe, and his career—after studying at the École des Beaux-Arts in Paris—could be described as a continuous journey through Europe with occasional side trips to the United States. He is best known as a brilliant portraitist of British and American society. His virtuoso technique is sometimes combined with insightful comment on the ironies of his subjects' lives and values. Sargent garnered many awards and honors, working steadily until his death at the age of sixty-nine.

Sargent's work in Holland, which took the form of several short excursions, comprises a minor although significant part of his long and active career. His first exploration of the Low Countries was probably an 1880 trip with two other American artists to visit Scheveningen and study the Frans Hals pictures in Haarlem. Hals's virtuoso brushwork must have been an inspiration to Sargent, whose later interest lay primarily in surface technique. On this first trip to Holland he practiced Hals-like bravura brushwork in his portrait of his cousin, the painter Ralph Curtis, lying on a sand dune. Curtis wears a bowler hat and suit and holds his walking stick in the air, forming a stark contrast with the informality of the pose. The combination of formal attire and casual pose, together with the rapid, sketchy technique, creates the effect of an unpremeditated snapshot moment. Curtis appears as a tourist on vacation. Through the next decades Sargent returned to the Hals Museum from time to time and also studied the old master pictures in Amsterdam, obtaining permission in 1901 to make a watercolor copy of Anthony van Dyck's *Magdalena* at the Rijksmuseum. Although Sargent's primary attraction to Holland was the opportunity to study the old masters, he occasionally also painted contemporary Dutch figures.

AS

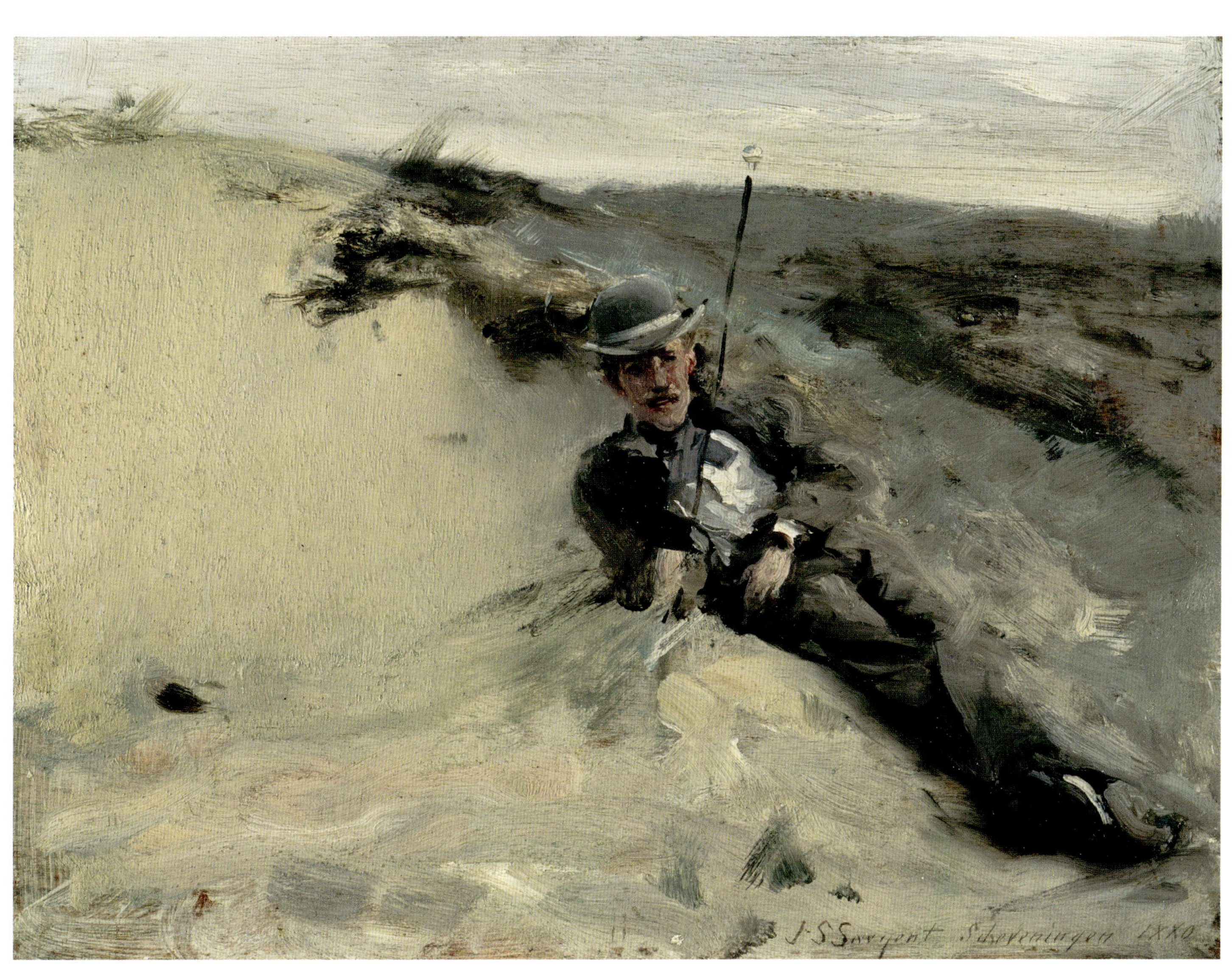
J. S. Sargent Scheveningen 1880

James Jebusa Shannon 1862–1923

58

George Hitchcock, c. 1895

Oil on canvas, 51⅛ × 35¼"
Signed: "J J Shannon"
Telfair Museum of Art, Savannah, Georgia
Museum purchase, 1909

BORN INTO AN IRISH AMERICAN FAMILY IN AUBURN, NEW YORK, James Jebusa Shannon would become one of the most celebrated portrait artists in Britain during the late Victorian and Edwardian periods. In 1878, at age sixteen, he moved to England to study at the National Art Training School in South Kensington (later the Royal College of Art) under Sir Edward Poynter, a respected academic artist. After only two years of study, Shannon received a gold medal for figure drawing in the national art school competition in Britain.[1] Shortly thereafter he was commissioned by Queen Victoria to paint portraits of her staff, which were exhibited at the Royal Academy in 1881 and 1882. Although he had originally intended to return home following his studies, he remained in Britain the rest of his life.

The commissions from Queen Victoria set the stage for Shannon's emergence as one of the most sought-after portrait artists of the late nineteenth century, a period of expanding wealth among the middle and upper classes. His chief rival was John Singer Sargent, whose elegant, bravado style may well have influenced Shannon's work. Shannon was patronized by many prominent citizens of his time, such as the Marchioness of Granby and Sarah Bernhardt. He was especially celebrated for his elegant portraits of women, sometimes depicted gazing at a vase or objet d'art in a manner reminiscent of works by James Abbott McNeill Whistler, whom he knew through the Royal Society of British Artists. Shannon also painted a number of charming pictures of his wife, Florence, and daughter, Kitty. His portrait of George Hitchcock was painted during a visit to the Egmonds in Holland, where Hitchcock (cat. 22–26) and Gari Melchers (cat. 37–45) resided. Although this portrait does not have a confirmed creation date, Shannon exhibited a portrait of Hitchcock in the Paris Salon of 1895, which may well have been this painting. The style of the work, showing the influence of impressionism in the vivid colors and loosely rendered leafy backdrop, also support that date.[2] Melchers purchased this portrait for the Telfair Museum of Art's collection some years later.

Compared to the studied, elegant works Shannon typically executed, his portrait of Hitchcock is frank and informal. The artist is shown in profile, bent knee-deep in a field of flowers, painting. Sporting a fashionable goatee and beret, Hitchcock reaches up, brush in hand, to mark the canvas. The canvas itself is not visible; Hitchcock's identity is defined by the act of painting, not its result. His determined, focused expression suggests his dedication to his task. In his other hand, Hitchcock holds additional brushes and a palette topped by a splotch of radiant white paint, referencing the bright color schemes of the artist who was known as the "painter of sunlight."[3] Completely surrounded by foliage and flowers, Hitchcock is immersed in nature, the chief inspiration for his work.

In 1892 Shannon purchased a studio in London's fashionable Holland Park district, which he remodeled in the Dutch Revival style. He would live there on and off for the rest of his life. In 1886 he became a founding member of the New English Art Club, a society of progressive academic painters influenced by continental art. A regular exhibitor at the Royal Academy from 1881 to 1922, Shannon was elected an associate in 1897 and a full academician in 1909. In 1910 he was elected the third president of the Royal Society of Portrait Painters, in which capacity he served until his death in 1923. The previous year, Shannon was knighted in honor of his achievements in art.

HKM

1. Christian Brinton, "A Painter of Fair Women," *Munsey's Magazine* 35, no. 2 (May 1906): 133–43.

2. Additionally, the screen of foliage in this portrait creates a flat, decorative space evidencing the influence of the "Studio style" of the 1890s, a British permutation of art nouveau. See Michael Quick, *American Expatriate Painters of the Late Nineteenth Century* (Dayton, Ohio: Dayton Art Institute, 1976), 132.

3. Christian Brinton, "George Hitchcock, Painter of Sunlight," *International Studio* 26, nos. 101–4 (July–October 1905): i–vi.

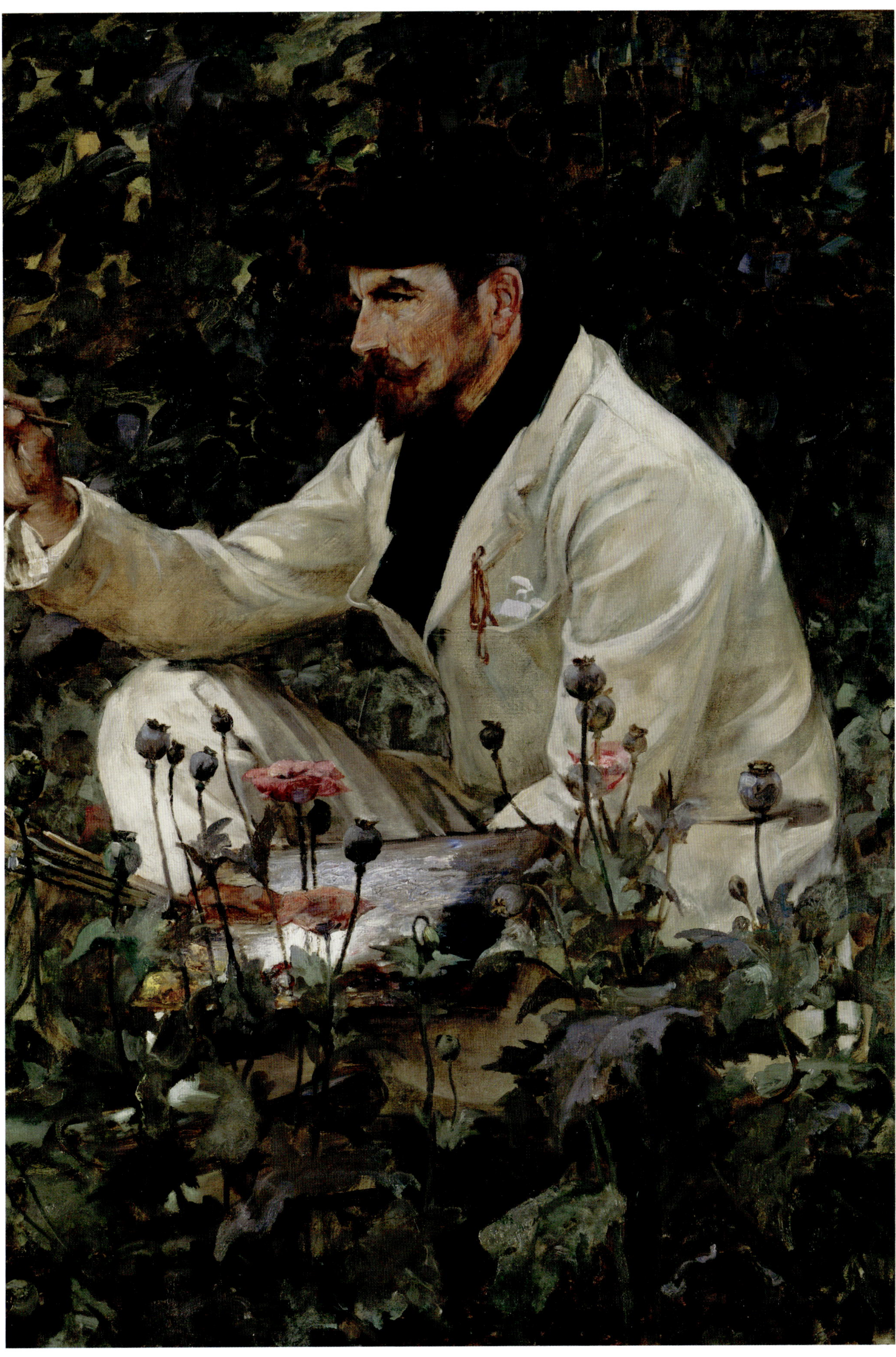

James Jebusa Shannon 1862–1923

59

On the Dunes (Lady Shannon and Kitty), c. 1900–10

Oil on canvas, 73⅜ × 56⅜"
Signed: "J J Shannon"
Smithsonian American Art Museum, Washington, D.C.
Gift of John Gellatly

ONE OF SEVERAL OF JAMES JEBUSA SHANNON'S PORTRAITS OF HIS WIFE and daughter, *On the Dunes (Lady Shannon and Kitty)* demonstrates the artist's ability to add tenderness and intimacy to the formal, elegant style of the commissioned portraits for which he was best known. At the time this painting was created, the American-born, British-educated Shannon had already secured his position as one of London's most highly regarded portraitists. He exhibited regularly at the Royal Academy, the Grosvenor Gallery, and the New English Art Club (of which he was a founding member). Shannon also maintained a studio in the fashionable neighborhood of Holland Park in Kensington, and had earned the patronage of Queen Victoria, the Marchioness of Granby, and other distinguished figures in London society. *On the Dunes* depicts Lady Shannon (born Florence Mary Cartwright, she and the artist had married in 1886) and daughter Kitty gracefully posed on the dunes of Egmond aan Zee, the small seaside village that was home to the first Dutch studio of American artists George Hitchcock (cat. 22–26) and Gari Melchers (cat. 37–45). Painted during one of the many holidays Shannon and his family spent visiting Hitchcock and Melchers, *On the Dunes* is unique in its depiction of Egmond aan Zee as neither fishing village nor artists' colony, but as a burgeoning seaside resort for the privileged classes. Lady Shannon is shown in elegant profile, her lips pursed as she reads aloud to her daughter. Kitty, her hat at her mother's feet and her hair in charming disarray, leans in closely to read along. The figures' flushed cheeks suggest that the sea air is as bracing and healthful as the town's newly formed tourist association would surely purport, while spectacular clouds billow overhead and their pet, a quintessentially English bulldog, sleeps calmly at their feet.

CM

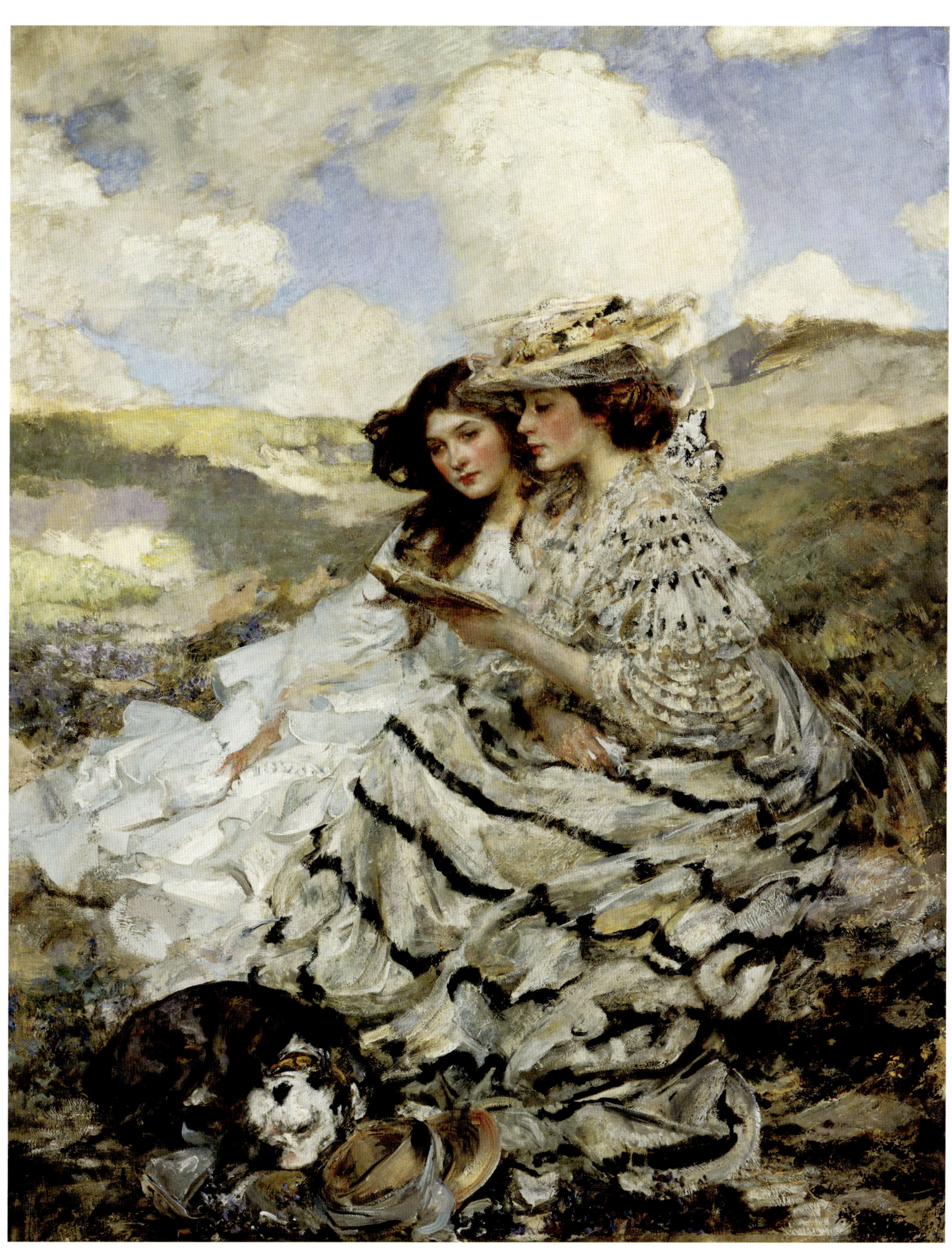

William Henry Singer Jr. 1868–1943

60

Heathland near the Tafelberg, Blaricum, 1902

Oil on canvas, 40 × 70"
Signed: "W. H. Singer Jr. Holland 1902"
Singer Laren Museum, the Netherlands

IN EARLY 1903 A PITTSBURGH NEWSPAPER RAN AN EXTENSIVE ARTICLE on William Singer and the paintings that he had made during his first sojourn in "the sleepy old hamlet of Laren." The article was occasioned by his first solo exhibition, *Recent Dutch Paintings,* at the local J. J. Gillespie gallery. As the son of a Pittsburgh steel manufacturer, Singer was destined to work in his father's company. Initially, he drew only as a hobby. However, a meeting with the artist Martin Borgord (cat. 2–3) was partly responsible for his decision to become a full-time artist. He took lessons drawing from models with Borgord at the Allegheny School of Art in Allegheny City, a suburb of Pittsburgh. His true passion, though, was landscape. Following a summer stay on Monhegan, an island off the coast of Maine, he left for France with his wife, Anna, and Borgord in 1901. In Paris, Singer studied at the Académie Julian with the history painter Jean-Paul Laurens. His interest in the work of the Hague School painter Anton Mauve, who was one of the first painters to work in Laren, may have been the reason why he too went to Laren in 1902. There, Singer painted subjects à la Mauve, such as *Heathland near the Tafelberg, Blaricum,* an exceptionally large and wide canvas that Singer most likely used to show off the panoramic breadth of the moors to good effect. Its subject, loose execution, and fairly somber tonalities are all related to Mauve. His interest in sheep also emerges from earlier studies and photographs he had made in America. Recently, some small panels were found that fit into the lid of his painting box which he used when he worked out of doors. They depict Laren village views with, for example, a country road, a farm, and a woman in Laren costume. These are the subjects he favored in the brief period that he worked in the spirit of the Hague School.

ERK

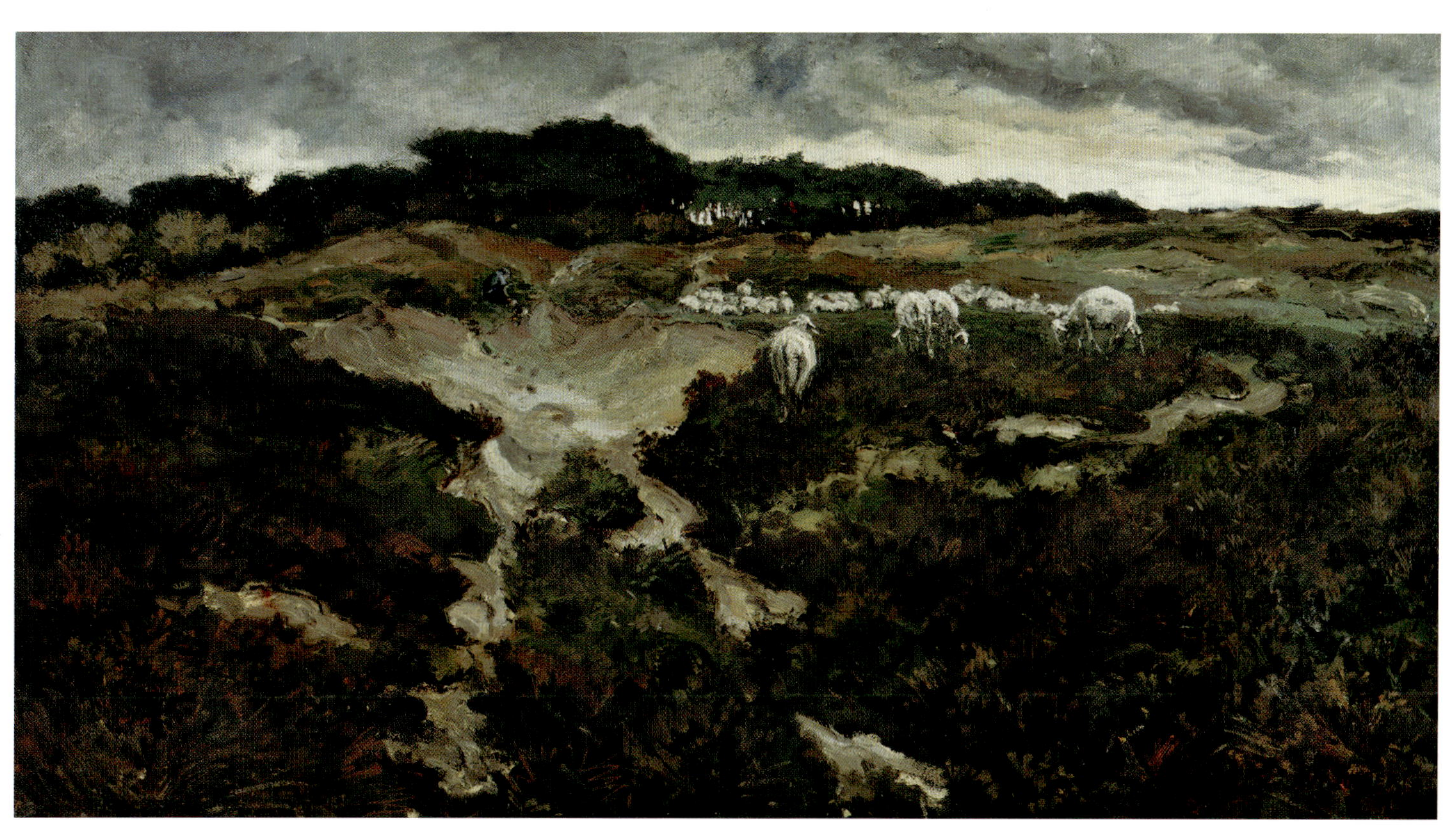

William Henry Singer Jr. 1868–1943

61

In My Garden, Spring, 1912

Oil on canvas, 18⅜ × 21⅞"

Inscribed on verso: "In my Garden Spring WH Singer JR"

Singer Laren Museum, the Netherlands

OVER THE YEARS, THE DARK TONES MARKING WILLIAM SINGER'S first period in Laren (1902–5) gave way to more color. In July 1903 Martin Borgord (cat. 2–3), who was of Norwegian origin, took the Singers to Norway. Singer was instantly captivated by the landscape with its mountains and fjords, and subsequently painted a great deal of his oeuvre there. Also crucial to his artistic development was a sojourn at the Old Lyme Art Colony in Connecticut in 1907. He met various American impressionists there, including Willard Metcalf. The much lighter and sometimes more colorful landscapes by these painters stimulated Singer to alter his palette. This shift is apparent in Norwegian landscapes done a mere year later, and even more conspicuous in a series of canvases dating after 1911. In that year the Singers built their home, De Wilde Zwanen, in Laren. Between 1911 and 1913 Singer painted pictures of the mansion and the garden on numerous occasions, using broad strokes and a wide range of colors. The theme (the garden) and brushwork accord entirely with American impressionism. Clearly his new living situation proved inspirational. *In My Garden, Spring* is one of his sunny paintings. The Singers received many Laren and American artist friends and also acquired works by them, which found a place in their home. With his wealth, Singer not only supported various artists, he was also a philanthropist.

ERK

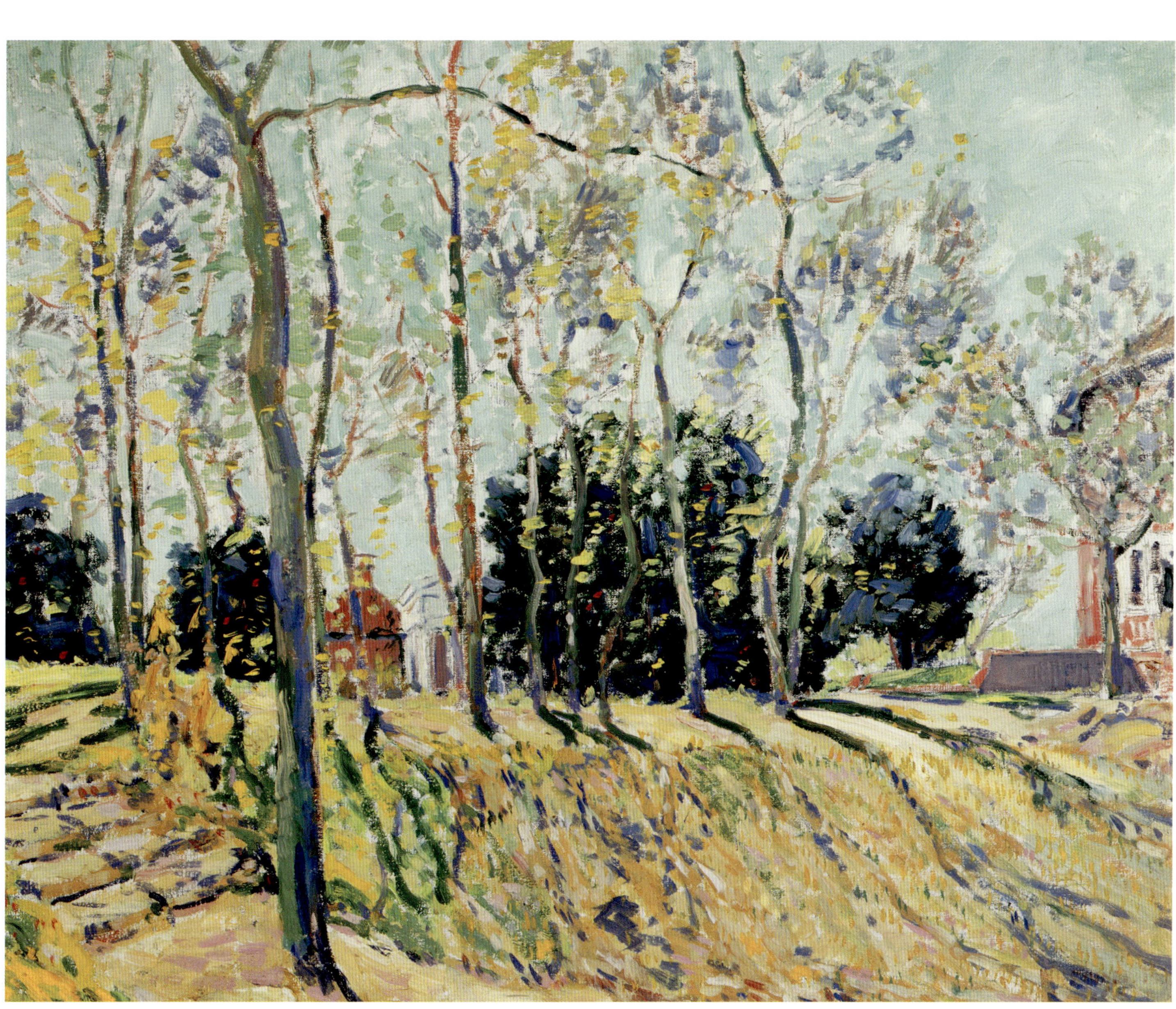

William Henry Singer Jr. 1868–1943

62

My Studio, 1913

Oil on canvas, 20 × 24"
Inscribed on verso: "'my studio.' 1913."
Singer Laren Museum, the Netherlands

WILLIAM SINGER HAD A LARGE STUDIO BUILDING IN THE GARDEN of De Wilde Zwanen with two spacious ateliers, one for Singer and one for Martin Borgord (cat. 2–3). Singer's painting *My Studio* gives an impression of the layout and old Dutch atmosphere of Singer's atelier; it had a fireplace faced with tiles, a chest, tall armchair, and various objects on the mantelpiece, table, and windowsill. The window, with its small leaded glass panes, also recalls seventeenth-century interiors. It is more or less a copy of the studio Singer had built at his home in Edgeworth, near Pittsburgh, in 1905. The Laren studio afforded a wonderful view of the garden, and the paintings Singer produced there met with great success at various exhibitions in New York. They were shown together with Norwegian landscapes, as Helen Schretlen noted in her 2008 monograph on William Singer.[1] After 1903 the Singers spent almost every summer in Norway, and in 1921 they built Villa Dalheim in Olden, where Singer painted mountain landscapes and the occasional still life. In the early 1930s he was again working in Laren, and in 1938 the couple built Villa Nederheem in Blaricum. William died in Olden, Norway, in 1943.

In the 1950s Anna Singer expanded De Wilde Zwanen with a theater and a museum, to which she donated a large share of their art collection. Singer Laren, as it is now called, was opened in 1956. Other parts of the Singers' collection, including paintings by Singer himself, Dutch contemporaries, Barbizon School masters, and bronzes by French sculptors such as Auguste Rodin, found their way to the Washington County Museum of Fine Arts in Hagerstown, Maryland, which opened in 1931; the West Norway Museum of Decorative Art in Bergen, Norway; and Villa Dalheim (Singerheimen) in Olden.

ERK

1. See Helen Schretlen, *American Impressionist William H. Singer Jr. 1868–1943* (Laren: Singer Laren Museum, 2008; Dutch and English edition).

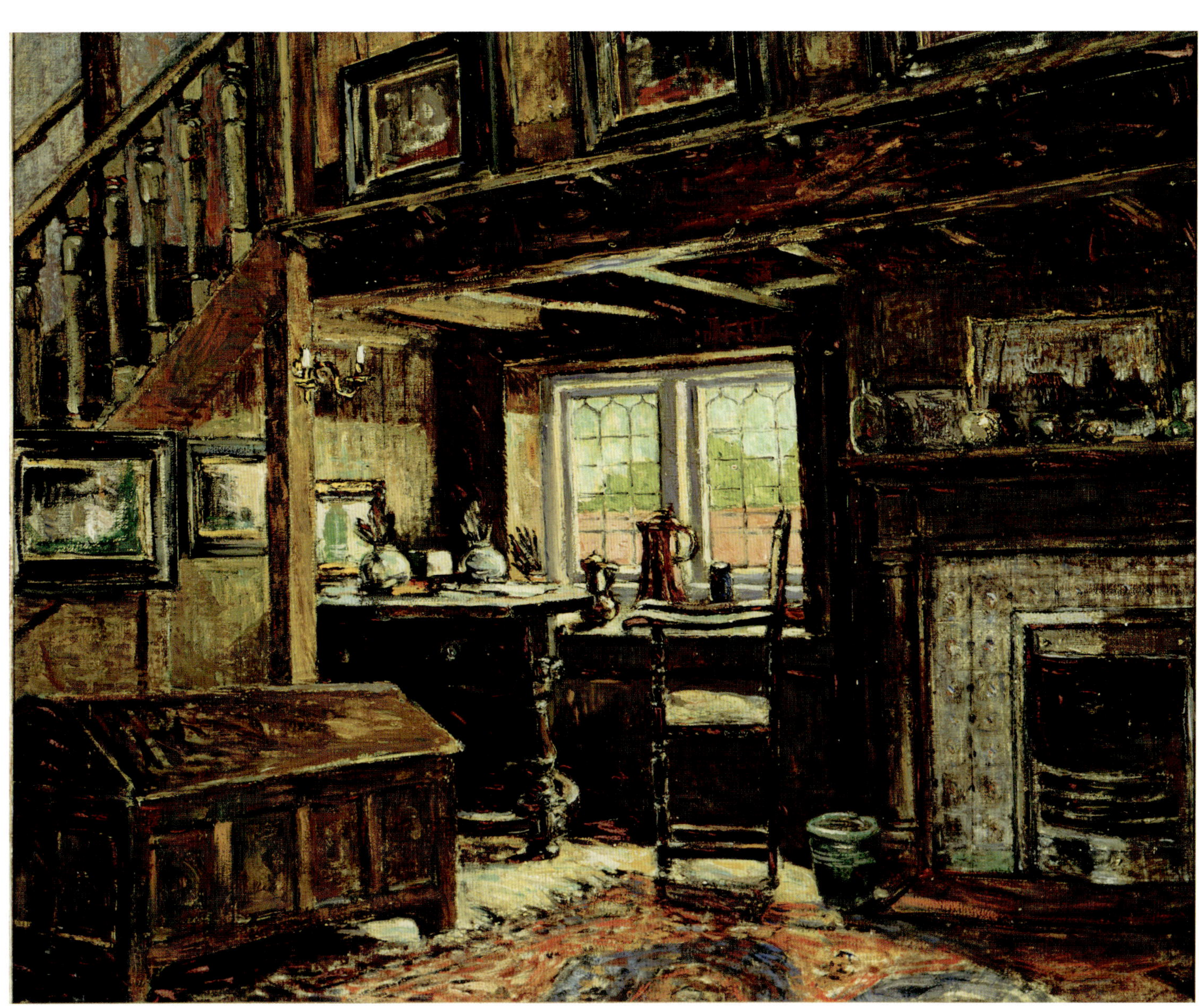

Letta Crapo Smith 1862–1921

63

The First Birthday, 1902

Oil on canvas, 57 × 43"

Signed: "L. Crapo Smith 1902"

Flint Institute of Arts, Flint, Michigan

DETROIT ARTIST LETTA CRAPO SMITH PAINTED THIS GENRE SCENE *en plein air* in 1902 during her second summer in Egmond aan den Hoef. Pleased with her accomplishment, she sent it to the Paris Salon the next year, where it was placed on the line—installed at eye level—so it was guaranteed to be noticed. It went on to garner a bronze medal at the Louisiana Purchase Exposition in St. Louis in 1904 and was included in the annual exhibition of the Pennsylvania Academy of the Fine Arts in 1906.

Crapo Smith was apparently inspired to paint this subject by an actual event. Egmonder Anna de Leeuw took in washing for the artists of the Egmond colony and modeled for their pictures. She had married Simon van den Berg in 1890 and their third child, Dirkje, was born on September 7, 1901.[1] On September 5, 1902, two days before Dirkje's first birthday, another Egmond art student wrote in her diary that she "helped Miss Crepo Smith [*sic*] carry her big canvas and saw her beginning," presumably on *The First Birthday*, Crapo Smith's only large canvas that summer.[2] The painting represents Anna and her daughter, Dirkje, seated under the trees on a sunny day. Dirkje occupies a typical Dutch highchair, built like a barrel on wheels. Anna has stopped knitting to watch her daughter play with a new doll. The child's rattle and a ball, perhaps birthday gifts, lie in the grass beside them. This is a typical maternal scene of a type frequently painted in the previous decades by Hague School artists such as Bernardus Johannes Blommers, but whereas they more often painted such scenes in humble interiors, Crapo Smith painted outdoors in sunlit tones that reflect her studies in Egmond with George Hitchcock (cat. 22–26).

Upon her return to Detroit, Crapo Smith was active in the Detroit Society of Women Painters and Sculptors, becoming its president in 1908. *The First Birthday* remained one of her most important pictures and, together with her 1902 Salon painting *A Daughter of Egmond*, she placed it on long-term loan at the Detroit Museum of Art where a local critic enthused:

> The atmosphere is fine, one feels that he can walk all around the chair, the tree and the house. The color is strikingly portrayed. The variegated notes,—the red crib, the greens in sunlight and shadow, the dull tones of the matron's dress, and the dull red of the tile and brick of the house, all combine to form one general tone with which no single note conflicts.[3]

The artist's niece, Mrs. Jay C. Thompson, inherited this picture and in 1967 gave it to the Flint Institute of Arts in Michigan.[4]

AS

1. Identification of the models and all genealogical information was kindly provided by Dirkje van den Berg's son, Ernst Mooij of Castricum, North Holland, through the good auspices of Ron van Vleuten. Dirkje gave Ernst a reproduction of this painting and the story of its creation.

2. Corinne Mackall diary, September 5, 1902 entry, Gari Melchers Studio and Museum, Fredericksburg, Virginia. *The Egmond Bad-Bode* recorded Miss L. Carpo Smith [*sic*] from America staying at Kraakman, August 1 and September 10, 1902.

3. "New Pictures in the Galleries," *Bulletin of the Detroit Museum of Art* (1907): 3.

4. Christopher R. Young, curator and registrar, Flint Institute of Arts, letter to Annette Stott, July 11, 1986.

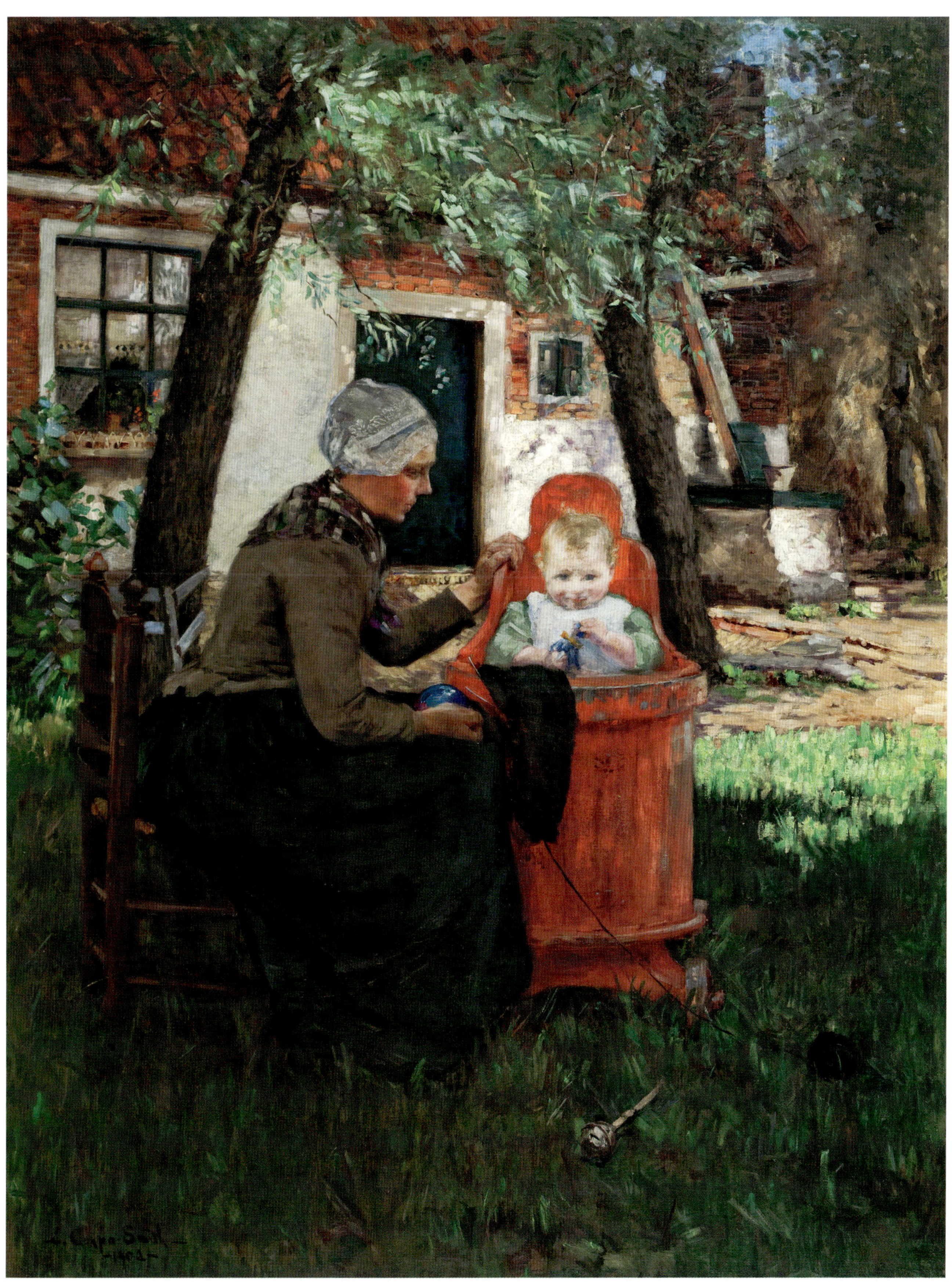

Anna Stanley 1864–1907

64

Girl Carrying Sheaves, c. 1895

Oil on canvas, 18 × 24"
Signed: "Anna Stanley"
Collection of Joanne Stanley Holbrook Patton,
South Hamilton, Massachusetts

ANNA STANLEY WAS AN EXCEPTIONAL YET LITTLE-KNOWN American impressionist painter who spent three seasons in the Netherlands. Born in 1864 to a distinguished army family in Ohio, Stanley proved a gifted artist at the Buffalo Academy for Girls. Under Ammi Merchant Farnham, she painted from photographs of European masters. She next attended the Pennsylvania Academy of the Fine Arts from 1882 to 1885 under the guidance of Thomas Eakins and Thomas Anshutz. Then in 1887 she arrived in Paris and studied for two and a half years at the Académie Julian under teachers Gustave Boulanger and Jules Lefebvre, and at the Académie Colarossi under the direction of André Rixen and Gustave Courtois. Stanley exhibited at the Salon first in 1888 with a charcoal drawing and in 1889 with an oil painting, both now lost. While in Paris, her new friendships with student artists from Chicago garnered her an invitation to study in the Netherlands under John Vanderpoel, of the Art Institute of Chicago. Stanley and most of her Paris classmates—Pauline Dohn, Alice Kellogg, Anna Page Scott, and Ida C. Haskell—spent two consecutive seasons (summer and fall) painting in Rijsoord. Vanderpoel's relatives, the Noorlanders, provided lodging in this pastoral setting untouched by the encroaching industrial world. The Dutch light and remote farming village inspired canvases that appealed to American buyers.

After Stanley exhibited in the United States as a professional artist, she returned to Holland for another season in 1895. *Girl Carrying Sheaves* captures the subject in motion and *en plein air.* The work reflects her matured impressionistic style. Her subjects, primarily women, were set against the typical Dutch landscape of windmills, canals, village houses, or as here, bucolic fields of harvested flax. The afternoon sky is hazy. The distant movement of a windswept tree almost urges the humble girl forward. Stanley's palette of blues, greens, and browns is muted in the background, while the rich foreground colors anchor the grass. *Girl Carrying Sheaves* was exhibited in 1895/96 at the National Academy of Design and at the Society of Washington Artists in 1896.

Anna Stanley married U.S. Army Lt. Willard Ames Holbrook (later first Chief of Cavalry). During her adult years she lived in San Antonio, Texas; Washington, D.C.; Arizona; the Oregon and California coasts; the Philippines; and finally in Chester, Pennsylvania. There she died unexpectedly of pneumonia in 1907 at the age of 42, leaving two young sons. She had stopped exhibiting early in her marriage, but she never stopped painting. During her active period, she exhibited at the Detroit Museum of Art, the Boston Art Club, O'Brien Galleries in Chicago, and at Veerhoff Galleries and the Grand Art Loan Exhibition, both in Washington, D.C.

ON

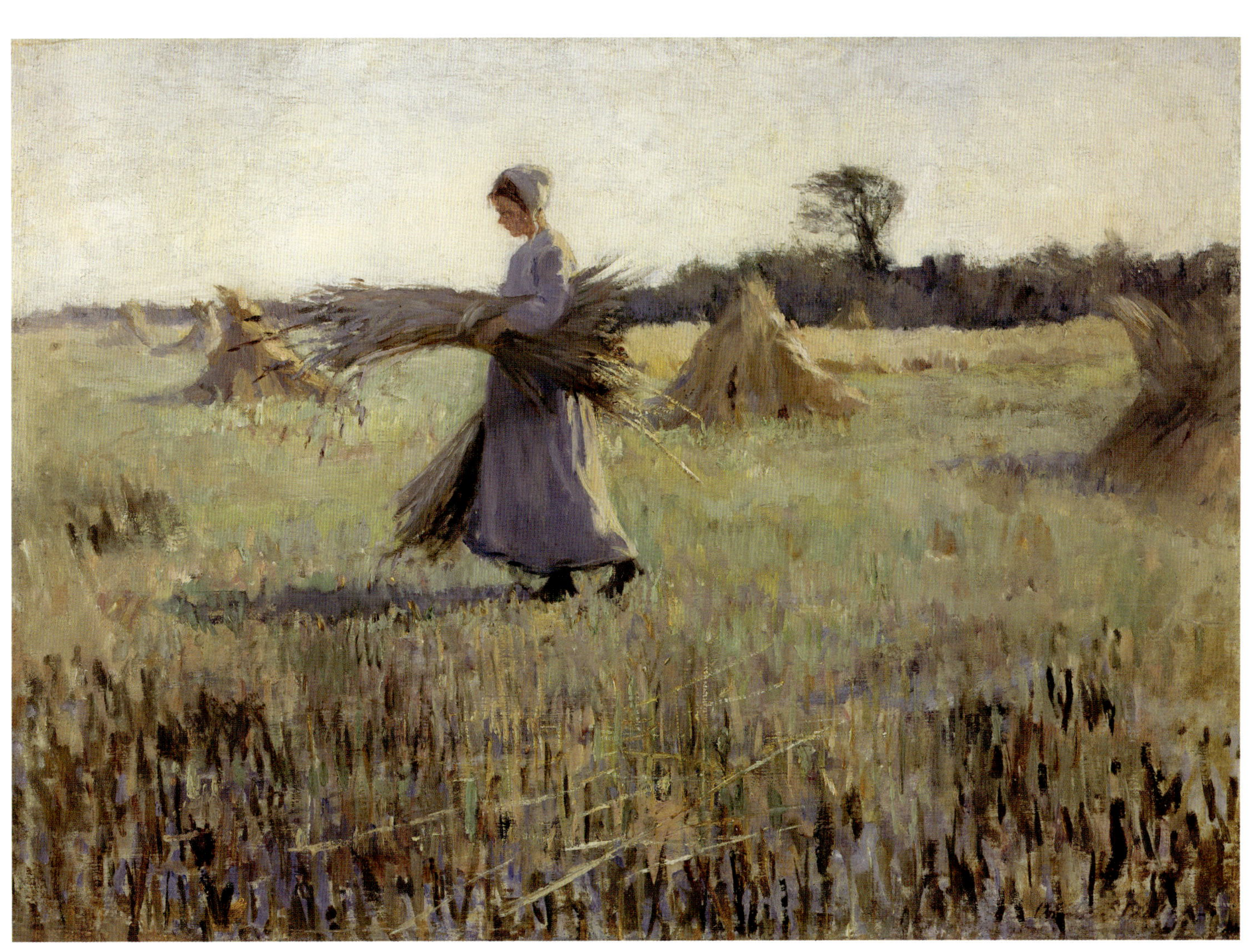

Dwight William Tryon 1849–1925

65

The River Maas at Dordrecht, 1881

Oil on canvas, 30⅝ × 48"
Signed: "D W Tryon 1881"
Collection of George and Betsy White, Waterford, Connecticut

DWIGHT WILLIAM TRYON BEGAN WORKING IN THE MEDIUM OF OILS at age fifteen, initially inspired by an 1864 exhibition that included art by the Dutch masters Jacob van Ruisdael and Rembrandt. The artist's passion for the sea is evident in his earliest works, predominantly shipping scenes of his hometown of Hartford, Connecticut. While working as a bookkeeper and calligrapher, Tryon auctioned his paintings and drawings to finance a formal education at the École des Beaux-Arts in Paris. While abroad from 1876 to 1881, Tryon and his wife visited Brittany, Normandy, Venice, and briefly Dordrecht in Holland.[1]

His homage to the Dutch marine genre, *The River Maas at Dordrecht* represents Tryon's transition from luminous harbor scenes following his French education. He made sketches and notes outdoors, but preferred to paint from imagination and memory in his studio. Tryon wrote that he spent three months during the summer of 1880 in Dordrecht making studies.[2] While there, he also studied the work of older Dutch artists at the Dordrecht Museum.[3] When Tryon returned to his Paris studio he used the sketches and studies to paint pictures of Dordrecht during the winter of 1880–81. This one is reminiscent of the similarly titled *River Maas at Dordrecht* (c. 1660, National Gallery of Art), by Aelbert Cuyp. Rather than representing a single moment in the life of the city, *The River Maas at Dordrecht* reflects the artist's idealized memories from his summer in Dordrecht. According to art historian Nina Lübbren, the relationship of artists and their audiences with rural places was imbued with nostalgia.[4] Indeed, Tryon stated, "It is good to travel and see what man has done in the past, to share the mind with the riches of bygone times and thereby formulate a standard by which we may gauge the work of the present."[5] The rosy hues of the sky serve as the composition's focal point, but nostalgia permeates the piece. Subtle red brick roofs recall the medieval architecture of Dordrecht with quick brushstrokes to suggest its impermanence. The juxtaposition of a hay boat, symbolic of the industrious Dutch nature, with a more leisurely paced sailboat reinforces the idyllic interpretation of a riverscape.

After his return to the United States, Tryon became head of the Smith College Art Department, to which he gave *The River Maas at Dordrecht* and several of its preparatory studies. The Smith College Museum sold the painting to Nelson C. White, son of Tryon's biographer, in 1956, and it has descended in his family.

MG

1. Linda Merrill, *An Ideal Country: Paintings by Dwight William Tryon in the Freer Gallery of Art* (Washington, D.C.: Smithsonian Institution, 1990), 24–29.

2. Dwight Tryon, quoted in Henry C. White, *The Life and Art of Dwight William Tryon* (New York: Houghton Mifflin, 1930), 48.

3. Tryon signed the Dordrecht Museum visitors' book in 1880, "D. W. Tryon, artist, U.S. of America."

4. Nina Lübbren, *Rural Artists' Colonies in Europe, 1870–1910* (New Brunswick, N.J.: Rutgers University Press, 2001), 14.

5. Tryon, quoted in White, *The Life and Art of Dwight William Tryon*, 50.

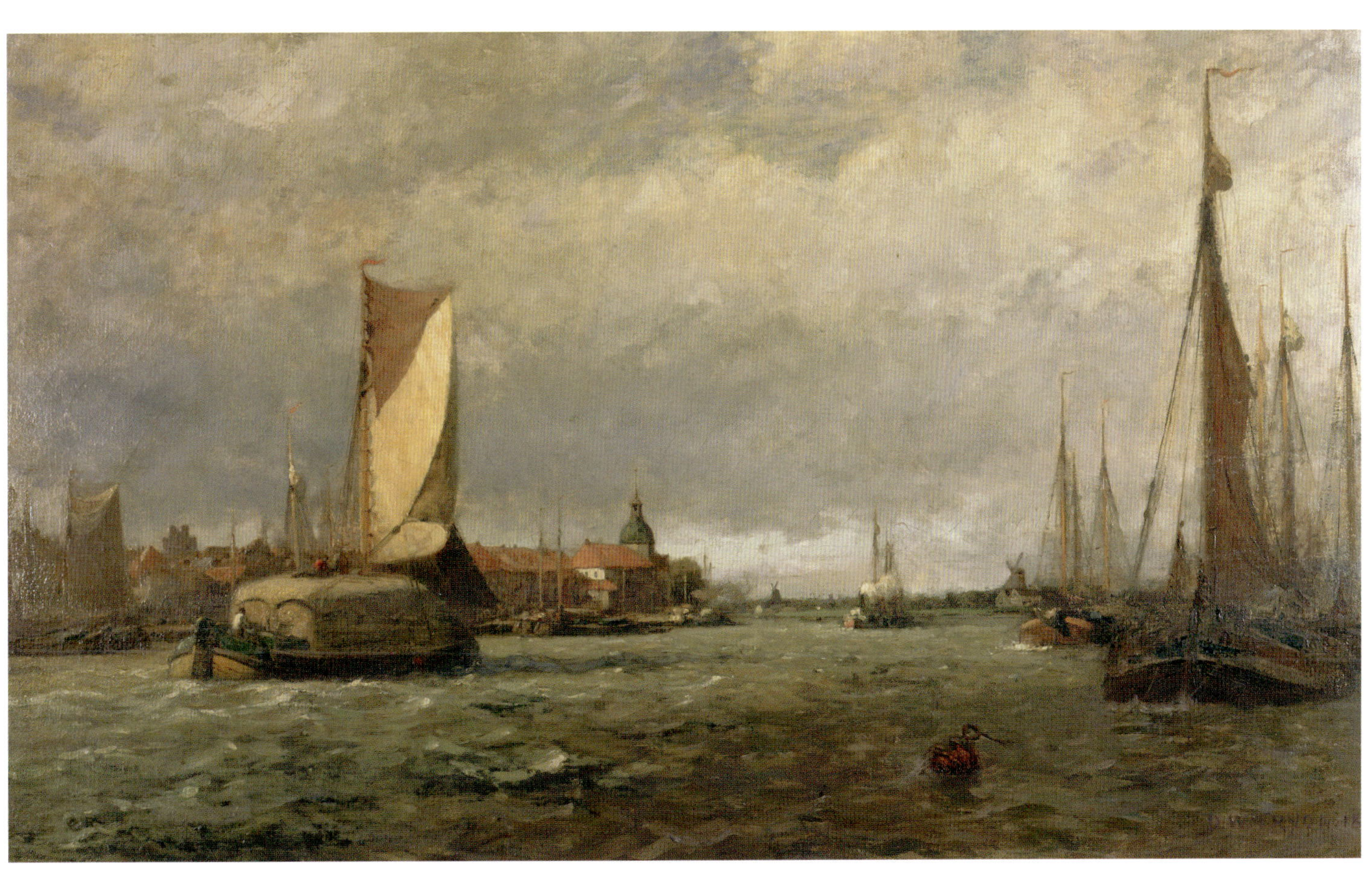

Stephen Salisbury Tuckerman 1830–1904

66

Marine View, 1885

Oil on canvas, 24 × 29"
Signed: "S S Tuckerman '85"
Cape Ann Museum,
Gloucester, Massachusetts

THE TURBULENT SEAS AND SKIES THAT THREATEN THE KATWIJK fishing boat in *Marine View* reveal the influence that the dramatic, atmospheric seascapes of Dutch Golden Age artists such as Willem van de Velde II and Ludolf Bakhuizen had on Stephen Salisbury Tuckerman's work. Given the popularity of these Dutch masters with late-nineteenth-century American audiences and the relative scarcity of their work on the market, Tuckerman's dynamic seascapes surely helped fulfill the needs of contemporary collectors for whom original seventeenth-century Dutch paintings were out of reach. Tuckerman was highly regarded during his lifetime as a leading marine painter, although his work is not nearly as well known today. He was born in Boston, where he was a student at Bronson Alcott's radical Temple School. As a young man he made several voyages to Calcutta, then studied art under William Morris Hunt, the renowned Boston artist generally credited with popularizing the work of the French Barbizon painters in America. Tuckerman continued his artistic training in his mother's hometown of Birmingham, England, before returning to Boston to head the New England School of Design, where one of his pupils was May Alcott, daughter of Bronson and sister of author Louisa. Tuckerman soon began to focus more seriously on his own painting and, sometime after the death of Fitz Henry Lane, moved his family into Lane's home in Gloucester, Massachusetts. The busy seaport town of Gloucester would become a thriving artists' colony later in the nineteenth century, but Tuckerman was one of the first artists after Lane to seek inspiration there: Winslow Homer would not arrive until around 1873, William Morris Hunt in 1875, and Frank Duveneck in 1898.[1]

Although his wife and children would remain in Gloucester, after 1872 Tuckerman spent the majority of his time in Europe, establishing a studio in The Hague and spending the summers of 1883, 1884, 1885, and 1887 in Katwijk. From 1882 through the end of the decade he participated in the contemporary Hague School artists' club, Pulchri Studio, to which he had been elected a member. He also continued to participate in group shows in the United States, exhibiting at the Centennial Exposition in Philadelphia in 1876, the National Academy of Design in 1882, and the Pennsylvania Academy of the Fine Arts in 1883. A group of fifty-three of Tuckerman's Dutch paintings, drawings, and watercolors were the subject of a solo exhibition held in Boston's Tremont Street studio building in the spring of 1886. The exhibition consisted primarily of marine scenes, many of which were set in stormy conditions and were likely comparable to *Marine View*. In addition to this painting from the collection of the Cape Ann Museum in Gloucester, examples of Tuckerman's work can be found in the Museum of Fine Arts, Boston, and the Butler Institute of American Art, Youngstown, Ohio.

CM

1. Thanks to Martha Oaks, curator of the Cape Ann Museum, for providing this chronology of artists' arrivals in Gloucester.

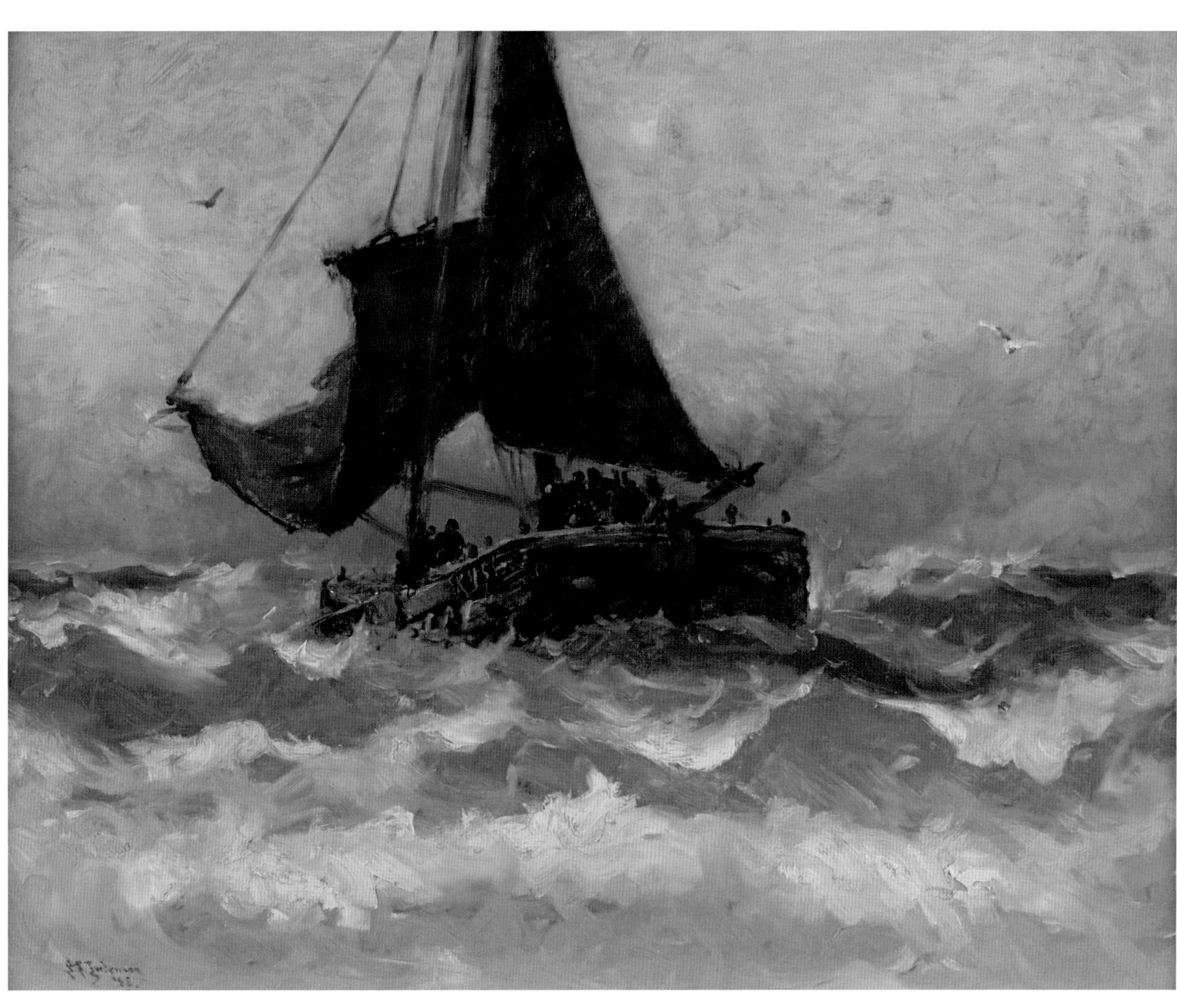

Charles Yardley Turner 1850–1919

67

The Grand Canal, Dordrecht, Holland, 1881

Oil on canvas, 38 × 65"
Collection of the Haling family, Jackson, Wyoming

BORN IN BALTIMORE AT MID-CENTURY, CHARLES YARDLEY TURNER worked in a local architect's office by day and studied art at the Maryland Institute by night during his teens. In 1872 he moved to New York City to study at the National Academy of Design, working for portrait photographers during the day and studying art at night. In 1875, when it was rumored that the Academy would close, he helped organize the Art Students League of New York. Three years later, Turner set forth for France to complete his training under Jean-Paul Laurens, Mihály Munkácsy, and Léon Bonnat. Like most Americans in Paris, he spent his summers sketching in the countryside. The summer of 1880 found him in Holland studying both old and contemporary Dutch masters in the museums of Dordrecht and Haarlem, and painting the city of Dordrecht.

The Grand Canal, Dordrecht, Holland was Charles Yardley Turner's first important oil painting. There is no Grand Canal in Dordrecht, so the exact location is a bit mysterious. He most likely composed it in his Paris studio from his summer sketches of country folk unloading milk cans at a quay, boats plying the rivers, and the architectural structure of the city's various canals. One of the women in the boat wears the headdress peculiar to this region of South Holland. *The Grand Canal, Dordrecht, Holland* was actually the second painting of this subject and title that Turner created, according to a contemporary, who wrote: "Dissatisfied with his original rendering of the subject, he destroyed the canvas, returned to Holland during the ensuing summer, and painted the picture anew."[1] This time, Turner was satisfied with his endeavor and upon his return to New York in 1882 he sent it to the fifty-seventh annual exhibition of the National Academy of Design. Charles Kurtz reproduced it in his illustrated catalog and it was purchased from the exhibition by no less illustrious a collector than John Taylor Johnston. Johnston had retired from his presidency of the Central Railroad of New Jersey five years earlier and now focused on other interests, including the Metropolitan Museum of Art, which he had helped to found and of which he was president. Representation in the personal collection of the president of the Metropolitan Museum of Art launched Turner's New York art career in a big way. Turner taught at the Art Students League, of which he became president, and exhibited with the Water Color Society, Society of American Artists, and the Salmagundi Club, which he helped to found. The National Academy of Design elected him to associate membership in 1893 and full membership in 1896. Turner served as assistant director of decorations for the Chicago World's Columbian Exposition in 1893, where he exhibited eleven paintings, including *The Grand Canal, Dordrecht, Holland,* on loan from Johnston.[2] When Johnston died that year, the painting probably stayed in the family but came on the market again as *Scene on Grand Canal* at Schultheis Art Galleries in New York City, where the great-grandfather of the current owner purchased it. As far as is known, this picture has not been publicly exhibited since 1893.

AS

1. Theodore Marburg, *Addresses delivered on the occasion of the unveiling of the mural decorations "The Burning of the Peggy Stewart" painted by Charles Yardley Turner and "Religious Toleration" painted by Edwin Howland Blashfield* (Baltimore: Municipal Art Society, n.d.), 18. My thanks to Danielle Lewis for this reference.

2. *Revisiting the White City: American Art at the 1893 World's Fair* (Washington, D.C.: National Museum of American Art and the National Portrait Gallery, Smithsonian Institution, 1993), 331–32. "Other Deaths," John Taylor Johnston, *New York Times,* March 25, 1893.

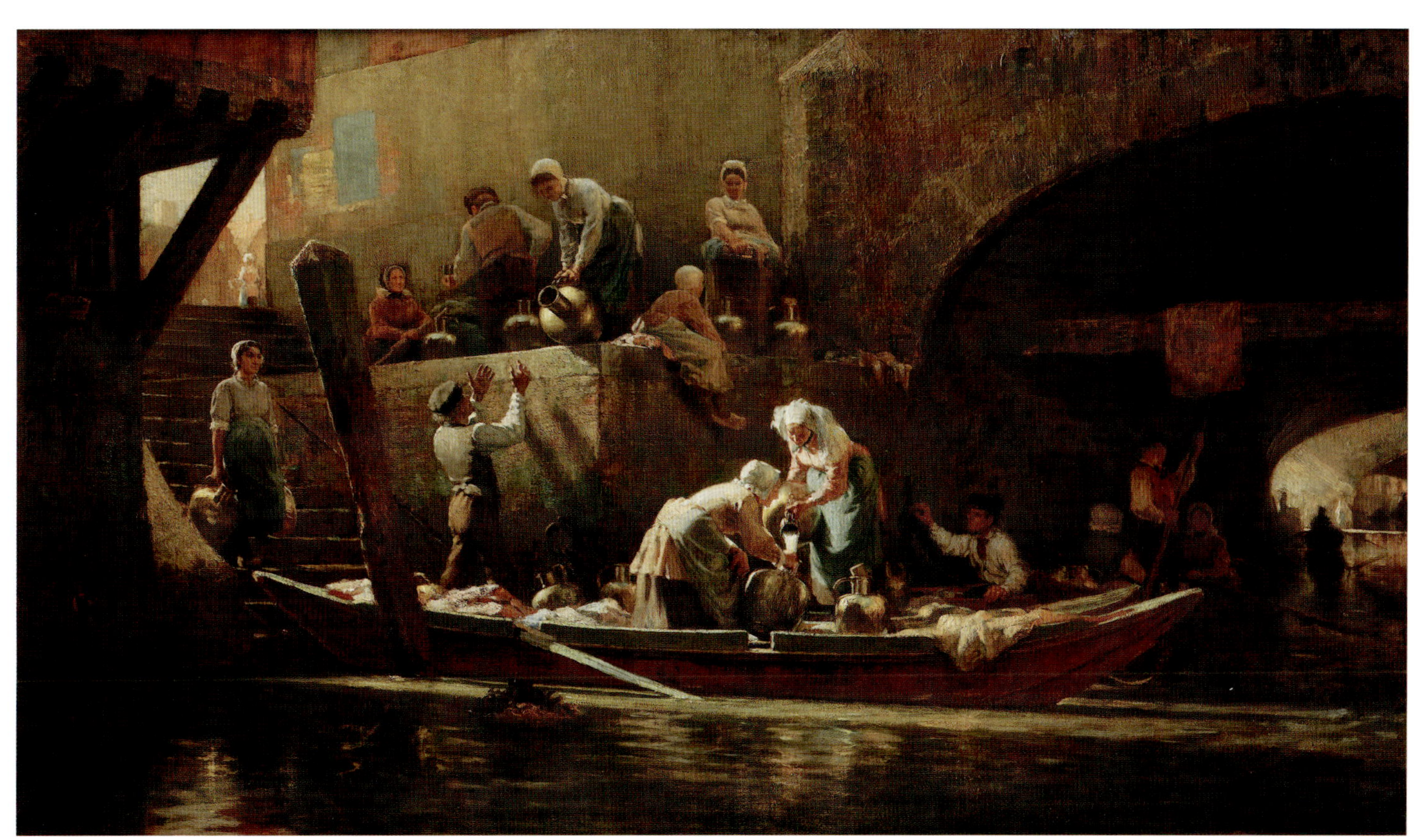

John Henry Twachtman 1853–1902

68

Dutch Landscape, c. 1881–85

Oil on canvas, 21 × 26"
Signed: "J H Twachtman"
Private Collection,
Kiawah Island, South Carolina

BORN IN CINCINNATI OF GERMAN PARENTS, JOHN HENRY TWACHTMAN began to study drawing while a teenager, entered Cincinnati's McMicken School of Design in 1871, and traveled to Munich with fellow Cincinnati artist Frank Duveneck, where he studied for the next two years. Work in Venice preceded his first trip to the Netherlands in 1881, which doubled as a sketching-painting sojourn and a honeymoon with his young artist bride, Martha Scudder. This proved to be an important trip for Twachtman. He studied the landscape of South Holland with its many rivers and canals, low-lying meadows, and wide open skies, pierced occasionally by the vertical accent of a windmill. Carrying a burin and small metal plates with him, he dashed off quick impressions to be printed at another time. He later attempted to record his sense of the moist gray days in oil paints. On this trip, Twachtman met the Hague School painter Anton Mauve, a master of Dutch atmospheric effects and quiet landscapes. Many of the Dutch scenes that Twachtman produced during and after this trip from his sketches reproduced the particular effect of cloudy, water-laden landscapes. At least one critic later confessed he thought Twachtman was Dutch because the artist's early pictures of Holland were so sympathetic to the Dutch methods of Paul Gabriël, Jan Hendrik Weissenbruch, and the Maris brothers.[1] Twachtman was also proud of the results of his experiments in the Netherlands, later writing "the Holland work remains the best."[2] From 1883 to 1885 he studied in France, where he further developed his tonal palette and *plein air* techniques. Then he returned to the Netherlands for additional summer work.

The undated painting now known as *Dutch Landscape* represents the experiments that Twachtman carried out during the first half of the 1880s as he simplified and abstracted nature to create a predominant mood. The harmonious palette of blue, green and gray, scaled down to a very narrow tonal range, conveys the sense of a moist day. The composition—a body of water in the foreground, rich gray-green meadows receding into the distance, at least two-thirds of the canvas devoted to sky, and one or more windmills against the horizon—was one that he repeated in several variations.

AS

1. "Artists Who Matter XXIV—John Twachtman," *The International Interpreter,* September 30, clipping in Twachtman curatorial file, Cincinnati Art Museum.

2. John Twachtman to J. Alden Weir, Avondale, March 5, 1882, Weir family papers, quoted in Lisa N. Peters, *John Henry Twachtman: An American Impressionist* (New York: Hudson Hills Press, 1999): 52.

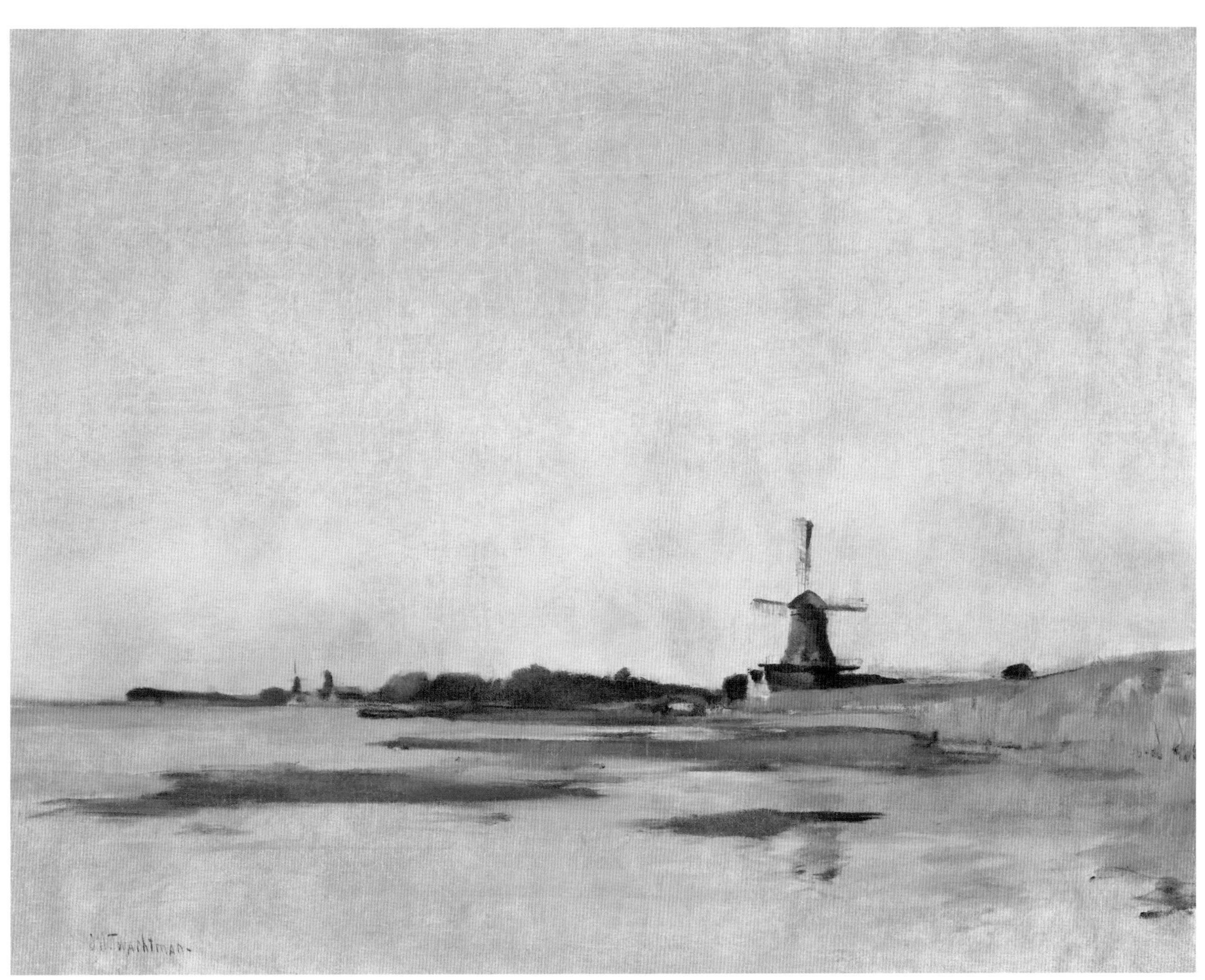

John Henry Twachtman 1853–1902

69

Windmills, c. 1885

Oil on canvas, 38 × 51½"
Signed: "J H Twachtman"
Collection of Mr. and Mrs. Stephen G. Vollmer, Cincinnati, Ohio

TWACHTMAN SIGNED THE GUEST BOOK OF THE FRANS HALS MUSEUM in Haarlem in June and again in September of 1885. In between those trips to refresh himself on the old Dutch masters, he worked steadily in and around Dordrecht, producing landscapes in a range of mediums. That winter he exhibited his oil paintings and pastels at the Chase Gallery in Boston. First on the list was a painting called *Hollandsch Diep* after the waterway south of Dordrecht that divides the province of South Holland from that of North Brabant. Twachtman's foremost biographer, Lisa N. Peters, has tentatively identified this as an early Dutch title for the picture that has been known ever since as *Windmills.*[1] Closely related to Twachtman's French landscape, *Arques-la-Bataille, Windmills* represents the successful culmination of all his European studies and a notable synthesis of his experiments with light, color, atmosphere, and composition to this date. His achievement was recognized by his peers when they awarded *Windmills* the Webb prize for the best landscape at the tenth annual exhibition of the Society of American Artists in 1888. Comparison with *Dutch Landscape* (cat. 68) suggests the technical range of Twachtman's Dutch windmill scenes. The greater complexity of the composition of *Windmills*, the variety of cloud formations, and stronger contrast may reveal a maturing style. Yet underlying *Windmills'* surface detail one sees the abstraction of elemental landscape forms and incipient tonalism of *Dutch Landscape.*

In a very general sense, both *Dutch Landscape* and *Windmills* suggest the appreciation for the premodern rural landscape evinced by so many artists at this time. No trace of the railroads that carried the artists to their destinations mars the tranquility of a space in which only nature moves, and at its own unhastening pace. This was the quality that the popular American preacher, historian, and lecturer William Elliot Griffis advocated to American tourists in Holland when he said "the country in general induces a spirit of quiet restfulness, so grateful to the overwrought American."[2] For all its strengths, *Windmills* did not sell during Twachtman's lifetime; he gave it to Smith College in Northampton, Massachusetts, sometime before his death in 1902. Since that time it has rarely been exhibited publicly.

AS

Research by RACHEL MILLER

TMA and TAFT

1. Lisa N. Peters, *John Twachtman (1853–1902): A "Painter's Painter"* (New York: Spanierman Gallery, 2006), 122–23.

2. William Elliot Griffis, *The American in Holland* (New York: Houghton Mifflin, 1899; 1907), 198–99.

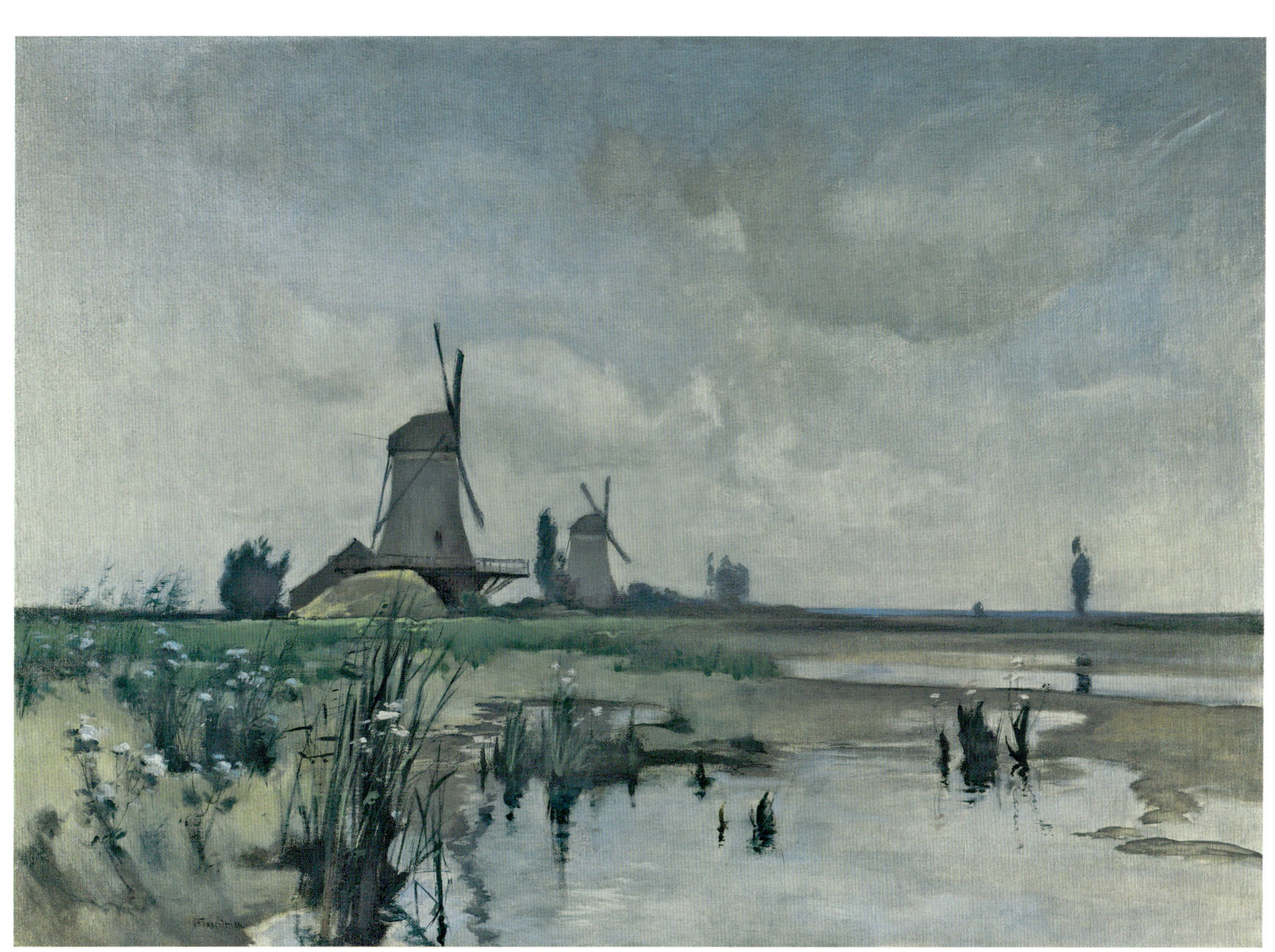

Charles Frederick Ulrich 1858–1908

70

The Village Printing Shop, Haarlem, Holland, 1884

Oil on panel, 21¼ × 23"
Signed: "Chas. F. Ulrich ANA"
Terra Foundation for American Art, Chicago, Illinois
Daniel J. Terra Collection, 1992.137

CHARLES FREDERICK ULRICH SPENT THE SUMMER OF 1884 working in Haarlem. Unlike many of his fellow artists who went there to absorb the lessons of the seventeenth-century master portrait painter Frans Hals, Ulrich showed more interest in the contemporary urban scene. He painted four pictures during the nearly five months he was there: children blowing bubbles in the Haarlem orphanage; a Dutch typesetter standing at his case by a partly curtained window; a boy counting papers in a print shop; and *The Village Printing Shop, Haarlem, Holland*, with the same boy drinking from a cup.[1] Haarlem was the site of one of the oldest continuous Dutch printing firms, Enschedé and Sons, which may have provided the setting for Ulrich's three print shop paintings. This was a town where the art and technology of printing were regularly celebrated in recognition of the claim that the seventeenth-century Haarlem printer Laurens Janszoon Coster invented moveable wooden type before Gutenberg. Ulrich could not have remained ignorant of these claims. It is also likely that many of his American viewers would have been reminded of Coster's story, of claims that Holland allowed refugees from England and the continent to print banned religious tracts in the seventeenth century, and of the general contention by some historians that the American ideals of free press, free speech, and freedom of religious expression originated in the Netherlands.[2] Ulrich brought this picture back to New York when he returned in November 1884 and sent it to the inaugural exhibition of the American Art Association's galleries in December. Seeing it there, a reviewer claimed:

> Admirable, too, is his "Village Printing Shop in Haarlem," although the interior is so much like that of an American country printing-office, and the 'prentice is so much like an American 'prentice, that the picture might be engraved as an illustration for that delightful chapter in "A Modern Instance" in which Mr. Howells introduces us to Bartley Hubbard and the sleepy town of Equity.[3]

These points of convergence in national identity—love of technology, inventiveness, Protestant work ethic, freedom of the press, and freedom of religion—are conveyed by the visual similarity between Ulrich's Dutch printing firm and the rural American print shop. Although the apprentice is taking a break from his labors, the men in the back are printing on a hand operated press and the whole air of the place is one of homey industry. Large-scale publishing in New York, with its mechanized, steam-driven presses, had lost some of the spirit of a community newspaper, so there is a hint of nostalgia in the painting and in the writer's reference to William Dean Howells's 1882 novel. In it, Hubbard gives up village life in Maine to seek his fortune in Boston, where greed and the evils of urban life destroy his marriage. Antimodernism and progressivism are blended in Ulrich's image of Dutchness, which looks so much like Americanness.

AS

1. The *New Amsterdam Gazette* followed his progress, vol. 2, August 4, September 5, October 9, and November 10, 1884.
2. Annette Stott, *Holland Mania: The Unknown Dutch Period in American Art and Culture* (Woodstock, N.Y.: Overlook Press, 1998), 78–100 on historical ties and 110–13 on this painting.
3. Montezuma, "My Note Book," *Art Amateur* 12 (January 1885): 28.

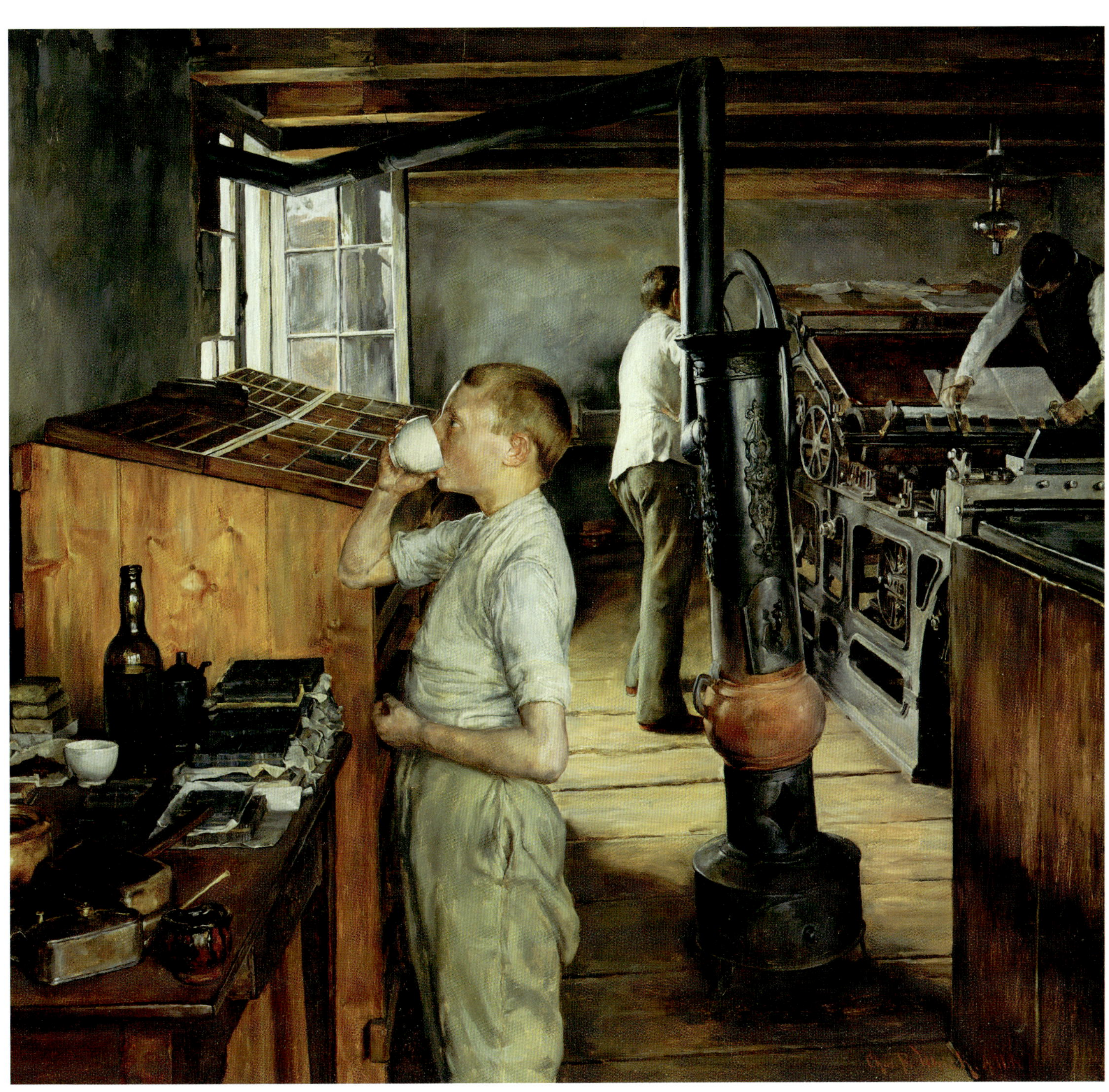

Julian Alden Weir 1852–1919

71

Milkmaid of Popindrecht, 1881

Oil on canvas, 76½ × 51"
Brigham Young University Museum of Art, Provo, Utah
Purchase/gift of Mahonri M. Young Estate

WHILE STUDYING IN FRANCE DURING THE 1870S, J. ALDEN WEIR made several trips to the Netherlands to seek out paintings by Frans Hals and Rembrandt. He does not appear to have considered the Dutch scenery and inhabitants as possible subjects for his own art at that time, but he absorbed the lessons of the older artists, whom he copied extensively. It was not until 1881 that he got a chance to return to Holland from New York and, in company with his brother John Ferguson Weir, his friend John Henry Twachtman (cat. 68–69), and Twachtman's new wife, printmaker Martha Scudder Twachtman, he set to work making paintings of the land and people in and around Dordrecht. Weir wrote to his father from Dordrecht on July 15, "I have today got a fine model who wears the curious costume—a large white cap, with gold curls each side of the head, like a cork-screw." Two weeks later, he added: "I have an immense canvas. I think larger than my *Good Samaritan*, of a peasant with her brass milk cans, standing in front of a door of a cottage. So far I think I have something quite interesting in the head."[1] Although he had second thoughts about painting such a large canvas that summer, he persevered and the result was *Milkmaid of Popindrecht*.[2] The Weir brothers may have worked side by side, for John's painting *Dutch Girl* represents the milkmaid in the same pose and setting, but with a slightly different tilt to her head and small alterations in costume and milk cans. It became a standard activity among artists to paint the women who lived in Papendrecht, just across the river from Dordrecht, whose job it was to milk the cows and help transport the dairy products to the city. Charles Yardley Turner (cat. 67), who was also in Dordrecht that summer working on his painting of milkmaids unloading their wares on the Grand Canal, painted *Dordrecht Milkmaid* (1882, gouache, private collection), which is very similar to Weir's, but set in the countryside. The characteristic South Holland headdress of long white veil over gold or silver helmet, with gold ornaments attached at the temples, proved attractive to artists and audiences alike. Weir exhibited his *Milkmaid of Popindrecht* at the National Academy of Design in 1882, where it was hailed as "one of the best pieces of work he has ever shown."[3] It must have made an interesting combination with Turner's *The Grand Canal, Dordrecht, Holland* (cat. 67) at the same exhibition.

AS

TMA, TAFT, GRAM

1. Notes in curatorial file, Brigham Young University Museum of Art, Provo, Utah.

2. Although the small town in the south of Holland referenced in the title of this work is correctly spelled "Papendrecht," Brigham Young University Museum of Art records indicate that Weir spelled it "Popindrecht" when he originally titled the work. This spelling was also used in an 1882 review of the work when it was exhibited at the National Academy of Design ("The Editor's Opera-Glass," *Frank Leslie's Popular Monthly* 13, no. 6 [June 1882]: 758).

3. Doreen Bolger Burke, *J. Alden Weir: An American Impressionist* (Newark, Del.: University of Delaware Press, 1983), 109.

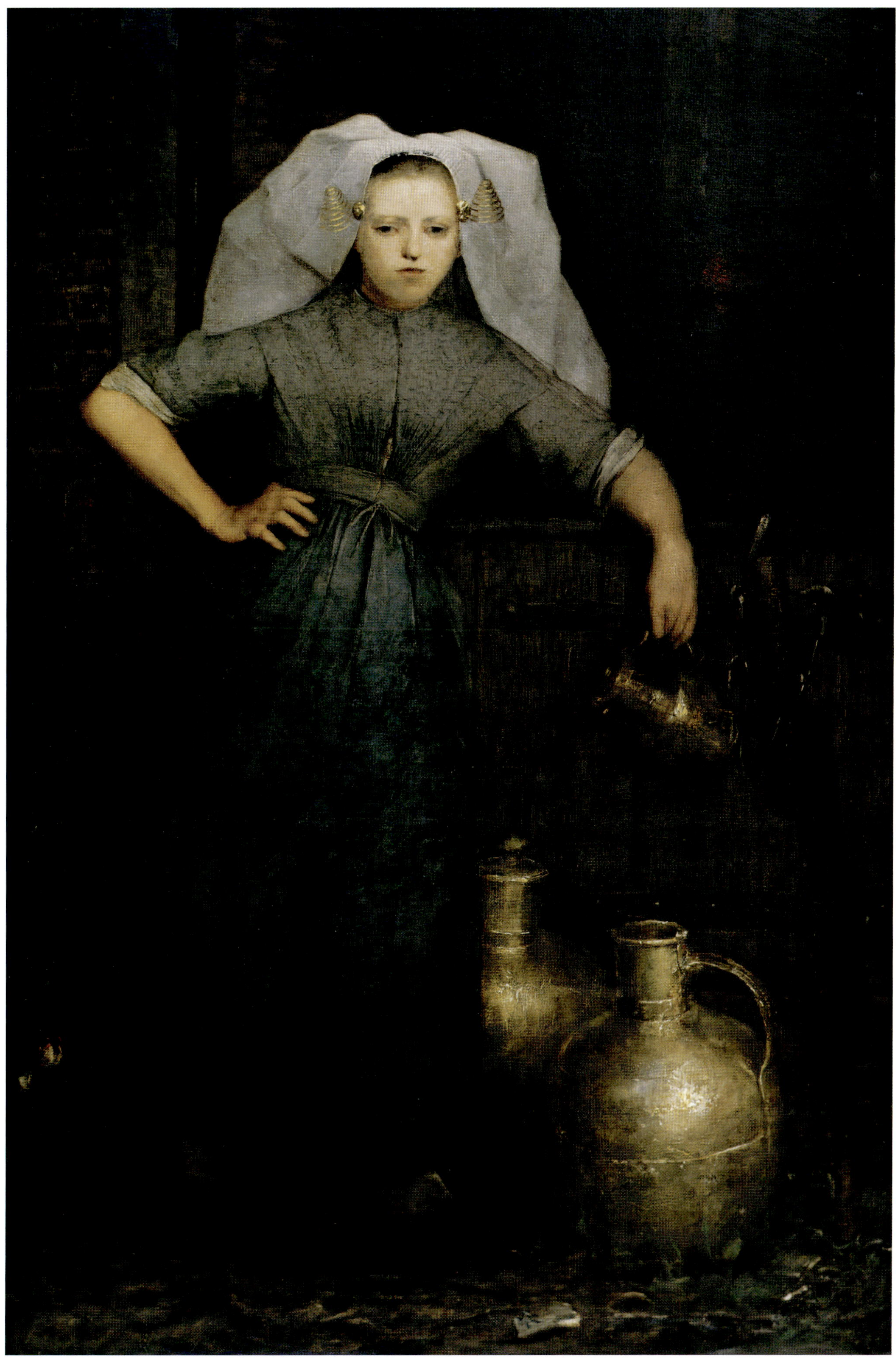

Charles Herbert Woodbury 1864–1940

72

Dutch Kermis (Dutch Fair), 1895

Oil on canvas, 20 × 27½"
Childs Gallery,
Boston, Massachusetts

THE TRADITION OF KERMIS (OR KERMESSE) BEGAN AS A CHRISTIAN FESTIVAL held on the anniversary of a church's founding, commonly celebrated in parts of Holland, Belgium, and northern France. By the seventeenth century, artists such as Peter Paul Rubens, Pieter Brueghel II, and both the elder and the younger Teniers had all depicted kermis as a more secular celebration, focused on eating, drinking, dancing, and merriment. Similarly festive, though rather less bacchanalian, is Woodbury's 1895 *Dutch Kermis*, which utilizes energetic strokes of vivid color to portray women and children in traditional costume surveying the vendors' stalls at the Volendam kermis. The vigorous brushwork and off-center composition of the painting lend it a freshness and originality, yet its subject is quintessentially Dutch, typical of what an American traveler of this period might expect to see during an excursion to the rural town of Volendam. In the early twentieth century, Americans had enough interest in the Dutch kermis that a number of American communities with significant Dutch American populations began establishing their own versions of the festival. These typically focused on traditional Dutch foods, costume, and other secular aspects of Dutch culture.

Charles Herbert Woodbury, best known for his dynamic, vigorous depictions of the New England seas and coast, began his career as a professional artist and teacher while still a teenager. Leaving his hometown of Lynn, Massachusetts, to study mechanical engineering at the Massachusetts Institute of Technology, the precocious Woodbury began exhibiting his work at the Boston Art Club in 1882, took evening life classes there in 1883, and taught his first private sketching class in 1885. A few months after his graduation from M.I.T. in 1886, he opened a studio in Boston and began accepting students. Woodbury's first trip to Europe occurred in 1890–91, shortly after his marriage to former student (and a recognized artist in her own right), Marcia Oakes (cat. 73). The newlyweds visited Belgium, Holland, Germany, Italy, Switzerland, and France. In Paris, Woodbury attended a few months of classes at the Académie Julian, his only formal artistic training. Holland became the Woodburys' preferred European destination; the couple would spend significant time in Volendam and Laren every year from 1892 until 1895, and would return to Holland for shorter visits in 1903 and 1907. Their time in the United States was typically divided between their homes in Boston and the coastal town of Ogunquit, Maine. *Dutch Kermis* was included in the Woodbury retrospective held five years after the artist's death at the Museum of Fine Arts, Boston, in 1945.

CM

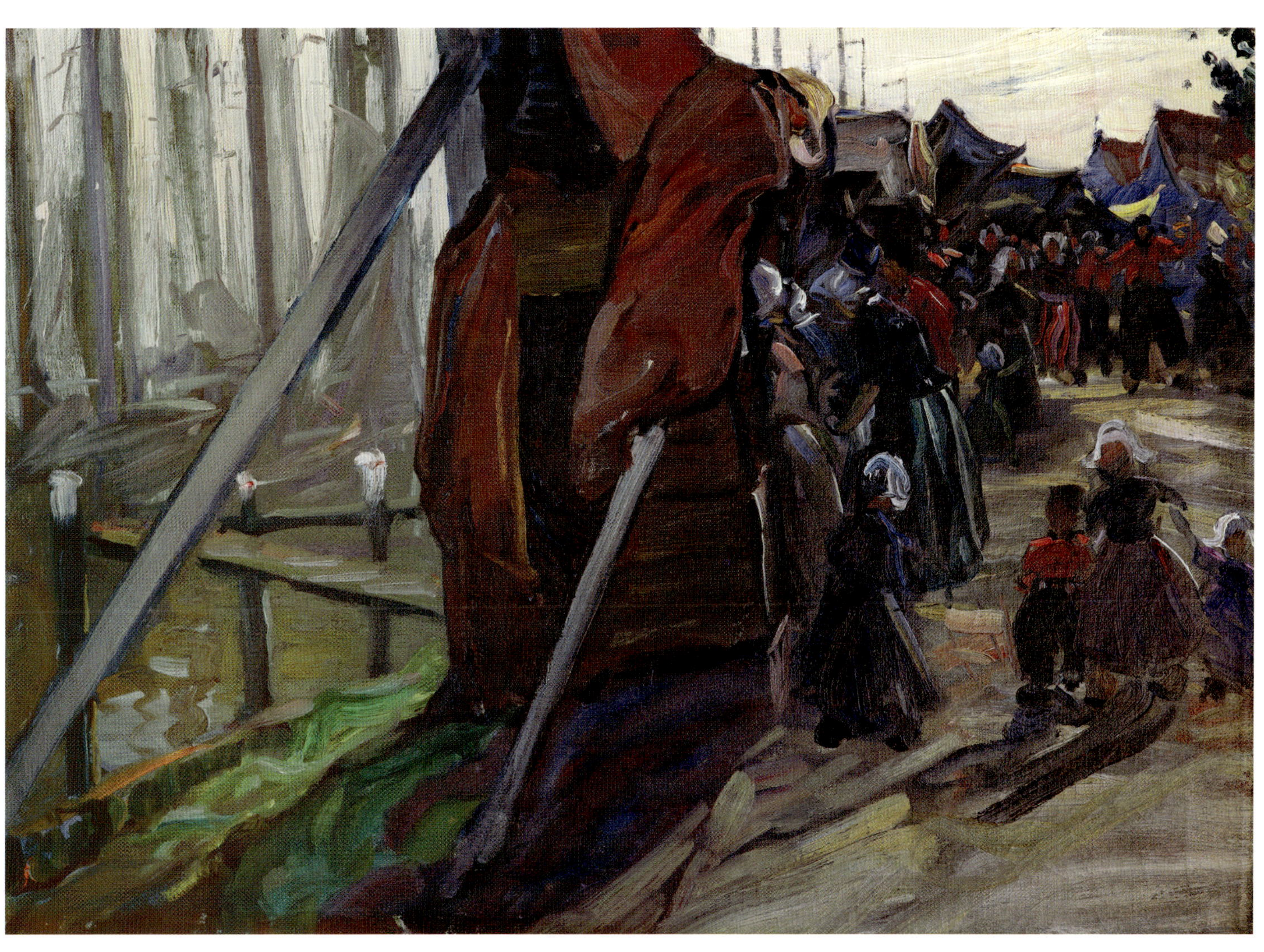

Marcia Oakes Woodbury 1865–1913

73

Moeder en Dochter: Het Geheele Leven (Mother and Daughter: The Whole of Life), 1894

Watercolor on paper,
26½ × 12" (left and right panels),
26½ × 24½" (center panel)
Signed: "Marcia Oakes Woodbury 94"
Museum of Fine Arts, Boston, Massachusetts
Gift of Charles H. Woodbury, 18.215

A REGULAR VISITOR TO HOLLAND, MARCIA OAKES WOODBURY SPECIALIZED in the portrayal of hard-working Dutch peasant women and their ruddy-cheeked children. Born Susan Marcia Oakes in South Berwick, Maine, she married her art teacher, Boston artist Charles H. Woodbury (cat. 72), in June 1890. The two made frequent voyages to Europe. Holland—where they spent time in Volendam, Laren, and Katwijk—quickly became their favorite destination. Woodbury's travel diaries are filled with accounts of days spent sketching local Dutch peasants, then creating watercolors and oils based on her accumulated sketches. Like many of the other American artists working in Holland at the time, Woodbury conspicuously omitted any references to contemporary urban life or industrialization from her work. This carefully tailored focus was well received by contemporary audiences; while reviewing a memorial exhibition held the year after Woodbury's death, a critic for the *Boston Transcript* admired her subjects' "quaintness of aspect, stolidity of character, and unsophisticated naturalness," and went on to declare Woodbury's pictures to be "not only veracious, intelligent and sympathetic, but in a measure ethnological documents."[1] Far from an insignificant statement, this description places Woodbury's Dutch peasant portraits beyond the realm of art, considering them in the greater context of cultural anthropology. The watercolor triptych *Mother and Daughter: The Whole of Life* is a prime example of the work that Woodbury produced in Holland, and was recognized as such by her contemporaries. Exhibited at the Art Club of Philadelphia in 1895, the Trans-Mississippi and International Exposition in 1898, and the Pan-American Exposition of 1901, it also received high acclaim when shown in the posthumous exhibition of Woodbury's work held at the Museum of Fine Arts, Boston, in 1914. The side panels contain solo portraits of a Dutch peasant woman, who grasps a set of rosary beads, and her daughter, who clutches a small book—most likely a Bible. Both are shown seated, wearing simple clothing, and staring modestly off into the middle distance. The middle panel of the triptych depicts the two figures together in an unadorned room, framed by the light from a single window. The mother labors at her spinning wheel while gazing toward her daughter, who cards wool in preparation for spinning. The subtitle of the triptych, *The Whole of Life*, suggests the artist's admiration for the generations of women who have spent their lives devoutly engaged in such wholesome and industrious domesticity.

CM

TMA and SL

1. "Mrs. Woodbury's Pictures: Memorial Exhibition of Her Watercolors and Oil Paintings at the Museum of Fine Arts," *Boston Transcript*, March 26, 1914.

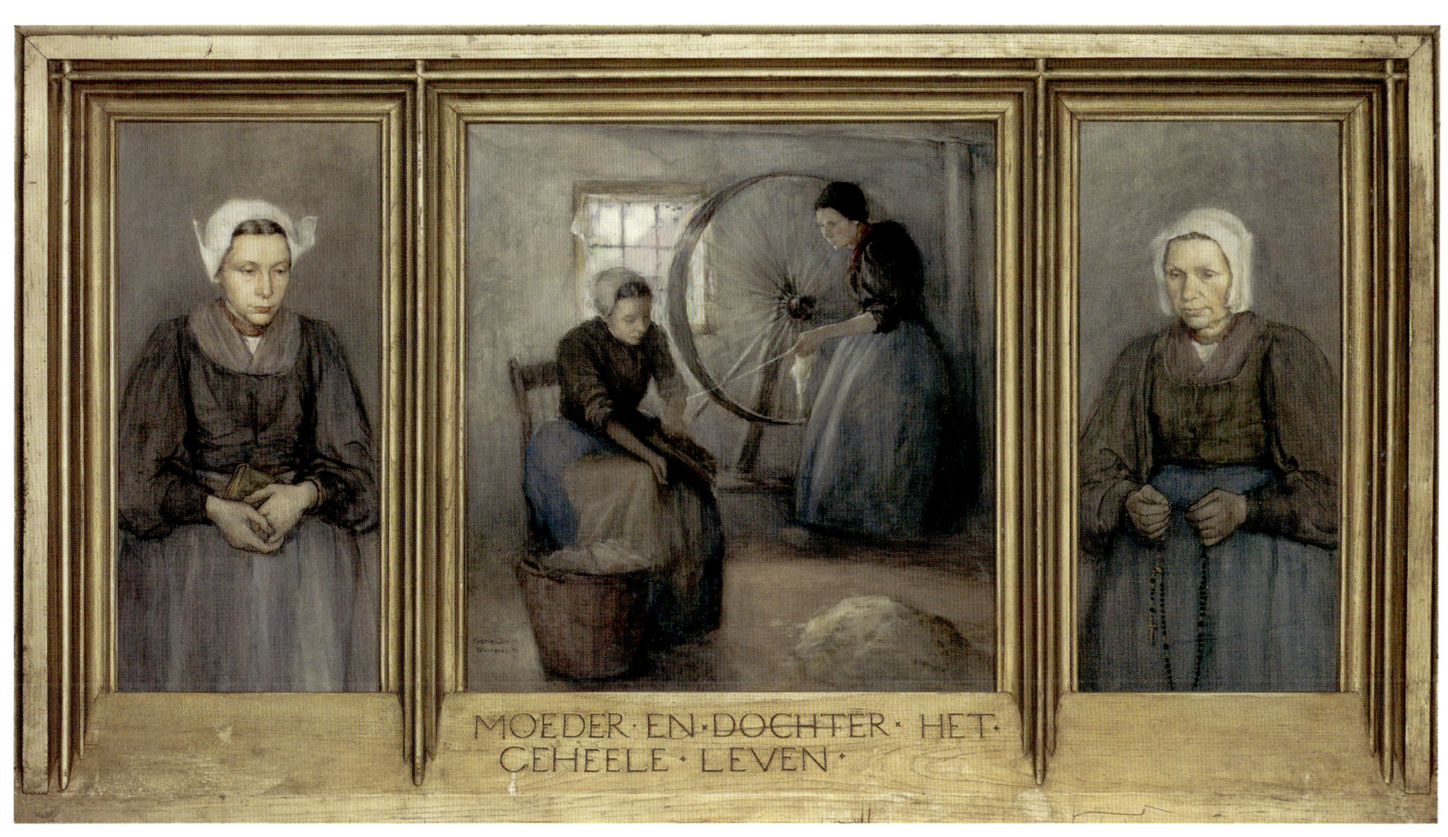
MOEDER · EN · DOCHTER · HET ·
GEHEELE · LEVEN ·

Lenders to the Exhibition

Aberdeen Art Gallery & Museums, Aberdeen, Scotland
Art Collection of the Municipality of Laren, the Netherlands
Brigham Young University Museum of Art, Provo, Utah
Cape Ann Museum, Gloucester, Massachusetts
Childs Gallery, Boston, Massachusetts
The Cleveland Museum of Art, Cleveland, Ohio
Robert and Connie Constant, Los Angeles, California
Currier Museum of Art, Manchester, New Hampshire
Dallas Museum of Art, Texas
Danforth Museum of Art, Framingham, Massachusetts
Frank van Dongen, Amstelveen, the Netherlands
William van Dongen, Utrecht, the Netherlands
Flint Institute of Arts, Flint, Michigan
Florence Griswold Museum, Old Lyme, Connecticut
Frye Art Museum, Seattle, Washington
Gari Melchers Home and Studio, Fredericksburg, Virginia
Grand Rapids Art Museum, Michigan
George Haigh, Cambridge, Massachusetts
Haling family, Jackson, Wyoming
Heckscher Museum of Art, Huntington, New York
High Museum of Art, Atlanta, Georgia
Huntsville Museum of Art, Alabama
Iris & B. Gerald Cantor Center for Visual Arts at Stanford University, Stanford, California
Katwijks Museum, Katwijk, the Netherlands
Memorial Art Gallery, University of Rochester, New York
Alice Miles, Providence, Rhode Island
Montgomery Gallery, San Francisco, California
Munson-Williams-Proctor Arts Institute, Utica, New York
Museum of Fine Arts, Boston, Massachusetts
Museum of Modern Art and Contemporary Art, Liège, Belgium
National Gallery of Art, Washington, D.C.
Patrimony Dutch Jesuit, The Hague, the Netherlands
Joanne Stanley Holbrook Patton, South Hamilton, Massachusetts
Payton Family Collection
Peabody Essex Museum, Salem, Massachusetts
Pennsylvania Academy of the Fine Arts, Philadelphia, Pennsylvania
Private Collection, Courtesy of Garzoli Gallery, San Rafael, California
Private Collection, Kiawah Island, South Carolina
Reading Public Museum, Reading, Pennsylvania
Royal Museum of Fine Arts, Antwerp, Belgium
Singer Laren Museum, the Netherlands
Jan Smit, Volendam, the Netherlands
Smithsonian American Art Museum, Washington, D.C.
Staatliche Museen zu Berlin (National Gallery), Berlin, Germany
Strong National Museum of Play, Rochester, New York
Tate, London, England
Telfair Museum of Art, Savannah, Georgia
Terra Foundation for American Art, Chicago, Illinois
Toledo Museum of Art, Toledo, Ohio
Union League Club of Chicago, Illinois
Mr. and Mrs. Stephen G. Vollmer, Cincinnati, Ohio
Westmoreland Museum of American Art, Greensburg, Pennsylvania
George and Betsy White, Waterford, Connecticut
Dr. Edward T. Wilson, Bethesda, Maryland

Selected Bibliography

Alpers, Svetlana. *The Art of Describing: Dutch Art in the Seventeenth Century.* Chicago: University of Chicago Press, 1983.

———. "Describe or Narrate? A Problem in Realistic Representation." *New Literary History* 8, no. 1 (1976): 15–41.

"An American Woman Painter Who Has Been Honored in Paris." *Current Literature* 48, no. 1 (January 1910).

"Amerikaanse schilders in Egmond (2)." *Geestgronden: Egmonds historisch tijdschrift* 2 (July 1995): 27–42.

Art Institute of Chicago. *Catalogue of Paintings Exhibited at the Opening of the New Galleries, February 24, 1890.* Chicago: S. W. Cor., 1890.

Bal, Mieke. *Narratology: Introduction to the Theory of Narrative.* 2nd ed. Toronto: University of Toronto Press, 1997.

Barthes, Roland. "On the Reality Effect in Descriptions." In *Realism,* edited by Lilian R. Furst. Harlow: Longman, 1992.

Beatty, John W. *The Relation of Art to Nature.* New York: William E. Rudge, 1922.

Bell, Arthur G. "Letters from Artists.—Sketching Grounds, No. 2.—Holland." *The Studio* 1, no. 3 (1893).

Bell, Ralcy Husted. *Art-Talks with Ranger.* New York: G. P. Putnam's Sons, 1914.

Bienenstock, Jennifer Martin. *The Forgotten Episode: Nineteenth Century American Art in Belgian Public Collections.* Brussels: The American Cultural Center, 1987.

Blaugrund, Annette, et al. *Paris 1889: American Artists at the Universal Exposition.* Philadelphia: Pennsylvania Academy of the Fine Arts and New York: Harry N. Abrams, 1989.

Booth, Bradford A., and Ernest Mehew, eds. *The Letters of Robert Louis Stevenson,* vol. 2. April 1874–July 1879. New Haven, Conn.: Yale University Press, 1994.

Boughton, George H. *Sketching Rambles in Holland.* New York: Harper and Brothers, 1885.

Boyle, Richard J. *John Twachtman.* New York: Watson-Guptill, 1979.

Brinkkemper, Dick, Peter Kersloot, and Kees Sier. *Volendam schildersdorp, 1880–1940.* Zwolle: Waanders, 2006.

Brinton, Christian. "George Hitchcock, Painter of Sunlight." *International Studio* 26, nos. 101–4 (July–October 1905).

———. "A Painter of Fair Women." *Munsey's Magazine* 35, no. 2 (May 1906).

Burke, Doreen Bolger. *J. Alden Weir: An American Impressionist.* Newark, Del.: University of Delaware Press, 1983.

Burke, Mary Alice Heekin. *Elizabeth Nourse, 1859–1938: A Salon Career.* Washington, D.C.: Smithsonian Institution Press, 1983.

Butterfield, Kenyon L. "Rural Life and the Family." *American Sociological Society Papers and Proceedings.* Third Annual Meeting, 106–10.

Carr, Carolyn Kinder, and Robert W. Rydell. *Revisiting the White City: American Art at the 1893 World's Fair.* Washington, D.C.: National Museum of American Art and the National Portrait Gallery, Smithsonian Institution, 1993.

Charles H. Woodbury N.A. (1864–1940). Marcia Oakes Woodbury (1865–1914). Boston: Vose Galleries of Boston, 1980.

Cincinnati Art Museum. *Catalogue of the Work of Elizabeth Nourse.* Cincinnati, Ohio: Cincinnati Museum Association, 1893.

Coenen, Jean. *Heeze: Geschiedenis van een schilderachtig dorp.* Weert: 1998.

Collectie Singer: Schilderijen. Laren: Singer Laren Museum and Zwolle: Waanders, 2002.

Corn, Wanda M. *The Great American Thing: Modern Art and National Identity, 1915–1935.* Berkeley: University of California Press, 1999.

Damon-Moore, Helen. *Magazines for the Millions: Gender and Commerce in the Ladies Home Journal and the Saturday Evening Post, 1880–1910.* Albany: State University of New York, 1994.

Davidson, Sandra C., and Ann H. Murray. *Eleanor Norcross. Amy Cross. Edith Loring Getchell.* Fitchburg, Mass.: Fitchburg Art Museum and Norton, Mass.: Watson Gallery, Wheaton College, 1980.

De Bodt, Saskia. *Schildersdorpen in Nederland.* Warnsveld: Terra and Laren: Singer Laren Museum, 2004.

De Cluny, Antoine. *Holland as Painted by Charles P. Gruppé.* Leiden: A.W. Sijthoff's Uitgevers-Maatschappij, n.d.

De Leeuw, Ronald, John Sillevis, and Charles Dumas, eds. *The Hague School: Dutch Masters of the Nineteenth Century.* The Hague: Gemeentemuseum, London: Royal Academy of Arts, and Paris: Grand Palais, 1983.

Denninger-Schreuder, Carole. *De Onvergankelijke Kijk op Kortenhoef: Een schildersdorp in beeld.* Bussum: Thoth, 1998.

———. *Schilders van Laren.* Bussum: Thoth, 2003.

Dennison, Mariea Caudill. "The American Girls' Club in Paris: The Propriety and Imprudence of Art Students, 1890–1914." *Woman's Art Journal* 26, no. 1 (Spring–Summer 2005).

Dorsey, Bruce. "Bibles, Public Schools, and Philadelphia's Bloody Riots of 1844." *Pennsylvania Legacies Magazine* (May 2008).

Dreiss, Joseph. *Gari Melchers: His Works in the Belmont Collection.* Charlottesville, Va.: University of Virginia, 1984.

Fink, Lois Marie. *American Art at the Nineteenth-Century Paris Salons.* Washington, D.C.: Smithsonian Institution and New York: Cambridge University Press, 1990.

Fischer, Diane P. *Paris 1900: The "American School" at the Universal Exposition.* New Brunswick, N.J.: Rutgers University Press and London: The Montclair Art Museum, 1999.

Fuchs, Heinrich. *Die österreichischen Maler des 19. Jahrhunderts.* Vienna: self-published, 1972.

Gaba-van Dongen, Alexandra. *Dromen van Rijsoord (Dreaming of Rijsoord): Wilhelmina Douglas Hawley, 1860–1958.* Bussum: Thoth, 2005.

Galassi, Peter. *Corot on Italy: Open-Air Painting and the Classical Landscape Tradition.* New Haven, Conn.: Yale University Press, 1991.

Gallati, Barbara Dayer. "Portraits of Artistry and Artifice: The Career of Sir James Jebusa Shannon, 1862–1923." 2 vols. PhD diss., City University of New York, 1992.

Genette, Gérard. *Narrative Discourse: An Essay in Method.* Ithaca, N.Y.: Cornell University Press, 1980.

George, Henry. *Social Problems.* Garden City, N.Y.: Doubleday Page, 1883.

Gerdts, William H. *American Impressionism.* New York: Abbeville Press, 1984.

Gerdts, William H., et al. *Mathias J. Alten: Journey of an American Painter.* Grand Rapids, Mich.: Grand Rapids Art Museum, 1998.

Goley, Mary Anne. *The Hague School and Its American Legacy.* Washington, D.C.: Federal Reserve, 1982.

Goodfriend, Joyce D., Benjamin Schmidt, and Annette Stott, eds. *Going Dutch: The Dutch Presence in America 1609–2009.* Leiden: Brill, 2008.

Green, Nicholas. *The Spectacle of Nature: Landscape and Bourgeois Culture in Nineteenth-Century France.* Manchester: Manchester University Press, 1990.

Griffis, William Elliot. *The American in Holland.* New York: Houghton Mifflin, 1899; 1907.

Grünzweig, Walter, and Andreas Solbach, eds. *Grenzüberschreitungen: Narratologie im Kontex/ Transcending Boundaries: Narratology in Context.* Tübingen: Gunter Narr Verlag, 1999.

Gurlitt, Cornelius. *Die Internationale Kunstausstellung zu Berlin 1891.* Munich: Franz Hanfstaengl Kunstverlag, 1891.

Herbert, Robert L. "City vs. Country: The Rural Image in French Painting from Millet to Gauguin." *Artforum* 8 (1970): 44–55.

Heyting, Lien. *De wereld in een dorp: Schilders, schrijvers en wereldverbeteraars in Laren en Blaricum 1880–1920.* Amsterdam: Meulenhoff, 1994.

Hitchcock, George. "The Picturesque Quality of Holland." *Scribner's Magazine* 2, no. 2 (August 1887): 160–68.

Hitchcock, George. "The Picturesque Quality of Holland: Interiors and Bric-a-Brac," *Scribner's Magazine* 5, no. 2 (February 1889): 162–71.

Hofstadter, Richard. *The Age of Reform.* New York: Vintage Books, 1955.

Huntington, David C. *The Quest for Unity: American Art Between the World's Fairs 1876–1893.* Detroit: Detroit Institute of Arts, 1983.

Irish, Sharon. *Cass Gilbert, Architect: Modern Traditionalist.* New York: Monacelli Press, 1999.

Jackman, Rilla Evelyn. *American Arts.* Chicago: Rand McNally, 1928.

James, Henry. *The American Scene.* London: Chapman and Hall, 1907.

Joseph Raphael (1869–1950): An Artistic Journey. New York: Spanierman Gallery, 2003.

Kane, Marie Louise. *A Bright Oasis: The Paintings of Richard E. Miller.* New York: Jordan-Volpe Gallery, 1997.

Katwijk in de schilderkunst. Katwijk: Katwijks Museum, 1995.

Knight, Laura. *Oil Paint and Grease Paint.* London: Ivor Nicholson and Watson, 1936.

Koel, D., G. Kouwenhoven, and H. Schulte Nordholt. *Schilders van Hattem.* Hattem: Stichting Streekmuseum Hatten Voermanhuis, 1991.

Kraan, Hans. *Dromen van Holland: buitenlandse kunstenaars schilderen Holland, 1800–1914.* Zwolle: Waanders and The Hague: Netherlands Institute for Art History, 2002.

Larkin, Susan G. *American Impressionism: The Beauty of Work.* Greenwich, Conn.: Bruce Museum of Arts and Sciences, 2005.

"The Late William Stanley Haseltine." *Evening Post* (New York). April 28, 1900. Originally published in *Il Giorno* (Rome), February 11, 1900.

Laurvik, J. Nilsen. *The Netherlands (Holland) Art Exhibition.* San Francisco: Independent Pressroom, 1916.

Leeds, Valerie Ann. *Robert Henri: The Painted Spirit.* New York: Gerald Peters Gallery, 2005.

Leeman, Kees. *Heel de wereld trekt naar Veere: kunst en cultuur in een klein zeeuws stadje, 1870–1970.* Goes: 2003.

Leroi, Paul. "The American Salon." *The Magazine of Art* (November 1886): 488.

Leroi, Paul. "Salon de 1894." *L'Art* 57 (1894).

Lesko, Diane, and Esther Persson, eds. *Gari Melchers: A Retrospective Exhibition.* St. Petersburg, Fla.: Museum of Fine Arts, 1990.

Licht, Walter. *Industrializing America: The Nineteenth Century.* Baltimore: Johns Hopkins University Press, 1995.

Low, Will Hicok. *A Chronicle of Friendships, 1873–1900.* London: Hodder and Stoughton, 1908.

Lowe, David Garrard. *Lost Chicago.* New York: Watson-Guptill, 2000.

Lübbren, Nina. "North to South: Paradigm Shifts in European Art and Tourism, 1880–1920." In *Visual Culture and Tourism,* edited by David Crouch and Nina Lübbren. Oxford: Berg, 2003.

———. *Rural Artists' Colonies in Europe, 1870–1910.* New Brunswick, N.J.: Rutgers University Press, 2001.

———. "'Toilers of the Sea:' Fisherfolk and the Geographies of Tourism in England, 1880–1900." In *The Geographies of English Art: Landscape and the National Past in English Art 1880–1940,* edited by David Peters Corbett, Ysanne Holt, and Fiona Russell. New Haven, Conn.: Yale University Press, 2000.

Marburg, Theodore. *Addresses delivered on the occasion of the unveiling of the mural decorations "The Burning of the Peggy Stewart" painted by Charles Yardley Turner and "Religious Toleration" painted by Edwin Howland Blashfield.* Baltimore: Municipal Art Society, n.d.

Martin, Frederick Townsend. *The Passing of the Idle Rich.* London: Doubleday, 1911.

Maxwell, Judith Kafka, ed. *Anna Richards Brewster: American Impressionist.* Berkeley: University of California Press, 2008.

McBride, Henry. "American Expatriates in Paris." *Dial* (April 1929).

"McEwen Dies: Noted As Artist For 60 Years." *New York Herald Tribune.* March 20, 1943.

McGerr, Michael. *A Fierce Discontent: The Rise and Fall of the Progressive Movement in America, 1870–1920.* New York: Oxford University Press, 2003.

Meltzer, Charles Henry. "A Painter of Sunlight." *Hearst's Magazine* 22, no. 7 (July 1912): 131–34.

Memorial Exhibition Castle Keith. Amsterdam / New York: Frans Buffa and Sons, 1929.

Merrill, Linda. *An Ideal Country: Paintings by Dwight William Tryon in the Freer Gallery of Art.* Washington, D.C.: Smithsonian Institution, 1990.

Moes, Wally. *Dorpsvertellingen.* The Hague: Nijgh and Van Ditmar, 1957.

———. *Heilig ongeduld: Herinneringen uit mijn Leven.* Amsterdam: Wereldbibliotheek, 1961.

———. *Nagelaten vertellingen.* Amsterdam: Scheltema and Holkema's Boekhandel, n.d. [1920].

"Mrs. Woodbury's Pictures: Memorial Exhibition of Her Watercolors and Oil Paintings at the Museum of Fine Arts." *Boston Transcript.* March 26, 1914.

The National Cyclopaedia of American Biography. New York: James T. White, 1916.

Neuhaus, Eugen. *The Galleries of the Exposition.* San Francisco: Paul Elder, 1915.

Peters, Lisa N. *John Henry Twachtman: An American Impressionist.* New York: Hudson Hills Press, 1999.

———. *John Twachtman (1853–1902): A "Painter's Painter."* New York: Spanierman Gallery, 2006.

Pisano, Ronald G. *A Leading Spirit in American Art: William Merritt Chase 1849–1916.* Seattle: University of Washington, Henry Art Gallery, 1983.

Preyer, David C. "George Elmer Browne, Painter." *Brush and Pencil* 14 (May 1904).

"Progress of Mural Art." *Chicago Sunday Tribune.* December 15, 1895.

Quick, Michael. *American Expatriate Painters of the Late Nineteenth Century.* Dayton, Ohio: Dayton Art Institute, 1976.

Raassen-Kruimel, Emke. "Bestaat er eigenlijk wel een Larense School?" *Tussen Vecht en Eem: Tijdschrift voor Regionale Geschiedenis* 24: 3 (September 2006): 179–84.

———. *Joseph Raphael 1869–1950.* Laren: Singer Laren Museum, 1981.

Ranger, Henry Ward. "Mr. H. W. Ranger on Sketching in Holland." *Art Amateur* 28 (1893).

Raynor, Vivien. *E. Ambrose Webster, 1869–1935: A Retrospective of Paintings.* New York: Babcock Galleries, 1965.

Riis, Jacob. *The Peril and Preservation of the Home.* Philadelphia: George W. Jacobs, 1903.

Roosevelt, Theodore. Speech made before the National Congress of Mothers, March 13, 1905, Washington, D.C.

Ruskin, John. *The Seven Lamps of Architecture.* London, 1849. Reprinted in Frank, Isabelle, ed. *The Theory of Decorative Art, 1750–1940: An Anthology of European and American Writings.* New Haven: Yale University Press, 2000.

Schlereth, Thomas J. *Victorian America: Transformations in Everyday Life, 1876–1915.* New York: Harper Perennial, 1991.

Schretlen, Helen. *American Impressionist William H. Singer Jr. 1868–1943.* Laren: Singer Laren Museum, 2008.

———. *Loving Art: The William & Anna Singer Collection.* Laren: Singer Laren Museum and Zwolle: Waanders, 2006.

Simpson, Marc, Andrea Henderson, and Sally Mills. *Expressions of Place: The Art of William Stanley Haseltine.* San Francisco: Fine Arts Museums of San Francisco, 1992.

Skillen, James W., and Stanley W. Carlson-Thies. "Religion and Political Development in Nineteenth-Century Holland." *Publis* 12, no. 3 (Summer 1982).

Smith, Joseph Coburn. *Charles Hovey Pepper.* Portland, Maine: Southworth-Anthoensen, 1945.

Spencer, Robert C., Jr. "The Architectural Club's Annual Exhibition at the Art Institute, Chicago." *Brush and Pencil* 4, no. 2 (May 1899).

Stott, Annette. "American Painters Who Worked in the Netherlands, 1880–1914." PhD diss. Boston University, 1986.

———. "Dutch Utopia: Paintings by Antimodern American Artists of the Nineteenth Century." *Smithsonian Studies in American Art* 3, no. 2 (Spring 1989): 47–61.

———. *Holland Mania: The Unknown Dutch Period in American Art and Culture.* Woodstock, N.Y.: Overlook Press, 1998.

Tentoonstelling van schilderijen en aquarellen: Charles P. Gruppe. The Hague: Frans Buffa and Sons, n.d.

Trask, John D., ed. *Catalogue de Luxe of the Department of Fine Arts, Panama-Pacific Exposition.* Vol. 1. San Francisco: Paul Elder, 1915.

Van den Berg, Dr. Peter J. H. *De Uitdaging van het Licht: George Hitchcock 1850–1913.* Bahlmond, 2009.

Van Hensbroek, Pieter Andreas Martin Boele. "Ch. P. Gruppe." *Elsevier's Geïllustreerd Maandschrift* 14, no. 28 (November 1904): 291.

Van Seumeren-Haerkens, Margriet. *Albert Neuhuys (1844–1914): Schilderijen, aquarellen en tekeningen.* Laren: Singer Laren Museum and Eindhoven: Museum Kempenland, 1987.

Van Seumeren, Margriet. *"Een mooi land": Wandelen door het kunstenaarsverleden van Laren en Blaricum.* Laren: Singer Laren Museum, 2000.

Van Vleuten, Ronald. "Egmond Remembers Gari Melchers." In *Gari Melchers: A Retrospective Exhibition,* edited by Diane Lesko and Esther Persson. St. Petersburg, Fla.: Museum of Fine Arts, 1990.

Verster, Cornelis Willem. "J. S. H. Kever." *Elsevier's Geïllustreerd Maandschrift* 22: 43 (1912): 116.

Weibe, Robert H. *The Search for Order.* New York: Hill and Wang, 1967.

Weisberg, Gabriel P. *Beyond Impressionism: The Naturalist Impulse.* New York: Harry N. Abrams, 1992.

White, Henry C. *The Life and Art of Dwight William Tryon.* New York: Houghton Mifflin, 1930.

Wilson, Woodrow. *The New Freedom: A Call for the Emancipation of the Generous Engines of a People.* New York: Doubleday Page, 1918.

Zaal, Wim. *Gerard Bilders: Vrolijk versterven. Een keuze uit zijn dagboek en brieven.* Amsterdam: Meulenhoff, 1974.

"Zij waren in Laren . . .": Buitenlandse kunstenaars in Laren en 't Gooi. Laren: Singer Laren Museum, 1989.

Index of Names

Italicized page references indicate figure illustrations. Boldfaced page references indicate catalogue illustrations. Boldfaced page ranges indicate full chapter topics. Endnotes are indicated with "n" followed by the endnote number.

General Index

Italicized page references indicate figure illustrations. Boldfaced page references indicate catalogue illustrations. Boldfaced page ranges indicate full chapter topics. Endnotes are indicated with "n" followed by the endnote number.

COPYRIGHT AND PHOTOGRAPHY CREDITS

Fig. 1 and comparative image in Cat. 25: Photography © The Art Institute of Chicago
Fig. 4: Photograph © 1980 The Detroit Institute of Arts
Figs. 5 and 12: Photography by Tom Haartsen
Fig. 11: The Bridgeman Art Library, PWI98045; Photography by Peter Willi
Fig. 19: The Bridgeman Art Library, BAL90200
Fig. 22: Photo © National Gallery of Canada
Fig. 23: Réunion des Musées Nationaux; Photography by Adélaïde Beaudoin
Fig. 24: Photograph © 2005 Clark Art Institute. All rights reserved
Figs. 33 and 41 and comparative image in Cat. 33: Photography by David Kaminsky
Fig. 36: Photograph by Bob Hashimoto. Reproduction © The Art Institute of Chicago
Fig. 37: Réunion des Musées Nationaux; Photography by Hervé Lewandowski
Fig. 38: Photography by Robert Bruce Langham III
Fig. 40: Photography by Ben Cohen
Cat. 2, 3, 47, 60, 61, and 62: Photography by Tom Haartsen
Cat. 4: © Tate, London 2008
Cat. 7: Photography by Walter Silver © Peabody Essex Museum
Cat. 14: Photography by Rob Howard
Cat. 20 and 42: Image courtesy of the Board of Trustees, National Gallery of Art, Washington, D.C.
Cat. 21 and 68: Photography by Rick Rhodes Photography & Imaging, LLC
Cat. 22, 36, and 44: Photography by Peter Harholdt
Cat. 30: Photography by Shane Photography
Cat. 39: Photography by Susan Dirk / Under the Light
Cat. 42: Photography by Andres Kilger
Cat. 45: Photography by Toni Marie Gonzalez for Toledo Museum of Art, 2008
Cat. 48: Photography by Plaza Studio Fotografie, Katwijk / Wim Zandbergen
Cat. 54: Photograhy by Thijs Quispel
Cat. 55: Photography by Brian Forrest
Cat. 56: Photography by Scot Gordon Photography
Cat. 58: Photography by Daniel L. Grantham Jr., Savannah, Georgia
Cat. 69: Photograph courtesy Spanierman Gallery, LLC, New York
Cat. 70: Photograph courtesy Terra Foundation for American Art, Chicago
Cat. 71: Courtesy of Brigham Young University Museum of Art. All rights reserved
Cat. 73: Photograph © 2009 Museum of Fine Arts, Boston

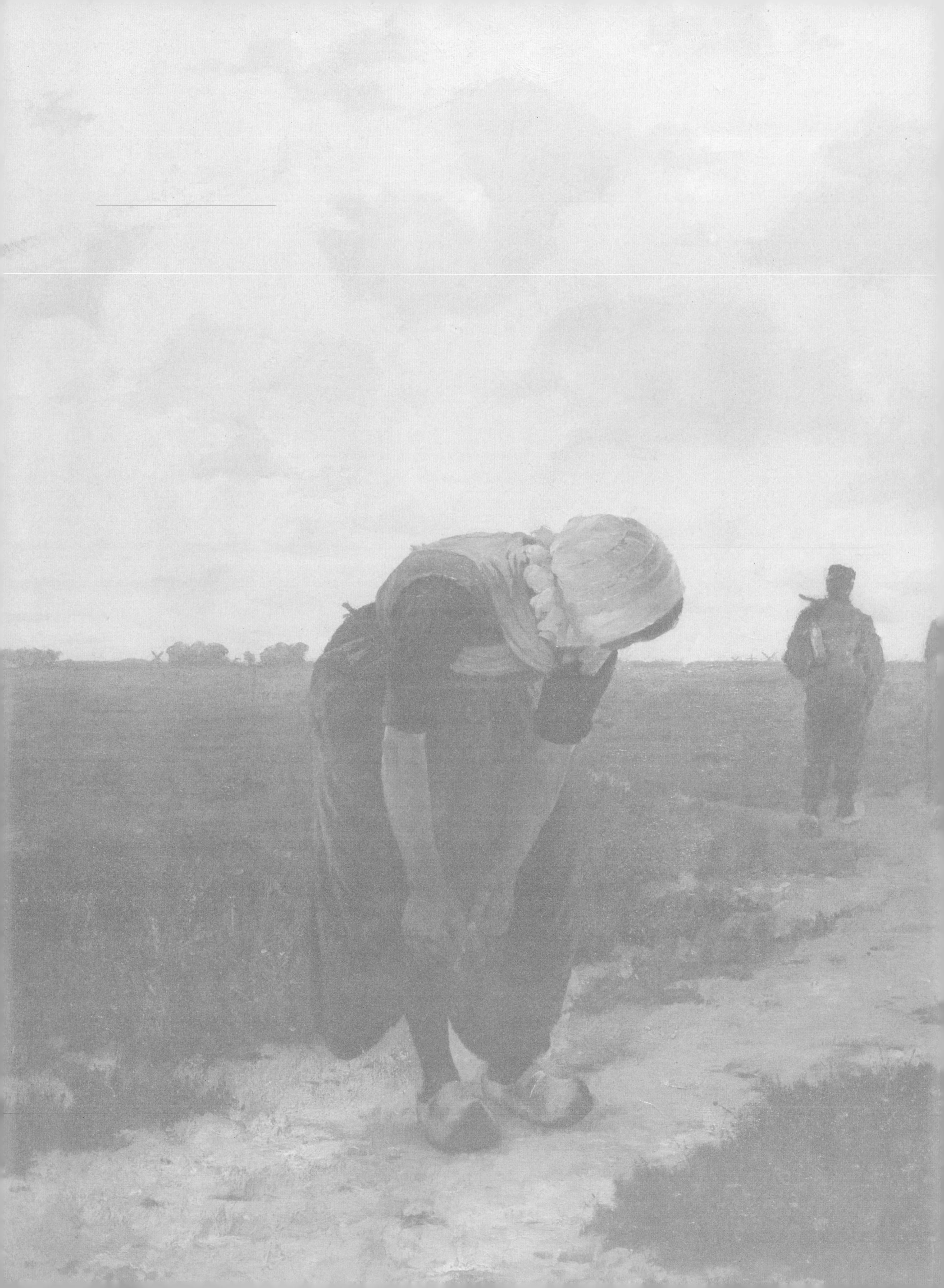